S0-DXH-109

THE WORLD AS WILL AND IDEA

VOLUME III

THE WORLD AS WILL AND IDEA

By

ARTHUR SCHOPENHAUER

VOLUME III

CONTAINING SUPPLEMENTS TO PART OF THE SECOND BOOK AND TO THE THIRD AND FOURTH BOOKS OF VOLUME I

LONDON
ROUTLEDGE & KEGAN PAUL LIMITED
BROADWAY HOUSE, 68 - 74 CARTER LANE, E.C.

Translated from the German by

R. B. HALDANE, M.A.

and

J. KEMP, M.A.

First Published 1883
Eleventh impression
1964

PRINTED IN GREAT BRITAIN BY
COMPTON PRINTING WORKS (LONDON) LTD
LONDON, N.1

CONTENTS.

SUPPLEMENTS TO THE SECOND BOOK.

CHAP.		PAGE
XXI.	Retrospect and More General View	1
XXII.	Objective View of the Intellect	5
XXIII.	On the Objectification of the Will in Unconscious Nature	32
XXIV.	On Matter	48
XXV.	Transcendent Considerations Concerning the Will as Thing in Itself	65
XXVI.	On Teleology	77
XXVII.	On Instinct and Mechanical Tendency	96
XXVIII.	Characterisation of the Will to Live	105

SUPPLEMENTS TO THE THIRD BOOK.

XXIX.	On the Knowledge of the Ideas	121
XXX.	On the Pure Subject of Knowledge	126
XXXI.	On Genius	138
XXXII.	On Madness	167
XXXIII.	Isolated Remarks on Natural Beauty	173
XXXIV.	On the Inner Nature of Art	176
XXXV.	On the Æsthetics of Architecture	182
XXXVI.	Isolated Remarks on the Æsthetics of the Plastic and Pictorial Arts	193
XXXVII.	On the Æsthetics of Poetry	200
XXXVIII.	On History	220
XXXIX.	On the Metaphysics of Music	231

SUPPLEMENTS TO THE FOURTH BOOK.

CHAP.		PAGE
XL.	Preface	247
XLI.	On Death and its Relation to the Indestructibility of our True Nature	249
XLII.	The Life of the Species	309
XLIII.	On Heredity	318
XLIV.	The Metaphysics of the Love of the Sexes	336
XLV.	On the Assertion of the Will to Live	376
XLVI.	On the Vanity and Suffering of Life	382
XLVII.	On Ethics	402
XLVIII.	On the Doctrine of the Denial of the Will to Live	420
XLIX.	The Way of Salvation	460
L.	Epiphilosophy	468

APPENDIX.

Analysis of "The Fourfold Root of the Principle of Sufficient Reason." 477

Index 487

SUPPLEMENTS TO THE SECOND BOOK.

CHAPTER XXI.

RETROSPECT AND MORE GENERAL VIEW.

If the *intellect* were not of a subordinate nature, as the two preceding chapters show, then everything which takes place without it, *i.e.*, without intervention of the idea, such as reproduction, the development and maintenance of the organism, the healing of wounds, the restoration or vicarious supplementing of mutilated parts, the salutary crisis in diseases, the works of the mechanical skill of animals, and the performances of instinct would not be done so infinitely better and more perfectly than what takes place with the assistance of intellect, all conscious and intentional achievements of men, which compared with the former are mere bungling. In general *nature* signifies that which operates, acts, performs without the assistance of the intellect. Now, that this is really identical with what we find in ourselves as *will* is the general theme of this second book, and also of the essay, "*Ueber den Willen in der Natur*." The possibility of this fundamental knowledge depends upon the fact that *in us* the will is directly lighted by the intellect, which here appears as self-consciousness; otherwise we could just as little arrive at a fuller knowledge of it *within us* as without us, and must for ever stop at inscrutable forces of nature. We have to abstract from the assistance of the *intellect* if we wish to comprehend the nature of the will in itself, and thereby, as far as is possible, penetrate to the inner being of nature.

On this account, it may be remarked in passing, my direct antipode among philosophers is Anaxagoras; for he assumed arbitrarily as that which is first and original, from which everything proceeds, a *νους*, an intelligence, a subject of ideas, and he is regarded as the first who promulgated such a view. According to him the world existed earlier in the mere idea than in itself; while according to me it is the unconscious *will* which constitutes the reality of things, and its development must have advanced very far before it finally attains, in the animal consciousness, to the idea and intelligence; so that, according to me, thought appears as the very last. However, according to the testimony of Aristotle (*Metaph.*, i. 4), Anaxagoras himself did not know how to begin much with his *νους*, but merely set it up, and then left it standing like a painted saint at the entrance, without making use of it in his development of nature, except in cases of need, when he did not know how else to help himself. All physico-theology is a carrying out of the error opposed to the truth expressed at the beginning of this chapter—the error that the most perfect form of the origin of things is that which is brought about by means of an *intellect*. Therefore it draws a bolt against all deep exploration of nature.

From the time of Socrates down to our own time, we find that the chief subject of the ceaseless disputations of the philosophers has been that *ens rationis*, called *soul.* We see the most of them assert its immortality, that is to say, its metaphysical nature; yet others, supported by facts which incontrovertibly prove the entire dependence of the intellect upon the bodily organism, unweariedly maintain the contrary. That soul is by all and before everything taken as *absolutely simple;* for precisely from this its metaphysical nature, its immateriality, and immortality were proved, although these by no means necessarily follow from it. For although we can only conceive the destruction of a formed body through breaking up of it into its parts, it does not follow from this that the destruction of a simple existence, of which besides we have no conception, may not be possible in some other way, perhaps by gradually vanishing. I, on the contrary, start by doing away with the presupposed simplicity of our subjectively conscious nature, or the *ego*, inasmuch as I show that the manifestations from which it was deduced have two very different sources, and that in any case the intellect is physically conditioned, the function of a material organ, therefore dependent upon it, and without it is just as impossible as the grasp without the hand; that accordingly it belongs to the mere phenomenon, and thus shares the fate of this,—that the *will*, on the contrary, is bound to no special organ, but is everywhere present, is everywhere that which moves and forms, and therefore is that which conditions the whole organism; that, in fact, it constitutes the metaphysical substratum of the whole phenomenon, consequently is not, like the intellect, a *Posterius* of it, but its *Prius*; and the phenomenon depends upon it, not it upon the phenomenon. But the body is reduced indeed to a mere idea, for it is only the manner in which the *will* exhibits itself in the perception of the intellect or brain. The *will*, again, which in all other systems, different as they are in other respects, appears as one of the last results, is with me the very first. The *intellect*, as mere function of the brain, is involved in the destruction of the body, but the *will* is by no means so. From this heterogeneity of the two, together with the subordinate nature of the intellect, it becomes conceivable that man, in the depths of his self-consciousness, feels himself to be eternal and indestructible, but yet can have no memory, either *a parte ante* or *a parte post*, beyond the duration of his life. I do not wish to anticipate here the exposition of the true indestructibility of our nature, which has its place in the fourth book, but have only sought to indicate the place where it links itself on.

But now that, in an expression which is certainly one-sided, yet from our standpoint true, the body is called a mere idea depends upon the fact than an existence in space, as something extended, and in time, as something that changes, and more closely determined in both through the causal-nexus, is only possible in the *idea*, for all those determinations rest upon its forms, thus in a brain, in which accordingly such an existence appears as something objective, *i.e.*, foreign; therefore even our own body can have this kind of existence only in a brain. For the knowledge which I have of my body as extended, space-occupying, and movable, is only *indirect:* it is a picture in my brain which is brought about by means of the senses and understanding. The body is given to me *directly* only in muscular action and in pain and pleasure, both of which primarily and directly belong to the *will*. But the combination of these two different kinds of knowledge of my own body afterwards affords the further insight that all other things which also have the objective existence described, which is primarily only in my brain, are not therefore entirely non-existent apart from it, but must also ultimately *in themselves* be that which makes itself known in self-consciousness as *will*.

CHAPTER XXII.[1]

OBJECTIVE VIEW OF THE INTELLECT.

THERE are two fundamentally different ways of regarding the intellect, which depend upon the difference of the point of view, and, much as they are opposed to each other in consequence of this, must yet be brought into agreement. One is the *subjective,* which, starting from *within* and taking the *consciousness* as the given, shows us by what mechanism the world exhibits itself in it, and how, out of the materials which the senses and the understanding provide, it constructs itself in it. We must look upon Locke as the originator of this method of consideration; Kant brought it to incomparably higher perfection; and our first book also, together with its supplements, are devoted to it.

The method of considering the intellect which is opposed to this is the *objective,* which starts from *without,* takes as its object not our own consciousness, but the beings given in outward experience, conscious of themselves and of the world, and now investigates the relation of their intellect to their other qualities, how it has become possible, how it has become necessary, and what it accomplishes for them. The standpoint of this method of consideration is the empirical. It takes the world and the animal existences present in it as absolutely given, in that it starts from them. It is accordingly primarily zoological, anatomical, physiological, and only becomes philosophical by connection with that first method of consideration, and

[1] This chapter is connected with the last half of § 27 of the first volume.

from the higher point of view thereby attained. The only foundations of this which as yet have been given we owe to zootomists and physiologists, for the most part French. Here Cabanis is specially to be named, whose excellent work, "*Des rapports du physique au moral,*" is initiatory of this method of consideration on the path of physiology. The famous Bichat was his contemporary, but his theme was a much more comprehensive one. Even Gall may be named here, although his chief aim was missed. Ignorance and prejudice have raised against this method of consideration the accusation of materialism, because, adhering simply to experience, it does not know the immaterial substance, soul. The most recent advances in the physiology of the nervous system, through Sir Charles Bell, Magendie, Marshall Hall, and others, have also enriched and corrected the material of this method of consideration. A philosophy which, like the Kantian, entirely ignores this point of view for the intellect is one-sided, and consequently inadequate. It leaves an impassable gulf between our philosophical and our physiological knowledge, with which we can never find satisfaction.

Although what I have said in the two preceding chapters concerning the life and the activity of the brain belongs to this method of consideration, and in the same way all the discussions to be found under the heading, "*Pflanzenphysiologie,*" in the essay, "*Ueber den Willen in der Natur,*" and also a portion of those under the heading "*Vergleichende Anatomie,*" are devoted to it, the following exposition of its results in general will be by no means superfluous.

We become most vividly conscious of the glaring contrast between the two methods of considering the intellect opposed to each other above if we carry the matter to the extreme and realise that what the one, as reflective thought and vivid perception, directly assumes and makes its material is for the other nothing more than the physiological function of an internal organ, the brain; nay, that we are justified in asserting that the whole objective world, so boundless in space, so infinite in time, so unsearchable in its perfection, is really only a certain movement or affection of the pulpy matter in the skull. We then ask in astonishment: what is this brain whose function produces such a phenomenon of all phenomena? What is the matter which can be refined and potentiated to such a pulp that the stimulation of a few of its particles becomes the conditional supporter of the existence of an objective world? The fear of such questions led to the hypothesis of the simple substance of an immaterial soul, which merely dwelt in the brain. We say boldly: this pulp also, like every vegetable or animal part, is an organic structure, like all its poorer relations in the inferior accommodation of the heads of our irrational brethren, down to the lowest, which scarcely apprehends at all; yet that organic pulp is the last product of nature, which presupposes all the rest. But in itself, and outside the idea, the brain also, like everything else, is *will. For existing for another is being perceived; being in itself is willing:* upon this it depends that on the purely objective path we never attain to the inner nature of things; but if we attempt to find their inner nature from without and empirically, this inner always becomes an outer again in our hands,—the pith of the tree, as well as its bark; the heart of the animal, as well as its hide; the white and the yolk of an egg, as well as its shell. On the other hand, upon the subjective path the inner is accessible to us at every moment; for we find it as the *will* primarily in ourselves, and must, by the clue of the analogy with our own nature, be able to solve that of others, in that we attain to the insight that a being in itself independent of being known, *i.e.*, of exhibiting itself in an intellect, is only conceivable as willing.

If now, in the *objective* comprehension of the intellect, we go back as far as we possibly can, we shall find that the necessity or the need of *knowledge in general* arises from the multiplicity and the *separate* existence of beings, thus from individuation. For suppose there only existed *a single* being, such a being would have no need of knowledge: because nothing would exist which was different from it, and whose existence it would therefore have to take up into itself indirectly through knowledge, *i.e.*, image and concept. It would *itself* already be all in all, and therefore there would remain nothing for it to know, *i.e.*, nothing foreign that could be apprehended as object. In the case of a multiplicity of beings, on the other hand, every individual finds itself in a condition of isolation from all the rest, and hence arises the necessity of knowledge. The nervous system, by means of which the animal individual primarily becomes conscious of itself, is bounded by a skin; yet in the brain that has attained to intellect it passes beyond this limit by means of its form of knowledge, causality, and thus there arises for it perception as a consciousness of *other* things, as an image of beings in space and time, which change in accordance with causality. In this sense it would be more correct to say, "Only the different is known by the different," than as Empedocles said, "Only the like is known by the like," which was a very indefinite and ambiguous proposition; although points of view may certainly also be conceived from which it is true; as, for instance, we may observe in passing that of Helvetius when he says so beautifully and happily: "*Il n'y a que l'esprit qui sente l'esprit: c'est une corde qui ne frémit qu'à l'unison,*" which corresponds with Xenophon's "σοφον ειναι δει τον επιγνωσομενον τον σοφον" (*sapientem esse opportet eum, qui sapientem agniturus sit*), and is a great sorrow. But now, again, from the other side we know that multiplicity of similars only becomes possible through time and space; thus through the forms of our knowledge. Space first arises in that the knowing subject sees externally; it is the manner in which the subject comprehends something as different from itself. But we also saw knowledge in general conditioned by multiplicity and difference. Thus knowledge and multiplicity, or individuation, stand and fall together, for they reciprocally condition each other. Hence it must be inferred that, beyond the phenomenon in the true being of all things, to which time and space, and consequently also multiplicity, must be foreign, there can also be no knowledge. Buddhism defines this as *Pratschna Paramita, i.e.,* that which is beyond all knowledge (J. J. Schmidt, "On the Maha-Jana and Pratschna Paramita"). A "knowledge of things in themselves," in the strictest sense of the word, would accordingly be already impossible from the fact that where the thing in itself begins knowledge ceases, and all knowledge is essentially concerned only with phenomena. For it springs from a limitation, by which it is made necessary, in order to extend the limits.

For the objective consideration the brain is the efflorescence of the organism; therefore only where the latter has attained its highest perfection and complexity does the brain appear in its greatest development. But in the preceding chapter we have recognised the organism as the objectification of the will; therefore the brain also, as a part of it, must belong to this objectification. Further, from the fact that the organism is only the visibility of the will, thus in itself is the will, I have deduced that every affection of the organism at once and directly affects the will, *i.e.,* is felt as agreeable or painful. Yet, with the heightening of sensibility, in the higher development of the nervous system, the possibility arises that in the nobler, *i.e.,* the *objective,* organs of sense (sight and hearing) the exquisitely delicate affections proper to them are perceived without in themselves and directly affecting the will, that is, without being either painful or agreeable, and that therefore they appear in consciousness as indifferent, merely perceived, sensations. But in the brain this heightening of sensibility reaches such a high degree that upon received impressions of sense a reaction even takes place, which does not proceed directly from the will, but is primarily a spontaneity of the function of understanding, which makes the transition from the directly perceived sensation of the senses to its *cause;* and since the brain then at once produces the form of space, there thus arises the perception of an *external object.* We may therefore regard the point at which the understanding makes the transition from the mere sensation upon the retina, which is still a mere affection of the body and therefore of the will, to the *cause* of that sensation, which it projects by means of its form of space, as something external and different from its own body, as the boundary between the world as will and the world as idea, or as the birthplace of the latter. In man, however, the spontaneity of the activity of the brain, which in the last instance is certainly conferred by the will, goes further than mere *perception* and immediate comprehension of causal relations. It extends to the construction of abstract conceptions out of these perceptions, and to operating with these conceptions, *i.e.*, to *thinking,* as that in which his *reason* consists. *Thoughts* are therefore furthest removed from the affections of the body, which, since the body is the objectification of the will, may, through increased intensity, pass at once into pain, even in the organs of sense. Accordingly idea and thought may also be regarded as the efflorescence of the will, because they spring from the highest perfection and development of the organism; but the organism, in itself and apart from the idea, is the *will.* Of course, in my explanation, the existence of the body presupposes the world of idea; inasmuch as it also, as body or real object, is only in this world; and, on the other hand, the idea itself just as much presupposes the body, for it arises only through the function of an organ of the body. That which lies at the foundation of the whole phenomenon, that in it which alone has being in itself and is original, is exclusively the *will;* for it is the will which through this very process assumes the form of the *idea*, *i.e.*, enters the secondary existence of an objective world, or the sphere of the knowable. Philosophers before Kant, with few exceptions, approached the explanation of the origin of our knowledge from the wrong side. They set out from a so-called soul, an existence whose inner nature and peculiar function consisted in thinking, and indeed quite specially in abstract thinking, with mere conceptions, which belonged to it the more completely the further they lay from all perception. (I beg to refer here to the note at the end of § 6 of my prize essay on the foundation of morals.) This soul has in some inconceivable manner entered the body, and there it is only disturbed in its pure thinking, first by impressions of the senses and perceptions, still more by the desires which these excite, and finally by the emotions, nay, passions, to which these desires develop; while the characteristic and original element of this soul is mere abstract thinking, and given up to this it has only universals, inborn conceptions, and *æternæ veritates* for its objects, and leaves everything perceptible lying far below it. Hence, also, arises the contempt with which even now "sensibility" and the "sensuous" are referred to by professors of philosophy, nay, are even made the chief source of immorality, while it is just the senses which are the genuine and innocent source of all our knowledge, from which all thinking must first borrow its material, for in combination with the *a priori* functions of the intellect they produce the *perception*. One might really suppose that in speaking of sensibility these gentlemen always think only of the pretended sixth sense of the French. Thus, as we have said, in the process of knowledge, its ultimate product was made that which is first and original in it, and accordingly the matter was taken hold of by the wrong end. According to my exposition, the intellect springs from the organism, and thereby from the will, and hence could not be without the latter. Thus, without the will it would also find no material to occupy it; for everything that is knowable is just the objectification of the will.

But not only the perception of the external world, or the consciousness of other things, is conditioned by the brain and its functions, but also self-consciousness. The will in itself is without consciousness, and remains so in the greater part of its phenomena. The secondary world of idea must be added, in order that it may become conscious of itself, just as light only becomes visible through the bodies which reflect it, and without them loses itself in darkness without producing any effect. Because the will, with the aim of comprehending its relations to the external world, produces a brain in the animal individual, the consciousness of its own self arises in it, by means of the subject of knowledge, which comprehends things as existing and the *ego* as willing. The sensibility, which reaches its highest degree in the brain, but is yet dispersed through its different parts, must first of all collect all the rays of its activity, concentrate them, as it were, in a focus, which, however, does not lie without, as in the case of the concave mirror, but within, as in the convex mirror. With this point now it first describes the line of time, upon which, therefore, all that it presents to itself as idea must exhibit itself, and which is the first and most essential form of all knowledge, or the form of inner sense. This focus of the whole activity of the brain is what Kant called the synthetic unity of apperception (*cf.* vol. ii. p. 475). Only by means of this does the will become conscious of itself, because this focus of the activity of the brain, or that which knows, apprehends itself as identical with its own basis, from which it springs, that which wills; and thus the *ego* arises. Yet this focus of the brain activity remains primarily a mere subject of knowledge, and as such capable of being the cold and impartial spectator, the mere guide and counsellor of the will, and also of comprehending the external world in a purely objective manner, without reference to the will and its weal or woe. But whenever it turns within, it recognises the will as the basis of its own phenomenon, and therefore combines with it in the consciousness of an *ego*. That focus of the activity of the brain (or the subject of knowledge) is indeed, as an indivisible point, simple, but yet is not on this account a substance (soul), but a mere condition or state. That of which it is itself a condition or state can only be known by it indirectly, as it were through reflection. But the ceasing of this state must not be regarded as the annihilation of that of which it is a state. This *knowing* and conscious *ego* is related to the will, which is the basis of its phenomenal appearance, as the picture in the focus of a concave mirror is related to the mirror itself, and has, like that picture, only a conditioned, nay, really a merely apparent, reality. Far from being the absolutely first (as, for example, Fichte teaches), it is at bottom tertiary, for it presupposes the organism, and the organism presupposes the will. I admit that all that is said here is really only an image and a figure, and in part also hypothetical; but we stand at a point to which thought can scarcely reach, not to speak of proof. I therefore request the reader to compare with this what I have adduced at length on this subject in chapter 20.

Now, although the true being of everything that exists consists in its will, and knowledge together with consciousness are only added at the higher grades of the phenomenon as something secondary, yet we find that the difference which the presence and the different degree of consciousness places between one being and another is exceedingly great and of important results. The subjective existence of the plant we must think of as a weak analogue, a mere shadow of comfort and discomfort; and even in this exceedingly weak degree the plant knows only of itself, not of anything outside of it. On the other hand, even the lowest animal standing next to it is forced by increased and more definitely specified wants to extend the sphere of its existence beyond the limits of its own body. This takes place through knowledge. It has a dim apprehension of its immediate surroundings, out of which the motives for its action with a view to its own maintenance arise. Thus accordingly the *medium of motives* appears, and this is—the world existing objectively in time and space, *the world as idea,* however weak, obscure, and dimly dawning this first and lowest example of it may be. But it imprints itself ever more and more distinctly, ever wider and deeper, in proportion as in the ascending scale of animal organisations the brain is ever more perfectly produced. This progress in the development of the brain, thus of the intellect, and of the clearness of the idea, at each of these ever higher grades is, however, brought about by the constantly increasing and more complicated *wants* of this phenomenon of the will. This must always first afford the occasion for it, for without necessity nature (*i.e.*, the will which objectifies itself in it) produces nothing, least of all the hardest of its productions—a more perfect brain: in consequence of its *lex parsimoniæ: natura nihil agit frustra et nihil facit supervacaneum.* It has provided every animal with the organs which are necessary for its sustenance and the weapons necessary for its conflict, as I have shown at length in my work, "*Ueber den Willen in der Natur,*" under the heading, "*Vergleichende Anatomie.*" According to this measure, therefore, it imparts to each the most important of those organs concerned with what is without, the brain, with its function the intellect. The more complicated, through higher development, its organisation became, the more multifarious and specially determined did its wants also become, and consequently the more difficult and the more dependent upon opportunity was the provision of what would satisfy them. Thus there was needed here a wider range of sight, a more accurate comprehension, a more correct distinction of things in the external world, in all their circumstances and relations. Accordingly we see the faculty of forming ideas, and its organs, brain, nerves, and special senses, appear ever more perfect the higher we advance in the scale of animals; and in proportion as the cerebral system develops, the external world appears ever more distinct, many-sided, and complete in consciousness. The comprehension of it now demands ever more attention, and ultimately in such a degree that sometimes its relation to the will must momentarily be lost sight of in order that it may take place more purely and correctly. Quite definitely this first appears in the case of man. With him alone does a *pure separation of knowing and willing* take place. This is an important point, which I merely touch on here in order to indicate its position, and be able to take it up again later. But, like all the rest, nature takes this last step also in extending and perfecting the brain, and thereby in increasing the powers of knowledge, only in consequence of the increased needs, thus in the service of the *will*. What this aims at and attains in man is indeed essentially the same, and not more than what is also its goal in the brutes—nourishment and propagation. But the requisites for the attainment of this goal became so much increased in number, and of so much higher quality and greater definiteness through the organisation of man, that a very much more considerable heightening of the intellect than the previous steps demanded was necessary, or at least was the easiest means of reaching the end. But since now the intellect, in accordance with its nature, is a tool of the most various utility, and is equally applicable to the most different kinds of ends, nature, true to her spirit of parsimony, could now meet through it alone all the demands of the wants which had now become so manifold. Therefore she sent forth man without clothing, without natural means of protection or weapons of attack, nay, with relatively little muscular power, combined with great frailty and little endurance of adverse influences and wants, in reliance upon that one great tool, in addition to which she had only to retain the hands from the next grade below him, the ape.

But through the predominating intellect which here appears not only is the comprehension of motives, their multiplicity, and in general the horizon of the aims infinitely increased, but also the distinctness with which the will is conscious *of itself* is enhanced in the highest degree in consequence of the clearness of the whole consciousness which has been brought about, which is supported by the capacity for abstract knowledge, and now attains to complete reflectiveness. But thereby, and also through the vehemence of the will, which is necessarily presupposed as the supporter of such a heightened intellect, an intensifying of all the *emotions* appears, and indeed the possibility of the *passions*, which, properly speaking, are unknown to the brute. For the vehemence of the will keeps pace with the advance of intelligence, because this advance really always springs from the increased needs and pressing demands of the will: besides this, however, the two reciprocally support each other. Thus the vehemence of the character corresponds to the greater energy of the beating of the heart and the circulation of the blood, which physically heighten the activity of the brain. On the other hand, the clearness of the intelligence intensifies the emotions, which are called forth by the outward circumstances, by means of the more vivid apprehension of the latter. Hence, for example, young calves quietly allow themselves to be packed in a cart and carried off; but young lions, if they are only separated from their mother, remain permanently restless, and roar unceasingly from morning to night; children in such a position would cry and vex themselves almost to death. The vivaciousness and impetuosity of the ape is in exact proportion to its greatly developed intellect. It depends just on this reciprocal relationship that man is, in general, capable of far greater sorrows than the brute, but also of greater joy in satisfied and pleasing emotions. In the same way his higher intelligence makes him more sensible to *ennui* than the brute; but it also becomes, if he is individually very complete, an inexhaustible source of entertainment. Thus, as a whole, the manifestation of the will in man is related to that in the brute of the higher species, as a note that has been struck to its fifth pitched two or three octaves lower. But between the different kinds of brutes also the differences of intellect, and thereby of consciousness, are great and endlessly graduated. The mere analogy of consciousness which we must yet attribute to plants will be related to the still far deader subjective nature of an unorganised body, very much as the consciousness of the lowest species of animals is related to the *quasi* consciousness of plants. We may present to our imagination the innumerable gradations in the degree of consciousness under the figure of the different velocity of points which are unequally distant from the centre of a revolving sphere. But the most correct, and indeed, as our third book teaches, the natural figure of that gradation is afforded us by the scale in its whole compass from the lowest audible note to the highest. It is, however, the grade of consciousness which determines the grade of existence of a being. For every immediate existence is subjective: the objective existence is in the consciousness of another, thus only for this other, consequently quite indirect. Through the grade of consciousness beings are as different as through the will they are alike, for the will is what is common to them all.

But what we have now considered between the plant and the animal, and then between the different species of animals, occurs also between man and man. Here also that which is secondary, the intellect, by means of the clearness of consciousness and distinctness of knowledge which depends upon it, constitutes a fundamental and immeasurably great difference in the whole manner of the existence, and thereby in the grade of it. The higher the consciousness has risen, the more distinct and connected are the thoughts, the clearer the perceptions the more intense the sensations. Through it everything gains more depth: emotion, sadness, joy, and sorrow. Commonplace blockheads are not even capable of real joy: they live on in dull insensibility. While to one man his consciousness only presents his own existence, together with the motives which must be apprehended for the purpose of sustaining and enlivening it, in a bare comprehension of the external world, it is to another a *camera obscura* in which the macrocosm exhibits itself:

> "He feels that he holds a little world
> Brooding in his brain,
> That it begins to work and to live,
> That he fain would give it forth."

The difference of the whole manner of existence which the extremes of the gradation of intellectual capacity establish between man and man is so great that that between a king and a day labourer seems small in comparison. And here also, as in the case of the species of animals, a connection between the vehemence of the will and the height of the intellect can be shown. Genius is conditioned by a passionate temperament, and a phlegmatic genius is inconceivable: it seems as if an exceptionally vehement, thus a violently longing, will must be present if nature is to give an abnormally heightened intellect, as corresponding to it; while the merely physical account of this points to the greater energy with which the arteries of the head move the brain and increase its turgescence. Certainly, however, the quantity, quality, and form of the brain itself is the other and incomparably more rare condition of genius. On the other hand, phlegmatic persons are as a rule of very moderate mental power; and thus the northern, cold-blooded, and phlegmatic nations are in general noticeably inferior in mind to the southern vivacious and passionate peoples; although, as Bacon[1] has most pertinently remarked, if once a man of a northern nation is highly gifted by nature, he can then reach a grade which no southern ever attains to. It is accordingly as perverse

[1] *De Augm. Scient.*, L. vi. c. 3.

as it is common to take the great minds of different nations as the standard for comparing their mental powers: for that is just attempting to prove the rule by the exceptions. It is rather the great majority of each nation that one has to consider: for one swallow does not make a summer. We have further to remark here that that very passionateness which is a condition of genius, bound up with its vivid apprehension of things, produces in practical life, where the will comes into play, and especially in the case of sudden occurrences, so great an excitement of the emotions that it disturbs and confuses the intellect; while the phlegmatic man in such a case still retains the full use of his mental faculties, though they are much more limited, and then accomplishes much more with them than the greatest genius can achieve. Accordingly a passionate temperament is favourable to the original quality of the intellect, but a phlegmatic temperament to its use. Therefore genius proper is only for theoretical achievements, for which it can choose and await its time, which will just be the time at which the will is entirely at rest, and no waves disturb the clear mirror of the comprehension of the world. On the other hand, genius is ill adapted and unserviceable for practical life, and is therefore for the most part unfortunate. Goethe's "Tasso" is written from this point of view. As now genius proper depends upon the *absolute* strength of the intellect, which must be purchased by a correspondingly excessive vehemence of disposition, so, on the other hand, the great preeminence in practical life that makes generals and statesmen depends upon the *relative* strength of the intellect, thus upon the highest degree of it that can be attained without too great excitability of the emotions, and too great vehemence of character, and that therefore can hold its own even in the storm. Great firmness of will and constancy of mind, together with a capable and fine understanding, are here sufficient; and whatever goes beyond this acts detrimentally, for too great a development of the intelligence directly impedes firmness of character and resolution of will. Hence this kind of eminence is not so abnormal, and is a hundred times less rare than the former kind; and accordingly we see great generals and great ministers appear in every age, whenever the merely external conditions are favourable to their efficiency. Great poets and philosophers, on the other hand, leave centuries waiting for them; and yet humanity may be contented even with this rare appearance of them, for their works remain, and do not exist only for the present, like the achievements of those other men. It is also quite in keeping with the law of the parsimony of nature referred to above that it bestows great eminence of mind in general upon very few, and genius only as the rarest of all exceptions, while it equips the great mass of the human race with no more mental power than is required for the maintenance of the individual and the species. For the great, and through their very satisfaction, constantly increasing needs of the human race make it necessary that the great majority of men should pass their lives in occupations of a coarsely physical and entirely mechanical description. And what would be the use to them of an active mind, a glowing imagination, a subtle understanding, and a profoundly penetrating intellect? These would only make them useless and unhappy. Therefore nature has thus gone about the most costly of all her productions in the least extravagant manner. In order not to judge unfairly one ought also to settle definitely one's expectations of the mental achievements of men generally from this point of view, and to regard, for example, even learned men, since as a rule they have become so only by the force of outward circumstances, primarily as men whom nature really intended to be tillers of the soil; indeed even professors of philosophy ought to be estimated according to this standard, and then their achievements will be found to come up to all fair expectations. It is worth noticing that in the south, where the necessities of life press less severely upon the human race, and more leisure is allowed, the mental faculties even of the multitude also become more active and finer. It is physiologically noteworthy that the preponderance of the mass of the brain over that of the spinal cord and the nerves, which, according to Sömmerring's acute discovery, affords the true and closest measure of the degree of intelligence both of species of brutes and of individual men, at the same time increases the direct power of moving, the agility of the limbs; because, through the great inequality of the relation, the dependence of all motor nerves upon the brain becomes more decided; and besides this the cerebellum, which is the primary controller of movements, shares the qualitative perfection of the cerebrum; thus through both all voluntary movements gain greater facility, rapidity, and manageableness, and by the concentration of the starting-point of all activity that arises which Lichtenberg praises in Garrick: "that he appeared to be present in all the muscles of his body." Hence clumsiness in the movement of the body indicates clumsiness in the movement of the thoughts, and will be regarded as a sign of stupidity both in individuals and nations, as much as sleepiness of the countenance and vacancy of the glance. Another symptom of the physiological state of the case referred to is the fact that many persons are obliged at once to stand still whenever their conversation with any one who is walking with them begins to gain some connection; because their brain, as soon as it has to link together a few thoughts, has no longer as much power over as is required to keep the limbs in motion by means of the motory nerves, so closely is everything measured with them.

It results from this whole objective consideration of the intellect and its origin, that it is designed for the comprehension of those ends upon the attainment of which depends the individual life and its propagation, but by no means for deciphering the inner nature of things and of the world, which exists independently of the knower.

What to the plant is the susceptibility to light, in consequence of which it guides its growth in the direction of it, that is, in kind, the knowledge of the brute, nay, even of man, although in degree it is increased in proportion as the needs of each of these beings demand. With them all apprehension remains a mere consciousness of their relations to other things, and is by no means intended to present again in the consciousness of the knower the peculiar, absolutely real nature of these things. Rather, as springing from the will, the intellect is also only designed for its service, thus for the apprehension of motives; it is adapted for this, and is therefore of a thoroughly practical tendency. This also holds good if we conceive the significance of life as ethical; for in this regard too we find man knowing only for the benefit of his conduct. Such a faculty of knowledge, existing exclusively for practical ends, will from its nature always comprehend only the relations of things to each other, but not the inner nature of them, as it is in itself. But to regard the complex of these relations as the absolute nature of the world as it is in itself, and the manner in which it necessarily exhibits itself in accordance with the laws predisposed in the brain as the eternal laws of the existence of all things, and then to construct ontology, cosmology, and theology in accordance with this view—this was really the old fundamental error, of which Kant's teaching has made an end. Here, then, our objective, and therefore for the most part physiological consideration of the intellect meets *his* transcendental consideration of it; nay, appears in a certain sense even as an *a priori* insight into it; for, from a point of view which we have taken up outside of it, our objective view enables us to know in its origin, and therefore as *necessary*, what that transcendental consideration, starting from facts of consciousness, presents only as a matter of fact. For it follows from our objective consideration of the intellect, that the world as idea, as it exists stretched out in space and time, and moves on regularly according to the strict law of causality, is primarily only a physiological phenomenon, a function of the brain, which brings it about, certainly upon the occasion of certain external stimuli, but yet in conformity with its own laws. Accordingly it is beforehand a matter of course, that what goes on in this function itself, and therefore through it and for it, must by no means be regarded as the nature of *things in themselves*, which exist independently of it and are entirely different from it, but primarily exhibits only the mode or manner of this function itself, which can always receive only a very subordinate modification through that which exists completely independently of it, and sets it in motion as a stimulus. As, then, Locke claimed for the organs of sense all that comes into our apprehension by means of the sensation, in order to deny that it belongs to things in themselves, so Kant, with the same intention, and pursuing the same path further, has proved all that makes *perception* proper possible, thus space, time, and causality, to be functions of the brain; although he has refrained from using this physiological expression, to which, however, our present method of investigation, coming from the opposite side, the side of the real, necessarily leads us. Kant arrived upon his analytical path at the result that what we know are mere *phenomena*. What this mysterious expression really means becomes clear from our objective and genetic investigation of the intellect. The phenomena are the motives for the aims of individual will as they exhibit themselves in the intellect which the will has produced for this purpose (which itself appears as a phenomenon objectively, as the brain), and which, when comprehended, as far as one can follow their concatenation, afford us in their connection the world which extends itself objectively in time and space, and which I call the world as idea. Moreover, from our point of view, the objectionable element vanishes which in the Kantian doctrine arises from the fact that, because the intellect knows merely phenomena instead of things as they are in themselves, nay, in consequence of this is led astray into paralogisms and unfounded hypostases by means of "sophistications, not of men but of the reason itself, from which even the wisest does not free himself, and if, perhaps indeed after much trouble, he avoids error, can yet never get quit of the illusion which unceasingly torments and mocks him"—because of all this, I say, the appearance arises that our intellect is intentionally designed to lead us into errors. For the objective view of the intellect given here, which contains a genesis of it, makes it conceivable that, being exclusively intended for practical ends, it is merely the *medium of motives*, and therefore fulfils its end by an accurate presentation of these, and that if we undertake to discover the nature of things in themselves, from the manifold phenomena which here exhibit themselves objectively to us, and their laws, we do this at our own peril and on our own responsibility. We have recognised that the original inner force of nature, without knowledge and working in the dark, which, if it has worked its way up to self-consciousness, reveals itself to this as *will*, attains to this grade only by the production of an animal brain and of knowledge, as its function, whereupon the phenomenon of the world of perception arises in this brain. But to explain this mere brain phenomenon, with the conformity to law which is invariably connected with its functions, as the objective inner nature of the world and the things in it, which is independent of the brain, existing before and after it, is clearly a spring which nothing warrants us in making. From this *mundus phænomenon*, however, from this perception which arises under such a variety of conditions, all our conceptions are drawn. They have all their content from it, or even only in relation to it. Therefore, as Kant says, they are only for immanent, not for transcendental, use; that is to say, these conceptions of ours, this first material of thought, and consequently still more the judgments which result from their combination, are unfitted for the task of thinking the nature of things in themselves, and the true connection of the world and existence; indeed, to undertake this is analogous to expressing the stereometrical content of a body in square inches. For our intellect, originally only intended to present to an individual will its paltry aims, comprehends accordingly mere *relations* of things, and does not penetrate to their inner being, to their real nature. It is therefore a merely superficial force, clings to the surface of things, and apprehends mere *species transitivas*, not the true being of things. From this it arises that we cannot understand and comprehend any single thing, even the simplest and smallest, through and through, but something remains entirely inexplicable to us in each of them. Just because the intellect is a product of nature, and is therefore only intended for its ends, the Christian mystics have very aptly called it "the light of nature," and driven it back within its limits; for nature is the object to which alone it is the subject. The thought from which the Critique of Pure Reason has sprung really lies already at the foundation of this expression. That we cannot comprehend the world on the direct path, *i.e.*, through the uncritical, direct application of the intellect and its data, but when we reflect upon it become ever more deeply involved in insoluble mysteries, points to the fact that the intellect, thus knowledge itself, is secondary, a mere product, brought about by the development of the inner being of the world, which consequently till then preceded it, and it at last appeared as a breaking through to the light out of the obscure depths of the unconscious striving the nature of which exhibits itself as *will* to the self-consciousness which now at once arises. That which preceded knowledge as its condition, whereby it first became possible, thus its own basis, cannot be directly comprehended by it; as the eye cannot see itself. It is rather the relations of one existence to another, exhibiting themselves upon the surface of things, which alone are its affair, and are so only by means of the apparatus of the intellect, its forms, space, time, and causality. Just because the world has made itself without the assistance of knowledge, its whole being does not enter into knowledge, but knowledge presupposes the existence of the world; on which account the origin of the world does not lie within its sphere. It is accordingly limited to the relations between the things which lie before it, and is thus sufficient for the individual will, for the service of which alone it appeared. For the intellect is, as has been shown, conditioned by nature, lies in it, belongs to it, and cannot therefore place itself over against it as something quite foreign to it, in order thus to take up into itself its whole nature, absolutely, objectively, and thoroughly. It can, if fortune favours it, understand all that is in nature, but not nature itself, at least not directly.

However discouraging to metaphysics this essential limitation of the intellect may be, which arises from its nature and origin, it has yet another side which is very consoling. It deprives the direct utterances of nature of their unconditional validity, in the assertion of which *naturalism* proper consists. If, therefore, nature presents to us every living thing as appearing out of nothing, and, after an ephemeral existence, returning again for ever to nothing, and if it seems to take pleasure in the unceasing production of new beings, in order that it may be able unceasingly to destroy, and, on the other hand, is unable to bring anything permanent to light; if accordingly we are forced to recognise *matter* as that which alone is permanent, which never came into being and never passes away, but brings forth all things from its womb, whence its name appears to be derived from *mater rerum*, and along with it, as the father of things, *form*, which, just as fleeting as matter is permanent, changes really every moment, and can only maintain itself so long as it clings as a parasite to matter (now to one part of it, now to another), but when once it entirely loses hold, disappears, as is shown by the palæotheria and the ichthyosaurians, we must indeed recognise this as the direct and genuine utterance of nature, but on account of the origin of the intellect explained above, and the nature of it which results from this origin, we cannot ascribe to this utterance an *unconditional truth*, but rather only an entirely *conditional* truth, which Kant has appropriately indicated as such by calling it the *phenomenon* in opposition to the *thing in itself*.

If, in spite of this essential limitation of the intellect, it is possible, by a circuitous route, to arrive at a certain understanding of the world and the nature of things, by means of reflection widely pursued, and the skilful combination of objective knowledge directed towards without, with the data of self-consciousness, this will yet be only a very limited, entirely indirect, and relative understanding, a parabolical translation into the forms of knowledge, thus a *quadam prodire tenus*, which must always leave many problems still unsolved. On the other hand, the fundamental error of the old *dogmatism* in all its forms, which was destroyed by Kant, was this, that it started absolutely from *knowledge*, i.e., *the world as idea*, in order to deduce and construct from its laws being in general, whereby it accepted that world of idea, together with its laws, as absolutely existing and absolutely real; while its whole existence is throughout relative, and a mere result or phenomenon of the true being which lies at its foundation,—or, in other words, that it constructed an ontology when it had only materials for a dianoiology. Kant discovered the subjectively conditioned and therefore entirely immanent nature of knowledge, *i.e.*, its unsuitableness for transcendental use, from the constitution of knowledge itself; and therefore he very appropriately called his doctrine the *Critique of Reason*. He accomplished this partly by showing the important and thoroughly *a priori* part of all knowledge, which, as throughout subjective, spoils all objectivity, and partly by professedly proving that if they were followed out to the end the principles of knowledge, taken as purely objective, led to contradictions. He had, however, hastily assumed that, apart from *objective* knowledge, *i.e.*, apart from the world as *idea,* there is nothing given us except conscience, out of which he constructed the little that still remained of metaphysics, his moral theology, to which, however, he attributed absolutely only a practical validity, and no theoretical validity at all. He had overlooked that although certainly objective knowledge, or the world as idea, affords nothing but phenomena, together with their phenomenal connection and regressus, yet our own nature necessarily also belongs to the world of things in themselves, for it must have its root in it. But here, even if the root itself cannot be brought to light, it must be possible to gather some data for the explanation of the connection of the world of phenomena with the inner nature of things. Thus here lies the path upon which I have gone beyond Kant and the limits which he drew, yet always restricting myself to the ground of reflection, and consequently of honesty, and therefore without the vain pretension of intellectual intuition or absolute thought which characterises the period of pseudo-philosophy between Kant and me. In his proof of the insufficiency of rational knowledge to fathom the nature of the world Kant started from knowledge as a *fact,* which our consciousness affords us, thus in this sense he proceeded *a posteriori.* But in this chapter, and also in my work, "*Ueber den Willen in der Natur,*" I have sought to show what knowledge is in its *nature and origin,* something secondary, designed for individual ends; whence it follows that it *must be* insufficient to fathom the nature of the world. Thus so far I have reached the same goal *a priori.* But one never knows anything wholly and completely until one has gone right round it for that purpose, and has got back to it from the opposite side from which one started. Therefore also, in the case of the important fundamental knowledge here considered, one must not merely go from the intellect to the knowledge of the world, as Kant has done, but also from the world, taken as given, to the intellect, as I have undertaken here. Then this physiological consideration, in the wider sense, becomes the supplement of that ideological, as the French say, or, more accurately, transcendental consideration.

In the above, in order not to break the thread of the exposition, I have postponed the explanation of one point which I touched upon. It was this, that in proportion as, in the ascending series of animals, the intellect appears ever more developed and complete, *knowledge* always separates itself more distinctly from *will*, and thereby becomes purer. What is essential upon this point will be found in my work, "*Ueber den Willen in der Natur*," under the heading, "*Pflanzenphysiologie*" (p. 68–72 of the second, and 74–77 of the third edition), to which I refer, in order to avoid repetition, and merely add here a few remarks. Since the plant possesses neither irritability nor sensibility, but the will objectifies itself in it only as plastic or reproductive power, it has neither muscle nor nerve. In the lowest grades of the animal kingdom, in zoophites, especially in polyps, we cannot as yet distinctly recognise the separation of these two constituent parts, but still we assume their existence, though in a state of fusion; because we perceive movements which follow, not, as in the case of plants, upon mere stimuli, but upon motives, *i.e.*, in consequence of a certain apprehension. Now in proportion as, in the ascending series of animals, the nervous and muscular systems *separate* ever more distinctly from each other, till in the vertebrate animals, and most completely in man, the former divides into an organic and a cerebral nervous system, and of these the latter again develops into the excessively complicated apparatus of the cerebrum and cerebellum, spinal marrow, cerebral and spinal nerves, sensory and motor nerve fascicles, of which only the cerebrum, together with the sensory nerves depending upon it, and the posterior spinal nerve fascicles are intended for the *apprehension of the motive* from the external world, while all the other parts are intended for the *transmission* of the motive to the muscles in which the will manifests itself directly; in the same proportion does the *motive* separate ever more distinctly in *consciousness* from the *act of will* which it calls forth, thus the *idea* from the *will;* and thereby the *objectivity* of consciousness constantly increases, for the ideas exhibit themselves ever more distinctly and purely in it. These two *separations* are, however, really only one and the same, which we have here considered from two sides, the objective and the subjective, or first in the consciousness of other things and then in self-consciousness. Upon the degree of this separation ultimately depends the difference and the gradation of intellectual capacity, both between different kinds of animals and between individual human beings; thus it gives the standard for the intellectual completeness of these beings. For the clearness of the consciousness of the external world, the objectivity of the perception, depends upon it. In the passage referred to above I have shown that the brute only perceives things so far as they are *motives* for its will, and that even the most intelligent of the brutes scarcely overstep these limits, because their intellect is too closely joined to the will from which it has sprung. On the other hand, even the stupidest man comprehends things in some degree *objectively;* for he recognises not merely what they are with reference to him, but also something of what they are with reference to themselves and to other things. Yet in the case of very few does this reach such a degree that they are in a position to examine and judge of anything purely objectively; but "that must I do, that must I say, that must I believe," is the goal to which on every occasion their thought hastens in a direct line, and at which their understanding at once finds welcome rest. For thinking is as unendurable to the weak head as the lifting of a burden to the weak arm; therefore both hasten to set it down. The objectivity of knowledge, and primarily of perceptive knowledge, has innumerable grades, which depend upon the energy of the intellect and its separation from the will, and the highest of which is *genius,* in which the comprehension of the external world becomes so pure and objective that to it even more reveals itself directly in the individual thing than the individual thing itself, namely, the nature of its whole *species, i.e.,* its Platonic Idea; which is brought about by the fact that in this case the will entirely vanishes from consciousness. Here is the point at which the present investigation, starting from physiological grounds, connects itself with the subject of our third book, the metaphysics of the beautiful, where æsthetic comprehension proper, which, in a high degree, is peculiar to genius alone, is fully considered as the condition of pure, *i.e.,* perfectly will-less, and on that account completely objective knowledge. According to what has been said, the rise of intelligence, from the obscurest animal consciousness up to that of man, is a progressive *loosening of the intellect from the will,* which appears complete, although only as an exception, in the *genius.* Therefore genius may be defined as the highest grade of the *objectivity* of knowledge. The condition of this, which so seldom occurs, is a decidedly larger measure of intelligence than is required for the service of the will, which constitutes its basis; it is accordingly this free surplus which first really properly comes to know the world, *i.e.,* comprehends it perfectly *objectively,* and now paints pictures, composes poems, and thinks in accordance with this comprehension.

CHAPTER XXIII.[1]

ON THE OBJECTIFICATION OF THE WILL IN UNCONSCIOUS NATURE.

THAT the will which we find within us does not proceed, as philosophy has hitherto assumed, first from knowledge, and indeed is a mere modification of it, thus something secondary, derived, and, like knowledge itself, conditioned by the brain; but that it is the *prius* of knowledge, the kernel of our nature, and that original force itself which forms and sustains the animal body, in that it carries out both its unconscious and its conscious functions;—this is the first step in the fundamental knowledge of my metaphysics. Paradoxical as it even now seems to many that the will in itself is without knowledge, yet the scholastics in some way already recognised and confessed it; for Jul. Cæs. Vaninus (that well-known sacrifice to fanaticism and priestly fury), who was thoroughly versed in their philosophy, says in his "*Amphitheatro*," p. 181: "*Voluntas potentia cœca est, ex scholasticorum opinione.*" That, further, it is that same will which in the plant forms the bud in order to develop the leaf and the flower out of it; nay, that the regular form of the crystal is only the trace which its momentary effort has left behind, and that in general, as the true and only *αυτοματον*, in the proper sense of the word, it lies at the foundation of all the forces of unorganised nature, plays, acts, in all their multifarious phenomena, imparts power to their laws, and even in the crudest mass manifests itself as gravity;—this insight is the second step in that fundamental knowledge, and is

[1] This chapter is connected with § 23 of the first volume.

brought about by further reflection. But it would be the grossest misunderstanding to suppose that this is a mere question of a word to denote an unknown quantity. It is rather the most real of all real knowledge which is here expressed in language. For it is the tracing back of that which is quite inaccessible to our immediate knowledge, and therefore in its essence foreign and unknown to us, which we denote by the words *force of nature*, to that which is known to us most accurately and intimately, but which is yet only accessible to us in our own being and directly, and must therefore be carried over from this to other phenomena. It is the insight that what is inward and original in all the changes and movements of bodies, however various they may be, is in its nature identical; that yet we have only one opportunity of getting to know it more closely and directly, and that is in the movements of our own body. In consequence of this knowledge we must call it *will*. It is the insight that that which acts and strives in nature, and exhibits itself in ever more perfect phenomena, when it has worked itself up so far that the light of knowledge falls directly upon it, *i.e.*, when it has attained to the state of self-consciousness—exists as that *will*, which is what is most intimately known to us, and therefore cannot be further explained by anything else, but rather affords the explanation of all other things. It is accordingly the *thing in itself* so far as this can ever be reached by knowledge. Consequently it is that which must express itself in some way in everything in the world, for it is the inner nature of the world and the kernel of all phenomena.

As my essay, "*Ueber den Willen in der Natur*," specially refers to the subject of this chapter, and also adduces the evidence of unprejudiced empiricists in favour of this important point of my doctrine, I have only to add now to what is said there a few supplementary remarks, which are therefore strung together in a somewhat fragmentary manner.

First, then, with reference to plant life, I draw attention to the remarkable first two chapters of Aristotle's work upon plants. What is most interesting in them, as is so often the case with Aristotle, are the opinions of earlier profound philosophers quoted by him. We see there that Anaxagoras and Empedocles quite rightly taught that plants have the motion of their growth by virtue of their indwelling *desires* (επιθυμια); nay, that they also attributed to them pleasure and pain, therefore sensation. But Plato only ascribed to them desires, and that on account of their strong appetite for nutrition (*cf.* Plato in the "*Timæus*," p. 403, Bip.) Aristotle, on the other hand, true to his customary method, glides on the surface of things, confines himself to single characteristics and conceptions fixed by current expressions, and asserts that without sensation there can be no desires, and that plants have not sensation. He is, however, in considerable embarrassment, as his confused language shows, till here also, "where fails the comprehension, a word steps promptly in as deputy," namely, το θρεπτικον, the faculty of nourishing. Plants have this, and thus a part of the so-called soul, according to his favourite division into *anima vegetativa, sensitiva*, and *intellectiva*. This, however, is just a scholastic *Quidditas,* and signifies *plantæ nutriuntur quia habent facultatem nutritivam.* It is therefore a bad substitute for the more profound research of his predecessors, whom he is criticising. We also see, in the second chapter, that Empedocles even recognised the sexuality of plants; which Aristotle then also finds fault with, and conceals his want of special knowledge behind general propositions, such as this, that plants could not have both sexes combined, for if so they would be more complete than animals. By quite an analogous procedure he displaces the correct astronomical system of the world of the Pythagoreans, and by his absurd fundamental principles, which he specially explains in the books *de Cœlo,* introduces the system of Ptolemy, whereby mankind was again deprived of an already discovered truth of the greatest importance for almost two thousand years.

I cannot refrain from giving here the saying of an excellent biologist of our own time who fully agrees with my teaching. It is G. R. Treviranus, who, in his work, "*Ueber die Erscheinungen und Gesetze des organischen Lebens,*" 1832, Bd. 2, Abth. 1, § 49, has said what follows: "A form of life is, however, conceivable in which the effect of the external upon the internal produces merely feelings of desire or dislike. Such is the life of plants. In the higher forms of animal life the external is felt as something objective." Treviranus speaks here from pure unprejudiced comprehension of nature, and is as little conscious of the metaphysical importance of his words as of the *contradictio in adjecto* which lies in the conception of something "felt as objective," a conception which indeed he works out at great length. He does not know that all feeling is essentially subjective, and all that is objective is, on the other hand, perception, and therefore a product of the understanding. Yet this does not detract at all from the truth and importance of what he says.

In fact, in the life of plants the truth that will can exist without knowledge is apparent—one might say palpably recognisable. For here we see a decided effort, determined by wants, modified in various ways, and adapting itself to the difference of the circumstances, yet clearly without knowledge. And just because the plant is without knowledge it bears its organs of generation ostentatiously in view, in perfect innocence; it knows nothing about it. As soon, on the other hand, as in the series of existences knowledge appears the organs of generation are transferred to a hidden part. Man, however, with whom this is again less the case, conceals them intentionally: he is ashamed of them.

Primarily, then, the vital force is identical with the will, but so also are all other forces of nature; though this is less apparent. If, therefore, we find the recognition of a desire, *i.e.*, of a will, as the basis of *plant life*, expressed at all times, with more or less distinctness of conception, on the other hand, the reference of the forces of *unorganised* nature to the same foundation is rarer in proportion as their remoteness from our own nature is greater. In fact, the boundary between the organised and the unorganised is the most sharply drawn in the whole of nature, and perhaps the only one that admits of no transgressions; so that *natura non facit saltus* seems to suffer an exception here. Although certain crystallisations display an external form resembling the vegetable, yet even between the smallest lichen, the lowest fungus, and everything unorganised there remains a fundamental and essential difference. In the *unorganised* body that which is essential and permanent, thus that upon which its identity and integrity rests, is the material, the *matter;* what is unessential and changing is, on the other hand, the *form*. With the *organised* body the case is exactly reversed; for its life, *i.e.*, its existence as an organised being, simply consists in the constant change of the *material*, while the *form* remains permanent. Its being and its identity thus lies in the *form* alone. Therefore the continuance of the *unorganised* body depends upon *repose* and exclusion from external influences: thus alone does it retain its existence; and if this condition is perfect, such a body lasts for ever. The continuance of the *organised* body, on the contrary, just depends upon continual *movement* and the constant reception of external influences. As soon as these are wanting and the movement in it stops it is dead, and thereby ceases to be organic, although the trace of the organism that has been still remains for a while. Therefore the talk, which is so much affected in our own day, of the life of what is unorganised, indeed of the globe itself, and that it, and also the planetary system, is an organism, is entirely inadmissible. The predicate life belongs only to what is organised. Every organism, however, is throughout organised, is so in all its parts; and nowhere are these, even in their smallest particles, composed by aggregation of what is unorganised. Thus if the earth were an organism, all mountains and rocks, and the whole interior of their mass, would necessarily be organised, and accordingly really nothing unorganised would exist; and therefore the whole conception of it would be wanting.

On the other hand, that the manifestation of a *will* is as little bound up with life and organisation as with knowledge, and that therefore the unorganised has also a will, the manifestations of which are all its fundamental qualities, which cannot be further explained,—this is an essential point in my doctrine; although the trace of such a thought is far seldomer found in writers who have preceded me than that of the will in plants, where, however, it is still unconscious.

In the forming of the crystal we see, as it were, a tendency towards an attempt at life, to which, however, it does not attain, because the fluidity of which, like a living thing, it is composed at the moment of that movement is not enclosed in a *skin*, as is always the case with the latter, and consequently it has neither vessels in which that movement could go on, nor does anything separate it from the external world. Therefore, rigidity at once seizes that momentary movement, of which only the trace remains as the crystal.

The thought that the will, which constitutes the basis of our own nature, is also the same will which shows itself even in the lowest unorganised phenomena, on account of which the conformity to law of both phenomena shows a perfect analogy, lies at the foundation of Goethe's "*Wahlverwandtschaften*," as the title indeed indicates, although he himself was unconscious of this.

Mechanics and astronomy specially show us how this will conducts itself so far as it appears at the lowest grade of its manifestation merely as gravity, rigidity, and inertia. Hydraulics shows us the same thing where rigidity is wanting and the fluid material is now unrestrainedly surrendered to its predominating passion, gravity. In this sense hydraulics may be conceived as a characteristic sketch of water, for it presents to us the manifestations of will to which water is moved by gravity; these always correspond exactly to the external influences, for in the case of all non-individual existences there is no particular character in addition to the general one; thus they can easily be referred to fixed characteristics, which are called laws, and which are learned by experience of water. These laws accurately inform us how water will conduct itself under all different circumstances, on account of its gravity, the unconditioned mobility of its parts, and its want of elasticity. Hydrostatics teaches how it is brought to rest through gravity; hydrodynamics, how it is set in motion; and the latter has also to take account of hindrances which adhesion opposes to the will of water: the two together constitute hydraulics. In the same way Chemistry teaches us how the will conducts itself when the inner qualities of materials obtain free play by being brought into a fluid state, and there appears that wonderful attraction and repulsion, separating and combining, leaving go of one to seize upon another, from which every precipitation originates, and the whole of which is denoted by "elective affinity" (an expression which is entirely borrowed from the conscious will). But Anatomy and Physiology allow us to see how the will conducts itself in order to bring about the phenomenon of life and sustain it for a while. Finally, the poet shows us how the will conducts itself under the influence of motives and reflection. He exhibits it therefore for the most part in the most perfect of its manifestations, in rational beings, whose character is individual, and whose conduct and suffering he brings before us in the Drama, the Epic, the Romance, &c. The more correctly, the more strictly according to the laws of nature his characters are there presented, the greater is his fame; hence Shakespeare stands at the top. The point of view which is here taken up corresponds at bottom to the spirit in which Goethe followed and loved the natural sciences, although he was not conscious of the matter in the abstract. Nay more, this not only appears from his writings, but is also known to me from his personal utterances.

If we consider the will, where no one denies it, in conscious beings, we find everywhere, as its fundamental effort, the *self-preservation* of every being: *omnis natura vult esse conservatrix sui.* But all manifestations of this fundamental effort may constantly be traced back to a seeking or pursuit and a shunning or fleeing from, according to the occasion. Now this also may be shown even at the lowest grades of nature, that is, of the objectification of the will, where the bodies still act only as bodies in general, thus are the subject-matter of mechanics, and are considered only with reference to the manifestations of impenetrability, cohesion, rigidity, elasticity, and gravity. Here also the *seeking* shows itself as gravitation, and the *shunning* as the receiving of motion; and the *movableness* of bodies by pressure or impact, which constitutes the basis of mechanics, is at bottom a manifestation of the effort after *self-preservation*, which dwells in them also. For, since as bodies they are impenetrable, this is the sole means of preserving their cohesion, thus their continuance at any time. The body which is impelled or exposed to pressure would be crushed to pieces by the impelling or pressing body if it did not withdraw itself from its power by flight, in order to preserve its cohesion; and when flight is impossible for it this actually happens. Indeed, one may regard *elastic* bodies as the more *courageous*, which seek to repel the enemy, or at least to prevent him from pursuing further. Thus in the one secret which (besides gravity) is left by mechanics otherwise so clear, in the communicability of motion, we see a manifestation of the fundamental effort of the will in all its phenomena, the effort after self-preservation, which shows itself even at the lowest grades as that which is essential.

In unorganised nature the will objectifies itself primarily in the universal forces, and only by means of these in the phenomena of the particular things which are called forth by causes. In § 26 of the first volume I have fully explained the relation between cause, force of nature, and will as thing in itself. One sees from that explanation that metaphysics never interrupts the course of physics, but only takes up the thread where physics leaves it, at the original forces in which all causal explanation has its limits. Only here does the metaphysical explanation from the will as the thing in itself begin. In the case of every physical phenomenon, of every *change* of material things, its cause is primarily to be looked for; and this cause is just such a particular *change* which has appeared immediately before it. Then, however, the original force of nature is to be sought by virtue of which this cause was capable of acting. And first of all the *will* is to be recognised as the inner nature of this force in opposition to its manifestation. Yet the will shows itself just as directly in the fall of a stone as in the action of the man; the difference is only that its particular manifestation is in the one case called forth by a motive, in the other by a mechanically acting cause, for example, the taking away of what supported the stone; yet in both cases with equal necessity; and that in the one case it depends upon an individual character, in the other upon an universal force of nature. This identity of what is fundamentally essential is even made palpable to the senses. If, for instance, we carefully observe a body which has lost its equilibrium, and on account of its special form rolls back and foward for a long time till it finds its centre of gravity again, a certain appearance of life forces itself upon us, and we directly feel that something analogous to the foundation of life is also active here. This is certainly the universal force of nature, which, however, in itself identical with the *will*, becomes here, as it were, the soul of a very brief *quasi* life. Thus what is identical in the two extremes of the manifestation of the will makes itself faintly known here even to direct perception, in that this raises a feeling in us that here also something entirely original, such as we only know in the acts of our own will, directly succeeded in manifesting itself.

We may attain to an intuitive knowledge of the existence and activity of the will in unorganised nature in quite a different and a sublime manner if we study the problem of the three heavenly bodies, and thus learn more accurately and specially the course of the moon round the earth. By the different combinations which the constant change of the position of these three heavenly bodies towards each other introduces, the course of the moon is now accelerated; now retarded, now it approaches the earth, and again recedes from it; and this again takes place differently in the perihelion of the earth from in its aphelion, all of which together introduces such irregularity into the moon's course that it really obtains a capricious appearance; for, indeed, Kepler's third law is no longer constantly valid, but in equal times it describes unequal areas. The consideration of this course is a small and separate chapter of celestial mechanics, which is distinguished in a sublime manner from terrestrial mechanics by the absence of all impact and pressure, thus of the *vis a tergo* which appears to us so intelligible, and indeed of the actually completed case, for besides *vis inertiæ* it knows no other moving and directing force, except only gravitation, that longing for union which proceeds from the very inner nature of bodies. If now we construct for ourselves in imagination the working of this given case in detail, we recognise distinctly and directly in the moving force here that which is given to us in self-consciousness as will. For the alterations in the course of the earth and the moon, according as one of them is by its position more or less exposed to the influence of the sun, are evidently analogous to the influence of newly appearing motives upon our wills, and to the modifications of our action which result.

The following is an illustrative example of another kind. Liebig (*Chemie in Anwendung auf Agrikultur*, p. 501), says: "If we bring moist copper into air which contains carbonic acid, the affinity of the metal for the oxygen of the air will be increased by the contact with this acid to such a degree that the two will combine with each other; its surface will be coated with green carbonic oxide of copper. But now two bodies which have the capacity of combining, the moment they meet assume opposite electrical conditions. Therefore if we touch the copper with iron, by producing a special electrical state, the capacity of the copper to enter into combination with the oxygen is destroyed; even under the above conditions it remains bright." The fact is well known and of technical use. I quote it in order to say that here the will of the copper, laid claim to and occupied by the electrical opposition to iron, leaves unused the opportunity which presents itself for its chemical affinity for oxygen and carbonic acid. Accordingly it conducts itself exactly as the will in a man who omits an action which he would otherwise feel himself moved to in order to perform another to which a stronger motive urges him.

I have shown in the first volume that the forces of nature lie outside the chain of causes and effects, because they constitute their accompanying condition, their metaphysical foundation, and therefore prove themselves to be eternal and omnipresent, *i.e.*, independent of time and space. Even in the uncontested truth that what is essential to a *cause* as such consists in this, that it will produce the same effect at any future time as it does now, it is already involved that something lies in the cause which is independent of the course of time, *i.e.*, is outside of all time; this is the force of nature which manifests itself in it. One can even convince oneself to a certain extent empirically and as a matter of fact of the *ideality* of this form of our perception by fixing one's eyes upon the powerlessness of time as opposed to natural forces. If, for example, a rotatory motion is imparted to a planet by some external cause, if no new cause enters to stop it, this motion will endure for ever. This could not be so if time were something in itself and had an objective, real existence; for then it would necessarily also produce some effect. Thus we see here, on the one hand, the *forces of nature,* which manifest themselves in that rotation, and, if it is once begun, carry it on for ever without becoming weary or dying out, prove themselves to be eternal or timeless, and consequently absolutely real and existing in themselves; and, on the other hand, *time* as something which consists only in the manner in which we apprehend that phenomenon, since it exerts no power and no influence upon the phenomenon itself; for *what does not act is not.*

We have a natural inclination whenever it is possible to explain every natural phenomenon *mechanically;* doubtless because mechanics calls in the assistance of the fewest original, and hence inexplicable, forces, and, on the other hand, contains much that can be known *a priori,* and therefore depends upon the forms of our own intellect, which as such carries with it the highest degree of comprehensibility and clearness. However, in the "Metaphysical First Principles of Natural Science" Kant has referred mechanical activity itself to a dynamical activity. On the other hand, the application of mechanical explanatory hypotheses, beyond what is demonstrably mechanical, to which, for example, Acoustics also belongs, is entirely unjustified, and I will never believe that even the simplest chemical combination or the dfference of the three states of aggregation will ever admit of mechanical explanation, much less the properties of light, of heat, and electricity. These will always admit only of a dynamical explanation, *i.e.,* one which explains the phenomenon from orginal forces which are entirely different from those of impact, pressure, weight, &c., and are therefore of a higher kind, *i.e.*, are more distinct objectifications of that will which obtains visible form in all things. I am of opinion that light is neither an emanation nor a vibration; both views are akin to that which explains transparency from pores, and the evident falseness of which is proved by the fact that light is subject to no mechanical laws. In order to obtain direct conviction of this one only requires to watch the effects of a storm of wind, which bends, upsets, and scatters everything, but during which a ray of light shooting down from a break in the clouds is entirely undisturbed and steadier than a rock, so that with great directness it imparts to us the knowledge that it belongs to another order of things than the mechanical: it stands there unmoved like a ghost. Those constructions of light from molecules and atoms which have originated with the French are indeed a revolting absurdity. An article by Ampère, who is otherwise so acute, upon light and heat, which is to be found in the April number of the "*Annales de chimie et physique*," of 1835, may be considered as a flagrant expression of this, and indeed of the whole of atomism in general. There the solid, the fluid, and the elastic consist of the same atoms, and all differences arise solely from their aggregation; nay, it is said that space indeed is infinitely divisible, but not matter; because, if the division has been carried as far as the atoms, the further divison must fall in the spaces between the atoms! Light and heat, then, are here vibrations of the atoms; and sound, on the other hand, is a vibration of the molecules composed of the atoms. In truth, however, these atoms are a fixed idea of the French savants, and therefore they just speak of them as if they had seen them. Otherwise one would necessarily marvel that such a matter-of-fact nation as the French can hold so firmly to a completely transcendent hypothesis, which is quite beyond the possibility of experience, and confidently build upon it up to the sky. This is just a consequence of the backward state of the metaphysics they shun so much, which is poorly represented by M. Cousin, who, with all good will, is shallow and very scantily endowed with judgment. At bottom they are still Lockeians, owing to the earlier influence of Condillac. Therefore for them the thing in itself is really matter, from the fundamental properties of which, such as impenetrability, form, hardness, and the other primary qualities, everything in the world must be ultimately explicable. They will not let themselves be talked out of this, and their tacit assumption is that matter can only be moved by mechanical forces. In Germany Kant's teaching has prevented the continuance of the absurdities of the atomistic and purely mechanical physics for any length of time; although at the present moment these views prevail here also, which is a consequence of the shallowness, crudeness, and folly introduced by Hegel. However, it cannot be denied that not only the evidently porous nature of natural bodies, but also two special doctrines of modern physics, apparently render assistance to the atomic nuisance. These are, Hauz's Crystallography, which traces every crystal back to its kernel form, which is an ultimate form, though only *relatively* indivisible; and Berzelius's doctrine of chemical atoms, which are yet mere expressions for combining proportions, thus only arithmetical quantities, and at bottom nothing more than counters. On the other hand, Kant's thesis in the second antinomy in defence of atoms, which is certainly only set up for dialectical purposes, is a mere sophism, as I have proved in my criticism of his philosophy, and our understanding itself by no means leads us necessarily to the assumption of atoms. For just as little as I am obliged to think that the slow but constant and uniform *motion* of a body before my eyes is composed of innumerable motions which are absolutely quick, but broken and interrupted by just as many absolutely short moments of rest, but. on the contrary, know very well that the stone that has been thrown flies more slowly than the projected bullet, yet never pauses for an instant on the way, so little am I obliged to think of the mass of a body as consisting of atoms and the spaces between them, *i.e.*, of absolute density and absolute vacuity; but I comprehend those two phenomena without difficulty as constant *continua*, one of which uniformly fills time and the other space. But just as the one motion may yet be quicker than another, *i.e.*, in an equal time can pass through more space, so also one body may have a greater specific gravity than another, *i.e.*, in equal space may contain more matter: in both cases the difference depends upon the intensity of the acting force; for Kant (following Priestley) has quite correctly reduced matter to forces. But even if the analogy here set up should not be admitted as valid, and it should be insisted upon that the difference of specific gravity can only have its ground in porosity, even this assumption would always lead, not to atoms, but only to a perfectly dense matter, unequally distributed among different bodies; a matter which would certainly be no longer *compressible*, when no pores ran through it, but yet, like the space which it fills, would always remain infinitely *divisible*. For the fact that it would have no pores by no means involves that no possible force could do away with the continuity of its spatial parts. For to say that everywhere this is only possible by extending the already existing intervals is a purely arbitrary assertion.

The assumption of atoms rests upon the two phenomena which have been touched upon, the difference of the specific gravity of bodies and that of their compressibility, for both are conveniently explained by the assumption of atoms. But then both must also always be present in like measure, which is by no means the case. For, for example, water has a far lower specific gravity than all metals properly so called. It must thus have fewer atoms and greater interstices between them, and consequently be very compressible: but it is almost entirely incompressible.

The defence of atoms might be conducted in this way. One may start from porosity and say something of this sort: All bodies have pores, and therefore so also have all parts of a body: now if this were carried out to infinity, there would ultimately be nothing left of a body but pores. The refutation would be that what remained over would certainly have to be assumed as without pores, and so far as absolutely dense, yet not on that account as consisting of absolutely indivisible particles, atoms; accordingly it would certainly be absolutely incompressible, but not absolutely indivisible. It would therefore be necessary that it should be asserted that the division of a body is only possible by penetrating into its pores; which, however, is entirely unproved. If, however, this is assumed, then we certainly have atoms, *i.e.*, absolutely indivisible bodies, thus bodies of such strong cohesion of their spatial parts that no possible power can separate them: but then one may just as well assume such bodies to be large as small, and an atom might be as big as an ox, if it only would resist all possible attacks upon it.

Imagine two bodies of very different kinds, entirely freed from all pores by compression, as by means of hammering, or by pulverisation;—would their specific gravity then be the same? This would be the criterion of dynamics.

CHAPTER XXIV.

ON MATTER.

MATTER has already been spoken of in the fourth chapter of the supplements to the first book, when we were considering the part of our knowledge of which we are conscious *a priori*. But it could only be considered there from a one-sided point of view, because we were then concerned merely with its relation to the forms of our intellect, and not to the thing in itself, and therefore we investigated it only from the subjective side, *i.e.*, so far as it is an idea, and not from the objective side, *i.e.*, with regard to what it may be in itself. In the first respect, our conclusion was that it is objective *activity* in general, yet conceived without fuller determination; therefore it takes the place of causality in the table of our *a priori* knowledge which is given there. For what is material is that which *acts* (the actual) in general, and regarded apart from the specific nature of its action. Hence also matter, merely as such, is not an object of *perception*, but only of *thought*, and thus is really an abstraction. It only comes into perception in connection with form and quality, as a body, *i.e.*, as a fully determined kind of activity. It is only by abstracting from this fuller determination that we think of matter as such, *i.e.*, separated from form and quality; consequently under matter we think of *acting* absolutely and in general, thus of *activity* in the abstract. The more fully determined acting we then conceive as the *accident* of matter; but only by means of this does matter become preceptible, *i.e.*, present itself as a body and an object of experience. Pure matter, on the other hand, which, as I have shown in the Criticism of the Kantian Philosophy, alone constitutes the true and admissible content of the conception of *substance*, is causality itself, thought objectively, consequently as in space, and therefore filling it. Accordingly the whole being of matter consists in *acting*. Only thus does it occupy space and last in time. It is through and through pure causality. Therefore wherever there is action there is matter, and the material is the active in general. But causality itself is the form of our understanding; for it is known to us *a priori*, as well as time and space. Thus matter also, *so far* and up to this point, belongs to the formal part of our knowledge, and is consequently that form of the understanding, *causality* itself, bound up with space and time, hence objectified, *i.e.*, conceived as that which fills space. (The fuller explanation of this doctrine will be found in the second edition of the essay on the principle of sufficient reason, p. 77; third edition, p. 82.) So far, however, matter is properly not the *object* but the *condition* of experience; like the pure understanding itself, whose function it so far is. Therefore of pure matter there is also only a *conception*, no *perception*. It enters into all external experience as a necessary constituent part of it; yet it cannot be given in any experience, but is only *thought*, and thought indeed as that which is absolutely inert, inactive, formless, and without qualities, and which is yet the supporter of all forms, qualities, and effects. Accordingly, of all fleeting phenomena, thus of all manifestations of natural forces and all living beings, matter is the *permanent substratum* which is necessarily produced by the forms of our intellect in which the world as *idea* exhibits itself. As such, and as having sprung from the forms of the intellect, it is entirely *indifferent* to those phenomena themselves, *i.e.*, it is just as ready to be the supporter of this force of nature as of that, whenever, under the guidance of causality, the necessary conditions appear; while it itself, just because its existence is really only *formal, i.e.*, is founded in the *intellect*, must be thought as that which under all that change is absolutely permanent, thus with regard to time is without beginning and without end. This is why we cannot give up the thought that anything may be made out of anything, for example, gold out of lead; for this would only require that we should find out and bring about the intermediate states which matter, in itself indifferent, would have to pass through upon that path. For *a priori* we can never see why the same matter which is now the supporter of the quality lead could not some time become the supporter of the quality gold. Matter, as that which is only *thought a priori*, is distinguished from the *a priori intuitions* or *perceptions* proper by the fact that we can also think it entirely away; space and time, on the contrary, never. But this only shows that we can present to ourselves space and time in imagination without matter. For the matter which has once been placed in them, and accordingly thought as *existing*, we can never again absolutely think away, *i.e.*, imagine it as vanished and annihilated, but are always forced to think of it merely as transferred to another space. So far, then, matter is as inseparably connected with our faculty of knowledge as space and time themselves. Yet even the difference that it must first be voluntarily thought as existing indicates that it does not belong so entirely and in every regard to the *formal* part of our knowledge as space and time, but also contains an element which is only given *a posteriori*. It is, in fact, the point of connection of the empirical part of our knowledge with the pure and *a priori* part, consequently the peculiar foundation-stone of the world of experience.

Only where all *a priori* assertions cease, therefore in the *entirely empirical* part of our knowledge of bodies, in their form, quality, and definite manner of acting, does that *will* reveal itself which we have already recognised and established as the true inner nature of things. But these forms and qualities always appear only as the properties and manifestations of that very *matter* the existence and nature of which depends upon the subjective forms of our intellect, *i.e.*, they only become visible in it, and therefore by means of it. For that which always exhibits itself to us is only *matter* acting in some specially determined manner. Out of the inner properties of such matter, properties which cannot be further explained, proceeds every definite kind of effect of given bodies; and yet the matter itself is never perceived, but only these effects, and the definite properties which lie at their foundation, after separating which, matter, as that which then remains over, is necessarily added in thought by us; for, according to the exposition given above, it is objectified *causality itself.* Accordingly matter is that whereby the *will,* which constitutes the inner nature of things, becomes capable of being apprehended, perceptible, *visible.* In this sense, then, matter is simply the *visibility* of the will, or the bond between the world as will and the world as idea. It belongs to the latter inasmuch as it is the product of the functions of the intellect, to the former inasmuch as that which manifests itself in all material existences, *i.e.*, phenomena is the will. Therefore every object is, as thing in itself, will, and as phenomenon, matter. If we could strip any given matter of all the properties that come to it *a priori, i.e.*, of all the forms of our perception and apprehension, we would have left the thing in itself, that which, by means of those forms, appears as the purely empirical in matter, but which would then itself no longer appear as something extended and active; *i.e.*, we would no longer have matter before us, but the will. This very thing in itself, or the will, in that it becomes a phenomenon, *i.e.*, enters the forms of our intellect, appears as matter, *i.e.*, as the invisible but necessarily assumed supporter of the properties which are only visible through it. In this sense, then, matter is the visibility of the *will.* Consequently Plotinus and Giordano Bruno were right, not only in their sense but also in ours, when they made the paradoxical assertion already referred to in chapter 4: Matter itself is not extended, consequently it is incorporeal. For space, which is our form of perception, imparts extension to matter, and corporeal existence consists in acting, which depends upon causality, and consequently upon the form of our understanding. On the other hand, every definite property, thus everything empirical in matter, even gravity, depends upon that which only becomes visible by means of matter, the thing in itself, the will. Gravity is yet the lowest of all grades of the objectification of the will; therefore it appears in all matter without exception, thus is inseparable from matter in general. Yet, just because it is a manifestation of the will, it belongs to knowledge *a posteriori*, not to knowledge *a priori*. Therefore we can always picture to ourselves matter without weight, but not without extension, repulsive force, and stability, for then it would be without impenetrability, and consequently would not occupy space, *i.e.*, it would be without *the power of acting*; but the nature of matter as such just consists in *acting*, *i.e.*, in causality in general; and causality depends upon the *a priori* form of our understanding, and therefore cannot be thought away.

Matter is accordingly the *will* itself, but no longer in itself, but so far as it is *perceived*, *i.e.*, assumes the form of the objective idea. Thus what objectively is matter is subjectively will. Exactly corresponding to this, as was proved above, our body is just the visibility, objectivity of our will, and so also every body is the objectivity of the will at some one of its grades. Whenever the will exhibits itself to objective knowledge it enters into the forms of perception of the intellect, time, space, and causality. But on account of this it exists at once as a *material* object. We can present to our minds form without matter, but not the reverse; because matter deprived of form would be the will itself, and the will only becomes objective by entering the forms of perception of our intellect, and therefore only by means of the assumption of form. Space is the form of perception of matter because the latter is the substance (Stoff) of mere form, but matter can *appear* only in form.

Since the will becomes objective, *i.e.*, passes over into the idea, matter is the universal substratum of this objectification, or rather it is this objectification itself taken abstractly, *i.e.*, regarded apart from all form. Matter is accordingly the *visibility* of the will in general, while the character of its definite manifestations has its expression in form and quality. Hence what in the manifestation, *i.e.*, for the idea, is *matter* is in itself *will*. Therefore, under the conditions of experience and perception, everything holds good of it that holds good of the will in itself, and it repeats all the relations and properties of the will in temporal images. Accordingly it is the substance of the world of perception, as the will is the inner nature of all things. The forms are innumerable, the matter is one; just as the will is one in all its objectifications. As the will never objectifies itself as general, *i.e.*, as absolute will, but always as particular, *i.e.*, under special determinations and a given character, so matter never appears as such, but always in connection with some particular form and quality. In the manifestation or objectification of the will matter represents its totality, it itself, which in all is one, as matter is one in all bodies. As the will is the inmost kernel of all phenomenal beings, so matter is the substance which remains after all the accidents have been taken away. As the will is that which is absolutely indestructible in all existence, so matter is that which is imperishable in time and permanent through all changes. That matter for itself, thus separated from form, cannot be perceived or presented in imagination depends upon the fact that in itself, and as the pure substantiality of bodies, it is really the *will* itself. But the will cannot be apprehended objectively, or perceived in itself, but only under all the conditions of the *idea*, and therefore only as *phenomenon*. Under these conditions, however, it exhibits itself at once as body, *i.e.*, as matter clothed in form and quality. But form is conditioned by space, and quality or power of acting by causality; thus both depend upon the functions of the intellect. Matter without them would just be the thing in itself, *i.e.*, the will itself. Therefore, as has been said, Plotinus and Giordano Bruno could only be brought by a completely objective path to the assertion that matter in and for itself is without extension, consequently without spatial properties, consequently incorporeal.

Because, then, matter is the visibility of the will, and every force in itself is will, no force can appear without a material substratum, and conversely no body can be without forces dwelling in it which constitute its quality. Therefore a body is the union of matter and form which is called substance (Stoff). Force and substance are inseparable because at bottom they are one; for, as Kant has shown, matter itself is given us only as the union of two forces, the force of expansion and that of attraction. Thus there is no opposition between force and substance, rather they are precisely one.

Led by the course of our consideration to this standpoint, and having attained to this metaphysical view of matter, we will confess without reluctance that the temporal *origin* of forms, shapes, or species cannot reasonably be sought elsewhere than in matter. Some time or other they must have come forth from it, just because it is the mere *visibility of the will* which constitutes the inner nature of all phenomena. In that the will manifests itself, *i.e.*, presents itself *objectively* to the intellect, matter, as its visibility, assumes *form* by means of the functions of the intellect. Hence the Schoolmen said: "*Materia appetit formam.*" That such was the origin of all forms of life cannot be doubted: we cannot even conceive it otherwise. Whether, however, now, since the paths to the perpetuation of the forms stand open, and are secured and sustained by nature with boundless care and jealousy, *generatio æquivoca* still takes place, can only be decided by experience; especially since the saying, *Natura nihil facit frustra*, might, with reference to the paths of regular propagation, be used as a valid argument against it. Yet in spite of the most recent objections to it, I hold that at very low grades *generatio æquivoca* is very probable, and primarily indeed in the case of entozoa and epizoa, particularly such as appear in consequence of special cachexia of the animal organism. For the conditions of their life only appear exceptionally; consequently their species cannot propagate itself in the regular manner, and therefore has always to arise anew whenever opportunity offers. Therefore as soon as the conditions of life of epizoa have appeared in consequence of certain chronic diseases, or cachexia, and in accordance with them, *pediculus capitis* or *pubis* or *corporis* appears entirely of itself, and without any egg; and this notwithstanding the complex structure of these insects, for the putrefaction of a living animal body affords material for higher productions than that of hay in water, which only produces infusoria. Or is it thought more likely that the eggs of the epizoa are constantly floating about in the air in expectation? (Fearful to think of!) Let us rather remember the disease of phthiriasis, which occurs even now. An analogous case takes place when through special circumstances the conditions of life appear of a species which up till then was foreign to that *place*. Thus August St. Hilaire saw in Brazil, after the burning of a primitive forest, as soon as ever the ashes had cooled, a number of plants grow up out of them, the species of which was not to be found far and wide; and quite recently Admiral Petit-Thouars informed the *Académie des sciences* that upon the growing coral islands in Polynesia a soil gradually deposits itself which is now dry, now lies in water, and which vegetation soon takes possession of, bringing forth trees which are absolutely peculiar to these islands (*Comptes rendus*, 17th Jan. 1859, p. 147). Whenever putrefaction takes place mould, fungi, and in liquids infusoria appear. The assumption now in favour that spores and eggs of the innumerable species of all those kinds of animal life are everywhere floating in the air, and wait through long years for a favourable opportunity, is more paradoxical than that of *generatio æquivoca*. Putrefaction is the decomposition of an organised body, first into its *more immediate* chemical constituents. Since now these are more or less the same in all living beings, the omnipresent will to live can possess itself of them, in order, in accordance with the circumstances, to produce new existences from them; and these forming themselves according to design, *i.e.*, objectifying the volition of the will at the time, solidify out of the chemical elements, as the chicken out of the fluidity of the egg. When, however, this does not take place, the putrefying matter is resolved into its *ultimate* constituent parts, which are the chemical elements, and now passes over again into the great course of nature. The war which has been waged for the last ten or fifteen years against *generatio æquivoca*, with its premature shouts of victory, was the prelude to the denial of the vital force, and related to it. Let no one, however, be deceived by dogmatic assertions and brazen assurances that the questions are decided, settled, and generally recognised. On the contrary, the whole mechanical and atomistic view of nature is approaching its bankruptcy, and its defenders have to learn that something more is concealed behind nature than action and reaction. The reality of *generatio æquivoca* and the folly of the extraordinary assumption that in the atmosphere, everywhere and always, billions of seeds of all possible kinds of fungi, and eggs of all possible kinds of infusoria, are floating about, till now one and then another by chance finds its suitable medium, has quite recently (1859) been thoroughly and victoriously shown by Pouchet before the French Academy, to the great vexation of the other members.

Our wonder at the origin of forms in matter is at bottom like that of the savage who looks for the first time in a mirror and marvels at his own image which he sees there. For our own inner nature is the will, whose mere *visibility* is matter. Yet matter never appears otherwise than with the *visible, i.e.*, under the outer shell of form and quality, and therefore is never directly apprehended, but always merely added in thought as that which is identical in all things, under all differences of quality and form. On this account it is more a metaphysical than a physical principle of explanation of things, and to make all existences arise from it is really to explain them from something which is very mysterious; which all know it to be except those who confound attacking with comprehending. In truth, the ultimate and exhaustive explanation of things is by no means to be sought in matter, although certainly the temporal origin both of unorganised forms and of organised beings is to be sought in it. Yet it seems that the origination of organised forms, the production of the species themselves, is almost as difficult for nature to accomplish as it is for us to comprehend. This is indicated by the entirely extravagant provision which nature always makes for maintaining the species which once exist. Yet on the present surface of this planet the will to live has gone through the scale of its objectification three times, quite independently of each other, in a different modulation, and also with great difference of perfection and fulness. The old world, America, and Australia have, it is well known, each their peculiar independent fauna, entirely different from that of the other two. Upon each of these great continents the species are throughout different, but yet, because all three belong to the same planet, they have a thorough analogy with each other running parallel through them; therefore the *genera* are for the most part the same. In Australia this analogy can only be very imperfectly followed because its fauna is very poor in mammalia, and contains neither beasts of prey nor apes. On the other hand, between the old world and America it is obvious, and in the following manner. In mammals America always produces the inferior analogue, but in birds and reptiles the better. Thus it has the advantage in the condor, the macaw, the humming-bird, and the largest batrachia and ophidia; but, for example, instead of the elephant it has only the tapir, instead of the lion the puma, instead of the tiger the jaguar, instead of the camel the lama, and instead of apes proper only monkeys. Even from this last defect it may be concluded that in America nature was not able to rise to man; for even from the nearest grade below man, the chimpanzee and the orang-outang or pongo, the step to man was still an excessively great one. Correspondingly we find that the three races of men which, both upon physiological and linguistic grounds, are undoubtedly equally original, the Caucasian, the Mongolian, and the Ethiopian, are only at home in the old world; while America, on the other hand, is peopled by a mixed or climatically modified Mongolian race, which must have come over from Asia. On the surface of the earth which immediately preceded the present surface apes were reached here and there, but not men.

From this standpoint of our consideration, which shows us matter as the direct visibility of the will which manifests itself in all things, nay, indeed, for the merely physical investigation which follows the guidance of time and causality, lets it pass as the origin of things, we are easily led to the question whether even in philosophy we could not just as well start from the objective as from the subjective side, and accordingly set up as the fundamental truth the proposition: "There is in general nothing but matter and its indwelling forces." But, with regard to these "indwelling forces" here so easily used, we must remember that their assumption leads every explanation back to a completely incomprehensible miracle, and then leaves it beside it, or rather leaves it to begin from it. For every definite, inexplicable force of nature which lies at the foundation of the most different kinds of effects of an unorganised body, not less than the vital force which manifests itself in every organised body, is such an incomprehensible miracle, as I have fully explained in chap. 17, and have also shown that physics can never be set upon the throne of metaphysics, just because it leaves quite untouched the assumption referred to and also many others; whereby from the beginning it renounces all claim to give an ultimate explanation of things. I must further remind the reader here of the proof of the insufficiency of materialism, which is given towards the end of the first chapter, because, as was said there, it is the philosophy of the subject which forgets itself in its calculation. But all these truths rest upon the fact that everything *objective*, everything external, since it is always only something apprehended, something known, remains also always indirect and secondary, therefore absolutely never can become the ultimate ground of explanation of things or the starting-point of philosophy. Philosophy necessarily requires what is absolutely immediate for its starting-point. But clearly only that which is given in *self-consciousness* fulfils this condition, that which is within, the *subjective*. And hence it is so eminent a merit of Descartes that he first made philosophy start from self-consciousness. Since then, upon this path, the genuine philosophers, especially Locke, Berkeley, and Kant, have gone even further, each in his own manner, and in consequence of their investigations I was led to recognise and make use, not of one, but of two completely different data of immediate knowledge in self-consciousness, the idea and the will, by the combined application of which one can go further in philosophy, in the same proportion as in the case of an algebraical problem one can accomplish more if two known quantities are given than if only one is given.

In accordance with what has been said, the ineradicable falseness of materialism primarily consists in the fact that it starts from a *petitio principii*, which when more closely considered turns out indeed to be a πρωτον φευδος. It starts from the assumption that matter is something absolutely and unconditionally given, something existing independently of the knowledge of the subject, thus really a thing in itself. It attributes to matter (and consequently also to its presuppositions time and space) an *absolute* existence, *i.e.*, an existence independent of the perceiving subject; this is its fundamental error. Then, if it will go honestly to work, it must leave the qualities inherent in the given materials, *i.e.*, in the substances, together with the natural forces which manifest themselves in these, and finally also the vital force, unexplained, as unfathomable *qualitates occultæ*, and start from them; as physics and physiology actually do, because they make no claim to be the ultimate explanation of things. But just to avoid this, materialism—at least as it has hitherto appeared—has not proceeded honestly. It denies all those original forces, for it pretends and seems to reduce them all, and ultimately also the vital force, to the mere mechanical activity of matter, thus to manifestations of impenetrability, form, cohesion, impulsive power, inertia, gravity, &c., qualities which certainly have least that is inexplicable in themselves, just because they partly depend upon what is known *a priori*, consequently on the forms of our own intellect, which are the principle of all comprehensibility. But the intellect as the condition of all objects, and consequently of the whole phenomenal world, is entirely ignored by materialism. Its plan is now to refer everything qualitative to something merely quantitative, for it attributes the former to mere *form* in opposition to *matter* proper. To matter it leaves, of the properly *empirical* qualities, only gravity, because it already appears as something quantitative, the only measure of the quantity of the matter. This path necessarily leads it to the fiction of atoms, which now become the material out of which it thinks to construct the mysterious manifestations of all original forces. But here it has really no longer to do with empirically *given* matter, but with a matter which is not to be found *in rerum natura*, but is rather a mere abstraction of that real matter, a matter which would absolutely have no other than those mechanical qualities which, with the exception of gravity, can be pretty well construed *a priori*, just because they depend upon the forms of space, time, and causality, and consequently upon our intellect; to this poor material, then, it finds itself reduced for the construction of its castle in the air.

In this way it inevitably becomes *atomism;* as happened to it already in its childhood in the hands of Leucippus and Democritus, and happens to it again now that it has come to a second childhood through age; with the French because they have never known the Kantian philosophy, and with the Germans because they have forgotten it. And indeed it carries it further in this its second childhood than in its first. Not merely *solid* bodies are supposed to consist of atoms, but liquids, water, air, gas, nay, even light, which is supposed to be the undulations of a completely hypothetical and altogether unproved ether, consisting of atoms, the difference of the rapidity of these undulations causing colours. This is an hypothesis which, like the earlier Newtonian seven-colour theory, starts from an analogy with music, entirely arbitrarily assumed, and then violently carried out. One must really be credulous to an unheard-of degree to let oneself be persuaded that the innumerable different ether vibrations proceeding from the infinite multiplicity of coloured surfaces in this varied world could constantly, and each in its own time, run through and everywhere cross each other without ever disturbing each other, but should rather produce through such tumult and confusion the profoundly peaceful aspect of illumined nature and art.

Credat Judæus Apella! Certainly the nature of light is to us a secret; but it is better to confess this than to bar the way of future knowledge by bad theories. That light is something quite different from a mere mechanical movement, undulation, or vibration and tremor, indeed that it is material, is shown by its chemical effects, a beautiful series of which was recently laid before the *Académie des sciences* by Chevreul, who let sunlight act upon different coloured materials. The most beautiful thing in these experiments is, that a white roll of paper which has been exposed to the sunlight exhibits the same effects, nay, does so even after six months, if during this time it has been secured in a firmly closed metal tube. Has, then, the tremulation paused for six months, and does it now fall into time again? (*Comptes rendus* of 20th December 1858.) This whole hypothesis of vibrating ether atoms is not only a chimera, but equals in awkward crudeness the worst of Democritus, and yet is shameless enough, at the present day, to profess to be an established fact, and has thus brought it about that it is orthodoxly repeated by a thousand stupid scribblers of all kinds, who are devoid of all knowledge of such things, and is believed in as a gospel. But the doctrine of atoms in general goes still further: it is soon a case of *Spartam, quam nactus es, orna!* Different perpetual motions are then ascribed to all the atoms, revolving, vibrating, &c., according to the office of each; in the same way every atom has its atmosphere of ether, or something else, and whatever other similar fancies there may be. The fancies of Schelling's philosophy of nature and its disciples were for the most part ingenious, lofty, or at least witty; but these, on the contrary, are clumsy, insipid, paltry, and awkward, the production of minds which, in the first place, are unable to think any other reality than a fabulous, qualityless matter, which is also an absolute object, *i.e.*, an object without a subject; and secondly can think of no other activity than motion and impact: these two alone are comprehensible to them, and that everything runs back to these is their *a priori* assumption; for these are their *thing in itself*. To attain this end the vital force is reduced to chemical forces (which are insidiously and unjustifiably called molecular forces), and all processes of unorganised nature to mechanism, *i.e.*, to action and reaction. And thus at last the whole world and everything in it becomes merely a piece of mechanical ingenuity, like the toys worked by levers, wheels, and sand, which represent a mine or the work on a farm. The source of the evil is, that through the amount of hand-work which experimenting requires the head-work of thinking has been allowed to get out of practice. The crucible and the voltaic pile are supposed to assume its functions; hence also the profound abhorrence of all philosophy.

But the matter might be put in this way. One might say that materialism, as it has hitherto appeared, has only failed because it did not adequately *know* the matter out of which it thought to construct the world, and therefore was dealing, not with matter itself, but with a propertyless substitute for it. If, on the contrary, instead of this, it had taken the actual and *empirically* given matter (*i.e.*, material substance, or rather substances), endowed as it is with all physical, chemical, electrical properties, and also with the power of spontaneously producing life out of itself, thus the true *mater rerum*, from the obscurity of whose womb all phenomena and forms come forth, to fall back into it some time again; from this, *i.e.*, from matter fully comprehended and exhaustively known, a world might have been constructed of which materialism would not need to be ashamed. Quite true: only the trick would then consist in this, that the *Quæsita* had been placed in the *Data*, for professedly what was taken as given, and made the starting-point of the deduction, was mere matter, but really it included all the mysterious forces of nature which cling to it, or more correctly, by means of it become visible to us, much the same as if under the name of the dish we understand what lies upon it. For in fact, for our knowledge, matter is really merely the *vehicle* of the qualities and natural forces, which appear as its accidents, and just because I have traced these back to the will I call matter the mere *visibility of the will.* Stripped of all these qualities, matter remains behind as that which is without qualities, the *caput mortuum* of nature, out of which nothing can honestly be made. If, on the contrary, in the manner referred to, one leaves it all these properties, one is guilty of a concealed *petitio principii*, for one has assumed the *Quæsita* beforehand as *Data.* But what is accomplished with *this* will no longer be a proper *materialism,* but merely *naturalism, i.e.,* an absolute system of *physics,* which, as was shown in chap. 17 already referred to, can never assume and fill the place of metaphysics, just because it only begins after so many assumptions, thus never undertakes to explain things from the foundation. Mere naturalism is therefore essentially based simply upon *qualitates occultæ*, which one can never get beyond except, as I have done, by calling in the aid of the *subjective* source of knowledge, which then certainly leads to the long and toilsome round-about path of metaphysics, for it presupposes the complete analysis of self-consciousness and of the intellect and will given in it. However, the starting from what is *objective,* at the foundation of which lies *external perception,* so distinct and comprehensible, is a path so natural and which presents itself of its own accord to man, that *naturalism,* and consequently, because this cannot satisfy as it is not exhaustive, *materialism,* are systems to which the speculative reason must necessarily have come, nay, must have come first of all. Therefore at the very beginning of the history of philosophy we meet naturalism, in the systems of the Ionic philosophers, and then materialism in the teaching of Leucippus and Democritus, and also later we see them ever appear anew from time to time.

CHAPTER XXV.

TRANSCENDENT CONSIDERATIONS CONCERNING THE WILL AS THING IN ITSELF.

EVEN the merely empirical consideration of nature recognises a constant transition from the simplest and most necessary manifestation of a universal force of nature up to the life and consciousness of man himself, through gentle gradations, and with only relative, and for the most part fluctuating, limits. Reflection, following this view, and penetrating somewhat more deeply into it, will soon be led to the conviction that in all these phenomena, the inner nature, that which manifests itself, that which appears, is one and the same, which comes forth ever more distinctly; and accordingly that what exhibits itself in a million forms of infinite diversity, and so carries on the most varied and the strangest play without beginning or end, this is one being which is so closely disguised behind all these masks that it does not even recognise itself, and therefore often treats itself roughly. Thus the great doctrine of the ἑν και παν early appeared both in the east and in the west, and, in spite of all contradiction, has asserted itself, or at least constantly revived. We, however, have now entered even deeper into the secret, since by what has already been said we have been led to the insight that when in any phenomenon a *knowing consciousness* is added to that inner being which lies at the foundation of all phenomena, a consciousness which when directed inwardly becomes *self-consciousness,* then that inner being presents itself to this self-consciousness as that which is so familiar and so mysterious, and is denoted by the word *will*. Accordingly we have called that universal fundamental nature of all phenomena *the will*, after that manifestation in which it unveils itself to us most fully; and by this word nothing is further from our intention than to denote an unknown x; but, on the contrary, we denote that which at least on one side is infinitely better known and more intimate than anything else.

Let us now call to mind a truth, the fullest and most thorough proof of which will be found in my prize essay on the freedom of the will—the truth that on account of the absolutely universal validity of the law of causality, the conduct or the action of all existences in this world is always strictly *necessitated* by the causes which in each case call it forth. And in this respect it makes no difference whether such an action has been occasioned by causes in the strictest sense of the word, or by stimuli, or finally by motives, for these differences refer only to the grade of the susceptibility of the different kinds of existences. On this point we must entertain no illusion: the law of causality knows no exception; but everything, from the movement of a mote in a sunbeam to the most deeply considered action of man, is subject to it with equal strictness. Therefore, in the whole course of the world, neither could a mote in a sunbeam describe any other line in its flight than it has described, nor a man act any other way than he has acted; and no truth is more certain than this, that all that happens, be it small or great, happens with absolute *necessity*. Consequently, at every given moment of time, the whole condition of all things is firmly and accurately determined by the condition which has just preceded it, and so is it with the stream of time back to infinity and on to infinity. Thus the course of the world is like that of a clock after it has been put together and wound up; thus from this incontestable point of view it is a mere machine, the aim of which we cannot see. Even if, quite without justification, nay, at bottom, in spite of all conceivability and its conformity to law, one should assume a first beginning, nothing would thereby be essentially changed. For the arbitrarily assumed first condition of things would at its origin have irrevocably determined and fixed, both as a whole and down to the smallest detail, the state immediately following it; this state, again, would have determined the one succeeding it, and so on *per secula seculorum*, for the chain of causality, with its absolute strictness—this brazen bond of necessity and fate—introduces every phenomenon irrevocably and unalterably, just as it is. The difference merely amounts to this, that in the case of the one assumption we would have before us a piece of clockwork which had once been wound up, but in the case of the other a perpetual motion; the necessity of the course, on the other hand, would remain the same. In the prize essay already referred to I have irrefutably proved that the action of man can make no exception here, for I showed how it constantly proceeds with strict necessity from two factors—his character and the motives which come to him. The character is inborn and unalterable; the motives are introduced with necessity under the guidance of causality by the strictly determined course of the world.

Accordingly then, from one point of view, which we certainly cannot abandon, because it is established by the objective laws of the world, which are *a priori* valid, the world, with all that is in it, appears as an aimless, and therefore incomprehensible, play of an eternal necessity, an inscrutable and inexorable *Αναγκη*. Now, what is objectionable, nay, revolting, in this inevitable and irrefutable view of the world cannot be thoroughly done away with by any assumption except this, that as in one aspect every being in the world is a phenomenon, and necessarily determined by the laws of the phenomenon, in another aspect it is in itself *will*, and indeed absolutely *free will*, for necessity only arises through the forms which belong entirely to the phenomenon, through the principle of sufficient reason in its different modes. Such a will, then, must be self-dependent, for, as free, *i.e.*, as a thing in itself, and therefore not subject to the principle of sufficient reason, it cannot depend upon another in its being and nature any more than in its conduct and action. By this assumption alone will as much *freedom* be supposed as is needed to counterbalance the inevitable strict *necessity* which governs the course of the world. Accordingly one has really only the choice either of seeing that the world is a mere machine which runs on of necessity, or of recognising a free will as its inner being whose manifestation is not directly the action but primarily the *existence and nature* of things. This freedom is therefore transcendental, and consists with empirical necessity, in the same way as the transcendental ideality of phenomena consists with their empirical reality. That only under this assumption the action of a man, in spite of the necessity with which it proceeds from his character and the motives, is yet *his own* I have shown in my prize essay on the freedom of the will; with this, however, self-dependency is attributed to his nature. The same relation holds good of all things in the world. The strictest *necessity*, carried out honestly with rigid consistency, and the most perfect *freedom*, rising to omnipotence, had to appear at once and together in philosophy; but, without doing violence to truth, this could only take place by placing the whole *necessity* in the *acting and doing* (*Operari*), and the whole *freedom* in the *being and nature* (*Esse*). Thereby a riddle is solved which is as old as the world, simply because it has hitherto always been held upside down and the freedom persistently sought in the *Operari*, the necessity in the *Esse*. I, on the contrary, say: Every being without exception *acts* with strict necessity, but it *exists* and is what it is by virtue of its *freedom*. Thus with me freedom and necessity are to be met with neither more nor less than in any earlier system; although now one and now the other must be conspicuous according as one takes offence that *will* is attributed to processes of nature which hitherto were explained from necessity, or that the same strict necessity is recognised in motivation as in mechanical causality. The two have merely changed places: freedom has been transferred to the *Esse*, and necessity limited to the *Operari*.

In short, *Determinism* stands firm. For fifteen hundred years men have wearied themselves in vain to shake it, influenced by certain crotchets, which are well known, but dare scarcely yet be called by their name. Yet in accordance with it the world becomes a mere puppet-show, drawn by wires (motives), without it being even possible to understand for whose amusement. If the piece has a plan, then fate is the director; if it has none, then blind necessity. There is no other deliverance from this absurdity than the knowledge that the *being and nature* of all things is the manifestation of a really *free will*, which knows itself in them; for their *doing and acting* cannot be delivered from necessity. To save freedom from fate and chance, it had to be transferred from the action to the existence.

As now necessity only affects the phenomenon, not the thing in itself, *i.e.*, the true nature of the world, so also does *multiplicity*. This is sufficiently explained in § 25 of the first volume. I have only to add here one remark in confirmation and illustration of this truth.

Every one knows only *one* being quite immediately—his own will in self-consciousness. Everything else he knows only indirectly, and then judges it by analogy with this; a process which he carries further in proportion to the grade of his reflective powers. Even this ultimately springs from the fact that there really is *only one being;* the illusion of multiplicity (*Maja*), which proceeds from the forms of external, objective comprehension, could not penetrate to inner, simple consciousness; therefore this always finds before it only one being.

If we consider the perfection of the works of nature, which can never be sufficiently admired, and which even in the lowest and smallest organisms, for example, in the fertilising parts of plants or in the internal construction of insects, is carried out with as infinite care and unwearied labour as if each work of nature had been its only one, upon which it was therefore able to expend all its art and power; if we yet find this repeated an infinite number of times in each one of innumerable individuals of every kind, and not less carefully worked out in that one whose dwelling-place is the most lonely, neglected spot, to which, till then, no eye had penetrated; if we now follow the combination of the parts of every organism as far as we can, and yet never come upon one part which is quite simple, and therefore ultimate, not to speak of one which is inorganic; if, finally, we lose ourselves in calculating the design of all those parts of the organism for the maintenance of the whole by virtue of which every living thing is complete in and for itself; if we consider at the same time that each of these masterpieces, itself of short duration, has already been produced anew an innumerable number of times, and yet every example of a species, every insect, every flower, every leaf, still appears just as carefully perfected as was the first of its kind; thus that nature by no means wearies and begins to bungle, but, with equally patient master-hand, perfects the last like the first: then we become conscious, first of all, that all human art is completely different, not merely in degree, but in kind, from the works of nature; and, next, that the working force, the *natura naturans,* in each of its innumerable works, in the least as in the greatest, in the last as in the first, *is immediately present whole and undivided,* from which it follows that, as such and in itself, it knows nothing of space and time. If we further reflect that the production of these hyperboles of all works of art costs nature absolutely nothing, so that, with inconceivable prodigality, she creates millions of organisms which never attain to maturity, and without sparing exposes every living thing to a thousand accidents, yet, on the other hand, if favoured by chance or directed by human purpose, readily affords millions of examples of a species of which hitherto there was only one, so that millions cost her no more than one; this also leads us to see that the multiplicity of things has its root in the nature of the knowledge of the subject, but is foreign to the thing in itself, *i.e.*, to the inner primary force which shows itself in things; that consequently space and time, upon which the possibility of all multiplicity depends, are mere forms of our perception; nay, that even that whole inconceivable ingenuity of structure associated with the reckless prodigality of the works upon which it has been expended ultimately springs simply from the way in which things are apprehended by us; for when the simple and indivisible original effort of the will exhibits itself as object in our cerebral knowledge, it must appear as an ingenious combination of separate parts, as means and ends of each other, accomplished with wonderful completeness.

The *unity of that will*, here referred to, which lies beyond the phenomenon, and in which we have recognised the inner nature of the phenomenal world, is a metaphysical unity, and consequently transcends the knowledge of it, *i.e.*, does not depend upon the functions of our intellect, and therefore can not really be comprehended by it. Hence it arises that it opens to the consideration an abyss so profound that it admits of no thoroughly clear and systematically connected insight, but grants us only isolated glances, which enable us to recognise this unity in this and that relation of things, now in the subjective, now in the objective sphere, whereby, however, new problems are again raised, all of which I will not engage to solve, but rather appeal here to the words *est quadam prodire tenus*, more concerned to set up nothing false or arbitrarily invented than to give a thorough account of all;—at the risk of giving here only a fragmentary exposition.

If we call up to our minds and distinctly go through in

thought the exceedingly acute theory of the origin of the planetary system, first put forth by Kant and later by Laplace, a theory of which it is scarcely possible to doubt the correctness, we see the lowest, crudest, and blindest forces of nature bound to the most rigid conformity to law, by means of their conflict for one and the same given matter, and the accidental results brought about by this produce the framework of the world, thus of the designedly prepared future dwelling-place of innumerable living beings, as a system of order and harmony, at which we are the more astonished the more distinctly and accurately we come to understand it. For example, if we see that every planet, with its present velocity, can only maintain itself exactly where it actually has its place, because if it were brought nearer to the sun it would necessarily fall into it, or if placed further from it would necessarily fly away from it; how, conversely, if we take the place as given, it can only remain there with its present velocity and no other, because if it went faster it would necessarily fly away from the sun, and if it went slower it would necessarily fall into it; that thus only one definite place is suitable to each definite velocity of a planet; and if we now see this solved by the fact that the same physical, necessary, and blindly acting cause which appointed it its place, at the same time and just by doing so, imparted to it exactly the only velocity suitable for this place, in consequence of the law of nature that a revolving body increases its velocity in proportion as its revolution becomes smaller; and, moreover, if finally we understand how endless permanence is assured to the whole system, by the fact that all the mutual disturbances of the course of the planets which unavoidably enter, must adjust themselves in time; how then it is just the irrationality of the periods of revolution of Jupiter and Saturn to each other that prevents their respective perturbations from repeating themselves at one place, whereby they would become dangerous, and brings it about that, appearing seldom and always at a different place, they must sublate themselves again, like dissonances in music which are again resolved into harmony. By means of such considerations we recognise a design and perfection, such as could only have been brought about by the freest absolute will directed by the most penetrating understanding and the most acute calculation. And yet, under the guidance of that cosmogony of Laplace, so well thought out and so accurately calculated, we cannot prevent ourselves from seeing that perfectly blind forces of nature, acting according to unalterable natural laws, through their conflict and aimless play among themselves, could produce nothing else but this very framework of the world, which is equal to the work of an extraordinarily enhanced power of combination. Instead now, after the manner of Anaxagoras, of dragging in the aid of an *intelligence* known to us only from animal nature, and adapted only to its aims, an intelligence which, coming from without, cunningly made use of the existing forces of nature and their laws in order to carry out its ends, which are foreign to these,—we recognise in these lowest forces of nature themselves that same, one will, which indeed first manifests itself in them, and already in this manifestation striving after its goal, through its original laws themselves works towards its final end, to which therefore all that happens according to blind laws of nature must minister and correspond. And this indeed cannot be otherwise, because everything material is nothing but just the phenomenal appearance, the visibility, the objectivity of the will to live which is one. Thus even the lowest forces of nature themselves are animated by that same will, which afterwards, in the individual beings provided with intelligence, marvels at its own work, as the somnambulist wonders in the morning at what he has done in his sleep; or, more accurately, which is astonished at its own form which it beholds in the mirror. This unity which is here proved of the accidental with the intentional, of the necessary with the free, on account of which the blindest chances, which, however, rest upon universal laws of nature, are as it were the keys upon which the world-spirit plays its melodies so full of significance,—this unity, I say, is, as has already been remarked, an abyss in the investigation into which even philosophy can throw no full light, but only a glimmer.

But I now turn to a *subjective* consideration belonging to this place, to which, however, I am able to give still less distinctness than to the objective consideration which has just been set forth; for I shall only be able to express it by images and similes. Why is our consciousness brighter and more distinct the further it extends towards without, so that its greatest clearness lies in sense perception, which already half belongs to things outside us,—and, on the other hand, grows dimmer as we go in, and leads, if followed to its inmost recesses, to a darkness in which all knowledge ceases? Because, I say, consciousness presupposes *individuality;* but this belongs to the mere phenomenon, for it is conditioned by the forms of the phenomenon, space and time, as multiplicity of the similar. Our inner nature, on the other hand, has its root in that which is no longer phenomenon, but thing in itself, to which, therefore, the forms of the phenomenon do not extend; and thus the chief conditions of individuality are wanting, and with these the distinctness of consciousness falls off. In this root of existence the difference of beings ceases, like that of the radii of a sphere in the centre; and as in the sphere the surface is produced by the radii ending and breaking off, so consciousness is only possible where the true inner being runs out into the phenomenon, through whose forms the separate individuality becomes possible upon which consciousness depends, which is just on that account confined to phenomena. Therefore all that is distinct and thoroughly comprehensible in our consciousness always lies without upon this surface of the sphere. Whenever, on the contrary, we withdraw entirely from this, consciousness forsakes us,—in sleep, in death, to a certain extent also in magnetic or magic influences; for these all lead through the centre. But just because distinct consciousness, being confined to the surface of the sphere, is not directed towards the centre, it recognises other individuals certainly as of the same kind, but not as identical, which yet in themselves they are. Immortality of the individual might be compared to a point of the surface flying off at a tangent. But immortality, by virtue of the eternal nature of the inner being of the whole phenomenon, may be compared to the return of that point, on the radius, to the centre, of which the whole surface is just the extension. The will as the thing in itself is whole and undivided in every being, as the centre is an integral part of every radius; while the peripherical end of this radius is in the most rapid revolution, with the surface, which represents time and its content, the other end, at the centre, which represents eternity, remains in the profoundest peace, because the centre is the point of which the rising half is not different from the sinking. Therefore in the Bhagavad-gita it is said: "*Haud distributum animantibus, et quasi distributum tamen insidens, animantiumque sustentaculum id cognoscendum, edax et rursus genitale*" (Lect. 13, 16 vers. Schlegel). Certainly we fall here into mystical and figurative language, but it is the only language in which anything can be said on this entirely transcendent theme. So this simile also may pass. The human race may be imagined as an *animal compositum*, a form of life of which many polypi, especially those which swim, such as *Veretillum*, *Funiculina*, and others, afford examples. As in these the head isolates each individual animal, and the lower part, with the common stomach, combines them all in the unity of one life process, so the brain with its consciousness isolates the human individual, while the unconscious part, the vegetative life with its ganglion system, into which in sleep the brain-consciousness disappears, like a lotus which nightly sinks in the flood, is a common life of all, by means of which in exceptional cases they can even communicate, as, for example, occurs when dreams communicate themselves directly, the thoughts of the mesmeriser pass into the somnambulist, and finally also in the magnetic or generally magical influence proceeding from intentional willing. Such an influence, if it occurs, is *toto genere* different from every other on account of the *influxus physicus* which takes place, for it is really an *actio in distans* which the will, certainly proceeding from the individual, yet performs in its metaphysical quality as the omnipresent substratum of the whole of nature. One might also say that as in the *generatio æquivoca* there sometimes and as an exception appears a weak residue of the original *creative power* of the will, which in the existing forms of nature has already done its work and is extinguished, so there may be, exceptionally, acting in these magical influences, as it were, a surplus of its original *omnipotence*, which completes its work and spends itself in the construction and maintenance of the organisms. I have spoken fully of this magical property of the will in "The Will in Nature," and I gladly omit here discussions which have to appeal to uncertain facts, which yet cannot be altogether ignored or denied.

CHAPTER XXVI.[1]

ON TELEOLOGY.

THE universal teleology or design of organised nature relative to the continuance of every existing being, together with the adaptation of organised to unorganised nature, cannot without violence enter into the connection of any philosophical system except that one which makes a *will* the basis of the existence of every natural being; a will which accordingly expresses its nature and tendency not merely in the actions, but already in the *form* of the phenomenal organism. In the preceding chapter I have merely indicated the account which our system of thought gives of this subject, since I have already expounded it in the passage of the first volume referred to below, and with special clearness and fulness in "The Will in Nature," under the rubric "Comparative Anatomy."

The astounding amazement which is wont to take possession of us when we consider the endless design displayed in the construction of organised beings ultimately rests upon the certainly natural but yet false assumption that that *adaptation* of the parts to each other, to the whole of the organism and to its aims in the external world, as we comprehend it and judge of it by means of *knowledge*, thus upon the path of the *idea*, has also come into being upon the same path; thus that as it exists *for* the intellect, it was also brought about *by* the intellect. We certainly can only bring about something

[1] This chapter and the following one are connected with § 28 of the first volume.

regular and conforming to law, such, for example, as every crystal is, under the guidance of the law and the rule; and in the same way, we can only bring about something designed under the guidance of the conception of the end; but we are by no means justified in imputing this limitation of ours to nature, which is itself prior to all intellect, and whose action is entirely different in kind from ours, as was said in the preceding chapter. It accomplishes that which appears so designed and planned without reflection and without conception of an end, because without idea, which is of quite secondary origin. Let us first consider what is merely according to rule, not yet adapted to ends. The six equal radii of a snowflake, separating at equal angles, are measured beforehand by no knowledge; but it is the simple tendency of the original will, which so exhibits itself to knowledge when knowledge appears. As now here the will brings about the regular figure without mathematics, so also without physiology does it bring about the form which is organised and furnished with organs evidently adapted to special ends. The regular form in space only exists for the perception, the perceptive form of which is space; so the design of the organism only exists for the knowing reason, the reflection of which is bound to the conceptions of end and means. If direct insight into the working of nature was possible for us, we would necessarily recognise that the wonder excited by teleology referred to above is analogous to that which that savage referred to by Kant in his explanation of the ludicrous felt when he saw the froth irresistibly foaming out of a bottle of beer which had just been opened, and expressed his wonder not that it should come out, but that any one had ever been able to get it in; for we also assume that the teleology of natural productions has been put in the same as it comes out for us. Therefore our astonishment at design may likewise be compared to that which the first productions of the art of printing excited in those who considered them under the supposition that they were works of the pen, and therefore had to resort to the assumption of the assistance of a devil in order to explain them. For, let it be said again, it is our intellect which by means of its own forms, space, time, and causality, apprehends as object the act of will, in itself metaphysical and indivisible, which exhibits itself in the phenomenon of an animal,—it is our intellect which first produces the multiplicity and diversity of the parts, and is then struck with amazement at their perfect agreement and conspiring together, which proceeds from the original unity; whereby then, in a certain sense, it marvels at its own work.

If we give ourselves up to the contemplation of the indescribably and infinitely ingenious construction of any animal, even if it were only the commonest insect, lose ourselves in admiration of it, and it now occurs to us that nature recklessly exposes even this exceedingly ingenious and highly complicated organism daily and by thousands to destruction by accident, animal rapacity, and human wantonness, this wild prodigality fills us with amazement; but our amazement is based upon an ambiguity of the conceptions, for we have in our minds the human work of art which is accomplished by the help of the intellect and by overcoming a foreign and resisting material, and therefore certainly costs much trouble. Nature's works, on the contrary, however ingenious they may be, cost her absolutely no trouble; for here the will to work is already the work itself, since, as has already been said, the organism is merely the visibility of the will which is here present, brought about in the brain.

In consequence of the nature of organised beings which has been set forth, teleology, as the assumption of the adaptation of every part to its end, is a perfectly safe guide in considering the whole of organised nature; on the other hand, in a metaphysical regard, for the explanation of nature beyond the possibility of experience, it must only be regarded as valid in a secondary and subsidiary manner for the confirmation of principles of explanation which are otherwise established: for here it belongs to the problems which have to be given account of. Accordingly, if in some animal a part is found of which we do not see any use, we must never venture the conjecture that nature has produced it aimlessly, perhaps trifling, or out of mere caprice. Certainly it is possible to conceive something of this kind under the Anaxagorean assumption that the disposition of nature has been brought about by means of an ordering understanding, which, as such, obeys a foreign will; but not under the assumption that the true inner being (*i.e.*, outside of our idea) of every organism is simply and solely *its own will;* for then the existence of every part is conditioned by the circumstance that in some way it serves the will which here lies at its foundation, expresses and realises some tendency of it, and consequently in some way contributes to the maintenance of this organism. For apart from *the will which manifests itself in it*, and the conditions of the external world under which this has voluntarily undertaken to live, for the conflict with which its whole form and disposition is already adapted, nothing can have influenced it and determined its form and parts, thus no arbitrary power, no caprice. On this account everything in it must be designed; and therefore final causes (*causæ finales*) are the clue to the understanding of organised nature, as efficient causes (*causæ efficientes*) are the clue to the understanding of unorganised nature. It depends upon this, that if in anatomy or zoology, we cannot find the end or aim of an existing part, our understanding receives a shock similar to that which it receives in physics from an effect whose cause remains concealed; and as we assume the latter as necessary, so also we assume the former, and therefore go on searching for it, however long we may already have done so in vain. This is, for example, the case with the spleen, as to the use of which men never cease inventing hypotheses, till some day one shall have proved itself correct. So is it also with the large spiral-formed teeth of the babyroussa, the horn-shaped excrescences of certain caterpillars, and more of the like. Negative cases are also judged by us according to the same rule; for example, that in a class which, as a whole, is so uniform as that of lizards, so important a part as the bladder is present in many species, while it is wanting in others; similarly that dolphins and certain cetacea related to them are entirely without olfactory nerves, while the rest of the cetacea and even fishes have them: there must be a reason which determines this.

Individual real exceptions to this universal law of design in organised nature have indeed been discovered, and with great surprise; but in these cases that *exceptio firmat regulam* applies, since they can be accounted for upon other grounds. Such, for example, is the fact that the tadpoles of the pipa toad have tails and gills, although, unlike all other tadpoles, they do not swim, but await their metamorphosis on the back of the mother; that the male kangaroo has the marsupial bones which in the female carry the pouch; that male mammals have breasts; that the *Mus typhlus*, a rat, has eyes, although very small ones, without any opening for them in the outer skin, which thus covers them, clothed with hair; and that the moles of the Apennines, and also two fishes—*Murena cæcilia* and *Gastrobrauchus cæcus*—are in the same case; of like kind is the *Proteus anguinus.* These rare and surprising exceptions to the rule of nature, which is otherwise so rigid, these contradictions with itself into which it falls, we must explain from the inner connection which the different kinds of phenomena have with each other, by virtue of the unity of that which manifests itself in them, and in consequence of which nature must hint at some thing in one, simply because another of the same type actually has it. Accordingly the male animal has a rudimentary form of an organ which is actually present in the female. As now here the difference of the *sex* cannot abolish the type of the *species*, so also the type of a whole order—for example, of the batrachia—asserts itself even where in one particular species (pipa) one of its determinations is superfluous. Still less can nature allow a determination (eyes) which belongs to the type of a whole division (Vertebrata) to vanish entirely without a trace, even if it is wanting in some particular species (*Mus typhlus*) as superfluous; but here also it must at least indicate in a rudimentary manner what it carries out in all the others.

Even from this point of view it is to some extent possible to see upon what depends that *homology* in the skeleton primarily of mammals, and in a wider sense of all vertebrates, which has been so fully explained, especially by Richard Owen in his "*Ostéologie comparée*," and on account of which, for example, all mammals have seven cervical vertebræ, every bone of the human hand and arm finds its analogue in the fin of the whale, the skull of the bird in the egg has exactly as many bones as that of the human fœtus, &c. All this points to a principle which is independent of teleology, but which is yet the foundation upon which teleology builds, or the already given material for its works, and just that which Geoffroy St. Hilaire has explained as the "anatomical element." It is the *unité de plan*, the fundamental type of the higher animal world, as it were the arbitrarily chosen key upon which nature here plays.

Aristotle has already correctly defined the difference between the efficient cause (*causa efficiens*) and the final cause (*causa finalis*) in these words: "Δυο τροποι της αιτιας, το οὗ ἑνεκα και το εξ αναγκης, και δει λεγοντας τυγχανειν μαλιστα μεν αμφοιν." (*Duo sunt causæ modi: alter cujus gratia, et alter e necessitate; ac potissimum utrumque eruere oportet.*) *De part. anim.*, i. 1. The efficient cause is that *whereby* something is, the final cause that *on account of which* it is; the phenomenon to be explained has, in time, the former *behind* it, and the latter *before* it. Only in the case of the voluntary actions of animal beings do the two directly unite, for here the final cause, the end, appears as the motive; a motive, however, is always the true and proper *cause* of the action, is wholly and solely its *efficient* cause, the change preceding it which calls it forth, by virtue of which it necessarily appears, and without which it could not happen; as I have shown in my prize essay upon freedom. For whatever of a physiological nature one might wish to insert between the act of will and the corporeal movement, the *will* always remains here confessedly that which moves, and what moves *it* is the *motive* coming from without, thus the *causa finalis;* which consequently appears here as *causa efficiens.* Besides, we know from what has gone before that the bodily movement is one with the act of will, for it is merely its phenomenal appearance in cerebral perception. This union of the *causa finalis* with the efficient cause in the one phenomenon *intimately* known to us, which accordingly remains throughout our typical phenomenon, is certainly to be firmly retained; for it leads precisely to the conclusion that at least in organised nature, the knowledge of which has throughout final causes for its clue, a *will* is the forming power. In fact, we cannot otherwise distinctly think a final cause except as an end in view, *i.e.*, a motive. Indeed, if we carefully consider the final causes in nature in order to express their transcendent nature, we must not shrink from a contradiction, and boldly say: the final cause is a motive which acts upon a being, by which it is not known. For certainly the termite nests are the motive which has produced the toothless muzzle of the ant-bear, and also its long extensile, glutinous tongue: the hard egg-shell which holds the chicken imprisoned is certainly the motive for the horny point with which its beak is provided in order to break through that shell, after which it throws it off as of no further use. And in the same way the laws of the reflection and refraction of light are the motive for the wonderfully ingenious and complex optical instrument, the human eye, which has the transparency of its cornea, the different density of its three humours, the form of its lens, the blackness of its choroid, the sensitiveness of its retina, the contracting power of its pupil, and its muscular system, accurately calculated according to those laws. But those motives acted before they were apprehended; it is not otherwise, however contradictory it may sound. For here is the transition of the physical into the metaphysical. But the latter we have already recognised in the *will;* therefore we must see that the will which extends an elephant's trunk towards an object is the same will which has also called it forth and formed it, anticipating objects.

It is in conformity with this that in the investigation of *organised* nature we are entirely referred to *final causes,* everywhere seek for these and explain everything from them. The *efficient causes,* on the contrary, here assume only a quite subordinate position as the mere tools of the final causes, and, just as in the case of the voluntary movement of the limbs, which is confessedly effected by external motives, they are rather assumed than pointed out. In explaining the physiological *functions* we certainly look about for the efficient causes, though for the most part in vain; but in explaining the origin of the parts we again look for them no more, but are satisfied with the final causes alone. At the most we have here some such general principle as that the larger the part is to be the stronger must be the artery that conducts blood to it; but of the actually efficient causes which bring about, for example, the eye, the ear, the brain, we know absolutely nothing. Indeed, even in explaining the mere functions the final cause is far more important and more to the point than the efficient; therefore, if the former alone is known we are instructed and satisfied with regard to the principal matter, while, on the other hand, the efficient cause alone helps us little. For example, if we really knew the *efficient cause* of the circulation of the blood, as we do not, but still seek it, this would help us little unless we knew the final cause, that the blood must go into the lungs for the purpose of oxidation, and again flow back for the purpose of nourishing; but by the knowledge of this, even without the knowledge of the efficient cause, we have gained much light. Moreover, I am of opinion, as was said above, that the circulation of the blood has no properly efficient cause, but that the will is here as immediately active as in muscular movement where motives determine it by means of nerve conduction, so that here also the movement is called forth directly by the final cause; thus by the need of oxidation in the lungs, which here to a certain extent acts as a motive upon the blood, yet so that the mediation of knowledge is in this case wanting, because everything takes place in the interior of the organism. The so-called metamorphosis of plants, a thought lightly thrown out by Kaspar Wolf, which, under this hyperbolic title, Goethe pompously and with solemn delivery expounds as his own production, belongs to the class of explanations of organic nature from the efficient cause; although ultimately he only says that nature does not in the case of every production begin from the beginning and create out of nothing, but as it were, writing on in the same style, adds on to what already exists, makes use of the earlier forms, developed, and raised to higher power, to carry its work further: just as it has done in the ascending series of animals entirely in accordance with the law: *Natura non facit saltus, et quod commodissimum in omnibus suis operationibus sequitur* (*Arist. de incessu animalium, c.* 2 *et* 8). Indeed, to explain the blossom by pointing out in all its parts the form of the leaf seems to me almost the same as explaining the structure of a house by showing that all its parts, storeys, balconies, and garrets, are only composed of bricks and mere repetitions of the original unity of the brick. And not much better, though much more problematical, seems to me the explanation of the skull from vertebræ, although even here also it is a matter of course that the covering or case of the brain will not be absolutely different and entirely disparate from that of the spinal cord, of which it is the continuation and terminal knob, but will rather be a carrying out of the same kind of thing. This whole method of consideration belongs to the Homology of Richard Owen referred to above. On the other hand, it seems to me that the following explanation of the nature of the flower from its *final cause,* suggested by an Italian whose name has escaped me, is a far more satisfactory account to give. The end of the *corolla* is—(1.) Protection of the pistil and the *stamina ;* (2.) by means of it the purified saps are prepared, which are concentrated in the *pollen* and *germs ;* (3.) from the glands of its base the essential oil distils which, for the most part as a fragrant vapour, surrounding the anthers and pistil, protects them to a certain extent from the influence of the damp air. It is also one of the advantages of final causes that every *efficient* cause always ultimately rests upon something that cannot be fathomed, a force of nature, *i.e.*, a *qualitas occulta*, and, therefore, it can only give a *relative* explanation ; while the final cause within its sphere affords a sufficient and perfect explanation. It is true we are only perfectly content when we know both the efficient cause, also called by Aristotle ἡ αιτια εξ αναγκης, and the final cause, ἡ χαριν του βελτιονος, at once and yet separately, as their concurrence, their wonderful working together, then surprises us, and on account of it the best appears as the absolutely necessary, and the necessary again as if it were merely the best and not necessary ; for then arises in us the dim perception that both causes, however different may be their origin, are yet connected in the root, in the nature of the thing in itself. But such a twofold knowledge is seldom attainable ; in *organised* nature, because the efficient cause is seldom known to us ; in *unorganised* nature, because the final cause remains problematical. However, I will illustrate this by a couple of examples as good as I find within the range of my physiological knowledge, for which physiologists may be able to substitute clearer and more striking ones. The louse of the negro is black. Final cause: its own safety. Efficient cause: because its nourishment is the black *rete Malpighi* of the negro. The multifarious, brilliant, and gay colouring of the plumage of tropical birds is explained, although only very generally, from the strong effect of the light in the tropics, as its efficient cause. As the final cause I would assign that those brilliant feathers are the gorgeous uniform in which the individuals of the innumerable species there, often belonging to the same genus, may recognise each other; so that each male may find his female. The same holds good of butterflies of different zones and latitudes. It has been observed that consumptive women, in the last stage of their illness, readily become pregnant, that the disease stops during pregnancy, but after delivery appears again worse than before, and now generally results in death: similarly that consumptive men generally beget another child in the last days of their life. The *final cause* here is that nature, always so anxiously concerned for the maintenance of the species, seeks to replace by a new individual the approaching loss of one in the prime of life; the *efficient cause*, on the other hand, is the unusually excited state of the nervous system which occurs in the last period of consumption. From the same final cause is to be explained the analogous phenomenon that (according to Oken, *Die Zeugung*, p. 65) flies poisoned with arsenic still couple, and die in the act of copulation. The final cause of the pubes in both sexes, and of the Mons Veneris in the female, is that even in the case of very thin subjects the Ossa pubis shall not be felt, which might excite antipathy; the efficient cause, on the other hand, is to be sought in the fact that wherever the mucous membrane passes over to the outer skin, hair grows in the vicinity; and, secondly, also that the head and the genitals are to a certain extent opposite poles of each other, and therefore have various relations and analogies between them, among which is that of being covered with hair. The same efficient cause holds good also of the beard of the man; the final cause of it, I suppose, lies in the fact that the pathogonomic signs, thus the rapid alterations of the countenance betraying every movement of the mind, are principally visible in the mouth and its vicinity; therefore, in order to conceal these from the prying eye of the adversary, as something dangerous in bargaining, or in sudden emergencies, nature gave man the beard (which shows that *homo homini lupus*). The woman, on the other hand, could dispense with this; for with her dissimulation and command of countenance are inborn. As I have said, there must be far more apt examples to be found to show how the completely blind working of nature unites in the result with the apparently intentional, or, as Kant calls it, the mechanism of nature with its technic; which points to the fact that both have their common origin beyond their difference in the will as the thing in itself. Much would be achieved for the elucidation of this point of view, if, for example, we could find the efficient cause which carries the driftwood to the treeless polar lands, or that which has concentrated the dry land of our planet principally in the northern half of it; while it is to be regarded as the final cause of this that the winter of that half, because it occurs in the perihelion which accelerates the course of the earth, is eight days shorter, and hereby is also milder. Yet in considering *unorganised* nature the final cause is always ambiguous, and, especially when the *efficient* cause is found, leaves us in doubt whether it is not a merely subjective view, an aspect conditioned by our point of view. In this respect, however, it may be compared to many works of art; for example, to coarse mosaics, theatre decorations, and to the god Apennine at Pratolino, near Florence, composed of large masses of rock, all of which only produce their effect at a distance, and vanish when we come near, because instead of them the efficient cause of their appearance now becomes visible: but the forms are yet actually existent, and are no mere imagination. Analogous to this, then, are the final causes in unorganised nature, if the efficient causes appear. Indeed, those who take a wide view of things would perhaps allow it to pass if I added that something similar is the case with omens.

For the rest, if any one desires to misuse the *external* design, which, as has been said, always remains ambiguous for physico-theological demonstrations, which is done even at the present day, though it is to be hoped only by Englishmen, there are in this class enough examples *in contrarium*, thus ateleological instances, to derange his conception. One of the strongest is presented by the unsuitableness of sea-water for drinking, in consequence of which man is never more exposed to the danger of dying of thirst than in the midst of the greatest mass of water on his planet. "Why, then, does the sea need to be salt?" let us ask our Englishman.

That in *unorganised* nature the final causes entirely withdraw into the background, so that an explanation from them alone is here no longer valid, but the efficient causes are rather indispensably required, depends upon the fact that the will which objectifies itself here also no longer appears in individuals which constitute a whole for themselves, but in forces of nature and their action, whereby end and means are too far separated for their relation to be clear and for us to recognise a manifestation of will in it. This already occurs in organised nature, in a certain degree, when the design is an external one, *i.e.*, the end lies in *one* individual and the means in *another*. Yet even here it remains unquestionable so long as the two belong to the same species, indeed it then becomes the more striking. Here we have first to count the reciprocally adapted organisation of the genitals of the two sexes, and then also many circumstances that assist the propagation of the species, for example, in the case of the *Lampyris noctiluca* (the glowworm) the circumstance that only the male, which does not shine, has wings to enable it to seek out the female; the wingless female, on the other hand, since it only comes out in the evening, possesses the phosphorescent light, so that the male may be able to find it. Yet in the case of the *Lampyris Italica* both sexes shine, which is an instance of the natural luxury of the South. But a striking, because quite special, example of the kind of design we are speaking of is afforded by the discovery made by Geoffroy St. Hilaire, in his last years, of the more exact nature of the sucking apparatus of the cetacea. Since all sucking requires the action of respiration, it can only take place in the respirable medium itself, and not under water, where, however, the sucking young of the whale hangs on to the teats of the mother; now to meet this the whole mammary apparatus of the cetacea is so modified that it has become an injecting organ, and placed in the mouth of the young injects the milk into it without it requiring to suck. When, on the contrary, the individual that affords essential help to another belongs to an entirely different species, and even to another kingdom of nature, we will doubt this external design just as in unorganised nature; unless it is evident that the maintenance of the species depends upon it. But this is the case with many plants whose fructification only takes place by means of insects, which either bear the pollen to the stigma or bend the stamina to the pistil. The common barberry, many kinds of iris, and *Aristolochia Clematitis* cannot fructify themselves at all without the help of insects (*Chr. Cour.* Sprengel, *Entdecktes Geheimniss, &c.*, 1793; Wildenow, *Grundriss der Kräuterkunde,* 353). Very many diœcia, monœcia, and polygamia are in the same position. The reciprocal support which the plant and the insect worlds receive from each other will be found admirably described in Burdach's large Physiology, vol. i. § 263. He very beautifully adds: "This is no mechanical assistance, no make-shift, as if nature had made the plants yesterday, and had committed an error which she tries to correct to-day through the insect; it is rather a deep-lying sympathy between the plant and the animal worlds. It ought to reveal the identity of the two. Both, children of one mother, ought to subsist with each other and through each other." And further on: "But the organised world stands in such a sympathy with the unorganised world also," &c. A proof of this *consensus naturæ* is also afforded by the observation communicated in the second volume of the "Introduction into Entomology" by Kirby and Spence, that the insect eggs that pass the winter attached to the twigs of the trees, which serve as nourishment for their larvæ, are hatched exactly at the time at which the twig buds; thus, for example, the aphis of the birch a month earlier than that of the ash. Similarly, that the insects of perennial plants pass the winter upon these as eggs; but those of mere annuals, since they cannot do this, in the state of pupæ.

Three great men have entirely rejected teleology, or the explanation from final causes, and many small men have echoed them. These three are, Lucretius, Bacon of Verulam, and Spinoza. But in the case of all three we know clearly enough the source of this aversion, namely, that they regarded it as inseparable from speculative theology, of which, however, they entertained so great a distrust (which Bacon indeed prudently sought to conceal) that they wanted to give it a wide berth. We find Leibnitz also entirely involved in this prejudice, for, with characteristic naïveté, he expresses it as something self-evident in his *Lettre à M. Nicaise* (*Spinozæ op. ed Paulus*, vol. ii. p. 672): "*Les causes finales, ou ce qui est la même chose, la considération de la sagesse divine dans l'ordre des choses.*" (The devil also *même chose!*) At the same point of view we find, indeed, Englishmen even at the present day. The Bridgewater-Treatise-men — Lord Brougham, &c. — nay, even Richard Owen also, in his "*Ostéologie Comparée,*" thinks precisely as Leibnitz, which I have already found fault with in the first volume. To all these teleology is at once also theology, and at every instance of design recognised in nature, instead of thinking and learning to understand nature, they break at once into the childish cry, "Design! design!" then strike up the refrain of their old wives' philosophy, and stop their ears against all rational arguments, such as, however, the great Hume has already advanced against them.[1]

The ignorance of the Kantian philosophy now, after seventy years, which is really a disgrace to Englishmen of learning, is principally responsible for this whole outcast position of the English; and this ignorance, again, depends, at least in great measure, upon the nefarious influence of the detestable English clergy, with whom stultification of every kind is a thing after their own hearts, so that only they may be able still to hold the English nation, otherwise so intelligent, involved in the most degrading bigotry; therefore, inspired by the basest obscurantism, they oppose with all their might the education of the people, the investigation of nature, nay, the advancement of all human knowledge in general; and both by means of their connections and by means of their scandalous, unwarrantable wealth, which increases the misery of the people, they extend their influence even to university teachers and authors, who accordingly (for example, Th. Brown, "On Cause and Effect") resort to suppressions and perversions of every kind simply in order to avoid opposing even in a distant manner that "cold superstition" (as Pückler very happily designates their religion, or the current arguments in its favour).

[1] Let me here remark in passing that, judging from the German literature since Kant, one would necessarily believe that Hume's whole wisdom had consisted in his obviously false scepticism with regard to the law of causality, for this alone is everywhere referred to. In order to know Hume one must read his "Natural History of Religion" and his "Dialogues on Natural Religion." There one sees him in his greatness, and these, together with Essay 21 "Of National Characters," are the writings on account of which—I know of nothing that says more for his fame—even to the present day, he is everywhere hated by the English clergy.

But, on the other hand, the three great men of whom we are speaking, since they lived long before the dawn of the Kantian philosophy, are to be pardoned for their distrust of teleology on account of its origin; yet even Voltaire regarded the physico-theological proof as irrefutable. In order, however, to go into this somewhat more fully: first of all, the polemic of Lucretius (iv. 824–858) against teleology is so crude and clumsy that it refutes itself and convinces us of the opposite. But as regards Bacon (*De augm. scient.*, iii. 4), he makes, in the first place, no distinction with reference to the use of final causes between organised and unorganised nature (which is yet just the principal matter), for, in his examples of final causes, he mixes the two up together. Then he banishes final causes from physics to metaphysics; but the latter is for him, as it is still for many at the present day, identical with speculative theology. From this, then, he regards final causes as inseparable, and goes so far in this respect that he blames Aristotle because he has made great use of final causes, yet without connecting them with speculative theology (which I shall have occasion immediately especially to praise). Finally, Spinoza (*Eth.* i. *prop.* 36, *appendix*) makes it abundantly clear that he identifies teleology so entirely with physico-theology, against which he expresses himself with bitterness, that he explains *Natura nihil frustra agere: hoc est, quod in usum hominum non sit:* similarly, *Omnia naturalia tanquam ad suum utile media considerant, et credunt aliquem alium esse, qui illa media paraverit;* and also: *Hinc statuerunt, Deos omnia in usum hominum fecisse et dirigere.* Upon this, then, he bases his assertion: *Naturam finem nullum sibi præfixum habere et omnes causas finales nihil, nisi humana esse figmenta.* His aim merely was to block the path of theism; and he had quite rightly recognised the physico-theological proof as its strongest weapon. But it was reserved for Kant really to refute this proof, and for me to give the correct exposition of its material, whereby

I have satisfied the maxim: *Est enim verum index sui et falsi.* But Spinoza did not know how else to help himself but by the desperate stroke of denying teleology itself, thus design in the works of nature—an assertion the monstrosity of which is at once evident to every one who has gained any accurate knowledge of organised nature. This limited point of view of Spinoza, together with his complete ignorance of nature, sufficiently prove his entire incompetence in this matter, and the folly of those who, upon his authority, believe they must judge contemptuously of final causes.

Aristotle, who just here shows his brilliant side, contrasts very advantageously with these modern philosophers. He goes unprejudiced to nature, knows of no physico-theology—such a thing has never entered his mind,—and he has never looked at the world for the purpose of seeing whether it was a bungled piece of work. He is in his heart pure from all this, for he also sets up hypotheses as to the origin of animals and men (*De generat. anim.*, iii. 11) without lighting upon the physico-theological train of thought. He always says: "ἡ φυσις ποιει (*natura facit*), never ἡ φυσις πεποιηται" (*natura facta est*). But after he has truly and diligently studied nature, he finds that it everywhere proceeds teleologically, and he says: "ματην ὁρωμεν ουδεν ποιουσαν την φυσιν" (*naturam nihil frustra facere cernimus*), *De respir.*, c. 10; and in the books, *De partibus animalium*, which are a comparative anatomy: "Ουδε περιεργον ουδεν, ουτε ματην ἡ φυσις ποιει.—Ἡ φυσις ἑνεκα του ποιει παντα.—Πανταχου δε λεγομεν τοδε τουδε ἑνεκα, ὁπου αν φαινηται τελος τι, προς ὁ ἡ κινησις περαινει· ὡστε ειναι φανερον, ὁτι εστι τι τοιουτον, ὁ δη και καλουμεν φυσιν. Επει το σωμα οργανον· ἑνεκα τινος γαρ ἑκαστον των μοριων, ομοιως τε και το ὁλον." (*Nihil supervacaneum, nihil frustra natura facit.—Natura rei alicujus gratia facit omnia.—Rem autem hanc esse illius gratia asserere ubique solemus, quoties finem intelligimus aliquem, in quem motus terminetur; quocirca ejusmodi aliquid esse constat, quod Naturam vocamus. Est enim corpus instrumentum: nam membrum unumquod-*

que rei alicujus gratia est, tum vero totum ipsum.) At greater length, p. 633 and 645 of the Berlin quarto edition, and also *De incessu animalium*, c. 2: "Ἡ φυσις ουδεν ποιει ματην, αλλ' αει, εκ των ενδεχομενων τῃ ουσιᾳ, περι ἑκαστον γενος ζωου το αριστον." (*Natura nihil frustra facit, sed semper ex iis, quæ cuique animalium generis essentiæ contingunt, id quod optimum est.*) But he expressly recommends teleology at the end of the books *De generatione animalium*, and blames Democritus for having denied it, which is just what Bacon, in his prejudice, praises in him. Especially, however, in the "Physica," ii. 8, p. 198, Aristotle speaks *ex professo* of final causes, and establishes them as the true principle of the investigation of nature. In fact, every good and regular mind must, in considering organised nature, hit upon teleology, but unless it is determined by the preconceived opinions, by no means either upon physico-theology or upon the anthropo-teleology condemned by Spinoza. With regard to Aristotle generally, I wish further to draw attention to the fact here, that his teaching, so far as it concerns *unorganised* nature, is very defective and unserviceable, as in the fundamental conceptions of mechanics and physics he accepts the most gross errors, which is the less pardonable, since before him the Pythagoreans and Empedocles had been upon the right path and had taught much better. Empedocles indeed, as we learn from Aristotle's second book, *De cœlo* (c. 1, p. 284), had already grasped the conception of a tangential force arising from rotation, and counteracting gravity, which Aristotle again rejects. Quite the reverse, however, is Aristotle's relation to the investigation of *organised* nature. This is his field; here the wealth of his knowledge, the keenness of his observation, nay, sometimes the depth of his insight, astonish us. Thus, to give just one example, he already knew the antagonism in which in the ruminants the horns and the teeth of the upper jaw stand to each other, on account of which, therefore, the latter are wanting where the former are found, and conversely (*De partib. anim.*, iii. 2). Hence then, also his correct estimation of final causes.

CHAPTER XXVII.

ON INSTINCT AND MECHANICAL TENDENCY.

It is as if nature had wished, in the mechanical tendencies of animals, to give the investigator an illustrative commentary upon her works, according to final causes and the admirable design of her organised productions which is thereby introduced. For these mechanical tendencies show most clearly that creatures can work with the greatest decision and definiteness towards an end which they do not know, nay, of which they have no idea. Such, for instance, is the bird's nest, the spider's web, the ant-lion's pitfall, the ingenious bee-hive, the marvellous termite dwelling, &c., at least for those individual animals that carry them out for the first time; for neither the form of the perfected work nor the use of it can be known to them. Precisely so, however, does *organising* nature work; and therefore in the preceding chapter I gave the paradoxical explanation of the final cause, that it is a motive which acts without being known. And as in working from mechanical tendency that which is active is evidently and confessedly the *will*, so is it also really the will which is active in the working of organising nature.

One might say, the will of animal creatures is set in motion in two different ways: either by motivation or by instinct; thus from without, or from within; by an external occasion, or by an internal tendency; the former is explicable because it lies before us without, the latter is inexplicable because it is merely internal. But, more closely considered, the contrast between the two is not so sharp, indeed ultimately it runs back into a difference of degree. The motive also only acts under the assumption of an inner tendency, *i.e.*, a definite quality of will which is called its *character*. The motive in each case only gives to this a definite direction—individualises it for the concrete case. So also instinct, although a definite tendency of the will, does not act entirely, like a spring, from within; but it also waits for some external circumstance necessarily demanded for its action, which at least determines the time of its manifestation; such is, for the migrating bird, the season of the year; for the bird that builds its nest, the fact of pregnancy and the presence of the material for the nest; for the bee it is, for the beginning of the structure, the basket or the hollow tree, and for the following work many individually appearing circumstances; for the spider, it is a well-adapted corner; for the caterpillar, the suitable leaf; for egg-laying insects, the for the most part very specially determined and often rare place, where the hatched larvæ will at once find their nourishment, and so on. It follows from this that in works of mechanical tendency it is primarily the instinct of these animals that is active, yet subordinated also to their intellect. The instinct gives the universal, the rule; the intellect the particular, the application, in that it directs the detail of the execution, in which therefore the work of these animals clearly adapts itself to the circumstances of the existing case. According to all this, the difference between instinct and mere character is to be fixed thus: Instinct is a character which is only set in motion by a *quite specially determined* motive, and on this account the action that proceeds from it is always exactly of the same kind; while the character which is possessed by every species of animal and every individual man is certainly a permanent and unalterable quality of will, which can yet be set in motion by very different motives, and adapts itself to these; and on account of this the action proceeding from it may, according to its material quality, be very different, but yet will always bear the stamp of the same character, and will therefore express and reveal this; so that for the knowledge of this character the material quality of the action in which it appears is essentially a matter of indifference. Accordingly we might explain instinct as a character which is beyond all measure one-sided and strictly determined. It follows from this exposition that being determined by mere motivation presupposes a certain width of the sphere of knowledge, and consequently a more fully developed intellect: therefore it is peculiar to the higher animals, quite pre-eminently, however, to man; while being determined by instinct only demands as much intellect as is necessary to apprehend the one quite specially determined motive, which alone and exclusively becomes the occasion for the manifestation of the instinct. Therefore it is found in the case of an exceedingly limited sphere of knowledge, and consequently, as a rule, and in the highest degree, only in animals of the lower classes, especially insects. Since, accordingly, the actions of these animals only require an exceedingly simple and small motivation from without, the medium of this, thus the intellect or the brain, is very slightly developed in them, and their outward actions are for the most part under the same guidance as the inner, follow upon mere stimuli, physiological functions, thus the ganglion system. This is, then, in their case excessively developed; their principal nerve-stem runs under the belly in the form of two cords, which at every limb of the body form a ganglion little inferior to the brain in size, and, according to Cuvier, this nerve-stem is an analogue not so much of the spinal cord as of the great sympathetic nerve. According to all this, instinct and action through mere motivation, stand in a certain antagonism, in consequence of which the former has its maximum in insects, and the latter in man, and the actuation of other animals lies between the two in manifold gradations according as in each the cerebral or the ganglion system is preponderatingly developed. Just because the instinctive action and the ingenious contrivances of insects are principally directed from the ganglion system, if we regard them as proceeding from the brain alone, and wish to explain them accordingly, we fall into absurdities, because we then apply a false key. The same circumstance, however, imparts to their action a remarkable likeness to that of somnambulists, which indeed is also explained as arising from the fact that, instead of the brain, the sympathetic nerve has undertaken the conduct of the outward actions also; insects are accordingly, to a certain extent, natural somnambulists. Things which we cannot get at directly we must make comprehensible to ourselves by means of an analogy. What has just been referred to will accomplish this in a high degree when assisted by the fact that in Kieser's "*Tellurismus*" (vol. ii. p. 250) a case is mentioned "in which the command of the mesmerist to the somnambulist to perform a definite action in a waking state was carried out by him when he awoke, without remembering the command." Thus it was as if he must perform that action without rightly knowing why. Certainly this has the greatest resemblance to what goes on in the case of mechanical instincts in insects. The young spider feels that it must spin its web, although it neither knows nor understands the aim of it. We are also reminded here of the dæmon of Socrates, on account of which he had the feeling that he must leave undone some action expected of him, or lying near him, without knowing why—for his prophetic dream about it was forgotten. We have in our own day quite well-authenticated cases analogous to this; therefore I only briefly call these to mind. One had taken his passage on a ship, but when it was about to sail he positively would not go on board without being conscious of a reason;—the ship went down. Another goes with companions to a powder magazine; when he has arrived in its vicinity he absolutely will not go any further, but turns hastily back, seized with anxiety he knows not why;—the magazine blows up. A third upon the ocean feels moved one night, without any reason, not to undress, but lays himself on the bed in his clothes and boots, and even with his spectacles on;—in the night the ship goes on fire, and he is among the few who save themselves in the boat. All this depends upon the dull after-effect of forgotten fatidical dreams, and gives us the key to an analogous understanding of instinct and mechanical tendencies.

On the other hand, as has been said, the mechanical tendencies of insects reflect much light upon the working of the unconscious will in the inner functions of the organism and in its construction. For without any difficulty we can see in the ant-hill or the beehive the picture of an organism explained and brought to the light of knowledge. In this sense Burdach says (*Physiologie*, vol. ii. p. 22): "The formation and depositing of the eggs is the part of the queen-bee, and the care for the cultivation of them falls to the workers; thus in the former the ovary, and in the latter the uterus, is individualised." In the insect society, as in the animal organism, the *vita propria* of each part is subordinated to the life of the whole, and the care for the whole precedes that for particular existence; indeed the latter is only conditionally willed, the former unconditionally; therefore the individuals are even sacrificed occasionally for the whole, as we allow a limb to be taken off in order to save the whole body. Thus, for example, if the path is closed by water against the march of the ants, those in front boldly throw themselves in until their corpses are heaped up into a dam for those that follow. When the drones have become useless they are stung to death. Two queens in the hive are surrounded, and must fight with each other till one of them loses its life. The ant-mother bites its own wings off after it has been impregnated, for they would only be a hindrance to it in the work that is before it of tending the new family it is about to found under the earth (Kirby and Spence, vol. i.) As the liver will do nothing more than secrete gall for the service of the digestion, nay, will only itself exist for this end—and so with every other part—the working bees also will do nothing more than collect honey, secrete wax, and make cells for the brood of the queen; the drones nothing more than impregnate; the queen nothing but deposit eggs; thus all the parts work only for the maintenance of the whole which alone is the unconditional end, just like the parts of the organism. The difference is merely that in the organism the will acts perfectly blindly in its primary condition; in the insect society, on the other hand, the thing goes on already in the light of knowledge, to which, however, a decided co-operation and individual choice is only left in the accidents of detail, where it gives assistance and adopts what has to be carried out to the circumstances. But the insects will the end as a whole without knowing it; just like organised nature working according to final causes; even the choice of the means is not as a whole left to their knowledge, but only the more detailed disposition of them. Just on this account, however, their action is by no means automatic, which becomes most distinctly visible if one opposes obstacles to their action. For example, the caterpillar spins itself in leaves without knowing the end; but if we destroy the web it skilfully repairs it. Bees adapt their hive at the first to the existing circumstances, and subsequent misfortunes, such as intentional destruction, they meet in the way most suitable to the special case (Kirby and Spence, *Introduc. to Entomol.;* Huber, *Des abeilles*). Such things excite our astonishment, because the apprehension of the circumstances and the adaptation to these is clearly a matter of knowledge; while we believe them capable once for all of the most ingenious preparation for the coming race and the distant future, well knowing that in this they are not guided by knowledge, for a forethought of that kind proceeding from knowledge demands an activity of the brain rising to the level of reason. On the other hand, the intellect even of the lower animals is sufficient for the modifying and arranging of the particular case according to the existing or appearing circumstances; because, guided by instinct, it has only to fill up the gaps which this leaves. Thus we see ants carry off their larvæ whenever the place is too damp, and bring them back again when it becomes dry. They do not know the aim of this, thus are not guided in it by knowledge; but the choice of the time at which the place is no longer suitable for the larvæ, and also of the place to which they now bring them, is left to their knowledge. I wish here also to mention a fact which some one related to me verbally from his own experience, though I have since found that Burdach quotes it from Gleditsch. The latter, in order to test the burying-beetle (*Necrophorus vespillo*), had tied a dead frog lying upon the ground to a string, the upper end of which was fastened to a stick stuck obliquely in the ground. Now after several burying-beetles had, according to their custom, undermined the frog, it could not, as they expected, sink into the ground; after much perplexed running hither and thither they undermined the stick also. To this assistance rendered to instinct, and that repairing of the works of mechanical tendency, we find in the organism the *healing power* of nature analogous, which not only heals wounds, replacing even bone and nerve substance, but, if through the injury of a vein or nerve branch a connection is interrupted, opens a new connection by means of enlargement of other veins or nerves, nay, perhaps even by producing new branches; which further makes some other part or function take the place of a diseased part or function; in the case of the loss of an eye sharpens the other, or in the case of the loss of one of the senses sharpens all the rest; which even sometimes closes an intestinal wound, in itself fatal, by the adhesion of the mesentery or the peritoneum; in short, seeks to meet every injury and every disturbance in the most ingenious manner. If, on the other hand, the injury is quite incurable, it hastens to expedite death, and indeed the more so the higher is the species of the organism, thus the greater its sensibility. Even this has its analogue in the instinct of insects. The wasps, for instance, who through the whole summer have with great care and labour fed their larvæ on the produce of their plundering, but now, in October, see the last generation of them facing starvation, sting them to death (Kirby and Spence, vol. i. p. 374). Nay, still more curious and special analogies may be found; for example, this: if the female humble-bee (*Apis terrestris, bombylius*) lays eggs, the working humble-bees are seized with a desire to devour them, which lasts from six to eight hours and is satisfied unless the mother keeps them off and carefully guards the eggs. But after this time the working humble-bees show absolutely no inclination to eat the eggs even when offered to them; on the contrary, they now become the zealous tenders and nourishers of the larvæ now being hatched out. This may without violence be taken as an analogue of children's complaints, especially teething, in which it is just the future nourishers of the organism making an attack upon it which so often costs it its life. The consideration of all these analogies between organised life and the instinct, together with the mechanical tendencies of the lower animals, serves ever more to confirm the conviction that the *will* is the basis of the one as of the other, for it shows here also the subordinate rôle of knowledge in the action of the will, sometimes more, sometimes less, confined, and sometimes wanting altogether.

But in yet another respect instincts and the animal organisation reciprocally illustrate each other: through the *anticipation of the future* which appears in both. By means of instincts and mechanical tendencies animals care for the satisfaction of wants which they do not yet feel, nay, not only for their own wants, but even for those of the future brood. Thus they work for an end which is as yet unknown to them. This goes so far, as I have illustrated by the example of the Bombex in "The Will in Nature" (second edit. p. 45, third edit. p. 47), that they pursue and kill in advance the enemies of their future eggs. In the same way we see the future wants of an animal, its prospective ends, anticipated in its whole corporisation by the organised implements for their attainment and satisfaction; from which, then, proceeds that perfect adaptation of the structure of every animal to its manner of life, that equipment of it with the needful weapons to attack its prey and to ward off its enemies, and that calculation of its whole form with reference to the element and the surroundings in which it has to appear as a pursuer, which I have fully described in my work on the will in nature under the rubric "Comparative Anatomy." All these anticipations, both in the instinct and in the organisation of animals, we might bring under the conception of a knowledge *a priori*, if *knowledge* lay at their foundation at all. But this is, as we have shown, not the case. Their source lies deeper than the sphere of knowledge, in the will as the thing in itself, which as such remains free even from the *forms* of knowledge; therefore with reference to it time has no significance, consequently the future lies as near it as the present.

CHAPTER XXVIII.[1]

CHARACTERISATION OF THE WILL TO LIVE.

OUR second book closed with the question as to the goal and aim of that will which had shown itself to be the inner nature of all things in the world. The following remarks may serve to supplement the answer to this question given there in general terms, for they lay down the character of the will as a whole.

Such a characterisation is possible because we have recognised as the inner nature of the world something thoroughly real and empirically given. On the other hand, the very name "world-soul," by which many have denoted that inner being, gives instead of this a mere *ens rationis;* for "soul" signifies an individual unity of consciousness which clearly does not belong to that nature, and in general, since the conception "soul" supposes knowing and willing in inseparable connection and yet independent of the animal organism, it is not to be justified, and therefore not to be used. The word should never be applied except in a metaphorical sense, for it is much more insidious than ψυχη or anima, which signify breath.

Much more unsuitable, however, is the way in which so-called pantheists express themselves, whose whole philosophy consists chiefly in this, that they call the inner nature of the world, which is unknown to them, "God;" by which indeed they imagine they have achieved much. According to this, then, the world would be a theophany. But let one only look at it: this world of constantly needy

[1] This chapter is connected with § 29 of the first volume.

creatures, who continue for a time only by devouring one another, fulfil their existence in anxiety and want, and often suffer terrible miseries, till at last they fall into the arms of death; whoever distinctly looks upon this will allow that Aristotle was right in saying: "ἡ φυσις δαιμονια, αλλ' ου θεια εστι" (*Natura dæmonia est, non divina*), *De divinat.*, c. 2, p. 463; nay, he will be obliged to confess that a God who could think of changing Himself into such a world as this must certainly have been tormented by the devil. I know well that the pretended philosophers of this century follow Spinoza in this, and think themselves thereby justified. But Spinoza had special reasons for thus naming his one substance, in order, namely, to preserve at least the word, although not the thing. The stake of Giordano Bruno and of Vanini was still fresh in the memory; they also had been sacrificed to that God for whose honour incomparably more human sacrifices have bled than on the altars of all heathen gods of both hemispheres together. If, then, Spinoza calls the world God, it is exactly the same thing as when Rousseau in the "*Contrat social*," constantly and throughout denotes the people by the word *le souverain;* we might also compare it with this, that once a prince who intended to abolish the nobility in his land, in order to rob no one of his own, hit upon the idea of ennobling all his subjects. Those philosophers of our day have certainly one other ground for the nomenclature we are speaking of, but it is no more substantial. In their philosophising they all start, not from the world or our consciousness of it, but from God, as something given and known; He is not their *quæsitum*, but their *datum*. If they were boys I would then explain to them that this is a *petitio principii*, but they know this as well as I do. But since Kant has shown that the path of the earlier dogmatism, which proceeded honestly, the path from the world to a God, does not lead there, these gentlemen now imagine they have found a fine way of escape and made it cunningly. Will the reader of a later age pardon me for detaining him with persons of whom he has never heard.

Every glance at the world, to explain which is the task of the philosopher, confirms and proves that *will to live*, far from being an arbitrary hypostasis or an empty word, is the only true expression of its inmost nature. Everything presses and strives towards *existence*, if possible *organised existence*, i.e., *life*, and after that to the highest possible grade of it. In animal nature it then becomes apparent that *will to live* is the keynote of its being, its one unchangeable and unconditioned quality. Let any one consider this universal desire for life, let him see the infinite willingness, facility, and exuberance with which the will to live presses impetuously into existence under a million forms everywhere and at every moment, by means of fructification and of germs, nay, when these are wanting, by means of *generatio æquivoca*, seizing every opportunity, eagerly grasping for itself every material capable of life: and then again let him cast a glance at its fearful alarm and wild rebellion when in any particular phenomenon it must pass out of existence; especially when this takes place with distinct consciousness. Then it is precisely the same as if in this single phenomenon the whole world would be annihilated for ever, and the whole being of this threatened living thing is at once transformed into the most desperate struggle against death and resistance to it. Look, for example, at the incredible anxiety of a man in danger of his life, the rapid and serious participation in this of every witness of it, and the boundless rejoicing at his deliverance. Look at the rigid terror with which a sentence of death is heard, the profound awe with which we regard the preparations for carrying it out, and the heartrending compassion which seizes us at the execution itself. We would then suppose there was something quite different in question than a few less years of an empty, sad existence, embittered by troubles of every kind, and always uncertain: we would rather be amazed that it was a matter of any consequence whether one attained a few years earlier to the place where after an ephemeral existence he has billions of years to be. In such phenomena, then, it becomes visible that I am right in declaring that *the will to live* is that which cannot be further explained, but lies at the foundation of all explanations, and that this, far from being an empty word, like the absolute, the infinite, the idea, and similar expressions, is the most real thing we know, nay, the kernel of reality itself.

But if now, abstracting for a while from this interpretation drawn from our inner being, we place ourselves as strangers over against nature, in order to comprehend it objectively, we find that from the grade of organised life upwards it has only one intention—that of the *maintenance of the species.* To this end it works, through the immense superfluity of germs, through the urgent vehemence of the sexual instinct, through its willingness to adapt itself to all circumstances and opportunities, even to the production of bastards, and through the instinctive maternal affection, the strength of which is so great that in many kinds of animals it even outweighs self-love, so that the mother sacrifices her life in order to preserve that of the young. The individual, on the contrary, has for nature only an indirect value, only so far as it is the means of maintaining the species. Apart from this its existence is to nature a matter of indifference; indeed nature even leads it to destruction as soon as it has ceased to be useful for this end. Why the individual exists would thus be clear; but why does the species itself exist? That is a question which nature when considered merely objectively cannot answer. For in vain do we seek by contemplating her for an end of this restless striving, this ceaseless pressing into existence, this anxious care for the maintenance of the species. The strength and time of the individuals are consumed in the effort to procure sustenance for themselves and their young, and are only just sufficient, sometimes even not sufficient, for this. Even if here and there a surplus of strength, and therefore of comfort—in the case of the *one* rational species also of knowledge—remains, this is much too insignificant to pass for the end of that whole process of nature. The whole thing, when regarded thus purely objectively, and indeed as extraneous to us, looks as if nature was only concerned that of all her (Platonic) *Ideas*, *i.e.*, permanent forms, none should be lost. Accordingly, as if she had so thoroughly satisfied herself with the fortunate discovery and combination of these Ideas (for which the three preceding occasions on which she stocked the earth's surface with animals were only the preparation), that now her only fear is lest any one of these beautiful fancies should be lost, *i.e.*, lest any one of these forms should disappear from time and the causal series. For the individuals are fleeting as the water in the brook; the Ideas, on the contrary, are permanent, like its eddies: but the exhaustion of the water would also do away with the eddies. We would have to stop at this unintelligible view if nature were known to us only from without, thus were given us merely *objectively*, and we accepted it as it is comprehended by knowledge, and also as sprung from knowledge, *i.e.*, in the sphere of the idea, and were therefore obliged to confine ourselves to this province in solving it. But the case is otherwise, and a glance at any rate is afforded us into the *interior of nature;* inasmuch as this is nothing else than *our own inner being*, which is precisely where nature, arrived at the highest grade to which its striving could work itself up, is now by the light of knowledge found directly in self-consciousness. Here the will shows itself to us as something *toto genere* different from the idea, in which nature appears unfolded in all her (Platonic) Ideas; and it now gives us, at one stroke, the explanation which could never be found upon the objective path of the idea. Thus the subjective here gives the key for the exposition of the objective. In order to recognise, as something original and unconditioned, that exceedingly strong tendency of all animals and men to retain life and carry it on as long as possible—a tendency which was set forth above as characteristic of the subjective, or of the will—it is necessary to make clear to ourselves that this is by no means the result of any objective *knowledge* of the worth of life, but is independent of all knowledge; or, in other words, that those beings exhibit themselves, not as drawn from in front, but as impelled from behind.

If with this intention we first of all review the interminable series of animals, consider the infinite variety of their forms, as they exhibit themselves always differently modified according to their element and manner of life, and also ponder the inimitable ingenuity of their structure and mechanism, which is carried out with equal perfection in every individual; and finally, if we take into consideration the incredible expenditure of strength, dexterity, prudence, and activity which every animal has ceaselessly to make through its whole life; if, approaching the matter more closely, we contemplate the untiring diligence of wretched little ants, the marvellous and ingenious industry of the bees, or observe how a single burying-beetle (*Necrophorus vespillo*) buries a mole of forty times its own size in two days in order to deposit its eggs in it and insure nourishment for the future brood (*Gleditsch, Physik. Bot. Œkon. Abhandl.*, iii. 220), at the same time calling to mind how the life of most insects is nothing but ceaseless labour to prepare food and an abode for the future brood which will arise from their eggs, and which then, after they have consumed the food and passed through the chrysalis state, enter upon life merely to begin again from the beginning the same labour; then also how, like this, the life of the birds is for the most part taken up with their distant and laborious migrations, then with the building of their nests and the collecting of food for the brood, which itself has to play the same rôle the following year; and so all work constantly for the future, which afterwards makes bankrupt;—then we cannot avoid looking round for the reward of all this skill and trouble, for the end which these animals have before their eyes, which strive so ceaselessly—in short, we are driven to ask: What is the result? what is attained by the animal existence which demands such infinite preparation? And there is nothing to point to but the satisfaction of hunger and the sexual instinct, or in any case a little momentary comfort, as it falls to the lot of each animal individual, now and then in the intervals of its endless need and struggle. If we place the two together, the indescribable ingenuity of the preparations, the enormous abundance of the means, and the insufficiency of what is thereby aimed at and attained, the insight presses itself upon us that life is a business, the proceeds of which are very far from covering the cost of it. This becomes most evident in some animals of a specially simple manner of life. Take, for example, the mole, that unwearied worker. To dig with all its might with its enormous shovel claws is the occupation of its whole life; constant night surrounds it; its embryo eyes only make it avoid the light. It alone is truly an *animal nocturnum;* not cats, owls, and bats, who see by night. But what, now, does it attain by this life, full of trouble and devoid of pleasure? Food and the begetting of its kind; thus only the means of carrying on and beginning anew the same doleful course in new individuals. In such examples it becomes clear that there is no proportion between the cares and troubles of life and the results or gain of it. The consciousness of the world of perception gives a certain appearance of objective worth of existence to the life of those animals which can see, although in their case this consciousness is entirely subjective and limited to the influence of motives upon them. But the *blind* mole, with its perfect organisation and ceaseless activity, limited to the alternation of insect larvæ and hunger, makes the disproportion of the means to the end apparent. In this respect the consideration of the animal world left to itself in lands uninhabited by men is also specially instructive. A beautiful picture of this, and of the suffering which nature prepares for herself without the interference of man, is given by Humboldt in his "*Ansichten der Natur*" (second edition, p. 30 *et seq.*); nor does he neglect to cast a glance (p. 44) at the analogous suffering of the human race, always and everywhere at variance with itself. Yet in the simple and easily surveyed life of the brutes the emptiness and vanity of the struggle of the whole phenomenon is more easily grasped. The variety of the organisations, the ingenuity of the means, whereby each is adapted to its element and its prey contrasts here distinctly with the want of any lasting final aim; instead of which there presents itself only momentary comfort, fleeting pleasure conditioned by wants, much and long suffering, constant strife, *bellum omnium*, each one both a hunter and hunted, pressure, want, need, and anxiety, shrieking and howling; and this goes on *in secula seculorum*, or till once again the crust of the planet breaks. Yunghahn relates that he saw in Java a plain far as the eye could reach entirely covered with skeletons, and took it for a battlefield; they were, however, merely the skeletons of large turtles, five feet long and three feet broad, and the same height, which come this way out of the sea in order to lay their eggs, and are then attacked by wild dogs (*Canis rutilans*), who with their united strength lay them on their backs, strip off their lower armour, that is, the small shell of the stomach, and so devour them alive. But often then a tiger pounces upon the dogs. Now all this misery repeats itself thousands and thousands of times, year out, year in. For this, then, these turtles are born. For whose guilt must they suffer this torment? Wherefore the whole scene of horror? To this the only answer is: it is thus that the will to live objectifies itself.[1] Let one

[1] In the *Siècle*, 10th April 1859, there appears, very beautifully written, the story of a squirrel that was magically drawn by a serpent into its very jaws: "Un voyageur qui vient de parcourir plusieurs provinces de l'ile de Java cite un exemple remarqueable du pouvoir facinateur des serpens. Le voyageur dont il est question commençait à

consider it well and comprehend it in all its objectifications; and then one will arrive at an understanding of its nature and of the world; but not if one frames general conceptions and builds card houses out of them. The comprehension of the great drama of the objectification of

gravir Junjind, un des monts appelés par les Hollandais Pepergebergte. Après avoir pénétré dans une épaisse forêt, il aperçut sur les branches d'un kijatile un écureuil de Java à tête blanche, folâtrant avec la grâce et l'agilité qui distinguent cette charmante espèce de rongeurs. Un nid sphérique, formé de brins flexible et de mousse, placé dans les parties les plus élevées de l'arbre, a l'enfourchure de deux branches, et une cavité dans le tronc, semblaient les points de mire de ses jeux. A peine s'en était-il éloigné qu'il y revenait avec une ardeur extrême. On était dans le mois de Juillet, et probablement l'écureuil avait en haut ses petits, et dans le bas le magasin à fruits. Bientôt il fut comme saisi d'effroi, ses mouvemens devinrent désordonnés, on eut dit qu'il cherchait toujours à mettre un obstacle entre lui et certaines parties de l'arbre : puis il se tapit et resta immobile entre deux branches. Le voyageur eut le sentiment d'un danger pour l'innocente bête, mais il ne pouvait deviner lequel. Il approcha, et un examen attentif lui fit découvrir dans un creux du tronc une couleuvre lieu, dardant ses yeux fixes dans la direction de l'écureuil. Notre voyageur trembla pour le pauvre écureuil. La couleuvre était si attentive à sa proie qu'elle ne semblait nullement remarquer la présence d'un homme. Notre voyageur, qui était armé, aurait donc prevenir en aide à l'infortuné rongeur en tuant le serpent. Mais la science l'emporta sur la pitié, et il voulut voir quelle issue aurait le drame. Le dénoûment fut tragique. L'écureuil ne tarda point à pousser un cri plaintif qui, pour tous ceux qui le connaissent, dénote le voisinage d'un serpent. Il avança un peu, essaya de reculer, revint encore en avant, tâche de retourner en arrière. Mais s'approcha toujours plus du reptile. La couleuvre, roulée en spirale, la tête au dessus des anneaux, et immobile comme un morceau de bois, ne le quittait pas du regard. L'écureuil, de branche en branche, et descendant toujours plus bas, arriva jusqu'à la partie nue du tronc. Alors le pauvre animal ne tenta même plus de fuir le danger. Attiré par une puissance invincible, et comme poussé par le vertige, il se précipita dans la gueule du serpent, qui s'ouvrit tout à coup démesurément pour le recevoir. Autant la couleuvre avait été inerte jusque là autant elle devint active dès qu'elle fut en possession de sa proie. Déroulant ses anneaux et prenant sa course de bas en haut avec une agilité inconcevable, sa reptation la porta en un clin d'œil au sommet de l'arbre, où elle alla sans doute digérer et dormir."

In this example we see what spirit animates nature, for it reveals itself in it, and how very true is the saying of Aristotle quoted above (p. 106). This story is not only important with regard to fascination, but also as an argument for pessimism. That an animal is surprised and attacked by another is bad; still we can console ourselves for that; but that such a poor innocent squirrel sitting beside its nest with its young is compelled, step by step, reluctantly, battling with itself and lamenting, to approach the wide, open jaws of the serpent and consciously throw itself into them is revolting and atrocious. What monstrous kind of nature is this to which we belong!

the will to live, and the characterisation of its nature, certainly demands somewhat more accurate consideration and greater thoroughness than the dismissal of the world by attributing to it the title of God, or, with a silliness which only the German fatherland offers and knows how to enjoy, explaining it as the "Idea in its other being," in which for twenty years the simpletons of my time have found their unutterable delight. Certainly, according to pantheism or Spinozism, of which the systems of our century are mere travesties, all that sort of thing reels itself off actually without end, straight on through all eternity. For then the world is a God, *ens perfectissimum, i.e.*, nothing better can be or be conceived. Thus there is no need of deliverance from it; and consequently there is none. But why the whole tragi-comedy exists cannot in the least be seen; for it has no spectators, and the actors themselves undergo infinite trouble, with little and merely negative pleasure.

Let us now add the consideration of the human race. The matter indeed becomes more complicated, and assumes a certain seriousness of aspect; but the fundamental character remains unaltered. Here also life presents itself by no means as a gift for enjoyment, but as a task, a drudgery to be performed; and in accordance with this we see, in great and small, universal need, ceaseless cares, constant pressure, endless strife, compulsory activity, with extreme exertion of all the powers of body and mind. Many millions, united into nations, strive for the common good, each individual on account of his own; but many thousands fall as a sacrifice for it. Now senseless delusions, now intriguing politics, incite them to wars with each other; then the sweat and the blood of the great multitude must flow, to carry out the ideas of individuals, or to expiate their faults. In peace industry and trade are active, inventions work miracles, seas are navigated, delicacies are collected from all ends of the world, the waves engulf thousands. All strive, some planning, others acting; the tumult is indescribable. But the ultimate aim of it all, what is it? To sustain ephemeral and tormented individuals through a short span of time in the most fortunate case with endurable want and comparative freedom from pain, which, however, is at once attended with ennui; then the reproduction of this race and its striving. In this evident disproportion between the trouble and the reward, the will to live appears to us from this point of view, if taken objectively, as a fool, or subjectively, as a delusion, seized by which everything living works with the utmost exertion of its strength for something that is of no value. But when we consider it more closely, we shall find here also that it is rather a blind pressure, a tendency entirely without ground or motive.

The law of motivation, as was shown in § 29 of the first volume, only extends to the particular actions, not to willing *as a whole and in general.* It depends upon this, that if we conceive of the human race and its action *as a whole and universally,* it does not present itself to us, as when we contemplate the particular actions, as a play of puppets who are pulled after the ordinary manner by threads outside them; but from this point of view, as puppets which are set in motion by internal clockwork. For if, as we have done above, one compares the ceaseless, serious, and laborious striving of men with what they gain by it, nay, even with what they ever can gain, the disproportion we have pointed out becomes apparent, for one recognises that that which is to be gained, taken as the motive-power, is entirely insufficient for the explanation of that movement and that ceaseless striving. What, then, is a short postponement of death, a slight easing of misery or deferment of pain, a momentary stilling of desire, compared with such an abundant and certain victory over them all as death? What could such advantages accomplish taken as actual moving causes of a human race, innumerable because constantly renewed, which unceasingly moves, strives, struggles, grieves, writhes, and performs the whole tragi-comedy of the history of the world, nay, what says more than all, *perseveres* in such a mock-existence as long as each one possibly can? Clearly this is all inexplicable if we seek the moving causes outside the figures and conceive the human race as striving, in consequence of rational reflection, or something analogous to this (as moving threads), after those good things held out to it, the attainment of which would be a sufficient reward for its ceaseless cares and troubles. The matter being taken thus, every one would rather have long ago said, "*Le jeu ne vaut pas la chandelle*," and have gone out. But, on the contrary, every one guards and defends his life, like a precious pledge intrusted to him under heavy responsibility, under infinite cares and abundant misery, even under which life is tolerable. The wherefore and the why, the reward for this, certainly he does not see; but he has accepted the worth of that pledge without seeing it, upon trust and faith, and does not know what it consists in. Hence I have said that these puppets are not pulled from without, but each bears in itself the clockwork from which its movements result. This is *the will to live*, manifesting itself as an untiring machine, an irrational tendency, which has not its sufficient reason in the external world. It holds the individuals firmly upon the scene, and is the *primum mobile* of their movements; while the external objects, the motives, only determine their direction in the particular case; otherwise the cause would not be at all suitable to the effect. For, as every manifestation of a force of nature has a cause, but the force of nature itself none, so every particular act of will has a motive, but the will in general has none: indeed at bottom these two are one and the same. The will, as that which is metaphysical, is everywhere the boundary-stone of every investigation, beyond which it cannot go. From the original and unconditioned nature of the will, which has been proved, it is explicable that man loves beyond everything else an existence full of misery, trouble, pain, and anxiety, and, again, full of ennui, which, if he considered and weighed it purely objectively, he would certainly abhor, and fears above all things the end of it, which is yet for him the one thing certain.[1] Accordingly we often see a miserable figure, deformed and shrunk with age, want, and disease, implore our help from the bottom of his heart for the prolongation of an existence, the end of which would necessarily appear altogether desirable if it were an objective judgment that determined here. Thus instead of this it is the blind will, appearing as the tendency to life, the love of life, and the sense of life; it is the same which makes the plants grow. This sense of life may be compared to a rope which is stretched above the puppet-show of the world of men, and on which the puppets hang by invisible threads, while apparently they are supported only by the ground beneath them (the objective value of life). But if the rope becomes weak the puppet sinks; if it breaks the puppet must fall, for the ground beneath it only seemed to support it: *i.e.*, the weakening of that love of life shows itself as hypochondria, spleen, melancholy: its entire exhaustion as the inclination to suicide, which now takes place on the slightest occasion, nay, for a merely imaginary reason, for now, as it were, the man seeks a quarrel with himself, in order to shoot himself dead, as many do with others for a like purpose;—indeed, upon necessity, suicide is resorted to without any special occasion. (Evidence of this will be found in Esquirol, *Des maladies mentales*, 1838.) And as with the persistence in life, so is it also with its action and movement. This is not something freely chosen; but while every one would really gladly rest, want and ennui are the whips that keep the top spinning. Therefore the whole and every individual bears the stamp of a forced condition; and every one, in that, inwardly weary, he longs for rest, but

[1] "*Augustini de civit. Dei*," L. xi. c. 27, deserves to be compared as an interesting commentary on what is said here.

yet must press forward, is like his planet, which does not fall into the sun only because a force driving it forward prevents it. Therefore everything is in continual strain and forced movement, and the course of the world goes on, to use an expression of Aristotle's (*De cœlo*, ii. 13), "ου φυσει, αλλα βιᾳ" (*Motu, non naturali sed violento*). Men are only apparently drawn from in front; really they are pushed from behind; it is not life that tempts them on, but necessity that drives them forward. The law of motivation is, like all causality, merely the form of the phenomenon. We may remark in passing that this is the source of the comical, the burlesque, the grotesque, the ridiculous side of life; for, urged forward against his will, every one bears himself as best he can, and the straits that thus arise often look comical enough, serious as is the misery which underlies them.

In all these considerations, then, it becomes clear to us that the will to live is not a consequence of the knowledge of life, is in no way a *conclusio ex præmissis*, and in general is nothing secondary. Rather, it is that which is first and unconditioned, the premiss of all premisses, and just on that account that from which philosophy must *start*, for the will to live does not appear in consequence of the world, but the world in consequence of the will to live.

I scarcely need to draw attention to the fact that the considerations with which we now conclude the second book already point forcibly to the serious theme of the fourth book, indeed would pass over into it directly if it were not that my architectonic symmetry makes it necessary that the third book, with its fair contents, should come between, as a second consideration of *the world as idea*, the conclusion of which, however, again points in the same direction.

Supplements to the Third Book.

"*Et is similis spectatori est, quod ab omni separatus spectaculum videt.*"

—Oupnekhat, vol. i. p. 304.

SUPPLEMENTS TO THE THIRD BOOK.

CHAPTER XXIX.[1]

ON THE KNOWLEDGE OF THE IDEAS.

THE intellect, which has hitherto only been considered in its original and natural condition of servitude under the will, appears in the third book in its deliverance from that bondage; with regard to which, however, it must at once be observed that we have not to do here with a lasting emancipation, but only with a brief hour of rest, an exceptional and indeed only momentary release from the service of the will. As this subject has been treated with sufficient fulness in the first volume, I have here only to add a few supplementary remarks.

As, then, was there explained, the intellect in its activity in the service of the will, thus in its natural function, knows only the mere *relations* of things; primarily to the will itself, to which it belongs, whereby they become motives of the will; but then also, just for the sake of the completeness of this knowledge, the relations of things to each other. This last knowledge first appears in some extent and importance in the human intellect; in the case of the brutes, on the other hand, even where the intellect is considerably developed, only within very narrow limits. Clearly even the apprehension of the relations which things have to each other only takes place,

[1] This chapter is connected with §§ 30–32 of the first volume.

indirectly, in the service of the will. It therefore forms the transition to the purely objective knowledge, which is entirely independent of the will; it is scientific knowledge, the latter is artistic knowledge. If many and various relations of an object are immediately apprehended, from these the peculiar and proper nature of the object appears ever more distinctly, and gradually constructs itself out of mere relations: although it itself is entirely different from them. In this mode of apprehension the subjection of the intellect to the will at once becomes ever more indirect and less. If the intellect has strength enough to gain the preponderance, and let go altogether the relations of things to the will, in order to apprehend, instead of them, the purely objective nature of a phenomenon, which expresses itself through all relations, it also forsakes, along with the service of the will, the apprehension of mere relations, and thereby really also that of the individual thing as such. It then moves freely, no longer belonging to a will. In the individual thing it knows only the *essential*, and therefore its whole *species;* consequently it now has for its object the *Ideas*, in my sense, which agrees with the original, Platonic meaning of this grossly misused word; thus the permanent, unchanging forms, independent of the temporal existence of the individuals, the *species rerum*, which really constitute what is purely objective in the phenomena. An Idea so apprehended is not yet indeed the essence of the thing in itself, just because it has sprung from knowledge of mere relations; yet, as the result of the sum of all the relations, it is the peculiar *character* of the thing, and thereby the complete expression of the essence which exhibits itself as an object of perception, comprehended, not in relation to an individual will, but as it expresses itself spontaneously, whereby indeed it determines all its relations, which till then alone were known. The Idea is the root point of all these relations, and thereby the complete and perfect phenomenon, or, as I have expressed it in the text, the adequate objectivity of the will at this grade of its manifestation. Form and colour, indeed, which in the apprehension of the Idea by perception are what is immediate, belong at bottom not to the Idea itself, but are merely the medium of its expression; for, strictly speaking, space is as foreign to it as time. In this sense the Neo-Platonist Olympiodorus already says in his commentary on Plato's Alcibiades (Kreuzer's edition of Proclus and Olympiodorus, vol. ii. p. 82): "*το ειδος μεταδεδωκε μεν της μορφης τῃ ὑλῃ· αμερες δε ον μετελαβεν εξ αυτης του δεαστατου*:" *i.e.*, the Idea, in itself unextended, imparted certainly the form to the matter, but first assumed extension from it. Thus, as was said, the Ideas reveal not the thing in itself, but only the objective character of things, thus still only the phenomenon; and we would not even understand this character if the inner nature of things were not otherwise known to us at least obscurely and in feeling. This nature itself cannot be understood from the Ideas, nor in general through any merely *objective* knowledge; therefore it would remain an eternal secret if we were not able to approach it from an entirely different side. Only because every knowing being is also an individual, and thereby a part of nature, does the approach to the inner being of nature stand open to him in his own self-consciousness, where, as we have found, it makes itself known in the most immediate manner as will.

Now what the Platonic Idea is, regarded as a merely objective image, mere form, and thereby lifted out of time and all relations—that, taken empirically and in time, is the *species* or kind. This, then, is the empirical correlative of the Idea. The Idea is properly eternal, but the species is of endless duration, although its appearance upon one planet may become extinct. Even the names of the two pass over into each other: *ιδεα*, *ειδος*, *species*, kind. The Idea is the species, but not the genus: therefore the *species* are the work of nature, the *genera* the work of man; they are mere conceptions. There are *species naturales,* but only *genera logica.* Of manufactured articles there are no Ideas, but only conceptions; thus *genera logica,* and their subordinate classes are *species logicæ.* To what is said in this reference in vol. i. § 41, I will add here that Aristotle also (*Metaph.* i. 9 and xiii. 5) says that the Platonists admitted no ideas of manufactured articles: "*οἱον οικια, και δακτυλιος, ὡν ου φασιν ειναι ειδη*" (*Ut domus et annulus, quorum ideas dari negant*). With which compare the Scholiast, p. 562, 563 of the Berlin quarto edition. Aristotle further says (*Metaph.* xi. 3): "*αλλ ειπερ* (Supple., *ειδη εστι*) *επι των φυσει* (*εστι·*) *διο δη ου κακως ὁ Πλατων εφη, ὁτι ειδη εστι ὁποσα φυσει*" (*Si quidem ideæ sunt, in iis sunt, quæ natura fiunt: propter quod non male Plato dixit, quod species eorum sunt, quæ natura sunt*). On which the Scholiast remarks, p. 800: "*και τουτο αρεσκει και αυτοις τοις τας ιδεας θεμενοις· των γαρ ὑπο τεχνης γινομενων ιδεας ειναι ουκ ελεγον, αλλα των ὑπο φυσεως*" (*Hoc etiam ipsis ideas statuentibus placet: non enim arte factorum ideas dari ajebant, sed natura procreatorum*). For the rest, the doctrine of Ideas originated with the Pythagoreans, unless we distrust the assertion of Plutarch in the book, *De placitis philosophorum,* L. i. c. 3.

The individual is rooted in the species, and time in eternity. And as every individual is so only because it has the nature of its species in itself, so also it has only temporal existence because it is in eternity. In the following book a special chapter is devoted to the life of the species.

In § 49 of the first volume I have sufficiently brought out the difference between the Idea and the conception. Their resemblance, on the other hand, rests upon the following ground: The original and essential unity of an Idea becomes broken up into the multiplicity of individual things through the perception of the knowing individual, which is subject to sensuous and cerebral conditions. But that unity is then restored through the reflection of the reason, yet only *in abstracto,* as a concept, *universale,* which indeed is equal to the Idea in extension, but has assumed quite a different *form*, and has thereby lost its perceptible nature, and with this its thorough determinateness. In this sense (but in no other) we might, in the language of the Scholastics, describe the Ideas as *universalia ante rem*, the conceptions as *universalia post rem*. Between the two stand the individual things, the knowledge of which is possessed also by the brutes. Without doubt the realism of the Scholastics arose from the confusion of the Platonic Ideas, to which, since they are also the species, an objective real being can certainly be attributed, with the mere concepts to which the Realists now wished to attribute such a being, and thereby called forth the victorious opposition of Nominalism.

CHAPTER XXX.[1]

ON THE PURE SUBJECT OF KNOWLEDGE.

THE comprehension of an Idea, the entrance of it into our consciousness, is only possible by means of a change in us, which might also be regarded as an act of self-denial; for it consists in this, that knowledge turns away altogether from our own will, thus now leaves out of sight entirely the valuable pledge intrusted to it, and considers things as if they could never concern the will at all. For thus alone does knowledge become a pure mirror of the objective nature of things. Knowledge conditioned in this way must lie at the foundation of every genuine work of art as its origin. The change in the subject which is required for this cannot proceed from the will, just because it consists in the elimination of all volition; thus it can be no act of the will, *i.e.*, it cannot lie in our choice. On the contrary, it springs only from a temporary preponderance of the intellect over the will, or, physiologically considered, from a strong excitement of the perceptive faculty of the brain, without any excitement of the desires or emotions. To explain this somewhat more accurately I remind the reader that our consciousness has two sides; partly, it is a consciousness of our *own selves*, which is the will; partly a consciousness of other things, and as such primarily, knowledge, *through perception*, of the external world, the apprehension of objects. Now the more one side of the whole consciousness comes to the front, the more the other side withdraws. Accordingly, the consciousness of *other things*, thus knowledge of perception, becomes the more

[1] This chapter is connected with §§ 33–34 of the first volume.

perfect, *i.e.*, the more objective, the less we are conscious of ourselves at the time. Here exists an actual antagonism. The more we are conscious of the object, the less we are conscious of the subject; the more, on the other hand, the latter occupies our consciousness, the weaker and more imperfect is our perception of the external world. The state which is required for pure objectivity of perception has partly permanent conditions in the perfection of the brain and the general physiological qualities favourable to its activity, partly temporary conditions, inasmuch as such a state is favoured by all that increases the attention and heightens the susceptibility of the cerebral nervous system, yet without exciting any passion. One must not think here of spirituous drinks or opium; what is rather required is a night of quiet sleep, a cold bath, and all that procures for the brain activity an unforced predominance by quieting the circulation and calming the passions. It is especially these natural means of furthering the cerebral nervous activity which bring it about, certainly so much the better the more developed and energetic in general the brain is, that the object separates itself ever more from the subject, and finally introduces the state of pure objectivity of perception, which of itself eliminates the will from consciousness, and in which all things stand before us with increased clearness and distinctness, so that we are conscious almost only of them and scarcely at all of ourselves; thus our whole consciousness is almost nothing more than the medium through which the perceived object appears in the world as an idea. Thus it is necessary for pure, will-less knowledge that the consciousness of ourselves should vanish, since the consciousness of other things is raised to such a pitch. For we only apprehend the world in a purely objective manner when we no longer know that we belong to it; and all things appear the more beautiful the more we are conscious merely of them and the less we are conscious of ourselves. Since now all suffering proceeds from the will, which constitutes the real self, with the withdrawal of this side of consciousness all possibility of suffering is also abolished; therefore the condition of the pure objectivity of perception is one which throughout gives pleasure; and hence I have shown that in it lies one of the two constituent elements of æsthetic satisfaction. As soon, on the other hand, as the consciousness of our own self, thus subjectivity, *i.e.*, the will, again obtains the upper hand, a proportional degree of discomfort or unrest also enters; of discomfort, because our corporealness (the organism which in itself is the will) is again felt; of unrest, because the will, on the path of thought, again fills the consciousness through wishes, emotions, passions, and cares. For the will, as the principle of subjectivity, is everywhere the opposite, nay, the antagonist of knowledge. The greatest concentration of subjectivity consists in the *act of will* proper, in which therefore we have the most distinct consciousness of our own self. All other excitements of the will are only preparations for this; the act of will itself is for subjectivity what for the electric apparatus is the passing of the spark. Every bodily sensation is in itself an excitement of the will, and indeed oftener of the *noluntas* than of the *voluntas*. The excitement of the will on the path of thought is that which occurs by means of motives; thus here the subjectivity is awakened and set in play by the objectivity itself. This takes place whenever any object is apprehended no longer in a purely objective manner, thus without participation in it, but, directly or indirectly, excites desire or aversion, even if it is only by means of a recollection, for then it acts as a motive in the widest sense of the word.

I remark here that abstract thinking and reading, which are connected with words, belong indeed in the wider sense to the consciousness *of other things*, thus to the objective employment of the mind; yet only indirectly, by means of conceptions. But the latter are the artificial product of the reason, and are therefore already a work of intention. Moreover, the will is the ruler of all abstract exercise of the mind, for, according to its aims, it imparts the direction, and also fixes the attention; therefore such mental activity is always accompanied by some effort; and this presupposes the activity of the will. Thus complete objectivity of consciousness does not exist with this kind of mental activity, as it accompanies the æsthetic apprehension, *i.e.*, the knowledge of the Ideas, as a condition.

In accordance with the above, the pure objectivity of perception, by virtue of which no longer the individual thing as such, but the Idea of its species is known, is conditioned by the fact that one is no longer conscious of oneself, but only of the perceived objects, so that one's own consciousness only remains as the supporter of the objective existence of these objects. What increases the difficulty of this state, and therefore makes it more rare, is, that in it the accident (the intellect) overcomes and annuls the substance (the will), although only for a short time. Here also lies the analogy and, indeed, the relationship of this with the denial of the will expounded at the end of the following book. Although knowledge, as was shown in the preceding book, is sprung from the will and is rooted in the manifestation of the will, the organism, yet it is just by the will that its purity is disturbed, as the flame is by the fuel and its smoke. It depends upon this that we can only apprehend the purely objective nature of things, the Ideas which appear in them, when we have ourselves no interest in them, because they stand in no relation to our will. From this, again, it arises that the Ideas of anything appeal to us more easily from a work of art than from reality. For what we behold only in a picture or in poetry stands outside all possibility of having any relation to our will; for in itself it exists only for knowledge and appeals immediately to knowledge alone. On the other hand, the apprehension of Ideas from reality assumes some measure of abstraction from our own volition, a rising above its interests which demands a special power of the intellect. In a high degree, and for some duration, this belongs only to genius, which consists indeed in this, that a greater measure of the power of knowledge exists than is required for the service of an individual will, and this surplus becomes free, and now comprehends the world without reference to the will. Thus that the work of art facilitates so greatly the apprehension of the Ideas, in which æsthetic satisfaction consists, depends not merely upon the fact that art, by giving prominence to what is essential and eliminating what is unessential, presents the things more distinctly and characteristically, but just as much on the fact that the absolute silence of the will, which is demanded for the purely objective comprehension of the nature of the things, is attained with the greatest certainty when the perceived object itself lies entirely outside the province of things which are capable of having a relation to the will, because it is nothing real, but a mere picture. Now this holds good, not only of the works of plastic and pictorial art, but also of poetry; the effect of which is also conditioned by indifferent, will-less, and thereby purely objective apprehension. It is exactly this which makes a perceived object *picturesque*, an event of actual life *poetical;* for it is only this that throws over the objects of the real world that magic gleam which in the case of sensibly perceived objects is called the picturesque, and in the case of those which are only perceived in imagination is called the poetical. If poets sing of the blithe morning, the beautiful evening, the still moonlight night, and many such things, the real object of their praise is, unknown to themselves, the pure subject of knowledge which is called forth by those beauties of nature, and on the appearance of which the will vanishes from consciousness, and so that peace of heart enters which, apart from this, is unattainable in the world. How otherwise, for example, could the verse—

"*Nox erat, et cœlo fulgebat luna sereno,*
Inter minora sidera,"

affect us so beneficently, nay, so magically? Further, that the stranger or the mere passing traveller feels the picturesque or poetical effect of objects which are unable to produce this effect upon those who live among them may be explained from the fact that the novelty and complete strangeness of the objects of such an indifferent, purely objective apprehension are favourable to it. Thus, for example, the sight of an entirely strange town often makes a specially agreeable impression upon the traveller, which it by no means produces in the inhabitant of it; for it arises from the fact that the former, being out of all relation to this town and its inhabitants, perceives it purely objectively. Upon this depends partly the pleasure of travelling. This seems also to be the reason why it is sought to increase the effect of narrative or dramatic works by transferring the scene to distant times or lands: in Germany, to Italy or Spain; in Italy, to Germany, Poland, or even Holland. If now perfectly objective, intuitive apprehension, purified from all volition, is the condition of the *enjoyment* of æsthetic objects, so much the more is it the condition of their *production*. Every good picture, every genuine poem, bears the stamp of the frame of mind described. For only what has sprung from perception, and indeed from purely objective perception, or is directly excited by it, contains the living germ from which genuine and original achievements can grow up: not only in plastic and pictorial art, but also in poetry, nay, even in philosophy. The *punctum saliens* of every beautiful work, of every great or profound thought, is a purely objective perception. Such perception, however, is absolutely conditioned by the complete silence of the will, which leaves the man simply the pure subject of knowledge. The natural disposition for the predominance of this state is genius.

With the disappearance of volition from consciousness,

the individuality also, and with it its suffering and misery, is really abolished. Therefore I have described the pure subject of knowledge which then remains over as the eternal eye of the world, which, although with very different degrees of clearness, looks forth from all living creatures, untouched by their appearing and passing away, and thus, as identical with itself, as constantly one and the same, is the supporter of the world of permanent Ideas, *i.e.*, of the adequate objectivity of the will; while the individual subject, whose knowledge is clouded by the individuality which springs from the will, has only particular things as its object, and is transitory as these themselves. In the sense here indicated a double existence may be attributed to every one. As will, and therefore as individual, he is only one, and this one exclusively, which gives him enough to do and to suffer. As the purely objective perceiver, he is the pure subject of knowledge in whose consciousness alone the objective world has its existence; as such he is *all things* so far as he perceives them, and in him is their existence without burden or inconvenience. It is *his* existence, so far as it exists in *his* idea; but it is there without will. So far, on the other hand, as it is will, it is not in him. It is well with every one when he is in that state in which he is all things; it is ill with him when in the state in which he is exclusively one. Every state, every man, every scene of life, requires only to be purely objectively apprehended and be made the subject of a sketch, whether with pencil or with words, in order to appear interesting, charming, and enviable; but if one is in it, if one is it oneself, then (it is often a case of) may the devil endure it. Therefore Goethe says—

> "What in life doth only grieve us,
> That in art we gladly see."

There was a period in the years of my youth when I was always trying to see myself and my action from without, and picture it to myself; probably in order to make it more enjoyable to me.

As I have never spoken before on the subject I have just been considering, I wish to add a psychological illustration of it.

In the immediate perception of the world and of life we consider things, as a rule, merely in their relations, consequently according to their relative and not their absolute nature and existence. For example, we will regard houses, ships, machines, and the like with the thought of their end and their adaptation to it; men, with the thought of their relation to us, if they have any such; and then with that of their relations to each other, whether in their present action or with regard to their position and business, judging perhaps their fitness for it, &c. Such a consideration of the relations we can follow more or less far to the most distant links of their chain: the consideration will thereby gain in accuracy and extent, but in its quality and nature it remains the same. It is the consideration of things in their relations, nay, *by means of these,* thus according to the principle of sufficient reason. Every one, for the most part and as a rule, is given up to this method of consideration; indeed I believe that most men are capable of no other. But if, as an exception, it happens that we experience a momentary heightening of the intensity of our intuitive intelligence, we at once see things with entirely different eyes, in that we now apprehend them no longer according to their relations, but according to that which they are in and for themselves, and suddenly perceive their absolute existence apart from their relative existence. At once every individual represents its species; and accordingly we now apprehend the universal of every being. Now what we thus know are the *Ideas of things;* but out of these there now speaks a higher wisdom than that which knows of mere relations. And we also have then passed out of the relations, and have thus become the pure subject of knowledge. But what now exceptionally brings about this state must be internal physiological processes, which purify the activity of the brain, and heighten it to such a degree that a sudden spring-tide of activity like this ensues. The external conditions of this are that we remain completely strange to the scene to be considered, and separated from it, and are absolutely not actively involved in it.

In order to see that a purely objective, and therefore correct, comprehension of things is only possible when we consider them without any personal participation in them, thus when the will is perfectly silent, let one call to mind how much every emotion or passion disturbs and falsifies our knowledge, indeed how every inclination and aversion alters, colours, and distorts not only the judgment, but even the original perception of things. Let one remember how when we are gladdened by some fortunate occurrence the whole world at once assumes a bright colour and a smiling aspect, and, on the contrary, looks gloomy and sad when we are pressed with cares; also, how even a lifeless thing, if it is to be made use of in doing something which we abhor, seems to have a hideous physiognomy; for example, the scaffold, the fortress, to which we have been brought, the surgeon's cases of instruments; the travelling carriage of our loved one, &c., nay, numbers, letters, seals, may seem to grin upon us horribly and affect us as fearful monstrosities. On the other hand, the tools for the accomplishment of our wishes at once appear to us agreeable and pleasing; for example, the hump-backed old woman with the love-letter, the Jew with the louis d'ors, the rope-ladder to escape by, &c. As now here the falsification of the idea through the will in the case of special abhorrence or love is unmistakable, so is it present in a less degree in every object which has any even distant relation to our will, that is, to our desire or aversion. Only when the will with its interests has left consciousness, and the intellect freely follows its own laws, and as pure subject mirrors the objective world, yet in doing so, although spurred on by no volition, is of its own inclination in the highest state of tension and activity, do the colours and forms of things appear in their true and full significance. Thus it is from such comprehension alone that genuine works of art can proceed whose permanent worth and ever renewed approval arises simply from the fact that they express the purely objective element, which lies at the foundation of and shines through the different subjective, and therefore distorted, perceptions, as that which is common to them all and alone stands fast; as it were the common theme of all those subjective variations. For certainly the nature which is displayed before our eyes exhibits itself very differently in different minds; and as each one sees it so alone can he repeat it, whether with the pencil or the chisel, or with words and gestures on the stage. Objectivity alone makes one capable of being an artist; but objectivity is only possible in this way, that the intellect, separated from its root the will, moves freely, and yet acts with the highest degree of energy.

To the youth whose perceptive intellect still acts with fresh energy nature often exhibits itself with complete objectivity, and therefore with perfect beauty. But the pleasure of such a glance is sometimes disturbed by the saddening reflection that the objects present which exhibit themselves in such beauty do not stand in a personal relation to this will, by virtue of which they could interest and delight him; he expects his life in the form of an interesting romance. "Behind that jutting cliff the well-mounted band of friends should await me,—beside that waterfall my love should rest; this beautifully lighted building should be her dwelling, and that vine-clad window hers;—but this beautiful world is for me a desert!" and so on. Such melancholy youthful reveries really demand something exactly contradictory to themselves; for the beauty with which those objects present themselves depends just upon the pure objectivity, *i.e.*, disinterestedness of their perception, and would therefore at once be abolished by the relation to his own will which the youth painfully misses, and thus the whole charm which now affords him pleasure, even though alloyed with a certain admixture of pain, would cease to exist. The same holds good, moreover, of every age and every relation; the beauty of the objects of a landscape which now delights us would vanish if we stood in personal relations to them, of which we remained always conscious. Everything is beautiful only so long as it does not concern us. (We are not speaking here of sensual passion, but of æsthetic pleasure.) Life is never beautiful, but only the pictures of life are so in the transfiguring mirror of art or poetry; especially in youth, when we do not yet know it. Many a youth would receive great peace of mind if one could assist him to this knowledge.

Why has the sight of the full moon such a beneficent, quieting, and exalting effect? Because the moon is an object of perception, but never of desire:

> "The stars we yearn not after
> Delight us with their glory."—G.

Further, it is sublime, *i.e.*, it induces a lofty mood in us, because, without any relation to us, it moves along for ever strange to earthly doings, and sees all while it takes part in nothing. Therefore, at the sight of it the will, with its constant neediness, vanishes from consciousness, and leaves a purely knowing consciousness behind. Perhaps there is also mingled here a feeling that we share this sight with millions, whose individual differences are therein extinguished, so that in this perception they are one, which certainly increases the impression of the sublime. Finally, this is also furthered by the fact that the moon lights without heating, in which certainly lies the reason why it has been called chaste and identified with Diana. In consequence of this whole beneficent impression upon our feeling, the moon becomes gradually our bosom friend. The sun, again, never does so; but is like an overplenteous benefactor whom we can never look in the face.

The following remark may find room here as an addition to what is said in § 38 of the first volume on the æsthetic pleasure afforded by light, reflection, and colours. The whole immediate, thoughtless, but also unspeakable, pleasure which is excited in us by the impression of colours, strengthened by the gleam of metal, and still more by transparency, as, for example, in coloured windows, and in a greater measure by means of the clouds and their reflection at sunset,—ultimately depends upon the fact that here in the easiest manner, almost by a physical necessity, our whole interest is won for knowledge, without any excitement of our will, so that we enter the state of pure knowing, although for the most part this consists here in a mere sensation of the affection of the retina, which, however, as it is in itself perfectly free from pain or pleasure, and therefore entirely without direct influence on the will, thus belongs to pure knowledge.

CHAPTER XXXI.

ON GENIUS.

WHAT is properly denoted by the name genius is the predominating capacity for that kind of knowledge which has been described in the two preceding chapters, the knowledge from which all genuine works of art and poetry, and even of philosophy, proceed. Accordingly, since this has for its objects the Platonic Ideas, and these are not comprehended in the abstract, but *only perceptibly*, the essence of genius must lie in the perfection and energy of the knowledge of *perception*. Corresponding to this, the works which we hear most decidedly designated works of genius are those which start immediately from perception and devote themselves to perception; thus those of plastic and pictorial art, and then those of poetry, which gets its perceptions by the assistance of the imagination. The difference between genius and mere talent makes itself noticeable even here. For talent is an excellence which lies rather in the greater versatility and acuteness of discursive than of intuitive knowledge. He who is endowed with talent thinks more quickly and more correctly than others; but the genius beholds another world from them all, although only because he has a more profound perception of the world which lies before them also, in that it presents itself in his mind more objectively, and consequently in greater purity and distinctness.

[1] This chapter is connected with § 36 of the first volume.

The intellect is, according to its destination, merely the medium of motives; and in accordance with this it originally comprehends nothing in things but their relations to the will, the direct, the indirect, and the possible. In the case of the brutes, where it is almost entirely confined to the direct relations, the matter is just on that account most apparent: what has no relation to their will does not exist for them. Therefore we sometimes see with surprise that even clever animals do not observe at all something conspicuous to them; for example, they show no surprise at obvious alterations in our person and surroundings. In the case of normal men the indirect, and even the possible, relations to the will are added, the sum of which make up the total of useful knowledge; but here also knowledge remains confined to the relations. Therefore the normal mind does not attain to an absolutely pure, objective picture of things, because its power of perception, whenever it is not spurred on by the will and set in motion, at once becomes tired and inactive, because it has not enough energy of its own elasticity and without an *end* in view to apprehend the world in a purely objective manner. Where, on the other hand, this takes place—where the brain has such a surplus of the power of ideation that a pure, distinct, objective image of the external world exhibits itself *without any aim;* an image which is useless for the intentions of the will, indeed, in the higher degrees, disturbing, and even injurious to them—there, the natural disposition, at least, is already present for that abnormity which the name genius denotes, which signifies that here a *genius* foreign to the will, *i.e.*, to the I proper, as it were coming from without, seems to be active. But to speak without a figure: genius consists in this, that the knowing faculty has received a considerably greater development than the *service of the will*, for which alone it originally appeared, demands. Therefore, strictly speaking, physiology might to a certain extent class such a superfluity of brain activity, and with it of brain itself, among the *monstra per exces-*

sum, which, it is well known, it co-ordinates with *monstra per defectum* and those *per situm mutatum*. Thus genius consists in an abnormally large measure of intellect, which can only find its use by being applied to the universal of existence, whereby it then devotes itself to the service of the whole human race, as the normal intellect to that of the individual. In order to make this perfectly comprehensible one might say: if the normal man consists of two-thirds will and one-third intellect, the genius, on the contrary, has two-thirds intellect and one-third will. This might, then, be further illustrated by a chemical simile: the base and the acid of a neutral salt are distinguished by the fact that in each of the two the radical has the converse relation to oxygen to that which it has in the other. The base or the alkali is so because in it the radical predominates with reference to oxygen, and the acid is so because in it oxygen predominates. In the same way now the normal man and the genius are related in respect of will and intellect. From this arises a thorough distinction between them, which is visible even in their whole nature and behaviour, but comes out most clearly in their achievements. One might add the difference that while that total opposition between the chemical materials forms the strongest affinity and attraction between them, in the human race the opposite is rather wont to be found.

The first manifestation which such a superfluity of the power of knowledge calls forth shows itself for the most part in the most original and fundamental knowledge, *i.e.*, in knowledge of *perception*, and occasions the repetition of it in an image; hence arises the painter and the sculptor. In their case, then, the path between the apprehension of genius and the artistic production is the shortest; therefore the form in which genius and its activity here exhibits itself is the simplest and its description the easiest. Yet here also the source is shown from which all genuine productions in every art, in poetry, and indeed in philosophy, have their origin, although in the case of these the process is not so simple.

Let the result arrived at in the first book be here borne in mind, that all perception is intellectual and not merely sensuous. If one now adds the exposition given here, and, at the same time, in justice considers that the philosophy of last century denoted the perceptive faculty of knowledge by the name "lower powers of the soul," we will not think it so utterly absurd nor so deserving of the bitter scorn with which Jean Paul quotes it in his "*Vorschule der Æsthetik*," that Adelung, who had to speak the language of his age, placed genius in "a remarkable strength of the lower powers of the soul." The work just referred to of this author, who is so worthy of our admiration, has great excellences, but yet I must remark that all through, whenever a theoretical explanation and, in general, instruction is the end in view, a style of exposition which is constantly indulging in displays of wit and hurrying along in mere similes cannot be well adapted to the purpose.

It is, then, *perception* to which primarily the peculiar and true nature of things, although still in a conditioned manner, discloses and reveals itself. All conceptions and everything thought are mere abstractions, consequently partial ideas taken from perception, and have only arisen by thinking away. All profound knowledge, even wisdom properly so called, is rooted in the *perceptive* apprehension of things, as we have fully considered in the supplements to the first book. A *perceptive* apprehension has always been the generative process in which every genuine work of art, every immortal thought, received the spark of life. All primary thought takes place in pictures. From conceptions, on the other hand, arise the works of mere talent, the merely rational thoughts, imitations, and indeed all that is calculated merely with reference to the present need and contemporary conditions.

But if now our perception were constantly bound to the

real present of things, its material would be entirely under the dominion of chance, which seldom produces things at the right time, seldom arranges them for an end and for the most part presents them to us in very defective examples. Therefore the *imagination* is required in order to complete, arrange, give the finishing touches to, retain, and repeat at pleasure all those significant pictures of life, according as the aims of a profoundly penetrating knowledge and of the significant work whereby they are to be communicated may demand. Upon this rests the high value of imagination, which is an indispensable tool of genius. For only by virtue of imagination can genius ever, according to the requirements of the connection of its painting or poetry or thinking, call up to itself each object or event in a lively image, and thus constantly draw fresh nourishment from the primary source of all knowledge, perception. The man who is endowed with imagination is able, as it were, to call up spirits, who at the right time reveal to him the truths which the naked reality of things exhibits only weakly, rarely, and then for the most part at the wrong time. Therefore the man without imagination is related to him, as the mussel fastened to its rock, which must wait for what chance may bring it, is related to the freely moving or even winged animal. For such a man knows nothing but the actual perception of the senses: till it comes he gnaws at conceptions and abstractions which are yet mere shells and husks, not the kernel of knowledge. He will never achieve anything great, unless it be in calculating and mathematics. The works of plastic and pictorial art and of poetry, as also the achievements of mimicry, may also be regarded as means by which those who have no imagination may make up for this defect as far as possible, and those who are gifted with it may facilitate the use of it.

Thus, although the kind of knowledge which is peculiar and essential to genius is knowledge of *perception*, yet the special object of this knowledge by no means consists of the particular things, but of the Platonic Ideas which manifest themselves in these, as their apprehension was analysed in chapter 29. Always to see the universal in the particular is just the fundamental characteristic of genius, while the normal man knows in the particular only the particular as such, for only as such does it belong to the actual which alone has interests for him, *i.e.*, relations to his *will*. The degree in which every one not merely thinks, but actually perceives, in the particular thing, only the particular, or a more or less universal up to the most universal of the species, is the measure of his approach to genius. And corresponding to this, only the nature of things generally, the universal in them, the whole, is the special object of genius. The investigation of the particular phenomena is the field of the talents, in the real sciences, whose special object is always only the relations of things to each other.

What was fully shown in the preceding chapter, that the apprehension of the Ideas is conditioned by the fact that the knower is the *pure subject* of knowledge, *i.e.*, that the will entirely vanishes from consciousness, must be borne in mind here. The pleasure which we have in many of Goethe's songs which bring the landscape before our eyes, or in Jean Paul's sketches of nature, depends upon the fact that we thereby participate in the objectivity of those minds, *i.e.*, the purity with which in them the world as idea separated from the world as will, and, as it were, entirely emancipated itself from it. It also follows from the fact that the kind of knowledge peculiar to genius is essentially that which is purified from all will and its relations, that the works of genius do not proceed from intention or choice, but it is guided in them by a kind of instinctive necessity. What is called the awaking of genius, the hour of initiation, the moment of inspiration, is nothing but the attainment of freedom by the intellect, when, delivered for a while from its service under the will, it does not now sink into inactivity or lassitude, but is active for a short time entirely alone and spontaneously. Then it is of the greatest purity, and becomes the clear mirror of the world; for, completely severed from its origin, the will, it is now the world as idea itself, concentrated in *one* consciousness. In such moments, as it were, the souls of immortal works are begotten. On the other hand, in all intentional reflection the intellect is not free, for indeed the will guides it and prescribes it its theme.

The stamp of commonness, the expression of vulgarity, which is impressed on the great majority of countenances consists really in this, that in them becomes visible the strict subordination of their knowledge to their will, the firm chain which binds these two together, and the impossibility following from this of apprehending things otherwise than in their relation to the will and its aims. On the other hand, the expression of genius which constitutes the evident family likeness of all highly gifted men consists in this, that in it we distinctly read the liberation, the manumission of the intellect from the service of the will, the predominance of knowledge over volition; and because all anxiety proceeds from the will, and knowledge, on the contrary, is in and for itself painless and serene, this gives to their lofty brow and clear, perceiving glance, which are not subject to the service of the will and its wants, that look of great, almost supernatural serenity which at times breaks through, and consists very well with the melancholy of their other features, especially the mouth, and which in this relation may be aptly described by the motto of Giordano Bruno: *In tristitia hilaris, in hilaritate tristis.*

The will, which is the root of the intellect, opposes itself to any activity of the latter which is directed to anything else but its own aims. Therefore the intellect is only capable of a purely objective and profound comprehension of the external world when it has freed itself at least for a while from this its root. So long as it remains bound to the will, it is of its own means capable of no activity, but sleeps in a stupor, whenever the will (the interests) does not awake it, and set it in motion. If, however, this happens, it is indeed very well fitted to recognise the relations of things according to the interest of the will, as the prudent mind does, which, however, must always be an awakened mind, *i.e.*, a mind actively aroused by volition; but just on this account it is not capable of comprehending the purely objective nature of things. For the willing and the aims make it so one-sided that it sees in things only that which relates to these, and the rest either disappears or enters consciousness in a falsified form. For example, the traveller in anxiety and haste will see the Rhine and its banks only as a line, and the bridges over it only as lines cutting it. In the mind of the man who is filled with his own aims the world appears as a beautiful landscape appears on the plan of a battlefield. Certainly these are extremes, taken for the sake of distinctness; but every excitement of the will, however slight, will have as its consequence a slight but constantly proportionate falsification of knowledge. The world can only appear in its true colour and form, in its whole and correct significance, when the intellect, devoid of willing, moves freely over the objects, and without being driven on by the will is yet energetically active. This is certainly opposed to the nature and determination of the intellect, thus to a certain extent unnatural, and just on this account exceedingly rare; but it is just in this that the essential nature of genius lies, in which alone that condition takes place in a high degree and is of some duration, while in others it only appears approximately and exceptionally. I take it to be in the sense expounded here that Jean Paul (*Vorschule der Æsthetik*, § 12) places the essence of genius in *reflectiveness.* The normal man is sunk in the whirl and tumult of life, to which he belongs through his will; his intellect is filled with the things and events of life; but he does not know these things nor life itself in their objective significance; as the merchant on 'Change in Amsterdam apprehends perfectly what his neighbour says, but does not hear the hum of the whole Exchange, like the sound of the sea, which astonishes the distant observer. From the genius, on the contrary, whose intellect is delivered from the will, and thus from the person, what concerns these does not conceal the world and things themselves; but he becomes distinctly conscious of them, he apprehends them in and for themselves in objective perception; in this sense he is *reflective.*

It is *reflectiveness* which enables the painter to repeat the natural objects which he contemplates faithfully upon the canvas, and the poet accurately to call up again the concrete present, by means of abstract conceptions, by giving it utterance and so bringing it to distinct consciousness, and also to express everything in words which others only feel. The brute lives entirely without reflection. It has consciousness, *i.e.*, it knows itself and its good and ill, also the objects which occasion these. But its knowledge remains always subjective, never becomes objective; everything that enters it seems a matter of course, and therefore can never become for it a theme (an object of exposition) nor a problem (an object of meditation). Its consciousness is thus entirely *immanent.* Not certainly the same, but yet of kindred nature, is the consciousness of the common type of man, for his apprehension also of things and the world is predominantly subjective and remains prevalently immanent. It apprehends the things in the world, but not the world; its own action and suffering, but not itself. As now in innumerable gradations the distinctness of consciousness rises, reflectiveness appears more and more; and thus it is brought about little by little that sometimes, though rarely, and then again in very different degrees of distinctness, the question passes through the mind like a flash, "What is all this?" or again, "How is it really fashioned?" The first question, if it attains great distinctness and continued presence, will make the philosopher, and the other, under the same conditions, the artist or the poet. Therefore, then, the high calling of both of these has its root in the reflectiveness which primarily springs from the distinctness with which they are conscious of the world and their own selves, and thereby come to reflect upon them. But the whole process springs from the fact that the intellect through its preponderance frees itself for a time from the will, to which it is originally subject.

The considerations concerning genius here set forth are connected by way of supplement with the exposition contained in chapter 21, of the *ever wider separation of the will and the intellect*, which can be traced in the whole series of existences. This reaches its highest grade in genius, where it extends to the entire liberation of the intellect from its root the will, so that here the intellect becomes perfectly free, whereby the *world as idea* first attains to complete objectification.

A few remarks now concerning the individuality of genius. Aristotle has already said, according to Cicero (*Tusc.*, i. 33), "*Omnes ingeniosos melancholicos esse;*" which without doubt is connected with the passage of Aristotle's "*Problemata,*" xxx. 1. Goethe also says: "My poetic rapture was very small, so long as I only encountered good; but it burnt with a bright flame when I fled from threatening evil. The tender poem, like the rainbow, is only drawn on a dark ground; hence the genius of the poet loves the element of melancholy."

This is to be explained from the fact that since the will constantly re-establishes its original sway over the intellect, the latter more easily withdraws from this under unfavourable personal relations; because it gladly turns from adverse circumstances, in order to a certain extent to divert itself, and now directs itself with so much the greater energy to the foreign external world, thus more easily becomes purely objective. Favourable personal relations act conversely. Yet as a whole and in general the melancholy which accompanies genius depends upon the fact that the brighter the intellect which enlightens the will to live, the more distinctly does it perceive the misery of its condition. The melancholy disposition of highly gifted minds which has so often been observed has its emblem in Mont Blanc, the summit of which is for the most part lost in clouds; but when sometimes, especially in the early morning, the veil of clouds is rent and now the mountain looks down on Chamounix from its height in the heavens above the clouds, then it is a sight at which the heart of each of us swells from its profoundest depths. So also the genius, for the most part melancholy, shows at times that peculiar serenity already described above, which is possible only for it, and springs from the most perfect objectivity of the mind. It floats like a ray of light upon his lofty brow: *In tristitia hilaris, in hilaritate tristis.*

All bunglers are so ultimately because their intellect, still too firmly bound to the will, only becomes active when spurred on by it, and therefore remains entirely in its service. They are accordingly only capable of personal aims. In conformity with these they produce bad pictures, insipid poems, shallow, absurd, and very often dishonest philosophemes, when it is to their interest to recommend themselves to high authorities by a pious disingenuousness. Thus all their action and thought is personal. Therefore they succeed at most in appropriating what is external, accidental, and arbitrary in the genuine works of others as mannerisms, in doing which they take the shell instead of the kernel, and yet imagine they have attained to everything, nay, have surpassed those works. If, however, the failure is patent, yet many hope to attain success in the end through their good intentions. But it is just this good will which makes success impossible; because this only pursues personal ends, and with these neither art nor poetry nor philosophy can ever be taken seriously.

Therefore the saying is peculiarly applicable to such persons: "They stand in their own light." They have no idea that it is only the intellect delivered from the government of the will and all its projects, and therefore freely active, that makes one capable of genuine productions, because it alone imparts true seriousness; and it is well for them that they have not, otherwise they would leap into the water. The *good will* is in *morality* everything; but in art it is nothing. In art, as the word itself indicates (*Kunst*), what alone is of consequence is ability (*Können*). It all amounts ultimately to this, where the true *seriousness* of the man lies. In almost all it lies exclusively in their own well-being and that of their families; therefore they are in a position to promote this and nothing else; for no purpose, no voluntary and intentional effort, imparts the true, profound, and proper seriousness, or makes up for it, or more correctly, takes its place. For it always remains where nature has placed it; and without it everything is only half performed. Therefore, for the same reason, persons of genius often manage so badly for their own welfare. As a leaden weight always brings a body back to the position which its centre of gravity thereby determined demands, so the true seriousness of the man always draws the strength and attention of the intellect back to that in which it lies; everything else the man does *without true seriousness*. Therefore only the exceedingly rare and abnormal men whose true seriousness does not lie in the personal and practical, but in the objective and theoretical, are in a position to apprehend what is essential in the things of the world, thus the highest truths, and reproduce them in any way. For such a seriousness of the individual, falling outside himself in the objective, is something foreign to the nature of man, something unnatural, or really supernatural: yet on account of this alone is the man *great;* and therefore what he achieves is then ascribed to a *genius* different from himself, which takes possession of him. To such a man his painting, poetry, or thinking is an *end;* to others it is a *means.* The latter thereby seek their own things, and, as a rule, they know how to further them, for they flatter their contemporaries, ready to serve their wants and humours; therefore for the most part they live in happy circumstances; the former often in very miserable circumstances. For he sacrifices his personal welfare to his *objective end;* he cannot indeed do otherwise, because his seriousness lies there. They act conversely; therefore they are *small,* but he is *great.* Accordingly his work is for all time, but the recognition of it generally only begins with posterity: they live and die with their time. In general he only is great who in his work, whether it is practical or theoretical, seeks *not his own concerns,* but pursues an *objective end* alone; he is so, however, even when in the practical sphere this end is a misunderstood one, and even if in consequence of this it should be a crime. *That he seeks not himself and his own concerns,* this makes him under all circumstances *great. Small,* on the other hand, is all action which is directed to personal ends; for whoever is thereby set in activity knows and finds himself only in his own transient and insignificant person. He who is great, again, finds himself in all, and therefore in the whole: he lives not, like others, only in the microcosm, but still more in the macrocosm. Hence the whole interests him, and he seeks to comprehend it in order to represent it, or to explain it, or to act practically upon it. For it is not strange to him; he feels that it concerns him. On account of this extension of his sphere he is called *great.* Therefore that lofty predicate belongs only to the true hero, in some sense, and to genius: it signifies that they, contrary to human nature, have not sought their own things, have not lived for themselves, but for all. As now clearly the great majority must *constantly* be small, and can *never* become great, the converse of this, that one should be great throughout, that is, constantly and every moment, is yet not possible—

"For man is made of common clay,
And custom is his nurse."

Every great man must often be only the individual, have only himself in view, and that means he must be small. Upon this depends the very true remark, that no man is a hero to his valet, and not upon the fact that the valet cannot appreciate the hero; which Goethe, in the "*Wahlverwandhschaften*" (vol. ii. chap. 5), serves up as an idea of Ottilie's.

Genius is its own reward: for the best that one is, one must necessarily be for oneself. "Whoever is born with a talent, to a talent, finds in this his fairest existence," says Goethe. When we look back at a great man of former times, we do not think, "How happy is he to be still admired by all of us!" but, "How happy must he have been in the immediate enjoyment of a mind at the surviving traces of which centuries revive themselves!" Not in the fame, but in that whereby it is attained, lies the value, and in the production of immortal children the pleasure. Therefore those who seek to show the vanity of posthumous fame from the fact that he who obtains it knows nothing of it, may be compared to the wiseacre who very learnedly tried to demonstrate to the man who cast envious glances at a heap of oyster-shells in his neighbour's yard the absolute uselessness of them.

According to the exposition of the nature of genius which has been given, it is so far contrary to nature, inasmuch as it consists in this, that the intellect, whose real destination is the service of the will, emancipates itself from this service in order to be active on its own account. Accordingly genius is an intellect which has become untrue to its destination. Upon this depend the *disadvantages* connected with it, for the consideration of which we shall now prepare the way by comparing genius with the less decided predominance of the intellect.

The intellect of the normal man, strictly bound to the service of the will, and therefore really only occupied with the apprehension of motives, may be regarded as a complex system of wires, by means of which each of these puppets is set in motion in the theatre of the world. From this arises the dry, grave seriousness of most people, which is only surpassed by that of the brutes, who never laugh. On the other hand, we might compare the genius, with his unfettered intellect, to a living man playing along with the large puppets of the famous puppet-show at Milan, who would be the only one among them who would understand everything, and would therefore gladly leave the stage for a while to enjoy the play from the boxes;—that is the reflectiveness of genius. But even the man of great understanding and reason, whom one might almost call wise, is very different from the genius, and in this way, that his intellect retains a *practical* tendency, is concerned with the choice of the best ends and means, therefore remains in the service of the will, and accordingly is occupied in a manner that is thoroughly in keeping with nature. The firm, practical seriousness of life which the Romans denoted *gravitas* presupposes that the intellect does not forsake the service of the will in order to wander away after that which does not concern the will; therefore it does not admit of that separation of the will and the intellect which is the condition of genius. The able, nay, eminent man, who is fitted for great achievements in the practical sphere, is so precisely because objects rouse his will in a lively manner, and spur him on to the ceaseless investigation of their relations and connections. Thus his intellect has grown up closely connected with his will. Before the man of genius, on the contrary, there floats in his objective comprehension the phenomenon of the world, as something foreign to him, an object of contemplation, which expels his will from consciousness. Round this point turns the distinction between the capacity for *deeds* and for *works*. The latter demand objectivity and depth of knowledge, which presupposes entire separation of the intellect from the will; the former, on the other hand, demands the application of knowledge, presence of mind, and decision, which required that the intellect should uninterruptedly attend to the service of the will. Where the bond between the intellect and the will is loosened, the intellect, turned away from its natural destination, will neglect the service of the will; it will, for example, even in the need of the moment, preserve its emancipation, and perhaps be unable to avoid taking in the picturesque impression of the surroundings, from which danger threatens the individual. The intellect of the reasonable and understanding man, on the other hand, is constantly at its post, is directed to the circumstances and their requirements. Such a man will therefore in all cases determine and carry out what is suitable to the case, and consequently will by no means fall into those eccentricities, personal slips, nay, follies, to which the genius is exposed, because his intellect does not remain exclusively the guide and guardian of his will, but sometimes more, sometimes less, is laid claim to by the purely objective. In the contrast of Tasso and Antonio, Goethe has illustrated the opposition, here explained in the abstract, in which these two entirely different kinds of capacity stand to each other. The kinship of genius and madness, so often observed, depends chiefly upon that separation of the intellect from the will which is essential to genius, but is yet contrary to nature. But this separation itself is by no means to be attributed to the fact that genius is accompanied by less intensity of will; for it is rather distinguished by a vehement and passionate character; but it is to be explained from this, that the practically excellent person, the man of deeds, has merely the whole, full measure of intellect required for an energetic will while most men lack even this; but genius consists in a completely abnormal, actual superfluity of intellect, such as is required for the service of no will. On this account the men of genuine works are a thousand times rarer than the men of deeds. It is just that abnormal superfluity of intellect by virtue of which it obtains the decided preponderance, sets itself free from the will, and now, forgetting its origin, is freely active from its own strength and elasticity; and from this the creations of genius proceed.

Now further, just this, that genius in working consists of the free intellect, *i.e.*, of the intellect emancipated from the service of the will, has as a consequence that its productions serve no useful ends. The work of genius is music, or philosophy, or paintings, or poetry; it is nothing to use. To be of no use belongs to the character of the works of genius; it is their patent of nobility. All other works of men are for the maintenance or easing of our existence; only those we are speaking of are not; they alone exist for their own sake, and are in this sense to be regarded as the flower or the net profit of existence. Therefore our heart swells at the enjoyment of them, for we rise out of the heavy earthly atmosphere of want. Analogous to this, we see the beautiful, even apart from these, rarely combined with the useful. Lofty and beautiful trees bear no fruit; the fruit-trees are small, ugly cripples. The full garden rose is not fruitful, but the small, wild, almost scentless roses are. The most beautiful buildings are not the useful ones; a temple is no dwelling-house. A man of high, rare mental endowments compelled to apply himself to a merely useful business, for which the most ordinary man would be fitted, is like a costly vase decorated with the most beautiful painting which is used as a kitchen pot; and to compare useful people with men of genius is like comparing building-stone with diamonds.

Thus the merely practical man uses his intellect for that for which nature destined it, the comprehension of the relations of things, partly to each other, partly to the will of the knowing individual. The genius, on the other hand, uses it, contrary to its destination, for the comprehension of the objective nature of things. His mind, therefore, belongs not to himself, but to the world, to the illumination of which, in some sense, it will contribute. From this must spring manifold *disadvantages* to the individual favoured with genius. For his intellect will in general show those faults which are rarely wanting in any tool which is used for that for which it has not been made. First of all, it will be, as it were, the servant of two masters, for on every opportunity it frees itself from the service to which it was destined in order to follow its own ends, whereby it often leaves the will very inopportunely in a fix, and thus the individual so gifted becomes more or less useless for life, nay, in his conduct sometimes reminds us of madness. Then, on account of its highly developed power of knowledge, it will see in things more the universal than the particular; while the service of the will principally requires the knowledge of the particular. But, again, when, as opportunity offers, that whole abnormally heightened power of knowledge directs itself with all its energy to the circumstances and miseries of the will, it will be apt to apprehend these too vividly, to behold all in too glaring colours, in too bright a light, and in a fearfully exaggerated form, whereby the individual falls into mere extremes. The following may serve to explain this more accurately. All great theoretical achievements, in whatever sphere they may be, are brought about in this way: Their author directs all the forces of his mind upon one point, in which he lets them unite and concentrate so strongly, firmly, and exclusively that now the whole of the rest of the world vanishes for him, and his object fills all reality. Now this great and powerful concentration which belongs to the privileges of genius sometimes appears for it also in the case of objects of the real world and the events of daily life, which then, brought under such a focus, are magnified to such a monstrous extent that they appear like the flea, which under the solar microscope assumes the stature of an elephant. Hence it arises that highly gifted individuals sometimes are thrown by trifles into violent emotions of the most various kinds, which are incomprehensible to others, who see them transported with grief, joy, care, fear, anger, &c., by things which leave the every-day man quite composed. Thus, then, the genius lacks *soberness*, which simply consists in this, that one sees in things nothing more than actually belongs to them, especially with reference to our possible ends; therefore no sober-minded man can be a genius. With the disadvantages which have been enumerated there is also associated hyper-sensibility, which an abnormally developed nervous and cerebral system brings with it, and indeed in union with the vehemence and passionateness of will which is certainly characteristic of genius, and which exhibits itself physically as energy of the pulsation of the heart. From all this very easily arises that extravagance of disposition, that vehemence of the emotions, that quick change of mood under prevailing melancholy, which Goethe has presented to us in Tasso. What reasonableness, quiet composure, finished surveyal, certainty and proportionateness of behaviour is shown by the well-endowed normal man in comparison with the now dreamy absentness, and now passionate excitement of the man of genius, whose inward pain is the mother's lap of immortal works! To all this must still be added that genius lives essentially alone. It is too rare to find its like with ease, and too different from the rest of men to be their companion. With them it is the will, with him it is knowledge, that predominates; therefore their pleasures are not his, and his are not theirs. They are merely moral beings, and have merely personal relations; he is at the same time a pure intellect, and as such belongs to the whole of humanity. The course of thought of the intellect which is detached from its mother soil, the will, and only returns to it periodically, will soon show itself entirely different from that of the normal intellect, still cleaving to its stem. For this reason, and also on account of the dissimilarity of the pace, the former is not adapted for thinking in common, *i.e.*, for conversation with the others: they will have as little pleasure in him and his oppressive superiority as he will in them. They will therefore feel more comfortable with their equals, and he will prefer the entertainment of his equals, although, as a rule, this is only possible through the works they have left behind them. Therefore Chamfort says very rightly: "*Il y a peu de vices qui empêchent un homme d'avoir beaucoup d'amis, autant que peuvent le faire de trop grandes qualités.*" The happiest lot that can fall to the genius is release from action, which is not his element, and leisure for production. From all this it results that although genius may highly bless him who is gifted with it, in the hours in which, abandoned to it, he revels unhindered in its delight, yet it is by no means fitted to procure for him a happy course of life; rather the contrary. This is also confirmed by the experience recorded in biographies. Besides this there is also an external incongruity, for the genius, in his efforts and achievements themselves, is for the most part in contradiction and conflict with his age. Mere men of talent come always at the right time; for as they are roused by the spirit of their age, and called forth by its needs, they are also capable only of satisfying these. They therefore go hand in hand with the advancing culture of their contemporaries or with the gradual progress of a special science: for this they reap reward and approval. But to the next generation their works are no longer enjoyable; they must be replaced by others, which again are not permanent. The genius, on the contrary, comes into his age like a comet into the paths of the planets, to whose well-regulated and comprehensible order its entirely eccentric course is foreign. Accordingly he cannot go hand in hand with the existing, regular progress of the culture of the age, but flings his works far out on to the way in front (as the dying emperor flung his spear among the enemy), upon which time has first to overtake them. His relation to the culminating men of talent of his time might be expressed in the words of the Evangelist: "*Ὁ καιρος ὁ εμος ουπω παρεστιν· ὁ δε καιρος ὁ ὑμετερος παντοτε εστιν ἑτοιμος*" (John vii. 6). The man of talent can achieve what is beyond the power of achievement of other men, but not what is beyond their power of apprehension: therefore he at once finds those who prize him. But the achievement of the man of genius, on the contrary, transcends not only the power of achievement, but also the power of apprehension of others; therefore they do not become directly conscious of him. The man of talent is like the marksman who hits a mark the others cannot hit; the man of genius is like the marksman who hits a mark they cannot even see to; therefore they only get news of him indirectly, and thus late; and even this they only accept upon trust and faith. Accordingly Goethe says in one of his letters, "Imitation is inborn in us; what to imitate is not easily recognised. Rarely is what is excellent found; still more rarely is it prized." And Chamfort says: "*Il en est de la valeur des hommes comme de celle des diamans, qui à une certaine mesure de grosseur, de pureté, de perfection, ont un prix fixe et marqué, mais qui, par-delà cette mesure, restent sans prix, et ne trouvent point d'acheteurs.*" And Bacon of Verulam has also expressed it: "*Infimarum virtutum, apud vulgus, laus est, mediarum admiratio, supremarum sensus nullus*" (*De augm. sc.*, L. vi. c. 3). Indeed, one might perhaps reply, *Apud vulgus!* But I must then come to his assistance with Machiavelli's assurance: "*Nel mondo non è se non volgo;*"[1] as also Thilo (*Ueber den Ruhm*) remarks, that to the vulgar herd there generally belongs one more than each of us believes. It is a consequence of this late recognition of the works of the man of genius that they are rarely enjoyed by their contemporaries, and accordingly in the freshness of colour which synchronism and presence imparts, but, like figs and dates, much more in a dry than in a fresh state.

[1] There is nothing else in the world but the vulgar.

If, finally, we consider genius from the somatic side, we find it conditioned by several anatomical and physiological qualities, which individually are seldom present in perfection, and still more seldom perfect together, but which are yet all indispensably required; so that this explains why genius only appears as a perfectly isolated and almost portentous exception. The fundamental condition is an abnormal predominance of sensibility over irritability and reproductive power; and what makes the matter more difficult, this must take place in a male body. (Women may have great talent, but no genius, for they always remain subjective.) Similarly the cerebral system must be perfectly separated from the ganglion system by complete isolation, so that it stands in complete opposition to the latter; and thus the brain pursues its parasitic life on the organism in a very decided, isolated, powerful, and independent manner. Certainly it will thereby very easily affect the rest of the organism injuriously, and through its heightened life and ceaseless activity wear it out prematurely, unless it is itself possessed of energetic vital force and a good constitution: thus the latter belong to the conditions of genius. Indeed even a good stomach is a condition on account of the special and close agreement of this part with the brain. But chiefly the brain must be of unusual development and magnitude, especially broad and high. On the other hand, its depth will be inferior, and the cerebrum will abnormally preponderate in proportion to the cerebellum. Without doubt much depends upon the configuration of the brain as a whole and in its parts; but our knowledge is not yet sufficient to determine this accurately, although we easily recognise the form of skull that indicates a noble and lofty intelligence. The texture of the mass of the brain must be of extreme fineness and perfection, and consist of the purest, most concentrated, tenderest, and most excitable nerve-substance; certainly the quantitative proportion of the white to the grey matter has a decided influence, which, however, we are also unable as yet to specify. However, the report of the *post-mortem* on the body of Byron[1] shows that in his case the white matter was in unusually large proportion to the grey, and also that his brain weighed six pounds. Cuvier's brain weighed five pounds; the normal weight is three pounds. In contrast to the superior size of the brain, the spinal cord and nerves must be unusually thin. A beautifully arched, high and broad skull of thin bone must protect the brain without in any way cramping it. This whole quality of the brain and nervous system is the inheritance from the mother, to which we shall return in the following book. But it is quite insufficient to produce the phenomenon of genius if the inheritance from the father is not added, a lively, passionate temperament, which exhibits itself somatically as unusual energy of the heart, and consequently of the circulation of the blood, especially towards the head. For, in the first place, that turgescence peculiar to the brain on account of which it presses against its walls is increased by this; therefore it forces itself out of any opening in these which has been occasioned by some injury; and secondly, from the requisite strength of the heart the brain receives that internal movement different from its constant rising and sinking at every breath, which consists in a shaking of its whole mass at every pulsation of the four cerebral arteries, and the energy of which must correspond to the here increased quantity of the brain, as this movement in general is an indispensable condition of its activity. To this, therefore, small stature and especially a short neck is favourable, because by the shorter path the blood reaches the brain with more energy; and on this account great minds have seldom large bodies. Yet that shortness of the distance is not indispensable; for example, Goethe was of more than middle height. If, however, the whole condition connected with the circulation of the blood, and therefore coming

[1] In Medwin's "Conversations of Lord Byron," p. 333.

from the father is wanting, the good quality of the brain coming from the mother, will at most produce a man of talent, a fine understanding, which the phlegmatic temperament thus introduced supports; but a phlegmatic genius is impossible. This condition coming from the father explains many faults of temperament described above. But, on the other hand, if this condition exists without the former, thus with an ordinarily or even badly constructed brain, it gives vivacity without mind, heat without light, hot-headed persons, men of unsupportable restlessness and petulance. That of two brothers only one has genius, and that one generally the elder, as, for example, in Kant's case, is primarily to be explained from the fact that the father was at the age of strength and passion only when he was begotten; although also the other condition originating with the mother may be spoiled by unfavourable circumstances.

I have further to add here a special remark on the *childlike* character of the genius, *i.e.*, on a certain resemblance which exists between genius and the age of childhood. In childhood, as in the case of genius, the cerebral and nervous system decidedly preponderates, for its development hurries far in advance of that of the rest of the organism; so that already at the seventh year the brain has attained its full extension and mass. Therefore, Bichat says: "*Dans l'enfance le système nerveux, comparé au musculaire, est proportionellement plus considérable que dans tous les âges suivans, tandis que par la suite, la plupart des autres systèmes prédominent sur celui-ci. On sait que, pour bien voir les nerfs, on choisit toujours les enfans*" (*De la vie et de la mort*, art. 8, § 6). On the other hand, the development of the genital system begins latest, and irritability, reproduction, and genital function are in full force only at the age of manhood, and then, as a rule, they predominate over the brain function. Hence it is explicable that children, in general, are so sensible, reasonable, desirous of information, and teachable, nay, on the whole, are more disposed and fitted for all theoretical occupation than grown-up people. They have, in consequence of that course of development, more intellect than will, *i.e.*, than inclinations, desire, and passion. For intellect and brain are one, and so also is the genital system one with the most vehement of all desires: therefore I have called the latter the focus of the will. Just because the fearful activity of this system still slumbers, while that of the brain has already full play, childhood is the time of innocence and happiness, the paradise of life, the lost Eden on which we look longingly back through the whole remaining course of our life. But the basis of that happiness is that in childhood our whole existence lies much more in knowing than in willing—a condition which is also supported from without by the novelty of all objects. Hence in the morning sunshine of life the world lies before us so fresh, so magically gleaming, so attractive. The small desires, the weak inclinations, and trifling cares of childhood are only a weak counterpoise to that predominance of intellectual activity. The innocent and clear glance of children, at which we revive ourselves, and which sometimes in particular cases reaches the sublime contemplative expression with which Raphael has glorified his cherubs, is to be explained from what has been said. Accordingly the mental powers develop much earlier than the needs they are destined to serve; and here, as everywhere, nature proceeds very designedly. For in this time of predominating intelligence the man collects a great store of knowledge for future wants which at the time are foreign to him. Therefore his intellect, now unceasingly active, eagerly apprehends all phenomena, broods over them and stores them up carefully for the coming time,—like the bees, who gather a great deal more honey than they can consume, in anticipation of future need. Certainly what a man acquires of insight and knowledge up to the age of puberty is, taken as a whole, more than all that he afterwards learns, however learned he may become; for it is the foundation of all human knowledge. Up till the same time plasticity predominates in the child's body, and later, by a metastasis, its forces throw themselves into the system of generation; and thus with puberty the sexual passion appears, and now, little by little, the will gains the upper hand. Then childhood, which is prevailingly theoretical and desirous of learning, is followed by the restless, now stormy, now melancholy, period of youth, which afterwards passes into the vigorous and earnest age of manhood. Just because that impulse pregnant with evil is wanting in the child is its volition so adapted and subordinated to knowledge, whence arises that character of innocence, intelligence, and reasonableness which is peculiar to the age of childhood. On what, then, the likeness between childhood and genius depends I scarcely need to express further: upon the surplus of the powers of knowledge over the needs of the will, and the predominance of the purely intellectual activity which springs from this. Really every child is to a certain extent a genius, and the genius is to a certain extent a child. The relationship of the two shows itself primarily in the naïveté and sublime simplicity which is characteristic of true genius; and besides this it appears in several traits, so that a certain childishness certainly belongs to the character of the genius. In Riemer's "*Mittheilungen über Goethe*" (vol. i. p. 184) it is related that Herder and others found fault with Goethe, saying he was always a big child. Certainly they were right in what they said, but they were not right in finding fault with it. It has also been said of Mozart that all his life he remained a child (Nissen's Biography of Mozart, p. 2 and 529). Schlichtegroll's "*Nekrology*" (for 1791, vol. ii. p. 109) says of him: "In his art he early became a man, but in all other relations he always remained a child." Every genius is even for this reason a big child; he looks out into the world as into something strange, a play, and therefore with purely objective interest. Accordingly he has just as little as the child that dull gravity of ordinary men, who, since they are capable only of subjective interests, always see in things mere motives for their action. Whoever does not to a certain extent remain all his life a big child, but becomes a grave, sober, thoroughly composed, and reasonable man, may be a very useful and capable citizen of this world; but never a genius. In fact, the genius is so because that predominance of the sensible system and of intellectual activity which is natural to childhood maintains itself in him in an abnormal manner through his whole life, thus here becomes perennial. A trace of this certainly shows itself in many ordinary men up to the period of their youth; therefore, for example, in many students a purely intellectual tendency and an eccentricity suggestive of genius is unmistakable. But nature returns to her track; they assume the chrysalis form and reappear at the age of manhood, as incarnate Philistines, at whom we are startled when we meet them again in later years. Upon all this that has been expounded here depends Goethe's beautiful remark: "Children do not perform what they promise; young people very seldom; and if they do keep their word, the world does not keep its word with them" (*Wahlverwandtschaften*, Pt. i. ch. 10)—the world which afterwards bestows the crowns which it holds aloft for merit on those who are the tools of its low aims or know how to deceive it. In accordance with what has been said, as there is a mere beauty of youth, which almost every one at some time possesses (*beauté du diable*), so there is a mere intellectuality of youth, a certain mental nature disposed and adapted for apprehending, understanding, and learning, which every one has in childhood, and some have still in youth, but which is afterwards lost, just like that beauty. Only in the case of a very few, the chosen, the one, like the other, lasts through the whole life; so that even in old age a trace of it still remains visible: these are the truly beautiful and the men of true genius.

The predominance of the cerebral nervous system and of intelligence in childhood, which is here under consideration, together with the decline of it in riper age, receives important illustration and confirmation from the fact that in the species of animals which stands nearest to man, the apes, the same relation is found in a striking degree. It has by degrees become certain that the highly intelligent orang-outang is a young pongo, which when it has grown up loses the remarkable human look of its countenance, and also its astonishing intelligence, because the lower and brutal part of its face increases in size, the forehead thereby recedes, large *cristæ*, muscular developments, give the skull a brutish form, the activity of the nervous system sinks, and in its place extraordinary muscular strength develops, which, as it is sufficient for its preservation, makes the great intelligence now superfluous. Especially important is what Fréd. Cuvier has said in this reference, and Flourens has illustrated in a review of the "*Histoire Naturelle*" of the former, which appeared in the September number of the "*Journal des Savans*" of 1839, and was also separately printed with some additions, under the title, "*Résumé analytique des observations de Fr. Cuvier sur l'instinct et l'intelligence des animaux*," *p. Flourens*, 1841. It is there said, p. 50: "*L'intelligence de l'orang-outang, cette intelligence si développée, et développée de si bonne heure, décroit avec l'âge. L'orang-outang, lorsqu'il est jeune, nous étonne par sa pénétration, par sa ruse, par son adresse ; l'orang-outang, devenu adulte, n'est plus qu'un animal grossier, brutal, intraitable. Et il en est de tous les singes comme de l'orang-outang. Dans tous, l'intelligence décroit à mesure que les forces s'accroissent. L'animal qui a le plus d'intelligence, n'a toute cette intelligence que dans le jeune âge.*" Further, p. 87: "*Les singes de tous les genres offrent ce rapport inverse de l'âge et de l'intelligence. Ainsi, par exemple, l'Entelle (espèce de guenon du sous-genre des Semno-pithèques et l'un des singes vénérés dans la religion des Brames) a, dans le jeune âge, le front large, le museau peu saillant, le crâne élevé, arrondi,"* etc. *Avec l'âge le front disparait, recule, le museau proémine; et le moral ne change pas moins que le physique: l'apathie, la violence, le besoin de solitude, remplacent la pénétration, la docilité, la confiance.* "*Ces différences sont si grandes,*" *dit Mr. Fréd. Cuvier,* "*que dans l'habitude où nous sommes de juger des actions des animaux par les nôtres, nous prendrions le jeune animal pour un individu de l'âge, où toutes les qualités morales de l'espèce sont acquises, et l'Entelle adulte pour un individu qui n'aurait encore que ses forces physiques. Mais la nature n'en agit pas ainsi avec ces animaux, qui ne doivent pas sortir de la sphère étroite, qui leur est fixée, et à qui il suffit en quelque sorte de pouvoir veiller à leur conservation. Pour cela l'intelligence était nécessaire, quand la force n'existait pas, et quand celle-ci est acquise, toute autre puissance perd de son utilité.*" And p. 118: "*La conservation des espèces ne repose pas moins sur les qualités intellectuelles des animaux, que sur leurs qualités organiques.*" This last confirms my principle that the intellect, like the claws and teeth, is nothing else than a weapon in the service of the will.

CHAPTER XXXII.[1]

ON MADNESS.

THE health of the mind properly consists in perfect recollection. Of course this is not to be understood as meaning that our memory preserves everything. For the past course of our life shrinks up in time, as the path of the wanderer looking back shrinks up in space: sometimes it is difficult for us to distinguish the particular years; the days have for the most part become unrecognisable. Really, however, only the exactly similar events, recurring an innumerable number of times, so that their images, as it were, conceal each other, ought so to run together in the memory that they are individually unrecognisable; on the other hand, every event in any way peculiar or significant we must be able to find again in memory, if the intellect is normal, vigorous, and quite healthy. In the text I have explained *madness* as the *broken thread* of this memory, which still runs on regularly, although in constantly decreasing fulness and distinctness. The following considerations may serve to confirm this.

The memory of a healthy man affords a certainty as to an event he has witnessed, which is regarded as just as firm and sure as his present apprehension of things; therefore, if sworn to by him, this event is thereby established in a court of law. On the other hand, the mere suspicion of madness will at once weaken the testimony

[1] This chapter is connected with the second half of § 36 of the first volume.

of a witness. Here, then, lies the criterion between the healthy mind and insanity. Whenever I doubt whether an event which I remember really took place, I throw upon myself the suspicion of madness: unless it is that I am uncertain whether it was not a mere dream. If another doubts the reality of an event, related by me as an eye-witness, without mistrusting my honesty, then he regards me as insane. Whoever comes at last, through constantly recounting an event which originally was fabricated by him, to believe in it himself is, in this one point, really insane. We may ascribe to an insane person flashes of wit, single clever thoughts, even correct judgments, but his testimony as to past events no man will consider valid. In the Lalita-vistara, well known to be the history of Buddha Sakya-Muni, it is related that at the moment of his birth all the sick became well, all the blind saw, all the deaf heard, and all mad people "recovered their memory." This last is mentioned in two passages.[1]

My own experience of many years has led me to the opinion that madness occurs proportionally most frequently among actors. But what a misuse they make of their memory! Daily they have to learn a new part or refresh an old one; but these parts are entirely without connection, nay, are in contradiction and contrast with each other, and every evening the actor strives to forget himself entirely and be some quite different person. This kind of thing paves the way for madness.

The exposition of the origin of madness given in the text will become more comprehensible if it is remembered how unwillingly we think of things which powerfully injure our interests, wound our pride, or interfere with our wishes; with what difficulty do we determine to lay such things before our own intellect for careful and serious investigation; how easily, on the other hand, we uncon-

[1] *Rgya Tcher Rol Pa, Hist. de Bouddha Chakya Mouni, trad. du Tibétain, p. Foucaux,* 1848, *p.* 91 *et* 99.

sciously break away or sneak off from them again; how, on the contrary, agreeable events come into our minds of their own accord, and, if driven away, constantly creep in again, so that we dwell on them for hours together. In that resistance of the will to allowing what is contrary to it to come under the examination of the intellect lies the place at which madness can break in upon the mind. Each new adverse event must be assimilated by the intellect, *i.e.*, it must receive a place in the system of the truths connected with our will and its interests, whatever it may have to displace that is more satisfactory. Whenever this has taken place, it already pains us much less; but this operation itself is often very painful, and also, in general, only takes place slowly and with resistance. However, the health of the mind can only continue so long as this is in each case properly carried out. If, on the contrary, in some particular case, the resistance and struggles of the will against the apprehension of some knowledge reaches such a degree that that operation is not performed in its integrity, then certain events or circumstances become for the intellect completely suppressed, because the will cannot endure the sight of them, and then, for the sake of the necessary connection, the gaps that thus arise are filled up at pleasure; thus madness appears. For the intellect has given up its nature to please the will: the man now imagines what does not exist. Yet the madness which has thus arisen is now the lethe of unendurable suffering; it was the last remedy of harassed nature, *i.e.*, of the will.

Let me mention here in passing a proof of my view which is worth noticing. Carlo Gozzi, in the "*Monstro turchino*," act i. scene 2, presents to us a person who has drunk a magic potion which produces forgetfulness, and this person appears exactly like a madman.

In accordance with the above exposition one may thus regard the origin of madness as a violent "casting out of the mind" of anything, which, however, is only possible by "taking into the head" something else. The converse process is more rare, that the "taking into the head" comes first, and the "casting out of the mind" second. It takes place, however, in those cases in which the occasion of insanity is kept constantly present to the mind and cannot be escaped from; thus, for example, in the case of many who have gone mad from love, erotomaniacs, where the occasion of their madness is constantly longed after; also in the case of madness which has resulted from the fright of some sudden horrible occurrence. Such patients cling, as it were, convulsively to the thought they have grasped, so that no other, or at least none opposed to it, can arise. In both processes, however, what is essential to madness remains the same, the impossibility of a uniformly connected recollection, such as is the basis of our healthy and rational reflection. Perhaps the contrast of the ways in which they arise, set forth here, might, if applied with judgment, afford a sharp and profound principle of division of delusions proper.

For the rest, I have only considered the physical origin of madness, thus what is introduced by external, objective occasions. More frequently, however, it depends upon purely physical causes, upon malformations or partial disorganisation of the brain or its membranes, also upon the influence which other parts affected with disease exercise upon the brain. Principally in the latter kind of madness false sense-perceptions, hallucinations, may arise. Yet the two causes of madness will generally partake of each other, particularly the psychical of the physical. It is the same as with suicide, which is rarely brought about by an external occasion alone, but a certain physical discomfort lies at its foundation; and according to the degree which this attains to a greater or less external occasion is required; only in the case of the very highest degree is no external occasion at all required. Therefore there is no misfortune so great that it would influence every one to suicide, and none so small that one like it has not already led to it. I have shown the psychical origin of madness as, at least according to all appearance, it is brought about in the healthy mind by a great misfortune. In the case of those who are already strongly disposed to madness physically a very small disappointment will be sufficient to induce it. For example, I remember a man in a madhouse who had been a soldier, and had gone out of his mind because his officer had addressed him as *Er*.[1] In the case of decided physical disposition no occasion at all is required when this has come to maturity. The madness which has sprung from purely psychical causes may, perhaps, by the violent perversion of the course of thought which has produced it, also introduce a kind of paralysis or other depravity of some part of the brain, which, if not soon done away with, becomes permanent. Therefore madness is only curable at first, and not after a longer time.

Pinel taught that there is a *mania sine delirio*, frenzy without insanity. This was controverted by Esquirol, and since then much has been said for and against it. The question can only be decided empirically. But if such a state really does occur, then it is to be explained from the fact that here the will periodically entirely withdraws itself from the government and guidance of the intellect, and consequently of motives, and thus it then appears as a blind, impetuous, destructive force of nature, and accordingly manifests itself as the desire to annihilate everything that comes in its way. The will thus let loose is like the stream which has broken through the dam, the horse that has thrown his rider, or a clock out of which the regulating screws have been taken. Yet only the reason, thus *reflective* knowledge, is included in that suspension, not *intuitive* knowledge also; otherwise the will would remain entirely without guidance, and consequently the man would be immovable. But, on the

[1] In German inferiors are sometimes addressed as *Er* instead of *Sie*. —*Trs.*

contrary, the man in a frenzy apprehends objects, for he breaks out upon them; thus he has also consciousness of his present action, and afterwards remembrance of it. But he is entirely without reflection, thus without any guidance of the reason, consequently quite incapable of any consideration or regard for the absent, the past, or the future. When the attack is over, and the reason has regained its command, its function is correct, because here its proper activity has not been perverted or destroyed, but only the will has found the means to withdraw itself from it entirely for a while.

CHAPTER XXXIII.[1]

ISOLATED REMARKS ON NATURAL BEAUTY.

WHAT contributes among other things to make the sight of a beautiful landscape so exceedingly delightful is the perfect *truth and consistency* of nature. Certainly nature does not follow here the guidance of logic in the connection of the grounds of knowledge, of antecedents and consequences, premisses and conclusions; but still it follows what is for it analogous to the law of causality in the visible connection of causes and effects. Every modification, even the slightest, which an object receives from its position, foreshortening, concealment, distance, lighting, linear and atmospheric perspective, &c., is, through its effect upon the eye, unerringly given and accurately taken account of: the Indian proverb, "Every corn of rice casts its shadow," finds here its confirmation. Therefore here everything shows itself so consistent, accurately regular, connected, and scrupulously right; here there are no evasions. If now we consider the sight of a beautiful view, merely as a brain-phenomenon, it is the only one among the complicated brain-phenomena which is always absolutely regular, blameless, and perfect; all the rest, especially our own mental operations, are, in form or material, affected more or less with defects or inaccuracies. From this excellence of the sight of beautiful nature, is the harmonious and thoroughly satisfying character of its impression to be explained, and also the favourable effect which

[1] This chapter is connected with § 38 of the first volume.

it has upon our whole thought, which in its formal part thereby becomes more correctly disposed, and to a certain extent purified, for that brain-phenomenon which alone is entirely faultless sets the brain in general in perfectly normal action; and now the thought seeks to follow that method of nature in the consistency, connectedness, regularity, and harmony of all its processes, after being brought by it into the right swing. A beautiful view is therefore a cathartic of the mind, as music, according to Aristotle, is of the feeling, and in its presence one will think most correctly.

That the sight of a mountain chain suddenly rising before us throws us so easily into a serious, and even sublime mood may partly depend upon the fact that the form of the mountains and the outline of the chain arising from it is the only constantly *permanent* line of the landscape, for the mountains alone defy the decay which soon sweeps away everything else, especially our own ephemeral person. Not that at the sight of the mountain chain all this appeared distinctly in our consciousness, but an obscure feeling of it is the fundamental note of our mood.

I would like to know why it is that while for the human form and countenance light from above is altogether the most advantageous, and light from below the most unfavourable, with regard to landscape nature exactly the converse holds good.

Yet how æsthetic is nature! Every spot that is entirely uncultivated and wild, *i.e.*, left free to itself, however small it may be, if only the hand of man remains absent, it decorates at once in the most tasteful manner, clothes it with plants, flowers, and shrubs, whose unforced nature, natural grace, and tasteful grouping bears witness that they have not grown up under the rod of correction of the great egoist, but that nature has here moved freely. Every neglected plant at once becomes beautiful. Upon this rests the principle of the English garden, which is as much as possible to conceal art, so that it may appear as if nature had here moved freely; for only then is it perfectly beautiful, *i.e.*, shows in the greatest distinctness the objectificaton of the still unconscious will to live, which here unfolds itself with the greatest naïveté, because the forms are not, as in the animal world, determined by external ends, but only immediately by the soil, climate, and a mysterious third influence on account of which so many plants which have originally sprung up in the same soil and climate yet show such different forms and characters.

The great difference between the English, or more correctly the Chinese, garden and the old French, which is now always becoming more rare, yet still exists in a few magnificent examples, ultimately rests upon the fact that the former is planned in an objective spirit, the latter in a subjective. In the former the will of nature, as it objectifies itself in tree and shrub, mountain and waterfall, is brought to the purest possible expression of these its Ideas, thus of its own inner being. In the French garden, on the other hand, only the will of the possessor of it is mirrored, which has subdued nature so that instead of its Ideas it bears as tokens of its slavery the forms which correspond to that will, and which are forcibly imposed upon it—clipped hedges, trees cut into all kinds of forms, straight alleys, arched avenues, &c.

CHAPTER XXXIV.[1]

ON THE INNER NATURE OF ART.

Not merely philosophy but also the fine arts work at bottom towards the solution of the problem of existence. For in every mind that once gives itself up to the purely objective contemplation of nature a desire has been excited, however concealed and unconscious it may be, to comprehend the true nature of things, of life and existence. For this alone has interest for the intellect as such, *i.e.*, for the pure subject of knowledge which has become free from the aims of the will; as for the subject which knows as a mere individual the aims of the will alone have interest. On this account the result of the purely objective apprehension of things is an expression more of the nature of life and existence, more an answer to the question, "What is life?" Every genuine and successful work of art answers this question in its own way with perfect correctness. But all the arts speak only the naive and childish language of perception, not the abstract and serious language of *reflection;* their answer is therefore a fleeting image: not permanent and general knowledge. Thus for *perception* every work of art answers that question, every painting, every statue, every poem, every scene upon the stage: music also answers it; and indeed more profoundly than all the rest, for in its language, which is understood with absolute directness, but which is yet untranslatable into that of the reason, the inner

[1] This chapter is connected with § 49 of the first volume.

nature of all life and existence expresses itself. Thus all the other arts hold up to the questioner a perceptible image, and say, "Look here, this is life." Their answer, however correct it may be, will yet always afford merely a temporary, not a complete and final, satisfaction. For they always give merely a fragment, an example instead of the rule, not the whole, which can only be given in the universality of the *conception*. For this, therefore, thus for reflection and in the abstract, to give an answer which just on that account shall be permanent and suffice for always, is the task of philosophy. However, we see here upon what the relationship of philosophy to the fine arts rests, and can conclude from that to what extent the capacity of both, although in its direction and in secondary matters very different, is yet in its root the same.

Every work of art accordingly really aims at showing us life and things as they are in truth, but cannot be directly discerned by every one through the mist of objective and subjective contingencies. Art takes away this mist.

The works of the poets, sculptors, and representative artists in general contain an unacknowledged treasure of profound wisdom; just because out of them the wisdom of the nature of things itself speaks, whose utterances they merely interpret by illustrations and purer repetitions. On this account, however, every one who reads the poem or looks at the picture must certainly contribute out of his own means to bring that wisdom to light; accordingly he comprehends only so much of it as his capacity and culture admit of; as in the deep sea each sailor only lets down the lead as far as the length of the line will allow. Before a picture, as before a prince, every one must stand, waiting to see whether and what it will speak to him; and, as in the case of a prince, so here he must not himself address it, for then he would only hear himself. It follows from all this that in the works of the representative arts all truth is certainly contained, yet only *virtualiter* or *implicite;* philosophy, on the other hand, endeavours to supply the same truth *actualiter* and *explicite*, and therefore, in this sense, is related to art as wine to grapes. What it promises to supply would be, as it were, an already realised and clear gain, a firm and abiding possession; while that which proceeds from the achievements and works of art is one which has constantly to be reproduced anew. Therefore, however, it makes demands, not only upon those who produce its works, but also upon those who are to enjoy them which are discouraging and hard to comply with. Therefore its public remains small, while that of art is large.

The co-operation of the beholder, which is referred to above, as demanded for the enjoyment of a work of art, depends partly upon the fact that every work of art can only produce its effect through the medium of the fancy; therefore it must excite this, and can never allow it to be left out of the play and remain inactive. This is a condition of the æsthetic effect, and therefore a fundamental law of all fine arts. But it follows from this that, through the work of art, everything must not be directly given to the senses, but rather only so much as is demanded to lead the fancy on to the right path; something, and indeed the ultimate thing, must always be left over for the fancy to do. Even the author must always leave something over for the reader to think; for Voltaire has very rightly said, "*Le secret d'être ennuyeux, c'est de tout dire.*" But besides this, in art the best of all is too spiritual to be given directly to the senses; it must be born in the imagination of the beholder, although begotten by the work of art. It depends upon this that the sketches of great masters often effect more than their finished pictures; although another advantage certainly contributes to this, namely, that they are completed offhand in the moment of conception; while the perfected painting is only produced through continued effort, by means of skilful deliberation and persistent intention, for the inspiration cannot last till it is completed. From the fundamental æsthetical law we are speaking of, it is further to be explained why wax figures never produce an æsthetic effect, and therefore are not properly works of fine art, although it is just in them that the imitation of nature is able to reach its highest grade. For they leave nothing for the imagination to do. Sculpture gives merely the form without the colour; painting gives the colour, but the mere appearance of the form; thus both appeal to the imagination of the beholder. The wax figure, on the other hand, gives all, form and colour at once; whence arises the appearance of reality, and the imagination is left out of account. Poetry, on the contrary, appeals indeed to the imagination alone, which it sets in action by means of mere words.

An arbitrary playing with the means of art without a proper knowledge of the end is, in every art, the fundamental characteristic of the dabbler. Such a man shows himself in the pillars that support nothing, aimless volutes, juttings and projections of bad architecture, in the meaningless runs and figures, together with the aimless noise of bad music, in the jingling of the rhymes of senseless poetry, &c.

It follows from the preceding chapter, and from my whole view of art, that its aim is the facilitating of the knowledge of the Ideas of the world (in the Platonic sense, the only one which I recognise for the word Idea). The Ideas, however, are essentially something perceptible, which, therefore, in its fuller determinations, is inexhaustible. The communication of such an Idea can therefore only take place on the path of perception, which is that of art. Whoever, therefore, is filled with the comprehension of an Idea is justified if he chooses art as the medium of its communication. The mere conception, on the other hand, is something completely determinable, therefore exhaustible, and distinctly thought, the whole content of which can be coldly and dryly expressed in words. Now to desire to communicate such a conception by means of a work of art is a very useless circumlocution, indeed belongs to that playing with the means of art without knowledge of its end which has just been condemned. Therefore a work of art which has proceeded from mere distinct conceptions is always ungenuine. If now, in considering a work of plastic art, or in reading a poem, or in hearing a piece of music (which aims at describing something definite), we see, through all the rich materials of art, the distinct, limited, cold, dry conception shine out, and at last come to the front, the conception which was the kernel of this work, the whole notion of which consequently consisted in the distinct thinking of it, and accordingly is absolutely exhausted by its communication, we feel disgusted and indignant, for we see ourselves deceived and cheated out of our interest and attention. We are only perfectly satisfied by the impression of a work of art when it leaves something which, with all our thinking about it, we cannot bring down to the distinctness of a conception. The mark of that hybrid origin from mere conceptions is that the author of a work of art could, before he set about it, give in distinct words what he intended to present; for then it would have been possible to attain his whole end through these words. Therefore it is an undertaking as unworthy as it is absurd if, as has often been tried at the present day, one seeks to reduce a poem of Shakspeare's or Goethe's to the abstract truth which it was its aim to communicate. Certainly the artist ought to think in the arranging of his work; but only that thought which was *perceived* before it was thought has afterwards, in its communication, the power of animating or rousing, and thereby becomes imperishable. We shall not refrain from observing here that certainly the work which is done at a stroke, like the sketches of painters already referred to, the work which is completed in the inspiration of its first conception, and as it were unconsciously dashed off, like the melody which comes entirely without reflection, and quite as if by inspiration, and finally, also the lyrical poem proper, the mere song, in which the deeply felt mood of the present, and the impression of the surroundings, as if involuntarily, pours itself forth in words, whose metre and rhyme come about of their own accord —that all these, I say, have the great advantage of being purely the work of the ecstasy of the moment, the inspiration, the free movement of genius, without any admixture of intention and reflection; hence they are through and through delightful and enjoyable, without shell and kernel, and their effect is much more inevitable than that of the greatest works of art, of slower and more deliberate execution. In all the latter, thus in great historical paintings, in long epic poems, great operas, &c., reflection, intention, and deliberate selection has had an important part; understanding, technical skill, and routine must here fill up the gaps which the conception and inspiration of genius has left, and must mix with these all kinds of necessary supplementary work as cement of the only really genuinely brilliant parts. This explains why all such works, only excepting the perfect masterpieces of the very greatest masters (as, for example, "Hamlet," "Faust," the opera of "Don Juan"), inevitably contain an admixture of something insipid and wearisome, which in some measure hinders the enjoyment of them. Proofs of this are the "Messiah," "*Gerusalemme liberata*," even "Paradise Lost" and the "Æneid;" and Horace already makes the bold remark, "*Quandoque dormitat bonus Homerus.*" But that this is the case is the consequence of the limitation of human powers in general.

The mother of the useful arts is necessity; that of the fine arts superfluity. As their father, the former have understanding; the latter genius, which is itself a kind of superfluity, that of the powers of knowledge beyond the measure which is required for the service of the will.

CHAPTER XXXV.[1]

ON THE ÆSTHETICS OF ARCHITECTURE.

In accordance with the deduction given in the text of the pure æsthetics of architecture from the lowest grades of the objectification of the will or of nature, the Ideas of which it seeks to bring to distinct perception, its one constant theme is *support and burden,* and its fundamental law is that no burden shall be without sufficient support, and no support without a suitable burden; consequently that the relation of these two shall be exactly the fitting one. The purest example of the carrying out of this theme is the column and entablature. Therefore the order or columnar arrangement has become, as it were, the thorough bass of the whole of architecture. In column and entablature the support and the burden are *completely separated;* whereby the reciprocal action of the two and their relation to each other becomes apparent. For certainly even every plain wall contains support and burden; but here the two are still fused together. All is here support and all is burden; hence there is no æsthetic effect. This first appears through the separation, and takes place in proportion to its degree. For between the row of columns and the plain wall there are many intermediate degrees. Even in the mere breaking up of the wall of a house by windows and doors one seeks at least to indicate that separation by flat projecting pilasters (*antæ*) with capitals, which are inserted under the mouldings, nay, in case of need, are represented by mere painting, in order to in-

[1] This chapter is connected with § 43 of the first volume.

dicate in some way the entablature and an order. Real pillars, and also consoles and supports of various kinds, realise more that pure separation of support and burden which is striven after throughout by architecture. In this respect, next to the column with the entablature, but as a special construction not imitating it, stands the vault with the pillar. The latter certainly is far from attaining to the æsthetic effect of the former, because here the support and the burden are not *purely separated*, but are fused, passing over into each other. In the vault itself every stone is at once burden and support, and even the pillars, especially in groined vaulting, are, at least apparently, held in position by the pressure of opposite arches; and also just on account of this lateral pressure not only vaults but even mere arches ought not to rest upon columns, but require the massive four-cornered pillars. In the row of columns alone is the separation complete, for here the entablature appears as pure burden, the column as pure support. Accordingly the relation of the colonnade to the plain wall may be compared to that which would exist between a scale ascending in regular intervals and a tone ascending little by little from the same depth to the same height without gradation, which would produce a mere howl. For in the one as in the other the material is the same, and the important difference proceeds entirely from the *pure separation.*

Moreover, the support is not adapted to the burden when it is only sufficient to bear it, but when it can do this so conveniently and amply that at the first glance we are quite at ease about it. Yet this superfluity of support must not exceed a certain degree; for otherwise we will perceive support without burden, which is opposed to the æsthetic end. As a rule for determining that degree the ancients devised the line of equilibrium, which is got by carrying out the diminution of the thickness of the column as it ascends till it runs out into an acute angle, whereby the column becomes a cone; now every cross section will leave the lower part so strong that it is sufficient to support the upper part cut off. Commonly, however, one builds with twentyfold strength, *i.e.*, one lays upon every support only $\frac{1}{20}$th of the maximum it could bear. A glaring example of burden without support is presented to the eye by the balconies at the corners of many houses built in the elegant style of the present day. We do not see what supports them; they seem to hang suspended, and disturb the mind.

That in Italy even the simplest and most unornamented buildings make an æsthetic impression, while in Germany this is not the case, depends principally upon the fact that in Italy the roofs are very flat. A high roof is neither support nor burden, for its two halves mutually support each other, but the whole has no weight corresponding to its extension. Therefore it presents to the eye an extended mass which is entirely foreign to the æsthetic end, serves merely a useful end, consequently disturbs the former, of which the theme is always only support and burden.

The form of the column has its sole ground in the fact that it affords the simplest and most suitable support. In the twisted column inappropriateness appears as if with intentional perversity, and therefore shamelessness: hence good taste condemns it at the first glance. The four-cornered pillar, since the diagonal exceeds the sides, has unequal dimensions of thickness which have no end as their motive, but are occasioned by the accident of greater feasibleness; and just on this account it pleases us so very much less than the column. Even the hexagonal or octagonal pillar is more pleasing, because it approaches more nearly to the round column; for the form of the latter alone is exclusively determined by the end. It is, however, also so determined in all its other proportions, primarily in the relation of its thickness to its height, within the limits permitted by the difference of the three columnar orders. Therefore its diminution from the first third of its height upwards, and also a slight increase of its thickness just at this place (*entasis vitr.*), depends upon the fact that the pressure of the burden is greatest there. It has hitherto been believed that this increase in thickness was peculiar to the Ionic and Corinthian columns alone, but recent measurements have shown it also in the Doric columns, even at Pæstum. Thus everything in the column, its thoroughly determined form, the proportion of its height to its thickness, of both to the intervals between the columns, and that of the whole series to the entablature and the burden resting upon it, is the exactly calculated result of the relation of the necessary support to the given burden. As the latter is uniformly distributed, so must also the support be; therefore groups of columns are tasteless. On the other hand, in the best Doric temples the corner column comes somewhat nearer to the next ones, because the meeting of the entablatures at the corner increases the burden; and in this the principle of architecture expresses itself distinctly, that the structural relations, *i.e.*, the relations between support and burden, are the essential ones, to which the relations of symmetry, as subordinate, must at once give way. According to the weight of the whole burden generally will the Doric or the two lighter orders of columns be chosen, for the first, not only by the greater thickness, but also by the closer position of the columns, which is essential to it, is calculated for heavier burdens, to which end also the almost crude simplicity of its capital is suited. The capitals in general serve the end of showing visibly that the columns bear the entablature, and are not stuck in like pins; at the same time they increase by means of their abacus the bearing surface. Since, then, all the laws of columnar arrangement, and consequently also the form and proportion of the column, in all its parts and dimensions down to the smallest details, follow from the thoroughly understood and consistently carried out conception of the amply adequate support of a given burden, thus so far are determined *a priori*, it comes out clearly how perverse is the thought, so often repeated, that the stems of trees, or even (which unfortunately even "Vitruvius," iv. 1, expresses) the human form has been the prototype of the column. For if the form of the column were for architecture a purely accidental one, taken from without, it could never appeal to us so harmoniously and satisfactorily whenever we behold it in its proper symmetry; nor, on the other hand, could every even slight disproportion of it be felt at once by the fine and cultivated sense as disagreeable and disturbing, like a false note in music. This is rather only possible because, according to the given end and means, all the rest is essentially determined *a priori*, as in music, according to the given melody and key, the whole harmony is essentially so determined. And, like music, architecture in general is also not an imitative art, although both are often falsely taken to be so.

Æsthetic satisfaction, as was fully explained in the text, always depends upon the apprehension of a (Platonic) Idea. For architecture, considered merely as a fine art, the Ideas of the lowest grades of nature, such as gravity, rigidity, and cohesion, are the peculiar theme; but not, as has hitherto been assumed, merely regular form, proportion, and symmetry, which, as something purely geometrical, properties of space, are not Ideas, and therefore cannot be the theme of a fine art. Thus in architecture also they are of secondary origin, and have a subordinate significance, which I shall bring out immediately. If it were the task of architecture as a fine art simply to exhibit these, then the model would have the same effect as the finished work. But this is distinctly not the case; on the contrary, the works of architecture, in order to act æsthetically, absolutely must have a considerable size; nay, they can never be too large, but may easily be too small. Indeed *ceteris paribus* the æsthetic effect is in exact proportion to the size of the building, because only great masses make the action of gravitation apparent and impressive in a high degree. But this confirms my view that the tendency and antagonism of those fundamental forces of nature constitute the special æsthetical material of architecture, which, according to its nature, requires large masses in order to become visible, and indeed capable of being felt. The forms in architecture, as was shown above in the case of the column, are primarily determined by the immediate structural end of each part. But so far as this leaves anything undetermined, the law of the most perfect clearness to perception, thus also of the easiest comprehensibility, comes in; for architecture has its existence primarily in our spatial perception, and accordingly appeals to our *a priori* faculty for this. But these qualities always result from the greatest regularity of the forms and rationality of their relations. Therefore beautiful architecture selects only regular figures composed of straight lines or regular curves, and also the bodies which result from these, such as cubes, parallelopipeda, cylinders, spheres, pyramids, and cones; but as openings sometimes circles or ellipses, yet, as a rule, quadrates, and still oftener rectangles, the latter of thoroughly rational and very easily comprehended relation of their sides (not, for instance, as 6 : 7, but as 1 : 2, 2 : 3), finally also blind windows or niches of regular and comprehensible proportions. For the same reason it will readily give to the buildings themselves and their large parts a rational and easily comprehended relation of height and breadth; for example, it will let the height of a façade be half the breadth, and place the pillars so that every three or four of them, with the intervals between them, will measure a line which is equal to the height, thus will form a quadrate. The same principle of perceptibility and easy comprehension demands also that a building should be easily surveyed. This introduces symmetry, which is further necessary to mark out the work as a whole, and to distinguish its essential from its accidental limitation; for sometimes, for example, it is only under the guidance of symmetry that one knows whether one has before one three buildings standing beside each other or only one. Thus only by means of symmetry does a work of architecture at once announce itself as individual unity, and as the development of a central thought.

Now although, as was cursorily shown above, architecture has by no means to imitate the forms of nature, such as the stems of trees or even the human figure, yet it ought to work in the spirit of nature, for it makes the law its own, *natura nihil agit frustra, nihilque supervacaneum, et quod commodissimum in omnibus suis operationibus sequitur*, and accordingly avoids everything which is even only apparently aimless, and always attains the end in view in each case, whether this is purely architectonic, *i.e.*, structural, or an end connected with usefulness, by the shortest and most natural path, and thus openly exhibits the end through the work itself. Thus it attains a certain grace, analogous to that which in living creatures consists in the ease and suitableness of every movement and position to its end. Accordingly we see in the good antique style of architecture every part, whether pillar, column, arch, entablature, or door, window, stair, or balcony, attain its end in the directest and simplest manner, at the same time displaying it openly and naively; just as organised nature also does in its works. The tasteless style of architecture, on the contrary, seeks in everything useless roundabout ways, and delights in caprices, thereby hits upon aimlessly broken and irregular entablatures, grouped columns, fragmentary cornices on door arches and gables, meaningless volutes, scrolls, and such like. It plays with the means of the art without understanding its aims, as children play with the tools of grown-up people. This was given above as the character of the bungler. Of this kind is every interruption of a straight line, every alteration in the sweep of a curve, without apparent end. On the other hand, it is also just that naive simplicity in the disclosure and attainment of the end, corresponding to the spirit in which nature works and fashions, that imparts such beauty and grace of form to antique pottery that it ever anew excites our wonder, because it contrasts so advantageously in original taste with our modern pottery, which bears the stamp of vulgarity, whether it is made of porcelain or common potter's clay. At the sight of the pottery and implements of the ancients we feel that if nature had wished to produce such things it would have done so in these forms. Since, then, we see that the beauty of architecture arises from the unconcealed exhibition of the ends, and the attainment of them by the shortest and most natural path, my theory here appears in direct contradiction with that of Kant, which places the nature of all beauty in an apparent design without an end.

The sole theme of architecture here set forth—support and burden—is so very simple, that just on this account this art, so far as it is a fine art (but not so far as it serves useful ends), is perfect and complete in essential matters, since the best Greek period, at least, is not susceptible of any important enrichment. On the other hand, the modern architect cannot noticeably depart from the rules and patterns of the ancients without already being on the path of deterioration. Therefore there remains nothing for him to do but to apply the art transmitted to him by the ancients, and carry out the rules so far as is possible under the limitations which are inevitably laid down for him by wants, climate, age, and country. For in this art, as in sculpture, the effort after the ideal unites with the imitation of the ancients.

I scarcely need to remind the reader that in all these considerations I have had in view antique architecture alone, and not the so-called Gothic style, which is of Saracen origin, and was introduced by the Goths in Spain to the rest of Europe. Perhaps a certain beauty of its own kind is not altogether to be denied to this style, but yet if it attempts to oppose itself to the former as its equal, then this is a barbarous presumption which must not be allowed for a moment. How beneficently, after contemplating such Gothic magnificence, does the sight of a building correctly carried out in the antique style act upon our mind! We feel at once that this alone is right and true. If one could bring an ancient Greek before our most celebrated Gothic cathedrals, what would he say to them?—*Βαρβαροι*! Our pleasure in Gothic works certainly depends for the most part upon the association of ideas and historical reminiscences, thus upon a feeling which is foreign to art. All that I have said of the true æsthetic end, of the spirit and the theme of architecture, loses in the case of these works its validity. For the freely lying entablature has vanished, and with it the columns: support and burden, arranged and distributed in order to give visible form to the conflict between rigidity and gravity, are here no longer the theme. Moreover, that thorough, pure rationality by virtue of which everything admits of strict account, nay, already presents it of its own accord to the thoughtful beholder, and which belongs to the character of antique architecture, can here no longer be found; we soon become conscious that here, instead of it, a will guided by other conceptions has moved; therefore much remains unexplained to us. For only the antique style of architecture is conceived in a purely *objective* spirit; the Gothic style is more in the subjective spirit. Yet as we have recognised the peculiar æsthetic fundamental thought of antique architecture in the unfolding of the conflict between rigidity and gravity, if we wish to discover in Gothic architecture also an analogous fundamental thought, it will be this, that here the entire overcoming and conquest of gravity by rigidity is supposed to be exhibited. For in accordance with this the horizontal line which is that of burden has entirely vanished, and the action of gravity only appears indirectly, disguised in arches and vaults, while the vertical line which is that of support, alone prevails, and makes palpable to the senses the victorious action of rigidity, in excessively high buttresses, towers, turrets, and pinnacles without number which rise unencumbered on high. While in antique architecture the tendency and pressure from above downwards is just as well represented and exhibited as that from below upwards, here the latter decidedly predominates; whence that analogy often observed with the crystal, whose crystallisation also takes place with the overcoming of gravity. If now we attribute this spirit and fundamental thought to Gothic architecture, and would like thereby to set it up as the equally justified antithesis of antique architecture, we must remember that the conflict between rigidity and gravity, which the antique architecture so openly and naïvely expresses, is an actual and true conflict founded in nature; the entire overcoming of gravity by rigidity, on the contrary, remains a mere appearance, a fiction accredited by illusion. Every one will easily be able to see clearly how from the fundamental thought given here, and the peculiarities of Gothic architecture noticed above, there arises that mysterious and hyperphysical character which is attributed to it. It principally arises, as was already mentioned, from the fact that here the abitrary has taken the place of the purely rational, which makes itself known as the thorough adaptation of the means to the end. The many things that are really aimless, but yet are so carefully perfected, raise the assumption of unknown, unfathomed, and secret ends, *i.e.*, give the appearance of mystery. On the other hand, the brilliant side of Gothic churches is the interior; because here the effect of the groined vaulting borne by slender, crystalline, aspiring pillars, raised high aloft, and, all burden having disappeared, promising eternal security, impresses the mind; while most of the faults which have been mentioned lie upon the outside. In antique buildings the external side is the most advantageous, because there we see better the support and the burden; in the interior, on the other hand, the flat roof always retains something depressing and prosaic. For the most part, also, in the temples of the ancients, while the outworks were many and great, the interior proper was small. An appearance of sublimity is gained from the hemispherical vault of a cupola, as in the Pantheon, of which, therefore, the Italians also, building in this style, have made a most extensive use. What determines this is, that the ancients, as southern peoples, lived more in the open air than the northern nations who have produced the Gothic style of architecture. Whoever, then, absolutely insists upon Gothic architecture being accepted as an essential and authorised style may, if he is also fond of analogies, regard it as the negative pole of architecture, or, again, as its minor key. In the interest of good taste I must wish that great wealth will be devoted to that which is objectively, *i.e.*, actually, good and right, to what in itself is beautiful, but not to that whose value depends merely upon the association of ideas. Now when I see how this unbelieving age so diligently finishes the Gothic churches left incomplete by the believing Middle Ages, it looks to me as if it were desired to embalm a dead Christianity.

CHAPTER XXXVI.[1]

ISOLATED REMARKS ON THE ÆSTHETICS OF THE PLASTIC AND PICTORIAL ARTS.

In sculpture beauty and grace are the principal things; but in painting expression, passion, and character predominate; therefore just so much of the claims of beauty must be neglected. For a perfect beauty of all forms, such as sculpture demands, would detract from the characteristic and weary by monotony. Accordingly painting may also present ugly faces and emaciated figures; sculpture, on the other hand, demands beauty, although not always perfect, but, throughout, strength and fulness of the figures. Consequently a thin Christ upon the Cross, a dying St. Jerome, wasted by age and disease, like the masterpiece of Domenichino, is a proper subject for painting; while, on the contrary, the marble figure by Donatello, in the gallery at Florence, of John the Baptist, reduced to skin and bone by fasting, has, in spite of the masterly execution, a repulsive effect. From this point of view sculpture seems suitable for the affirmation, painting for the negation, of the will to live, and from this it may be explained why sculpture was the art of the ancients, while painting has been the art of the Christian era.

In connection with the exposition given in § 45 of the first volume, that the discovery, recognition, and retention of the type of human beauty depends to a certain extent upon an anticipation of it, and therefore in

[1] This chapter is connected with §§ 44–50 of the first volume.

part has an *a priori* foundation, I find that I have yet to bring out clearly the fact that this anticipation nevertheless requires experience, by which it may be stirred up; analogous to the instinct of the brutes, which, although guiding the action *a priori*, yet requires determination by motives in the details of it. Experience and reality present to the intellect of the artist human forms, which, in one part or another, are more or less true to nature, as it were asking for his judgment concerning them, and thus, after the Socratic method, call forth from that obscure anticipation the distinct and definite knowledge of the ideal. Therefore it assisted the Greek sculptors very much that the climate and customs of their country gave them opportunity the whole day of seeing half-naked forms, and in the gymnasium entirely naked forms. In this way every limb presented its plastic significance to criticism, and to comparison with the ideal which lay undeveloped in their consciousness. Thus they constantly exercised their judgment with regard to all forms and limbs, down to their finest shades of difference; and thus, little by little, their originally dull anticipation of the ideal of human beauty was raised to such distinct consciousness that they became capable cf objectifying it in works of art. In an entirely analogous manner some experience is useful and necessary to the poet for the representation of characters. For although he does not work according to experience and empirical data, but in accordance with the clear consciousness of the nature of humanity, as he finds it within himself, yet experience serves this consciousness as a pattern, incites it and gives it practice. Accordingly his knowledge of human nature and its varieties, although in the main it proceeds *a priori* and by anticipation, yet first receives life, definiteness, and compass through experience. But, supporting ourselves upon the preceding book and chapter 44 in the following book, we can go still deeper into the ground of that marvellous sense of beauty of the Greeks which made them alone of all nations upon earth capable of discovering the true normal type of the human form, and accordingly of setting up the pattern of beauty and grace for the imitation of all ages, and we can say: The same thing which, if it remains unseparated from the *will*, gives sexual instinct with its discriminating selection, *i.e.*, *sexual love* (which it is well known was subject among the Greeks to great aberrations), becomes, if, by the presence of an abnormally preponderating intellect, it separates itself from the will and yet remains active, *the objective sense of beauty* of the human form, which now shows itself primarily as a critical artistic sense, but can rise to the discovery and representation of the norm of all parts and proportions; as was the case in Phidias, Praxiteles, Scopas, &c. Then is fulfilled what Goethe makes the artist say—

> "That I with mind divine
> And human hand
> May be able to form
> What with my wife,
> As animal, I can and must."

And again, analogous to this, that which in the poet, if it remained unseparated from the will, would give only worldly prudence, becomes, if it frees itself from the will by abnormal preponderance of the intellect, the capacity for objective, dramatic representation.

Modern sculpture, whatever it may achieve, is still analogous to modern Latin poetry, and, like this, is a child of imitation, sprung from reminiscences. If it presumes to try to be original, it at once goes astray, especially upon the bad path of forming according to nature as it lies before it, instead of according to the proportions of the ancients. Canova, Thorwaldsen, and many others may be compared to Johannes Secundus and Owenus. It is the same with architecture, only there it is founded in the art itself, the purely æsthetic part of which is of small compass, and was already exhausted by the ancients; therefore the modern architect can only distinguish himself in the wise application of it; and he ought to know that he removes himself from good taste just so far as he departs from the style and pattern of the Greeks.

The art of the painter, considered only so far as it aims at producing the appearance of reality, may ultimately be referred to the fact that he understands how to separate purely what in seeing is the mere sensation, thus the affection of the retina, *i.e.*, the only directly given *effect*, from its *cause*, *i.e.*, the objective external world, the perception of which first rises in the understanding from this effect; whereby, if he has technical skill, he is in a position to produce the same effect in the eye through an entirely different cause, the patches of applied colour, from which then in the understanding of the beholder the same perception again arises through the unavoidable reference of the effect to the ordinary cause.

If we consider how there lies something so entirely idiosyncratic, so thoroughly original, in every human countenance, and that it presents a whole which can only belong to a unity consisting entirely of necessary parts, by virtue of which we recognise a known individual out of so many thousands, even after long years, although the possible variations of human features, especially of one race, lie within very narrow limits, we must doubt whether anything of such essential unity and such great originality could ever proceed from any other source than from the mysterious depths of the inner being of nature; but from this it would follow that no artist could be capable of really reproducing the original peculiarity of a human countenance, or even of composing it according to nature from recollection. Accordingly what he produced of this kind would always be only a half true, nay, perhaps an impossible composition; for how should he compose an actual physiognomical unity when the principle of this unity is really unknown to him? Therefore, in the case of every face which has merely been imagined by an artist, we must doubt whether it is in fact a possible face, and whether nature, as the master of all masters, would not show it to be a bungled production by pointing out complete contradictions in it. This would, of course, lead to the principle that in historical paintings only portraits ought to figure, which certainly would then have to be selected with the greatest care and in some degree idealised. It is well known that great artists have always gladly painted from living models and introduced many portraits.

Although, as is explained in the text, the real end of painting, as of art in general, is to make the comprehension of the (Platonic) Ideas of the nature of the world easier for us, whereby we are at once thrown into the state of pure, *i.e.*, will-less, knowing, there yet belongs to it besides this an independent beauty of its own, which is produced by the mere harmony of the colours, the pleasingness of the grouping, the happy distribution of light and shade, and the tone of the whole picture. This accompanying subordinate kind of beauty furthers the condition of pure knowing, and is in painting what the diction, the metre, and rhyme are in poetry; both are not what is essential, but what acts first and immediately.

I have some further evidence to give in support of my judgment given in the first volume, § 50, on the inadmissibleness of allegory in painting. In the Borghese palace at Rome there is the following picture by Michael Angelo Caravaggio: Jesus, as a child of about ten years old, treads upon the head of a serpent, but entirely without fear and with great calmness; and His mother, who accompanies Him, remains quite as indifferent. Close by stands St. Elizabeth, looking solemnly and tragically up to heaven. Now what could be thought of this kyriological hieroglyphic by a man who had never heard anything about the seed of the woman that should bruise the head of the serpent? At Florence, in the library of the palace Riccardi, we find the following allegory upon the ceiling, painted by Luca Giordano, which is meant to signify that science frees the understanding from the bonds of ignorance: the understanding is a strong man bound with cords, which are just falling off; a nymph holds a mirror in front of him, another hands him a large detached wing; above sits science on a globe, and beside her, with a globe in her hand, the naked truth. At Ludwigsburg, near Stuttgart, there is a picture which shows us time, as Saturn, cutting off with a pair of shears the wings of Cupid. If this is meant to signify that when we grow old love proves unstable, this no doubt has its truth.

The following may serve to strengthen my solution of the problem as to why Laocoon does not cry out. One may practically convince oneself of the faulty effect of the representation of shrieking by the works of the plastic and pictorial arts, which are essentially dumb, by a picture of the slaughter of the innocents, by Guido Reni, which is to be found in the Academy of Arts at Bologna, and in which this great artist has committed the mistake of painting six shrieking wide-open mouths. Let any one who wants to have this more distinct think of a pantomimic representation on the stage, and in one of the scenes an urgent occasion for one of the players to shriek; if now the dancer who is representing this part should express the shriek by standing for a while with his mouth wide open, the loud laughter of the whole house would bear witness to the absurdity of the thing. Accordingly, since the shrieking of Laocoon had to be avoided for reasons which did not lie in the objects to be represented, but in the nature of the representing art, the task thus arose for the artist so to present this not-shrieking as to make it plausible to us that a man in such a position should not shriek. He solves this problem by representing the bite of the snake, not as having already taken place, nor yet as still threatening, but as just happening now in the side; for thereby the lower part of the body is contracted, and shrieking made impossible. This immediate but only subordinate reason was correctly discovered by Goethe, and is expounded at the end of the eleventh book of his autobiography, and also in the paper on Laocoon in the first part of the Propylæa; but the ultimate, primary reason, which conditions this one, is that which I have set forth. I cannot refrain from remarking that I here stand in the same relation to Goethe as with reference to the theory of colours. In the collection of the Duke of Aremberg at Brussels there is an antique head of Laocoon which was found later. However, the head in the world-renowned group is not a restored one which follows from Goethe's special table of all the restorations of this group, which is given at the end of the first volume of the Propylæa, and is also confirmed by the fact that the head which was found later resembles that of the group very much. Thus we must assume that another antique repetition of the group has existed to which the Aremberg head belonged. In my opinion the latter excels both in beauty and expression that of the group. It has the mouth decidedly wider open than in the group, yet not really to the extent of shrieking.

CHAPTER XXXVII.[1]

ON THE ÆSTHETICS OF POETRY.

I MIGHT give it as the simplest and most correct definition of poetry, that it is the art of bringing the imagination into play by means of words. How it brings this to pass I have shown in the first volume, § 51. A special confirmation of what is said there is afforded by the following passage in a letter of Wieland's to Merck, which has since then been published: "I have spent two days and a half upon a single stanza, in which the whole thing ultimately depended upon a single word which I wanted and could not find. I revolved and turned about the thing and my brain in all directions, because naturally, where a picture was in question, I desired to bring the same definite vision, which floated before my own mind into the mind of my reader also, and for this all often depends, *ut nosti*, upon a single touch or suggestion or reflex" (*Briefe an Merck*, edited by Wagner, 1835, p. 193). From the fact that the imagination of the reader is the material in which poetry exhibits its pictures, it has the advantage that the fuller development of these pictures and their finer touches, take place in the imagination of every one just as is most suitable to his individuality, his sphere of knowledge, and his humour, and therefore move him in the most lively manner; instead of which plastic and pictorial art cannot so adapt itself, but here *one* picture, *one* form, must satisfy all. And yet this will always bear in some respect the stamp of the individuality of the artist or of his model, as a subjective

[1] This chapter is connected with § 51 of the first volume.

or accidental and inefficient addition; although always less so the more objective, *i.e.*, the more of a genius, the artist is. This, to some extent, explains why works of poetry exercise a much stronger, deeper, and more universal effect than pictures and statues; the latter, for the most part, leave the common people quite cold; and, in general, the plastic arts are those which have the weakest effect. A remarkable proof of this is afforded by the frequent discovery and disclosure of pictures by great masters in private houses and all kinds of localities, where they have been hanging for many generations, not buried and concealed, but merely unheeded, thus without any effect. In my time (1823) there was even discovered in Florence a Madonna of Raphael's, which had hung for a long series of years on the wall of the servants' hall of a palace (in the *Quartiere di S. Spirito*); and this happens among Italians, the nation which is gifted beyond all others with the sense of the beautiful. It shows how little direct and immediate effect the works of plastic and pictorial art have, and that it requires more culture and knowledge to prize them than the works of all other arts. How unfailingly, on the contrary, a beautiful melody that touches the heart makes its journey round the world, and an excellent poem wanders from people to people. That the great and rich devote their powerful support just to the plastic and pictorial arts, and expend considerable sums upon *their* works only; nay, at the present day, an idolatry, in the proper sense of the term, gives the value of a large estate for a picture of a celebrated old master—this depends principally upon the rarity of the masterpieces, the possession of which therefore gratifies pride; and then also upon the fact that the enjoyment of them demands very little time and effort, and is ready at any moment, for a moment; while poetry and even music make incomparably harder conditions. Corresponding to this, the plastic and pictorial arts may be dispensed with; whole nations—for example, the Mohammedan peoples—

are without them, but no people is without music and poetry.

But the intention with which the poet sets our imagination in motion is to reveal to us the Ideas, *i.e.*, to show us by an example what life and what the world is. The first condition of this is that he himself has known it; according as his knowledge has been profound or superficial so will his poem be. Therefore, as there are innumerable degrees of profoundness and clearness in the comprehension of the nature of things, so are there of poets. Each of these, however, must regard himself as excellent so far as he has correctly represented what he knew, and his picture answers to *his* original: he must make himself equal with the best, for even in the best picture he does not recognise more than in his own, that is, as much as he sees in nature itself; for his glance cannot now penetrate deeper. But the best himself recognises himself as such in the fact that he sees how superficial was the view of the others, how much lay beyond it which they were not able to repeat, because they did not see it, and how much further his own glance and picture reaches. If he understood the superficial poets as little as they do him, then he would necessarily despair; for just because it requires an extraordinary man to do him justice, but the inferior poets can just as little esteem him as he can them, he also has long to live upon his own approval before that of the world follows it. Meanwhile he is deprived even of his own approval, for he is expected to be very modest. It is, however, as impossible that he who has merit, and knows what it costs, should himself be blind to it, as that a man who is six feet high should not observe that he rises above others. If from the base of the tower to the summit is 300 feet, then certainly it is just as much from the summit to the base. Horace, Lucretius, Ovid, and almost all the ancients have spoken proudly of themselves, and also Dante, Shakspeare, Bacon of Verulam, and many more. That one can be a great man without observing anything of it is an absurdity of which only hopeless incapacity can persuade itself, in order that it may regard the feeling of its own insignificance as modesty. An Englishman has wittily and correctly observed that merit and modesty have nothing in common except the initial letter.[1] I have always a suspicion about modest celebrities that they may very well be right; and Corneille says directly—

> "La fausse humilité ne met plus en crédit :
> Je sçais ce que je vaux, et crois ce qu'on m'en dit."

Finally, Goethe has frankly said, "Only good-for-nothings are modest." But the assertion would be still more certain that those who so eagerly demand modesty from others, urge modesty, unceasingly cry, "Only be modest, for God's sake, only be modest!" are positively good-for-nothings, *i.e.*, persons entirely without merit, manufactures of nature, ordinary members of the great mass of humanity. For he who himself has merit also concedes merit—understands himself truly and really. But he who himself lacks all excellence and merit wishes there was no such thing: the sight of it in others stretches him upon the rack; pale, green, and yellow envy consumes his heart: he would like to annihilate and destroy all those who are personally favoured; but if unfortunately he must let them live, it must only be under the condition that they conceal, entirely deny, nay, abjure their advantages. This, then, is the root of the frequent eulogising of modesty. And if the deliverers of these eulogies have the opportunity of suppressing merit as it arises, or at least of hindering it from showing itself or being known, who can doubt that they will do it? For this is the practice of their theory.

Now, although the poet, like every artist, always brings before us only the particular, the individual, what he has

[1] Lichtenberg ("*Vermischte Schriften*," new edition, Göttingen, 1884, vol. iii. p. 19) quotes Stanislaus Leszczynski as having said, "*La modestie devroit être la vertu de ceux, a qui les autres manquent.*"

known, and wishes by his work to make us know, is the (Platonic) Idea, the whole species; therefore in his images, as it were, the type of human characters and situations will be impressed. The narrative and also the dramatic poet takes the whole particular from life, and describes it accurately in its individuality, but yet reveals in this way the whole of human existence; for although he seems to have to do with the particular, in truth he is concerned with that which is everywhere and at all times. Hence it arises that sentences, especially of the dramatic poets, even without being general apophthegms, find frequent application in actual life. Poetry is related to philosophy as experience is related to empirical science. Experience makes us acquainted with the phenomenon in the particular and by means of examples, science embraces the whole of phenomena by means of general conceptions. So poetry seeks to make us acquainted with the (Platonic) Ideas through the particular and by means of examples. Philosophy aims at teaching, as a whole and in general, the inner nature of things which expresses itself in these. One sees even here that poetry bears more the character of youth, philosophy that of old age. In fact, the gift of poetry really only flourishes in youth; and also the susceptibility for poetry is often passionate in youth: the youth delights in verses as such, and is often contented with small ware. This inclination gradually diminishes with years, and in old age one prefers prose. By that poetical tendency of youth the sense of the real is then easily spoiled. For poetry differs from reality by the fact that in it life flows past us, interesting and yet painless; while in reality, on the contrary, so long as it is painless it is uninteresting, and as soon as it becomes interesting, it does not remain without pain. The youth who has been initiated into poetry earlier than into reality now desires from the latter what only the former can achieve; this is a principal source of the discomfort which oppresses the most gifted youths.

Metre and rhyme are a fetter, but also a veil which the poet throws round him, and under which he is permitted to speak as he otherwise dared not do; and that is what gives us pleasure. He is only half responsible for all that he says; metre and rhyme must answer for the other half. Metre, or measure, as mere rhythm, has its existence only in time, which is a pure perception *a priori,* thus, to use Kant's language, belongs merely to *pure sensibility;* rhyme, on the other hand, is an affair of sensation, in the organ of hearing, thus of *empirical sensibility.* Therefore rhythm is a much nobler and more worthy expedient than rhyme, which the ancients accordingly despised, and which found its origin in those imperfect languages which arose from the corruption of earlier ones and in barbarous times. The poorness of French poetry depends principally upon the fact that it is confined to rhyme alone without metre, and it is increased by the fact that in order to conceal its want of means it has increased the difficulty of rhyming by a number of pedantic laws, such as, for example, that only syllables which are written the same way rhyme, as if it were for the eye and not for the ear that the hiatus is forbidden; that a number of words must not occur; and many such, to all of which the new school of French poetry seeks to put an end. In no language, however, at least on me, does the rhyme make such a pleasing and powerful impression as in Latin; the rhymed Latin poems of the Middle Ages have a peculiar charm. This must be explained from the fact that the Latin language is incomparably more perfect, more beautiful and noble, than any modern language, and now moves so gracefully in the ornaments and spangles which really belong to the latter, and which it itself originally despised.

To serious consideration it might almost appear as high treason against our reason that even the slightest violence should be done to a thought or its correct and pure expression, with the childish intention that after some syllables the same sound of word should be heard, or even that these syllables themselves should present a kind of rhythmical beat. But without such violence very few verses would be made; for it must be attributed to this that in foreign languages verses are much more difficult to understand than prose. If we could see into the secret workshops of the poets, we would find that the thought is sought for the rhyme ten times oftener than the rhyme for the thought; and even when the latter is the case, it is not easily accomplished without pliability on the part of the thought. But the art of verse bids defiance to these considerations, and, moreover, has all ages and peoples upon its side, so great is the power which metre and rhyme exercise upon the feeling, and so effective the mysterious *lenocinium* which belongs to them. I would explain this from the fact that a happily rhymed verse, by its indescribably emphatic effect, raises the feeling as if the thought expressed in it lay already predestined, nay, performed in the language, and the poet has only had to find it out. Even trivial thoughts receive from rhythm and rhyme a touch of importance; cut a figure in this attire, as among girls plain faces attract the eye by finery. Nay, even distorted and false thoughts gain through versification an appearance of truth. On the other hand, even famous passages from famous poets shrink together and become insignificant when they are reproduced accurately in prose. If only the true is beautiful, and the dearest ornament of truth is nakedness, then a thought which appears true and beautiful in prose will have more true worth than one which affects us in the same way in verse. Now it is very striking, and well worth investigating, that such trifling, nay, apparently childish, means as metre and rhyme produce so powerful an effect. I explain it to myself in the following manner: That which is given directly to the sense of hearing, thus the mere sound of the words, receives from rhythm and rhyme a certain completeness and significance in itself for it thereby becomes a kind of music; therefore it seems now to exist for its own sake, and no longer as a mere means, mere signs of something signified, the sense of the words. To please the ear with its sound seems to be its whole end, and therefore with this everything seems to be attained and all claims satisfied. But that it further contains a meaning, expresses a thought, presents itself now as an unexpected addition, like words to music—as an unexpected present which agreeably surprises us—and therefore, since we made no demands of this kind, very easily satisfies us; and if indeed this thought is such that, in itself, thus said in prose, it would also be significant, then we are enchanted. I can remember, in my early childhood, that I had delighted myself for a long time with the agreeable sound of verse before I made the discovery that it all also contained meaning and thoughts. Accordingly there is also, in all languages, a mere doggerel poetry almost entirely devoid of meaning. Davis, the Sinologist, in the preface to his translation of the "*Laou-sang-urh,*" or "An Heir in Old Age" (London, 1817), observes that the Chinese dramas partly consist of verses which are sung, and adds: "The meaning of them is often obscure, and, according to the statements of the Chinese themselves, the end of these verses is especially to flatter the ear, and the sense is neglected, and even entirely sacrificed to the harmony." Who is not reminded here of the choruses of many Greek tragedies which are often so hard to make out?

The sign by which one most immediately recognises the genuine poet, both of the higher and lower species, is the unforced nature of his rhymes. They have appeared of themselves as if by divine arrangement; his thoughts come to him already in rhyme. The homely, prosaic man on the contrary, seeks the rhyme for the thought; the bungler seeks the thought for the rhyme. Very often one can find out from a couple of rhymed verses which of the two had the thought and which had the rhyme as its father. The art consists in concealing the latter, so that such lines may not appear almost as mere stuffed out *boutsrimés.*

According to my feeling (proofs cannot here be given) rhyme is from its nature binary: its effect is limited to one single recurrence of the same sound, and is not strengthened by more frequent repetition. Thus whenever a final syllable has received the one of the same sound its effect is exhausted; the third recurrence of the note acts merely as a second rhyme which accidentally hits upon the same sound, but without heightening the effect; it links itself on to the existing rhyme, yet without combining with it to produce a stronger impression. For the first note does not sound through the second on to the third: therefore this is an æsthetic pleonasm, a double courage which is of no use. Least of all, therefore, do such accumulations of rhymes merit the heavy sacrifices which they cost in the octave rhyme, the terza rima, and the sonnet, and which are the cause of the mental torture under which we sometimes read such productions, for poetical pleasure is impossible under the condition of racking our brains. That the great poetical mind sometimes overcomes even these forms, and moves in them with ease and grace, does not extend to a recommendation of the forms themselves, for in themselves they are as ineffectual as they are difficult. And even in good poets, when they make use of these forms, we frequently see the conflict between the rhyme and the thought, in which now one and now the other gains the victory; thus either the thought is stunted for the sake of the rhyme, or the rhyme has to be satisfied with a weak *à peu près.* Since this is so, I do not regard it as an evidence of ignorance, but as a proof of good taste, that Shakspeare in his sonnets has given different rhymes to each quatraine. At any rate, their acoustic effect is not in the least diminished by it, and the thought obtains its rights far more than it could have done if it had had to be laced up in the customary Spanish boots.

It is a disadvantage for the poetry of a language if it has many words which cannot be used in prose, and, on the other hand, dare not use certain words of prose. The former is mostly the case in Latin and Italian poetry, and the latter in French, where it has recently been very aptly called, "*La bégeulerie de la langue française;*" both are to be found less in English, and least in German. For such words belonging exclusively to poetry remain foreign to our heart, do not speak to us directly, and therefore leave us cold. They are a conventional language of poetry, and as it were mere painted sensations instead of real ones: they exclude genuine feeling.

The distinction, so often discussed in our own day, between *classic* and *romantic* poetry seems to me ultimately to depend upon the fact that the former knows no other motives than those which are purely human, actual, and natural; the latter, on the other hand, also treats artificial conventional, and imaginary motives as efficient. To such belong the motives which spring from the Christian mythus, also from the chivalrous over-strained fantastical law of honour, further from the absurd and ludicrous Germano-Christian veneration of women, and lastly from doting and mooning hyperphysical amorousness. But even in the best poets of the romantic class, *e.g.*, in Calderon, we can see to what ridiculous distortions of human relations and human nature these motives lead. Not to speak of the Autos, I merely refer to such pieces as "*No siempre el peor es cierto*" (The worst is not always certain), and "*El postrero duelo en España*" (The last duel in Spain), and similar comedies *en capa y espada:* with the elements mentioned there is here further associated the scholastic subtility so often appearing in the conversation which at that time belonged to the mental culture of the higher classes. How decidedly advantageous, on the contrary, is the position of the poetry of the ancients, which always remains true to nature; and the result is that classical poetry has an unconditional, romantic poetry only a conditional, truth and correctness; analogous to Greek and Gothic architecture. Yet, on the other hand, we must remark here that all dramatic or narrative poems which transfer their scene to ancient Greece or Rome lose by this from the fact that our knowledge of antiquity, especially in what concerns the details of life, is insufficient, fragmentary, and not drawn from perception. This obliges the poet to avoid much and to content himself with generalities, whereby he becomes abstract, and his work loses that concreteness and individualisation which is throughout essential to poetry. It is this which gives all such works the peculiar appearance of emptiness and tediousness. Only Shakspeare's works of this kind are free from it; because without hesitation he has presented, under the names of Greeks and Romans, Englishmen of his own time.

It has been objected to many masterpieces of lyrical poetry, especially some Odes of Horace (see, for example, the second of the third book) and several of Goethe's songs (for example, "The Shepherd's Lament"), that they lack proper connection and are full of gaps in the thought. But here the logical connection is intentionally neglected, in order that the unity of the fundamental sensation and mood may take its place, which comes out more clearly just by the fact that it passes like a thread through the separate pearls, and brings about the quick changes of the objects of contemplation, in the same way as in music the transition from one key to another is brought about by the chord of the seventh, through which the still sounding fundamental note becomes the dominant of the new key. Most distinctly, even exaggeratedly, the quality here described is found in the Canzone of Petrarch which begins, "*Mai non vo' più cantar, com' io soleva.*"

Accordingly, as in the lyrical poem the subjective element predominates, so in the drama, on the contrary, the objective element is alone and exclusively present.

Between the two epic poetry in all its forms and modifications, from the narrative romance to the epos proper, has a broad middle path. For although in the main it is objective, yet it contains a subjective element, appearing now more and now less, which finds its expression in the tone, in the form of the delivery, and also in scattered reflections. We do not so entirely lose sight of the poet as in the drama.

The end of the drama in general is to show us in an example what is the nature and existence of man. The sad or the bright side of these can be turned to us in it, or their transitions into each other. But the expression, "nature and existence of man," already contains the germ of the controversy whether the nature, *i.e.*, the character, or the existence, *i.e.*, the fate, the adventures, the action, is the principal thing. Moreover, the two have grown so firmly together that although they can certainly be separated in conception, they cannot be separated in the representation of them. For only the circumstances, the fate, the events, make the character manifest its nature, and only from the character does the action arise from which the events proceed. Certainly, in the representation, the one or the other may be made more prominent; and in this respect the piece which centres in the characters and the piece which centres in the plot are the two extremes.

The common end of the drama and the epic, to exhibit, in significant characters placed in significant situations, the extraordinary actions brought about by both, will be most completely attained by the poet if he first introduces the characters to us in a state of peace, in which merely their general colour becomes visible, and allows a motive to enter which produces an action, out of which a new and stronger motive arises, which again calls forth a more significant action, which, in its turn, begets new and even stronger motives, whereby, then, in the time suitable to the form of the poem, the most passionate excitement takes the place of the original peace, and in this now the important actions occur in which the qualities of the characters which have hitherto slumbered are brought clearly to light, together with the course of the world.

Great poets transform themselves into each of the persons to be represented, and speak out of each of them like ventriloquists; now out of the hero, and immediately afterwards out of the young and innocent maiden, with equal truth and naturalness: so Shakspeare and Goethe. Poets of the second rank transform the principal person to be represented into themselves. This is what Byron does; and then the other persons often remain lifeless, as is the case even with the principal persons in the works of mediocre poets.

Our pleasure in tragedy belongs, not to the sense of the beautiful, but to that of the sublime; nay, it is the highest grade of this feeling. For, as at the sight of the sublime in nature we turn away from the interests of the will, in order to be purely perceptive, so in the tragic catastrophe we turn away even from the will to live. In tragedy the terrible side of life is presented to us, the wail of humanity, the reign of chance and error, the fall of the just, the triumph of the wicked; thus the aspect of the world which directly strives against our will is brought before our eyes. At this sight we feel ourselves challenged to turn away our will from life, no longer to will it or love it. But just in this way we become conscious that then there still remains something over to us, which we absolutely cannot know positively, but only negatively, as that which does not will life. As the chord of the seventh demands the fundamental chord; as the colour red demands green, and even produces it in the eye; so every tragedy demands an entirely different kind of existence, another world, the knowledge of which can only be given us indirectly just as here by such a demand. In the moment of the tragic catastrophe the conviction becomes more distinct to us than ever that life is a bad dream from which we have to awake. So far the effect of the tragedy is analogous to that of the dynamical sublime, for like this it lifts us above the will and its interests, and puts us in such a mood that we find pleasure in the sight of what tends directly against it. What gives to all tragedy, in whatever form it may appear, the peculiar tendency towards the sublime is the awakening of the knowledge that the world, life, can afford us no true pleasure, and consequently is not worthy of our attachment. In this consists the tragic spirit: it therefore leads to resignation.

I admit that in ancient tragedy this spirit of resignation seldom appears and is expressed directly. Œdipus Colonus certainly dies resigned and willing; yet he is comforted by the revenge on his country. Iphigenia at Aulis is very willing to die; yet it is the thought of the welfare of Greece that comforts her, and occasions the change of her mind, on account of which she willingly accepts the death which at first she sought to avoid by any means. Cassandra, in the Agamemnon of the great Æschylus, dies willingly, *αρκειτω βιος* (1306); but she also is comforted by the thought of revenge. Hercules, in the Trachiniæ, submits to necessity, and dies composed, but not resigned. So also the Hippolytus of Euripides, in whose case it surprises us that Artemis, who appears to comfort him, promises him temples and fame, but never points him to an existence beyond life, and leaves him in death, as all gods forsake the dying:—in Christianity they come to him; and so also in Brahmanism and Buddhism, although in the latter the gods are really exotic. Thus Hippolytus, like almost all the tragic heroes of the ancients, shows submission to inevitable fate and the inflexible will of the gods, but no surrender of the will to live itself. As the Stoic equanimity is fundamentally distinguished from Christian resignation by the fact that it teaches only patient endurance and composed expectation of unalterably necessary evil, while Christianity teaches renunciation, surrender of the will; so also the tragic heroes of the ancients show resolute subjection under the unavoidable blows of fate, while Christian tragedy, on the contrary, shows the surrender of the whole will to live, joyful forsaking of the world in the consciousness of its worthlessness and vanity. But I am also entirely of opinion that modern tragedy stands higher than that of the ancients. Shakspeare is much greater than Sophocles; in comparison with Goethe's Iphigenia one might find that of Euripides almost crude and vulgar. The Bacchæ of Euripides is a revolting composition in favour of the heathen priests. Many ancient pieces have no tragic tendency at all, like the Alcestis and Iphigenia in Tauris of Euripides; some have disagreeable, or even disgusting motives, like the Antigone and Philocteles. Almost all show the human race under the fearful rule of chance and error, but not the resignation which is occasioned by it, and delivers from it. All because the ancients had not yet attained to the summit and goal of tragedy, or indeed of the view of life itself.

Although, then, the ancients displayed little of the spirit of resignation, the turning away of the will from life, in their tragic heroes themselves, as their frame of mind, yet the peculiar tendency and effect of tragedy remains the awakening of that spirit in the beholder, the calling up of that frame of mind, even though only temporarily. The horrors upon the stage hold up to him the bitterness and worthlessness of life, thus the vanity of all its struggle. The effect of this impression must be that he becomes conscious, if only in obscure feeling, that it is better to tear his heart free from life, to turn his will from it, to love not the world nor life; whereby then in his deepest soul, the consciousness is aroused that for another kind of willing there must also be another existence. For if this were not so, then the tendency of tragedy would not be this rising above all the ends and good things of life, this turning away from it and its seductions, and the turning towards another kind of existence, which already lies in this, although an existence which is for us quite inconceivable. How would it, then, in general, be possible that the exhibition of the most terrible side of life, brought before our eyes in the most glaring light, could act upon us beneficently, and afford us a lofty satisfaction? Fear and sympathy, in the excitement of which Aristotle places the ultimate end of tragedy, certainly do not in themselves belong to the agreeable sensations: therefore they cannot be the end, but only the means. Thus the summons to turn away the will from life remains the true tendency of tragedy, the ultimate end of the intentional exhibition of the suffering of humanity, and is so accordingly even where this resigned exaltation of the mind is not shown in the hero himself, but is merely excited in the spectator by the sight of great, unmerited, nay, even merited suffering. Many of the moderns also are, like the ancients, satisfied with throwing the spectator into the mood which has been described, by the objective representation of human misfortune as a whole; while others exhibit this through the change of the frame of mind of the hero himself, effected by suffering. The former give, as it were, only the premisses, and leave the conclusion to the spectator; while the latter give the conclusion, or the moral of the fable, also, as the change of the frame of mind of the hero, and even also as reflection, in the mouth of the chorus, as, for example, Schiller in "The Bride of Messina:" "Life is not the highest good." Let me remark here that the genuine tragic effect of the catastrophe, thus the resignation and exaltation of the mind of the hero which is brought about by it, seldom appears so purely motived and so distinctly expressed as in the opera of "Norma," where it comes in in the duet, "*Qual cor tradisti, qual cor perdesti,*" in which the change of the will is distinctly indicated by the quietness which is suddenly introduced into the music. In general, this piece—regarded apart altogether from its excellent music, and also from the diction which can only be that of a libretto, and considered only according to its motives and its inner economy—is a highly perfect tragedy, a true pattern of tragic disposition of the motives, tragic progress of the action, and tragic development, together with the effect of these upon the frame of mind of the hero, raising it above the world, and which is then also communicated to the spectator; indeed the effect attained here is the less delusive and the more indicative of the true nature of tragedy that no Christians, nor even Christian ideas, appear in it.

The neglect of the unity of time and place with which the moderns are so often reproached is only a fault when it goes so far that it destroys the unity of the action; for then there only remains the unity of the principal character, as, for example, in Shakspeare's "Henry VIII." But even the unity of the action does not need to go so far that the same thing is spoken of throughout, as in the French tragedies which in general observe this so strictly that the course of the drama is like a geometrical line without breadth. There it is constantly a case of "Only get on! *Pensez à votre affaire!*" and the thing is expedited and hurried on in a thoroughly business fashion, and no one detains himself with irrelevances which do not belong to it, or looks to the right or the left. The Shakspearian tragedy, on the other hand, is like a line which has also breadth: it takes time, *exspatiatur:* speeches and even whole scenes occur which do not advance the action, indeed do not properly concern it, by which, however, we get to know the characters or their circumstances more fully, and then understand the action also more thoroughly. This certainly remains the principal thing, yet not so exclusively that we forget that in the last instance what is aimed at is the representation of human nature and existence generally.

The dramatic or epic poet ought to know that he is

fate, and should therefore be inexorable, as it is; also that he is the mirror of the human race, and should therefore represent very many bad and sometimes profligate characters, and also many fools, buffoons, and eccentric persons; then also, now and again, a reasonable, a prudent, an honest, or a good man, and only as the rarest exception a truly magnanimous man. In the whole of Homer there is in my opinion no really magnanimous character presented, although many good and honest. In the whole of Shakspeare there may be perhaps a couple of noble, though by no means transcendently noble, characters to be found; perhaps Cordelia, Coriolanus—hardly more; on the other hand, his works swarm with the species indicated above. But Iffland's and Kotzebue's pieces have many magnanimous characters; while Goldoni has done as I recommended above, whereby he shows that he stands higher. On the other hand, Schiller's "Minna von Barnhelm" labours under too much and too universal magnanimity; but so much magnanimity as the one Marquis Posa displays is not to be found in the whole of Goethe's works together. There is, however, a small German piece called "Duty for Duty's Sake" (a title which sounds as if it had been taken from the Critique of Practical Reason), which has only three characters, and yet all the three are of most transcendent magnanimity.

The Greeks have taken for their heroes only royal persons; and so also for the most part have the moderns. Certainly not because the rank gives more worth to him who is acting or suffering; and since the whole thing is just to set human passions in play, the relative value of the objects by which this happens is indifferent, and peasant huts achieve as much as kingdoms. Moreover, civic tragedy is by no means to be unconditionally rejected. Persons of great power and consideration are yet the best adapted for tragedy on this account, that the misfortune in which we ought to recognise the fate of humanity must have a sufficient magnitude to appear terrible to the spectator, whoever he may be. Euripides himself says, "φευ, φευ, τα μεγαλα, μεγαλα και πασχει κακα" (*Stob. Flor.*, vol. ii. p. 299). Now the circumstances which plunge a citizen family into want and despair are in the eyes of the great or rich, for the most part, very insignificant, and capable of being removed by human assistance, nay, sometimes even by a trifle: such spectators, therefore, cannot be tragically affected by them. On the other hand, the misfortunes of the great and powerful are unconditionally terrible, and also accessible to no help from without; for kings must help themselves by their own power, or fall. To this we have to add that the fall is greatest from a height. Accordingly persons of the rank of citizens lack height to fall from.

If now we have found the tendency and ultimate intention of tragedy to be a turning to resignation, to the denial of the will to live, we shall easily recognise in its opposite, comedy, the incitement to the continued assertion of the will. It is true the comedy, like every representation of human life, without exception, must bring before our eyes suffering and adversity; but it presents it to us as passing, resolving itself into joy, in general mingled with success, victory, and hopes, which in the end preponderate; moreover, it brings out the inexhaustible material for laughter of which life, and even its adversities themselves are filled, and which under all circumstances ought to keep us in a good humour. Thus it declares, in the result, that life as a whole is thoroughly good, and especially is always amusing. Certainly it must hasten to drop the curtain at the moment of joy, so that we may not see what comes after; while the tragedy, as a rule, so ends that nothing can come after. And moreover, if once we contemplate this burlesque side of life somewhat seriously, as it shows itself in the naïve utterances and gestures which trifling embarrassment, personal fear, momentary anger, secret envy, and many similar emotions force upon the forms of the real life that mirrors itself here, forms which deviate considerably from the type of beauty, then from this side also, thus in an unexpected manner, the reflective spectator may become convinced that the existence and action of such beings cannot itself be an end; that, on the contrary, they can only have attained to existence by an error, and that what so exhibits itself is something which had better not be.

CHAPTER XXXVIII.[1]

ON HISTORY.

In the passage of the first volume referred to below I have fully shown that more is achieved for our knowledge of mankind by poetry than by history, and why this is so; inasmuch as more real instruction was to be expected from the former than from the latter. Aristotle has also confessed this, for he says: "*και φιλοσοφωτερον και σπουδαιοτερον ποιησις ἱστοριας εστιν*" (*et res magis philosophica, et melior poësis est quam historia*[2]), *De poët.*, c. 9. Yet, in order to cause no misunderstanding as to the value of history, I wish here to express my thoughts about it.

In every class and species of things the facts are innumerable, the individuals infinite in number, the variety of their differences unapproachable. At the first glance at them the curious mind becomes giddy; however much it investigates, it sees itself condemned to ignorance. But then comes science: it separates the innumerable multitude, arranges it under generic conceptions, these again under conceptions of species, whereby it opens the path to a knowledge of the general and the particular, which also comprehends the innumerable individuals, for it holds good of all without one being obliged to consider each particular for itself. Thus it promises satisfaction to the investigating mind. Then all

[1] This chapter is connected with § 51 of the first volume.

[2] Let me remark in passing that from this opposition of *ποιησις* and *ἱστορια* the origin, and also the peculiar significance, of the first word comes out with more than ordinary distinctness; it signifies that which is made, invented, in opposition to what is discovered.

sciences place themselves together, and above the real world of individual things, as that which they have divided among them. Over them all, however, moves philosophy, as the most general, and therefore important, rational knowledge, which promises the conclusions for which the others have only prepared the way. History alone cannot properly enter into that series, since it cannot boast of the same advantage as the others, for it lacks the fundamental characteristic of science, the subordination of what is known, instead of which it can only present its co-ordination. Therefore there is no system of history, as there is of every other science. It is therefore certainly rational knowledge, but it is not a science. For it never knows the particular by means of the general, but must comprehend the particular directly, and so, as it were, creeps along the ground of experience; while the true sciences move above it, because they have obtained comprehensive conceptions by means of which they command the particular, and, at least within certain limits, anticipate the possibility of things within their sphere, so that they can be at ease even about what may yet have to come. The sciences, since they are systems of conceptions, speak always of species; history speaks of individuals. It would accordingly be a science of individuals, which is a contradiction. It also follows that the sciences all speak of that which always is: history, on the other hand, of that which is once, and then no more. Since, further, history has to do with the absolutely particular and individuals, which from its nature is inexhaustible, it knows everything only imperfectly and half. Besides, it must also let itself be taught by every new day in its trivial commonplaceness what as yet it did not know at all. If it should be objected that in history also there is subordination of the particular under the general, because the periods, the governments, and other general changes, or political revolutions, in short, all that is given in historical tables, is the general, to which the special subordinates itself, this would rest upon a false comprehension of the conception of the general. For the general in history here referred to is merely *subjective, i.e.*, its generality springs merely from the inadequacy of the individual knowledge of the things, but not *objective, i.e.*, a conception in which the things would actually already be thought together. Even the most general in history is in itself only a particular and individual, a long period of time, or an important event; therefore the special is related to this as the part to the whole, but not as the case to the rule; which, on the contrary, takes place in all the sciences proper because they afford conceptions and not mere facts. On this account in these sciences by a correct knowledge of the general we can determine with certainty the particular that arises. If, for example, I know the laws of the triangle in general, I can then also tell what must be the properties of the triangle laid before me; and what holds good of all mammals, for example, that they have double ventricles of the heart, exactly seven cervical vertebræ, lungs, diaphragm, bladder, five senses, &c., I can also assert of the strange bat which has just been caught, before dissecting it. But not so in history, where the general is no objective general of the conception, but merely a subjective general of my knowledge, which can only be called general inasmuch as it is superficial. Therefore I may always know in general of the Thirty Years' War that it was a religious war, waged in the seventeenth century; but this general knowledge does not make me capable of telling anything more definite about its course. The same opposition is also confirmed by the fact that in the real sciences the special and individual is that which is most certain, because it rests upon immediate apprehension; the general truths, again, are only abstracted from it; therefore something false may be more easily assumed in the latter. But in history, conversely, the most general is the most certain; for example, the periods, the succession of the kings, the revolutions, wars, and treaties of peace; the particulars, again, of the events and their connection is uncertain, and becomes always more so the further one goes into details. Therefore history is the more interesting the more special it is, but the less to be trusted, and approaches then in every respect to the romance. For the rest, what importance is to be attached to the boasted pragmatic teaching of history he will best be able to judge who remembers that sometimes it was only after twenty years that he understood the events of his own life in their true connection, although the data for this were fully before him, so difficult is the combination of the action of the motives under the constant interferences of chance and the concealment of the intentions. Since now history really always has for its object only the particular, the individual fact, and regards this as the exclusively real, it is the direct opposite and counterpart of philosophy, which considers things from the most general point of view, and has intentionally the general as its object, which remains identical in every particular; therefore in the particular philosophy sees only the general, and recognises the change in its manifestation as unessential: φιλοκαθολου γαρ ὁ φιλοσοφος (*generalium amator philosophus*). While history teaches us that at every time something else has been, philosophy tries to assist us to the insight that at all times exactly the same was, is, and shall be. In truth, the essence of human life, as of nature in general, is given complete in every present time, and therefore only requires depth of comprehension in order to be exhaustively known. But history hopes to make up for depth by length and breadth; for it every present time is only a fragment which must be supplemented by the past, the length of which is, however, infinite, and to which again an infinite future is joined. Upon this rests the opposition between philosophical and historical minds; the former want to go to the bottom, the latter want to go through the whole series. History shows on every side only the same under different forms; but whoever does not come to know this in one or a few will hardly attain to a knowledge of it by going through all the forms. The chapters of the history of nations are at bottom only distinguished by the names and dates; the really essential content is everywhere the same.

Now since the material of art is the *Idea,* and the material of science the *concept,* we see both occupied with that which always exists and constantly in the same manner, not something which now is and now is not, now is thus and now otherwise; therefore both have to do with that which Plato set up as the exclusive object of real rational knowledge. The material of history, on the other hand, is the particular in its particularity and contingency, which at one time is, and then for ever is no more, the transient complexities of a human world moved like clouds in the wind, a world which is often entirely transformed by the most trifling accident. From this point of view the material of history appears to us as scarcely a worthy object of the serious and painful consideration of the human mind, the human mind which, just because it is so transitory, ought to choose for its consideration that which passes not away.

Finally, as regards the endeavour—specially introduced by the Hegelian pseudo-philosophy, everywhere so pernicious and stupefying to the mind—to comprehend the history of the world as a planned whole, or, as they call it, "to construe it organically," a crude and positive realism lies at its foundation, which takes the phenomenon for the inner being of the world, and imagines that this phenomenon, its forms and events, are the chief concern; in which it is secretly supported by certain mythological notions which it tacitly assumes: otherwise one might ask for what spectators such a comedy was really produced. For, since only the individual, and not the human race, has actual, immediate unity of consciousness, the unity of the course of life of the race is a mere fiction. Besides, as in nature only the species are real, and the genera are mere abstractions, so in the human race only the individuals and their course of life are real, the peoples and their lives mere abstractions. Finally, constructive histories, guided by a positive optimism, always ultimately end in a comfortable, rich, fat State, with a well-regulated constitution, good justice and police, useful arts and industries, and, at the most, in intellectual perfection; for this, in fact, is alone possible, since what is moral remains essentially unaltered. But it is the moral element which, according to the testimony of our inmost consciousness, is the whole concern: and this lies only in the individual as the tendency of his will. In truth, only the life of each individual has unity, connection, and true significance: it is to be regarded as an instruction, and the meaning of it is moral. Only the incidents of our *inner* life, since they concern the will, have true reality, and are actual events; because the will alone is the thing in itself. In every microcosm lies the whole macrocosm, and the latter contains nothing more than the former. Multiplicity is phenomenal, and external events are mere configurations of the phenomenal world, and have therefore directly neither reality nor significance, but only indirectly through their relation to the wills of the individuals. The endeavour to explain and interpret them directly is accordingly like the endeavour to see in the forms of the clouds groups of men and animals. What history narrates is in fact only the long, heavy, and confused dream of humanity.

The Hegelians, who regard the philosophy of history as indeed the chief end of all philosophy, are to be referred to Plato, who unweariedly repeats that the object of philosophy is that which is unchangeable and always remains, not that which now is thus and now otherwise. All those who set up such constructions of the course of the world, or, as they call it, of history, have failed to grasp the principal truth of all philosophy, that what is is at all times the same, all becoming and arising are only seeming; the Ideas alone are permanent; time ideal. This is what Plato holds, this is what Kant holds. One ought therefore to seek to understand what exists, what really *is*, to-day and always, *i.e.*, to know the Ideas (in Plato's sense). Fools, on the contrary, imagine that something must first become and happen. Therefore they concede to history the chief place in their philosophy, and construct it according to a preconceived plan of the world, according to which everything is ordered for the best, which is then supposed *finaliter* to appear, and will be a glorious thing. Accordingly they take the world as perfectly real, and place the end of it in the poor earthly happiness, which, however much it may be fostered by men and favoured by fate, is a hollow, deceptive, decaying, and sad thing, out of which neither constitutions and legal systems nor steam-engines and telegraphs can ever make anything that is essentially better. The said philosophers and glorifiers of history are accordingly simple realists, and also optimists and eudæmonists, consequently dull fellows and incarnate philistines; and besides are really bad Christians, for the true spirit and kernel of Christianity, as also of Brahmanism and Buddhism, is the knowledge of the vanity of earthly happiness, the complete contempt for it, and the turning away from it to an existence of another, nay, an opposite, kind. This, I say, is the spirit and end of Christianity, the true "humour of the matter;" and not, as they imagine, monotheism; therefore even atheistic Buddhism is far more closely related to Christianity than optimistic Judaism or its variety Islamism.

A true philosophy of history ought not therefore to consider, as all these do, what (to use Plato's language) always *becomes* and never *is*, and hold this to be the true nature of things; but it ought to fix its attention upon that which always is and never becomes nor passes away. Thus it does not consist in raising the temporal ends of men to eternal and absolute ends, and then with art and imagination constructing their progress through all complications; but in the insight that not only in its development, but in its very nature, history is mendacious; for, speaking of mere individuals and particular events, it pretends always to relate something different, while from beginning to end it repeats always the same thing under different names and in a different dress. The true philosophy of history consists in the insight that in all these endless changes and their confusion we have always before us only the same, even, unchanging nature, which to-day acts in the same way as yesterday and always; thus it ought to recognise the identical in all events, of ancient as of modern times, of the east as of the west; and, in spite of all difference of the special circumstances, of the costume and the customs, to see everywhere the same humanity. This identical element which is permanent through all change consists in the fundamental qualities of the human heart and head—many bad, few good. The motto of history in general should run: *Eadem, sed aliter.* If one has read Herodotus, then in a philosophical regard one has already studied history enough. For everything is already there that makes up the subsequent history of the world: the efforts, action, sufferings, and fate of the human race as it proceeds from the qualities we have referred to, and the physical earthly lot.

If in what has been said we have recognised that history, regarded as a means for the knowledge of the nature of man, is inferior to poetry; then, that it is not in the proper sense a science; finally, that the endeavour to construct it as a whole with beginning, middle, and end, together with a significant connection, is vain, and based upon misunderstanding: it would look as if we wished to deny it all value if we did not show in what its value consists. Really, however, there remains for it, after this conquest by art and rejection by science, a quite special province, different from both, in which it exists most honourably.

What reason is to the individual that is history to the human race. By virtue of reason, man is not, like the brute, limited to the narrow, perceptible present, but also knows the incomparably more extended past, with which it is linked, and out of which it has proceeded; and only thus has he a proper understanding of the present itself, and can even draw inferences as to the future. The brute, on the other hand, whose knowledge, devoid of reflection, is on this account limited to the present, even when it is tamed, moves about among men ignorant, dull, stupid, helpless, and dependent. Analogous to this is the nation that does not know its own history, is limited to the present of the now living generation, and therefore does not understand itself and its own present, because it cannot connect it with a past, and explain it from this; still less can it anticipate the future. Only through history does a nation become completely conscious of itself. Accordingly history is to be regarded as the rational consciousness of the human race, and is to the race what the reflected and connected consciousness is to the individual who is conditioned by reason, a consciousness through the want of which the brute is confined to the narrow, perceptible present. Therefore every gap in history is like a gap in the recollective self-consciousness of a man; and in the presence of a monument of ancient times which has outlived the knowledge of itself, as, for example, the Pyramids, or temples and palaces in Yucatan, we stand as senseless and stupid as the brute in the presence of the action of man, in which it is implicated in his service; or as a man before something written in an old cipher of his own, the key to which he has forgotten; nay, like a somnambulist who finds before him in the morning what he has done in his sleep. In this sense, then, history is to be regarded as the reason, or the reflected consciousness, of the human race, and takes the place of an immediate self-consciousness common to the whole race, so that only by virtue of it does the human race come to be a whole, come to be a humanity. This is the true value of history, and accordingly the universal and predominating interest in it depends principally upon the fact that it is a personal concern of the human race. Now, what language is for the reason of individuals, as an indispensable condition of its use, writing is for the reason of the whole race here pointed out; for only with this does its real existence begin, as that of the individual reason begins first with language. Writing serves to restore unity to the consciousness of the human race, which is constantly interrupted by death, and therefore fragmentary; so that the thought which has arisen in the ancestor is thought out by his remote descendant; it finds a remedy for the breaking up of the human race and its consciousness into an innumerable number of ephemeral individuals, and so bids defiance to the ever hurrying time, in whose hand goes forgetfulness. As an attempt to accomplish this we must regard not only written, but also *stone* monuments, which in part are older than the former. For who will believe that those who, at incalculable cost, set in action the human powers of many thousands for many years in order to construct the pyramids, monoliths, rock tombs, obelisks, temples, and palaces which have already existed for thousands of years, could have had in view the short span of their own life, too short to let them see the finishing of the construction, or even the ostensible end which the ignorance of the many required them to allege? Clearly their real end was to speak to their latest descendants, to put themselves in connection with these, and so to establish the unity of the consciousness of humanity. The buildings of the Hindus, the Egyptians, even the Greeks and Romans, were calculated to last several thousand years, because through higher culture their horizon was a wider one; while the buildings of the Middle Ages and of modern times have only been intended, at the most, to last a few centuries; which, however, is also due to the fact that men trusted more to writing after its use had become general, and still more since from its womb was born the art of printing. Yet even in the buildings of more recent times we see the desire to speak to posterity ; and, therefore, it is shameful if they are destroyed or disfigured in order to serve low utilitarian ends. Written monuments have less to fear from the elements, but more to fear from barbarians, than stone ones ; they accomplish far more. The Egyptians wished to combine the two, for they covered their stone monuments with hieroglyphics, nay, they added paintings in case the hieroglyphics should no longer be understood.

CHAPTER XXXIX.[1]

ON THE METAPHYSICS OF MUSIC.

THE outcome, or result, of my exposition of the peculiar significance of this wonderful art, which is given in the passage of the first volume referred to below, and which will here be present to the mind of the reader, was, that there is indeed no resemblance between its productions and the world as idea, *i.e.*, the world of nature, but yet there must be a distinct *parallelism*, which was then also proved. I have yet to add some fuller particulars with regard to this parallelism, which are worthy of attention.

The four voices, or parts, of all harmony, the bass, the tenor, the alto, and the soprana, or the fundamental note, the third, the fifth, and the octave, correspond to the four grades in the series of existences, the mineral kingdom, the vegetable kingdom, the brute kingdom, and man. This receives an additional and striking confirmation in the fundamental rule of music, that the bass must be at a much greater distance below the three upper parts than they have between themselves; so that it must never approach nearer to them than at the most within an octave of them, and generally remains still further below them. Hence, then, the correct triad has its place in the third octave from the fundamental note. Accordingly the effect of *extended* harmony, in which the bass is widely separated from the other parts, is much more powerful and beautiful than that of *close* harmony, in which it is moved up nearer to them, and which is only introduced on account of the

[1] This chapter is connected with § 52 of the first volume.

limited compass of the instruments. This whole rule, however, is by no means arbitrary, but has its root in the natural source of the tonal system; for the nearest consonant intervals that sound along with the fundamental note by means of its vibrations are the octave and its fifth. Now, in this rule we recognise the analogue of the fundamental characteristic of nature on account of which organised beings are much more nearly related to each other than to the inanimate, unorganised mass of the mineral kingdom, between which and them exists the most definite boundary and the widest gulf in the whole of nature. The fact that the high voice which sings the melody is yet also an integral part of the harmony, and therein accords even with the deepest fundamental bass, may be regarded as the analogue of the fact that *the same* matter which in a human organism is the supporter of the Idea of man must yet also exhibit and support the Ideas of gravitation and chemical qualities, that is, of the lowest grades of the objectification of will.

That music acts directly upon the will, *i.e.*, the feelings, passions, and emotions of the hearer, so that it quickly raises them or changes them, may be explained from the fact that, unlike all the other arts, it does not express the Ideas, or grades of the objectification of the will, but directly the *will itself*.

As surely as music, far from being a mere accessory of poetry, is an independent art, nay, the most powerful of all the arts, and therefore attains its ends entirely with means of its own, so surely does it not stand in need of the words of the song or the action of an opera. Music as such knows the tones or notes alone, but not the causes which produce these. Accordingly, for it even the human voice is originally and essentially nothing else than a modified tone, just like that of an instrument; and, like every other tone, it has the special advantages and disadvantages which are a consequence of the instrument that produces it. Now, in this case, that this same instrument, as the organ of speech, also serves to communicate conceptions is an accidental circumstance, which music can certainly also make use of, in order to enter into a connection with poetry; but it must never make this the principal matter, and concern itself entirely with the expression of what for the most part, nay (as Diderot gives us to understand in *Le Neveu de Rameau*), essentially are insipid verses. The words are and remain for the music a foreign addition, of subordinate value, for the effect of the tones is incomparably more powerful, more infallible, and quicker than that of the words. Therefore, if words become incorporated in music, they must yet assume an entirely subordinate position, and adapt themselves completely to it. But the relation appears reversed in the case of the given poetry, thus the song or the libretto of an opera to which music is adapted. For the art of music at once shows in these its power and higher fitness, disclosing the most profound ultimate and secret significance of the feeling expressed in the words or the action presented in the opera, giving utterance to their peculiar and true nature, and teaching us the inmost soul of the actions and events whose mere clothing and body is set before us on the stage. With regard to this superiority of the music, and also because it stands to the libretto and the action in the relation of the universal to the particular, of the rule to the example, it might perhaps appear more fitting that the libretto should be written for the music than that the music should be composed for the libretto. However, in the customary method, the words and actions of the libretto lead the composer to the affections of the will which lie at their foundation, and call up in him the feelings to be expressed; they act, therefore, as a means of exciting his musical imagination. Moreover, that the addition of poetry to music is so welcome to us, and a song with intelligible words gives us such deep satisfaction, depends upon the fact that in this way our most direct and most indirect ways of knowing are called into play at once and in connection. The most direct is that for which music expresses the emotions of the will itself, and the most indirect that of conceptions denoted by words. When the language of the feelings is in question the reason does not willingly sit entirely idle. Music is certainly able with the means at its own disposal to express every movement of the will, every feeling; but by the addition of words we receive besides this the objects of these feelings, the motives which occasion them. The music of an opera, as it is presented in the score, has a completely independent, separate, and, as it were, abstract existence for itself, to which the incidents and persons of the piece are foreign, and which follows its own unchanging rules; therefore it can produce its full effect without the libretto. But this music, since it was composed with reference to the drama, is, as it were, the soul of the latter; for, in its connection with the incidents, persons, and words, it becomes the expression of the inner significance of all those incidents, and of their ultimate and secret necessity which depends upon this significance. The pleasure of the spectator, unless he is a mere gaper, really depends upon an indistinct feeling of this. Yet in the opera music also shows its heterogeneous nature and higher reality by its entire indifference to the whole material of the incidents; in consequence of which it everywhere expresses the storm of the passions and the pathos of the feelings in the same way, and its tones accompany the piece with the same pomp, whether Agamemnon and Achilles or the dissensions of a bourgeois family form its material. For only the passions, the movements of the will, exist for it, and, like God, it sees only the hearts. It never assimilates itself to the natural; and therefore, even when it accompanies the most ludicrous and extravagant farces of the comic opera, it still preserves its essential beauty, purity, and sublimity; and its fusion with these incidents is unable to draw it down from its height, to which all absurdity is really foreign. Thus the profound and serious significance of our existence hangs over the farce and the endless miseries of human life, and never leaves it for a moment.

If we now cast a glance at purely instrumental music, a symphony of Beethoven presents to us the greatest confusion, which yet has the most perfect order at its foundation, the most vehement conflict, which is transformed the next moment into the most beautiful concord. It is *rerum concordia discors*, a true and perfect picture of the nature of the world which rolls on in the boundless maze of innumerable forms, and through constant destruction supports itself. But in this symphony all human passions and emotions also find utterance; joy, sorrow, love, hatred, terror, hope, &c., in innumerable degrees, yet all, as it were, only *in abstracto*, and without any particularisation; it is their mere form without the substance, like a spirit world without matter. Certainly we have a tendency to realise them while we listen, to clothe them in imagination with flesh and bones, and to see in them scenes of life and nature on every hand. Yet, taken generally, this is not required for their comprehension or enjoyment, but rather imparts to them a foreign and arbitrary addition: therefore it is better to apprehend them in their immediacy and purity.

Since now, in the foregoing remarks, and also in the text, I have considered music only from the metaphysical side, that is, with reference to the inner significance of its performances, it is right that I should now also subject to a general consideration the means by which, acting upon our mind, it brings these about; therefore that I should show the connection of that metaphysical side of music, and the physical side, which has been fully investigated, and is well known, I start from the theory which is generally known, and has by no means been shaken by recent objections, that all harmony of the notes depends upon the coincidence of their vibrations, which when two notes sound together occurs perhaps at every second, or at every third, or at every fourth vibration, according to which, then, they are the octave, the fifth, or the fourth of each other, and so on. So long as the vibrations of two notes have a rational relation to each other, which can be expressed in small numbers, they can be connected together in our apprehension through their constantly recurring coincidence: the notes become blended, and are thereby in consonance. If, on the other hand, that relation is an irrational one, or one which can only be expressed in larger numbers, then no coincidence of the vibrations which can be apprehended occurs, but *obstrepunt sibi perpetuo,* whereby they resist being joined together in our apprehension, and accordingly are called a dissonance. Now, according to this theory, music is a means of making rational and irrational relations of numbers comprehensible, not like arithmetic by the help of the concept, but by bringing them to a knowledge which is perfectly directly and simultaneously sensible. Now the connection of the metaphysical significance of music with this its physical and arithmetical basis depends upon the fact that what resists our *apprehension*, the irrational relation, or the dissonance, becomes the natural type of what resists our *will;* and, conversely, the consonance, or the rational relation, which easily adapts itself to our apprehension, becomes the type of the satisfaction of the will. And further, since that rational and irrational element in the numerical relations of the vibrations admits of innumerable degrees, shades of difference, sequences, and variations, by means of it music becomes the material in which all the movements of the human heart, *i.e.*, of the will, movements whose essential nature is always satisfaction and dissatisfaction, although in innumerable degrees. can be faithfully portrayed and rendered in all their finest shades and modifications, which takes place by means of the invention of the melody. Thus we see here the movements of the will transferred to the province of the mere idea, which is the exclusive scene of the achievements of the fine arts, for they absolutely demand that the *will itself* shall not interfere, and that we shall conduct ourselves as pure *knowing* subjects. Therefore the affections of the will itself, thus actual pain and actual pleasure, must not be excited, but only their substitutes, that which is agreeable to *the intellect*, as a *picture* of the satisfaction of the will, and that which is more or less repugnant to it, as a *picture* of greater or less pain. Only thus does music never cause us actual sorrow, but even in its most melancholy strains is still pleasing, and we gladly hear in its language the secret history of our will, and all its emotions and strivings, with their manifold protractions, hindrances, and griefs, even in the saddest melodies. When, on the other hand, in reality and its terrors, it is our *will itself* that is roused and tormented, we have not then to do with tones and their numerical relations, but are rather now ourselves the trembling string that is stretched and twanged.

But, further, because, in consequence of the physical theory which lies at its foundation, the musical quality of the notes is in the proportion of the rapidity of their vibrations, but not in their relative strength, the musical ear always follows by preference, in harmony, the highest note, not the loudest. Therefore, even in the case of the most powerful orchestral accompaniment, the soprano comes out clearly, and thus receives a natural right to deliver the melody. And this is also supported by its great flexibility, which depends upon the same rapidity of the vibrations, and shows itself in the ornate passages, whereby the soprano becomes the suitable representative of the heightened sensibility, susceptible to the slightest impression, and determinable by it, consequently of the most highly developed consciousness standing on the uppermost stage of the scale of being. Its opposite, from converse causes, is the bass, inflexible, rising and falling only in great intervals, thirds, fourths, and fifths, and also at every step guided by rigid rules.

It is therefore the natural representative of the inorganic kingdom of nature, which is insensible, insusceptible to fine impressions, and only determinable according to general laws. It must indeed never rise by one tone, for example, from a fourth to a fifth, for this produces in the upper parts the incorrect consecutive fifths and octaves; therefore, originally and in its own nature, it can never present the melody. If, however, the melody is assigned to it, this happens by means of counterpoint, *i.e.*, it is an *inverted* bass—one of the upper parts is lowered and disguised as a bass; properly speaking, it then requires a second fundamental bass as its accompaniment. This unnaturalness of a melody lying in the bass is the reason why bass airs, with full accompaniment, never afford us pure, undisturbed pleasure, like the soprano air, which, in the connection of harmony, is alone natural. We may remark in passing that such a melodious bass, forcibly obtained by invertion, might, in keeping with our metaphysic of music, be compared to a block of marble to which the human form has been imparted: and therefore it is wonderfully suitable to the stone guest in " Don Juan."

But now we shall try to get somewhat nearer the foundation of the genesis of melody, which can be accomplished by analysing it into its constituent parts, and in any case will afford us the pleasure which arises from bringing to abstract and distinct consciousness what every one knows in the concrete, so that it gains the appearance of novelty.

Melody consists of two elements, the one rhythmical, the other harmonious. The former may also be described as the quantitative, the latter as the qualitative element, since the first is concerned with the duration, and the second with the pitch of the notes. In the writing of music the former depends upon the perpendicular, and the latter upon the horizontal lines. Purely arithmetical relations, thus relations of time, lie at the foundation of both; in the one case the relative duration of the notes, in the other the relative rapidity of their vibrations. The rhythmical element is the essential; for it can produce a kind of melody of itself alone, and without the other, as, for example, on the drum; yet complete melody requires both elements. It consists in an alternating *disunion and reconciliation* of them, as I shall show immediately; but first, since I have already spoken of the harmonious element in what has been said, I wish to consider the rhythmical element somewhat more closely.

Rhythm is in time what *symmetry* is in space, division into equal parts corresponding to each other. First, into larger parts, which again fall into smaller parts, subordinate to the former. In the series of the arts given by me *architecture* and *music* are the two extreme ends. Moreover, according to their inner nature, their power, the extent of their spheres, and their significance, they are the most heterogeneous, indeed true antipodes. This opposition extends even to the form of their appearance, for architecture is in space alone, without any connection with time; and music is in time alone, without any connection with space.[1] Now hence springs their one point of analogy, that as in architecture that which orders and holds together is *symmetry*, in music it is *rhythm*, and thus here also it holds true that extremes meet. As the ultimate constituent parts of a building are the exactly similar stones, so the ultimate constituent parts of a musical composition are the exactly similar beats; yet by being weak or strong, or in general by the measure, which denotes the species of time, these are divided into equal parts, which may be compared to the dimensions of the stone. The musical period consists of several bars, and it has also two equal parts, one rising, aspiring, generally going to the

[1] It would be a false objection that sculpture and painting are also merely in space; for their works are connected, not directly, but yet indirectly, with time, for they represent life, movement, action. And it would be just as false to say that poetry, as speech, belongs to time alone: this is also true only indirectly of the words; its matter is all existent, thus spatial.

dominant, and one sinking, quieting, returning to the fundamental note. Two or several periods constitute a part, which in general is also symmetrically doubled by the sign of repetition; two parts make a small piece of music, or only a movement of a larger piece; and thus a concerto or sonata usually consists of three movements, a symphony of four, and a mass of five. Thus we see the musical composition bound together and rounded off as a whole, by symmetrical distribution and repeated division, down to the beats and their fractions, with thorough subordination, superordination, and co-ordination of its members, just as a building is connected and rounded off by its symmetry. Only in the latter that is exclusively in space which in the former is exclusively in time. The mere feeling of this analogy has in the last thirty years called forth the oft-repeated, daring witticism, that architecture is frozen music. The origin of this can be traced to Goethe; for, according to Eckermann's "Conversations," vol. ii. p. 88, he said: "I have found among my papers a page on which I call architecture a rigidified music; and really there is something in it; the mood which is produced by architecture approaches the effect of music." Probably he let fall this witticism much earlier in conversation, and in that case it is well known that there were never wanting persons to pick up what he so let fall that they might afterwards go about decked with it. For the rest, whatever Goethe may have said, the analogy of music and architecture, which is here referred by me to its sole ground, the analogy of rhythm with symmetry, extends accordingly only to the outward form, and by no means to the inner nature of the two arts, which is entirely different. Indeed it would be absurd to wish to put on the same level in essential respects the most limited and the weakest of all the arts, and the most far-reaching and powerful. As an amplification of the analogy pointed out, we might add further, that when music, as it were in a fit of desire for independence, seizes the opportunity of a pause to free itself from the control of rhythm, to launch out into the free imagination of an ornate *cadenza*, such a piece of music divested of all rhythm is analogous to the ruin which is divested of symmetry, and which accordingly may be called, in the bold language of the witticism, a frozen *cadenza*.

After this exposition of *rhythm*, I have now to show how the nature of melody consists in the constantly renewed *disunion and reconciliation* of the rhythmical, and the harmonious elements of it. Its harmonious element has as its assumption the fundamental note, as the rhythmical element has the species of time, and consists in a wandering from it through all the notes of the scale, until by shorter or longer digressions it reaches a harmonious interval, generally the dominant or sub-dominant, which affords it an incomplete satisfaction; and then follows, by a similarly long path, its return to the fundamental note, with which complete satisfaction appears. But both must so take place that the attainment of the interval referred to and the return to the fundamental note correspond with certain favourite points of the rhythm, otherwise it will not work. Thus, as the harmonious succession of sounds requires certain notes, first of all the tonic, next to it the dominant, and so on, so rhythm, on its part, requires certain *points of time*, certain numbered bars, and certain parts of these bars, which are called strong or good beats, or the accented parts of the bar, in opposition to the weak or bad beats, or unaccented parts of the bar. Now the disunion of these two fundamental elements consists in this, that because the demand of one is satisfied that of the other is not; and their reconciliation consists in this, that both are satisfied at once and together. That wandering of the notes until they find a more or less harmonious interval must so take place that this interval is attained only after a definite number of bars, and also at an accented part of the bar, and in this way becomes for it a kind of resting-point; and similarly the return to the keynote must take place after a like number of bars, and also at an accented part of the bar, and thus complete satisfaction is then attained. So long as this required coincidence of the satisfaction of both elements is not attained, the rhythm, on the one hand, may follow its regular course, and, on the other hand, the required notes may occur often enough, but yet they will remain entirely without that effect through which melody arises. The following very simple example may serve to illustrate this:—

Here the harmonious sequence of notes finds the keynote just at the end of the first bar; but it does not receive any satisfaction from this, because the rhythm is caught at the least accented part of the bar. Immediately afterwards, in the second bar, the rhythm has the accented part of the bar, but the sequence of notes has arrived at the seventh. Thus here the two elements of melody are entirely *disunited;* and we feel disquieted. In the second half of the period everything is reversed, and in the last note they are *reconciled.* This kind of thing can be shown in every melody, although generally in a much more extended form. Now the constant disunion and reconciliation of its two elements which there takes place is, when metaphysically considered, the copy of the origination of new wishes, and then of their satisfaction. Thus, by flattery, music penetrates into our hearts, for it presents the image of the complete satisfaction of its wishes. More closely considered, we see in this procedure of melody a condition which, to a certain extent, is *inward* (the harmonious) meet with an *outward* condition (the rhythmical), as if by an *accident,*—which is certainly brought about by the composer, and which may, so far, be compared to rhyme in poetry. But this is just the copy of the meeting of our wishes with the favourable outward circumstances which are independent of them, and is thus the picture of happiness. The effect of the *suspension* also deserves to be considered here. It is a dissonance which delays the final consonance, which is awaited with certainty; and thus the longing for it is strengthened, and its appearance satisfies all the more. Clearly an analogue of the heightened satisfaction of the will through delay. The complete cadence requires the preceding chord of the seventh on the dominant; because the most deeply felt satisfaction and the most entire relief can only follow the most earnest longing. Thus, in general, music consists of a constant succession of more or less disquieting chords, *i.e.*, chords which excite longing, and more or less quieting and satisfying chords; just as the life of the heart (the will) is a constant succession of greater or less disquietude through desire and aversion, and just as various degrees of relief. Accordingly the harmonious sequence of chords consists of the correct alternation of dissonance and consonance. A succession of merely consonant chords would be satiating, wearisome, and empty, like the languor produced by the satisfaction of all wishes. Therefore dissonances must be introduced, although they disquiet us and affect us almost painfully, but only in order to be resolved again in consonances with proper preparation. Indeed, in the whole of music there are really only two fundamental chords, the dissonant chord of the seventh and the consonant triad, to which all chords that occur can be referred. This just corresponds to the fact, that for the will there are at bottom only dissatisfaction and satisfaction, under however many forms they may present themselves. And as there are two general fundamental moods of the mind, serenity, or at least healthiness, and sadness, or even oppression, so music has two general keys, the major and the minor, which correspond to these, and it must always be in one of the two. But it is, in fact, very wonderful that there is a sign of pain which is neither physically painful nor yet conventional, but which nevertheless is suitable and unmistakable: the minor. From this we may measure how deeply music is founded in the nature of things and of man. With northern nations, whose life is subject to hard conditions, especially with the Russians, the minor prevails, even in the church music. Allegro in the minor is very common in French music, and is characteristic of it; it is as if one danced while one's shoe pinched.

I add further a few subsidiary remarks. When the key-note is changed, and with it the value of all the intervals, in consequence of which the same note figures as the second, the third, the fourth, and so on, the notes of the scale are analogous to actors, who must assume now one *rôle*, now another, while their person remains the same. That the actors are often not precisely suited to these *rôles* may be compared to the unavoidable impurity of every harmonic system (referred to at the end of § 52 of the first volume) which the equal temperament has introduced.

Perhaps some may be offended, that, according to this metaphysic of it, music, which so often exalts our minds, which seems to us to speak of other and better worlds than ours, yet really only flatters the will to live, because it exhibits to it its nature, deludes it with the image of its success, and at the end expresses its satisfaction and contentment. The following passage from the "*Vedas*" may serve to quiet such doubts: "*Etanand sroup, quod forma gaudii est, τον pram Atma ex hoc dicunt, quod quocunque loco gaudium est, particula e gaudio ejus est*" (*Oupnekhat*, vol. i. p. 405; *et iterum*, vol. ii. p. 215).

Supplements to the Fourth Book.

"*Tous les hommes désirent uniquement de se délivrer de la mort: ils ne savent pas se délivrer de la vie.*"

—*Lao-tsen-Tao-te-King*, ed. STAN. JULIEN, p. 184.

SUPPLEMENTS TO THE FOURTH BOOK.

CHAPTER XL.

PREFACE.

THE supplements to this fourth book would be very considerable if it were not that two of its principal subjects which stand specially in need of being supplemented—the freedom of the will and the foundation of ethics—have, on the occasion of prize questions being set by two Scandinavian Academies, been fully worked out by me in the form of a monograph, which was laid before the public in the year 1841 under the title, "The Two Fundamental Problems of Ethics." Accordingly I assume an acquaintance on the part of my readers with the work which has just been mentioned, just as unconditionally as in the supplements to the second book I have assumed it with regard to the work "On the Will in Nature." In general I make the demand that whoever wishes to make himself acquainted with my philosophy shall read every line of me. For I am no voluminous writer, no fabricator of compendiums, no earner of pecuniary rewards, not one whose writings aim at the approbation of a minister; in a word, not one whose pen is under the influence of personal ends. I strive after nothing but the truth, and write as the ancients wrote, with the sole intention of preserving my thoughts, so that they may be for the benefit of those who understand how to meditate upon them and prize them. Therefore I have written little, but that little with reflection and at long intervals, and accordingly I have also confined within the smallest possible limits those repetitions which in philosophical works are sometimes unavoidable on account of the connection, and from which no single philosopher is free; so that by far the most of what I have to say is only to be found in one place. On this account, then, whoever wishes to learn from me and understand me must leave nothing unread that I have written. Yet one can judge me and criticise me without this, as experience has shown; and to this also I further wish much pleasure.

Meanwhile the space gained by the said elimination of two important subjects will be very welcome to us. For since those explanations, which every man has more at heart than anything else, and which therefore in every system, as ultimate results, form the apex of its pyramid, are also crowded together in *my* last book, a larger space will gladly be granted to every firmer proof or more accurate account of these. Besides this we have been able to discuss here, as belonging to the doctrine of the "assertion of the will to live," a question which in our fourth book itself remained untouched, as it was also entirely neglected by all philosophers before me: it is the inner significance and real nature of the sexual love, which sometimes rises to a vehement passion—a subject which it would not have been paradoxical to take up in the ethical part of philosophy if its importance had been known.

CHAPTER XLI.[1]

ON DEATH AND ITS RELATION TO THE INDESTRUCTIBILITY OF OUR TRUE NATURE.

DEATH is the true inspiring genius, or the muse of philosophy, wherefore Socrates has defined the latter as *θανατου μελετη*. Indeed without death men would scarcely philosophise. Therefore it will be quite in order that a special consideration of this should have its place here at the beginning of the last, most serious, and most important of our books.

The brute lives without a proper knowledge of death; therefore the individual brute enjoys directly the absolute imperishableness of the species, for it is only conscious of itself as endless. In the case of men the terrifying certainty of death necessarily entered with reason. But as everywhere in nature with every evil a means of cure, or at least some compensation, is given, the same reflection which introduces the knowledge of death also assists us to *metaphysical* points of view, which comfort us concerning it, and of which the brute has no need and is incapable. All religious and philosophical systems are principally directed to this end, and are thus primarily the antidote to the certainty of death, which the reflective reason produces out of its own means. Yet the degree in which they attain this end is very different, and certainly *one* religion or philosophy will, far more than the others, enable men to look death in the face with a quiet glance.

[1] This chapter is connected with § 54 of the first volume.

Brahmanism and Buddhism, which teach man to regard himself as himself, the original being, the Brahm, to which all coming into being and passing away is essentially foreign, will achieve much more in this respect than such as teach that man is made out of nothing, and actually begins at birth his existence derived from another. Answering to this we find in India a confidence and a contempt for death of which one has no conception in Europe. It is, in fact, a hazardous thing to force upon a man, by early imprinting them, weak and untenable conceptions in this important regard, and thereby making him for ever incapable of taking up correct and stable ones. For example, to teach him that he recently came out of nothing, and consequently through an eternity has been nothing, but yet for the future will be imperishable, is just the same as to teach him that although he is through and through the work of another, yet he will be held responsible through all eternity for his actions. If, then, when the mind ripens and reflection appears, the untenable nature of such doctrines forces itself upon him, he has nothing better to put in its place, nay, is no longer capable of understanding anything better, and thus loses the comfort which nature had destined for him also, as a compensation for the certainty of death. In consequence of such a process, we see even now in England (1844), among ruined factory hands, the Socialists, and in Germany, among ruined students, the young Hegelians, sink to the absolutely physical point of view, which leads to the result: *edite, bibite, post mortem nulla voluptas,* and so far may be defined as bestialism.

However, after all that has been taught concerning death, it cannot be denied that, at least in Europe, the opinion of men, nay, often even of the same individual, very frequently vacillates between the conception of death as absolute annihilation and the assumption that we are, as it were, with skin and hair, immortal. Both are equally false: but we have not so much to find a correct mean as rather to gain the higher point of view from which such notions disappear of themselves.

In these considerations I shall first of all start from the purely empirical standpoint. Here there primarily lies before us the undeniable fact that, according to the natural consciousness, man not only fears death for his own person more than anything else, but also weeps violently over the death of those that belong to him, and indeed clearly not egotistically, for his own loss, but out of sympathy for the great misfortune that has befallen them. Therefore he also censures those who in such a case neither weep nor show sadness as hard-hearted and unloving. It is parallel with this that revenge, in its highest degree, seeks the death of the adversary as the greatest evil that can be inflicted. Opinions change with time and place; but the voice of nature remains always and everywhere the same, and is therefore to be heeded before everything else. Now here it seems distinctly to say that death is a great evil. In the language of nature death means annihilation. And that death is a serious matter may be concluded from the fact that, as every one knows, life is no joke. We must indeed deserve nothing better than these two.

In fact, the fear of death is independent of all knowledge; for the brute has it, although it does not know death. Everything that is born brings it with it into the world. But this fear of death is *a priori* only the reverse side of the will to live, which indeed we all are. Therefore in every brute the fear of its destruction is inborn, like the care for its maintenance. Thus it is the fear of death, and not the mere avoidance of pain, which shows itself in the anxious carefulness with which the brute seeks to protect itself, and still more its brood, from everything that might become dangerous. Why does the brute flee, trembling, and seek to conceal itself? Because it is simply the will to live, but, as such, is forfeited to death, and wishes to gain time. Such also, by nature, is man.

The greatest evil, the worst that can anywhere threaten, is death; the greatest fear is the fear of death. Nothing excites us so irresistibly to the most lively interest as danger to the life of others; nothing is so shocking as an execution. Now the boundless attachment to life which appears here cannot have sprung from knowledge and reflection; to these it rather appears foolish, for the objective worth of life is very uncertain, and at least it remains doubtful whether it is preferable to not being, nay, if experience and reflection come to be expressed, not being must certainly win. If one knocked on the graves, and asked the dead whether they wished to rise again, they would shake their heads. Such is the opinion of Socrates in "Plato's Apology," and even the gay and amiable Voltaire cannot help saying, "*On aime la vie; mais le néant ne laisse pas d'avoir du bon;*" and again, "*Je ne sais pas ce que c'est que la vie éternelle, mais celle-ci est une mauvaise plaisanterie.*" Besides, life must in any case soon end; so that the few years which perhaps one has yet to be vanish entirely before the endless time when one will be no more. Accordingly it appears to reflection even ludicrous to be so anxious about this span of time, to tremble so much if our own life or that of another is in danger, and to compose tragedies the horror of which has its strength in the fear of death. That powerful attachment to life is therefore irrational and blind; it can only be explained from the fact that our whole inner nature is itself will to live, to which, therefore, life must appear as the highest good, however embittered, short, and uncertain it may always be; and that that will, in itself and originally, is unconscious and blind. Knowledge, on the contrary, far from being the source of that attachment to life, even works against it, for it discloses the worthlessness of life, and thus combats the fear of death. When it conquers, and accordingly the man faces death courageously and composedly, this is honoured as great and noble, thus we hail then the triumph of knowledge over the blind will to live, which is yet the kernel of our own being. In the same way we despise him in whom knowledge is defeated in that conflict, and who therefore clings unconditionally to life, struggles to the utmost against approaching death, and receives it with despair;[1] and yet in him it is only the most original being of ourselves and of nature that expresses itself. We may here ask, in passing, how could this boundless love of life and endeavour to maintain it in every way as long as possible be regarded as base, contemptible, and by the adherents of every religion as unworthy of this, if it were the gift of good gods, to be recognised with thankfulness? And how could it then seem great and noble to esteem it lightly? Meanwhile, what is confirmed by these considerations is—(1.) that the will to live is the inmost nature of man; (2.) that in itself it is unconscious and blind; (3.) that knowledge is an adventitious principle, which is originally foreign to the will; (4.) that knowledge conflicts with the will, and that our judgment applauds the victory of knowledge over the will.

If what makes death seem so terrible to us were the thought of not being, we would necessarily think with equal horror of the time when as yet we were not. For it is irrefutably certain that not being after death cannot be different from not being before birth, and consequently is also no more deplorable. A whole eternity has run its course while as yet we were not, but that by no means disturbs us. On the other hand, we find it hard, nay, unendurable, that after the momentary intermezzo of an ephemeral existence, a second eternity should follow in which we shall no longer be. Should, then, this thirst for existence have arisen because we have now tasted it and have found it so delightful? As was already briefly explained above, certainly not; far sooner

[1] *In gladiatoriis pugnis timidos et supplices, et, ut vivere liceat, obsecrantes etiam odisse solemus; fortes et animosos, et se acriter ipsos morti offerentes servare cupimus* (*Cic. pro Milone*, c. 34).

could the experience gained have awakened an infinite longing for the lost paradise of non-existence. To the hope, also, of the immortality of the soul there is always added that of a "better world"—a sign that the present world is not much good. Notwithstanding all this, the question as to our state after death has certainly been discussed, in books and verbally, ten thousand times oftener than the question as to our state before birth. Yet theoretically the one is just as near at hand and as fair a problem as the other; and besides, whoever had answered the one would soon see to the bottom of the other. We have fine declamations about how shocking it would be to think that the mind of man, which embraces the world, and has so many very excellent thoughts, should sink with him into the grave; but we hear nothing about this mind having allowed a whole eternity to pass before it came into being with these its qualities, and how the world must have had to do without it all that time. Yet no question presents itself more naturally to knowledge, uncorrupted by the will, than this: An infinite time has passed before my birth; what was I during this time? Metaphysically, it might perhaps be answered, "I was always I; that is, all who during that time said I, were just I." But let us look away from this to our present entirely empirical point of view, and assume that I did not exist at all. Then I can console myself as to the infinite time after my death, when I shall not be, with the infinite time when I already was not, as a well-accustomed, and indeed very comfortable, state. For the eternity *a parte post* without me can be just as little fearful as the eternity *a parte ante* without me, since the two are distinguished by nothing except by the interposition of an ephemeral dream of life. All proofs, also, for continued existence after death may just as well be applied *in partem ante*, where they then demonstrate existence before life, in the assumption of which the Hindus and Buddhists therefore show themselves very consistent. Kant's ideality of time alone solves all these riddles. But we are not speaking of that now. This, however, results from what has been said, that to mourn for the time when one will be no more is just as absurd as it would be to mourn over the time when as yet one was not; for it is all the same whether the time which our existence does not fill is related to that which it does fill, as future or as past.

But, also, regarded entirely apart from these temporal considerations, it is in and for itself absurd to look upon not being as an evil; for every evil, as every good, presupposes existence, nay, even consciousness: but the latter ceases with life, as also in sleep and in a swoon; therefore the absence of it is well known to us, and trusted, as containing no evil at all: its entrance, however, is always an affair of a moment. From this point of view Epicurus considered death, and therefore quite rightly said, "*ὁ θανατος μηδεν προς ἡμας*" (Death does not concern us); with the explanation that when we are death is not, and when death is we are not (*Diog. Laert.*, x. 27). To have lost what cannot be missed is clearly no evil. Therefore ceasing to be ought to disturb us as little as not having been. Accordingly from the standpoint of knowledge there appears absolutely no reason to fear death. But consciousness consists in knowing; therefore, for consciousness death is no evil. Moreover, it is really not this *knowing* part of our *ego* that fears death, but the *fuga mortis* proceeds entirely and alone from the blind *will*, of which everything living is filled. To this, however, as was already mentioned above, it is essential, just because it is will to live, whose whole nature consists in the effort after life and existence, and which is not originally endowed with knowledge, but only in consequence of its objectification in animal individuals. If now the will, by means of knowledge, beholds death as the end of the phenomenon with which it has identified itself, and to which, therefore, it sees itself limited, its whole nature struggles against it with all its might. Whether now it has really something to fear from death we will investigate further on, and will then remember the real source of the fear of death, which has been shown here along with the requisite distinction of the willing and the knowing part of our nature.

Corresponding to this, then, what makes death so terrible to us is not so much the end of life—for this can appear to no one specially worthy of regret—but rather the destruction of the organism; really because this is the will itself exhibiting itself as body. But we only really feel this destruction in the evils of disease or of old age; death itself, on the other hand, consists for the *subject* only in the moment when consciousness vanishes because the activity of the brain ceases. The extension of the stoppage to all the other parts of the organism which follows this is really already an event after death. Thus death, in a subjective regard, concerns the consciousness alone. Now what the vanishing of this may be every one can to a certain extent judge of from going to sleep; but it is still better known to whoever has really fainted, for in this the transition is not so gradual, nor accompanied by dreams, but first the power of sight leaves us, still fully conscious, and then immediately the most profound unconsciousness enters; the sensation that accompanies it, so far as it goes, is anything but disagreeable; and without doubt, as sleep is the brother of death, so the swoon is its twin-brother. Even violent death cannot be painful, for even severe wounds are not felt at all till some time afterwards, often not till the outward signs of them are observed. If they are rapidly mortal, consciousness will vanish before this discovery; if they result in death later, then it is the same as with other illnesses. All those also who have lost consciousness in water, or from charcoal fumes, or through hanging are well known to say that it happened without pain. And now, finally, the death which is properly in accordance with nature, death from old age, euthanasia, is a gradual vanishing and sinking out of existence in an imperceptible manner. Little by little in old age, the passions and desires, with the susceptibility for their objects, are extinguished; the emotions no longer find anything to excite them; for the power of presenting ideas to the mind always becomes weaker, its images fainter; the impressions no longer cleave to us, but pass over without leaving a trace, the days roll ever faster, events lose their significance, everything grows pale. The old man stricken in years totters about or rests in a corner now only a shadow, a ghost of his former self. What remains there for death to destroy? One day a sleep is his last, and his dreams are ——. They are the dreams which Hamlet inquires after in the famous soliloquy. I believe we dream them even now.

I have here also to remark that the maintenance of the life process, although it has a metaphysical basis, does not go on without resistance, and consequently not without effort. It is this to which the organism yields every night, on account of which it then suspends the brain function and diminishes certain secretions, the respiration, the pulse, and the development of heat. From this we may conclude that the entire ceasing of the life process must be a wonderful relief to its motive force; perhaps this has some share in the expression of sweet contentment on the faces of most dead persons. In general the moment of death may be like the moment of awaking from a heavy dream that has oppressed us like a nightmare.

Up to this point the result we have arrived at is that death, however much it may be feared, can yet really be no evil. But often it even appears as a good thing, as something wished for, as a friend. All that have met with insuperable obstacles to their existence or their efforts, that suffer from incurable diseases or inconsolable griefs, have as a last refuge, which generally opens to them of its own accord, the return into the womb of nature, from which they arose for a short time, enticed by the hope of more favourable conditions of existence than have fallen to their lot, and the same path out of which constantly remains open. That return is the *cessio bonorum* of life. Yet even here it is only entered upon after a physical and moral conflict: so hard does one struggle against returning to the place from which one came out so lightly and readily, to an existence which has so much suffering and so little pleasure to offer. The Hindus give the god of death, Yama, two faces; one very fearful and terrible, and one very cheerful and benevolent. This partly explains itself from the reflections we have just made.

At the empirical point of view at which we still stand, the following consideration is one which presents itself of its own accord, and therefore deserves to be accurately defined by illustration, and thereby referred to its proper limits. The sight of a dead body shows me that sensibility, irritability, circulation of the blood, reproduction, &c., have here ceased. I conclude from this with certainty that what actuated these hitherto, which was yet always something unknown to me, now actuates them no longer, thus has departed from them. But if I should now wish to add that this must have been just what I have known only as consciousness, consequently as intelligence (soul), this would be not only an unjustified but clearly a false conclusion. For consciousness has always showed itself to me not as the cause, but as the product and result of the organised life, for it rose and sank in consequence of this in the different periods of life, in health and sickness, in sleep, in a swoon, in awaking, &c., thus always appeared as effect, never as cause of the organised life, always showed itself as something which arises and passes away, and again arises, so long as the conditions of this still exist, but not apart from them. Nay, I may also have seen that the complete derangement of consciousness, madness, far from dragging down with it and depressing the other forces, or indeed endangering life, heightens these very much, especially irritability or muscular force, and rather lengthens than shortens life, if other causes do not come in. Then, also: I knew individuality as a quality of everything organised, and therefore, if this is a self-conscious organism, also of consciousness. But there exists no occasion now to conclude that individuality was inherent in that vanished principle, which imparts life, and is completely unknown to me; all the less so as I see that everywhere in nature each particular phenomenon is the work of a general force which is active in thousands of similar phenomena. But, on the other hand, there is just as little occasion to conclude that because the organised life has ceased here that force which hitherto actuated it has also become nothing; as little as to infer the death of the spinner from the stopping of the spinning-wheel. If a pendulum, by finding its centre of gravity, at last comes to rest, and thus its individual apparent life has ceased, no one will imagine that gravitation is now annihilated; but every one comprehends that, after as before, it is active in innumerable phenomena. Certainly it might be urged against this comparison, that here also, in this pendulum, gravitation has not ceased to be active, but only to manifest its activity palpably; whoever insists on this may think, instead, of an electrical body, in which, after its discharge, electricity has actually ceased to be active. I only wished to show in this that we ourselves recognise in the lowest forces of nature an eternity and ubiquity with regard to which the transitory nature of their fleeting phenomena never makes us err for a moment. So much the less, then, should it come into our mind to regard the ceasing of life as the annihilation of the living principle, and consequently death as the entire destruction of the man. Because the strong arm which, three thousand years ago, bent the bow of Ulysses is no more, no reflective and well-regulated understanding will regard the force which acted so energetically in it as entirely annihilated, and therefore, upon further reflection, will also not assume that the force which bends the bow to-day first began with this arm. The thought lies far nearer us, that the force which earlier actuated the life which now has vanished is the same which is active in the life which now flourishes: nay, this is almost inevitable. Certainly, however, we know that, as was explained in the second book, only that is perishable which is involved in the causal series; but only the states and forms are so involved. On the other hand, untouched by the change of these which is introduced by causes, there remain on the one side matter, and on the other side natural forces: for both are the presupposition of all these changes. But the principle of our life we must, primarily at least, conceive as a force of nature, until perhaps a more profound investigation has brought us to know what it is in itself. Thus, taken simply as a force of nature, the vital force remains entirely undisturbed by the change of forms and states, which the bond of cause and effect introduces and carries off again, and which alone are subject to the process of coming into being and passing away, as it lies before us in experience. Thus so far the imperishable nature of our true being can be proved with certainty. But it is true this will not satisfy the claims which are wont to be made upon proofs of our continued existence after death, nor insure the consolation which is expected from such proofs. However, it is always something; and whoever fears death as an absolute annihilation cannot afford to despise the perfect certainty that the inmost principle of his life remains untouched by it. Nay, the paradox might be set up, that that second thing also which, just like the forces of nature, remains untouched by the continual change under the guidance of causality, thus matter, by its absolute permanence, insures us indestructibility, by virtue of which whoever was incapable of comprehending any other might yet confidently trust in a certain imperishableness. "What!" it will be said, "the permanence of the mere dust, of the crude matter, is to be regarded as a continuance of our being?" Oh! do you know this dust, then? Do you know what it is and what it can do? Learn to know it before you despise it. This matter which now lies there as dust and ashes will soon, dissolved in water, form itself as a crystal, will shine as metal, will then emit electric sparks, will by means of its galvanic intensity manifest a force which, decomposing the closest combinations, reduces earths to metals; nay, it will, of its own accord, form itself into plants and animals, and from its mysterious womb develop that life for the loss of which you, in your narrowness, are so painfully anxious. Is it, then, absolutely nothing to continue to exist as such matter? Nay, I seriously assert that even this permanence of matter affords evidence of the indestructibility of our true nature, though only as in an image or simile, or, rather, only as in outline. To see this we only need to call to mind the explanation of matter given in chapter 24, from which it resulted that mere formless matter—this basis of the world of experience which is never perceived for itself alone, but assumed as constantly remaining—is the immediate reflection, the visibility in general, of the thing in itself, thus of the will. Therefore, whatever absolutely pertains to the will as such holds good also of matter, and it reflects the true eternal nature of the will under the image of temporal imperishableness. Because, as has been said, nature does not lie, no view which has sprung from a purely objective comprehension of it, and been logically thought out, can be absolutely false, but at the most only very one-sided and imperfect. Such, however, is, indisputably, consistent materialism; for instance, that of Epicurus, just as well as the absolute idealism opposed to it, like that of Berkeley, and in general every philosophical point of view which has proceeded from a correct *apperçu*, and been honestly carried out. Only they are all exceedingly one-sided comprehensions, and therefore, in spite of their opposition, they are all true, each from a definite point of view; but as soon as one has risen above this point of view, then they only appear as relatively and conditionally true. The highest standpoint alone, from which one surveys them all and knows them in their relative truth, but also beyond this, in their falseness, can be that of absolute truth so far as this is in general attainable. Accordingly we see, as was shown above, that in the very crude, and therefore very old, point of view of materialism proper the indestructibility of our true nature in itself is represented, as by a mere shadow of it, the imperishableness of matter; as in the already higher naturalism of an absolute physics it is represented by the ubiquity and eternity of the natural forces, among which the vital force is at least to be counted. Thus even these crude points of view contain the assertion that the living being suffers no absolute annihilation through death, but continues to exist in and with the whole of nature.

The considerations which have brought us to this point, and to which the further explanations link themselves on, started from the remarkable fear of death which fills all living beings. But now we will change the standpoint and consider how, in contrast to the individual beings, the *whole* of nature bears itself with reference to death. In doing this, however, we still always remain upon the ground of experience.

Certainly we know no higher game of chance than that for death and life. Every decision about this we watch with the utmost excitement, interest, and fear; for in our eyes all in all is at stake. On the other hand, nature, which never lies, but is always straightforward and open, speaks quite differently upon this theme, speaks like Krishna in the Bhagavadgita. What it says is: The death or the life of the individual is of no significance. It expresses this by the fact that it exposes the life of every brute, and even of man, to the most insignificant accidents without coming to the rescue. Consider the insect on your path; a slight, unconscious turning of your step is decisive as to its life or death. Look at the wood-snail, without any means of flight, of defence, of deception, of concealment, a ready prey for all. Look at the fish carelessly playing in the still open net; the frog restrained by its laziness from the flight which might save it; the bird that does not know of the falcon that soars above it; the sheep which the wolf eyes and examines from the thicket. All these, provided with little foresight, go about guilelessly among the dangers that threaten their existence every moment. Since now nature exposes its organisms, constructed with such inimitable skill, not only to the predatory instincts of the stronger, but also to the blindest chance, to the humour of every fool, the mischievousness of every child without reserve, it declares that the annihilation of these individuals is indifferent to it, does it no harm, has no significance, and that in these cases the effect is of no more importance than the cause. It says this very distinctly, and it does not lie; only it makes no comments on its utterances, but rather expresses them in the laconic style of an oracle. If now the all-mother sends forth her children without protection to a thousand threatening dangers, this can only be because she knows that if they fall they fall back into her womb, where they are safe; therefore their fall is a mere jest. Nature does not act otherwise with man than with the brutes. Therefore its declaration extends also to man: the life and death of the individual are indifferent to it. Accordingly, in a certain sense, they ought also to be indifferent to us, for we ourselves are indeed nature. Certainly, if only we saw deep enough, we would agree with nature, and regard life and death as indifferently as it does. Meanwhile, by means of reflection, we must attribute that carelessness and indifference of nature towards the life of the individuals to the fact that the destruction of such a phenomenon does not in the least affect its true and proper nature.

If we further ponder the fact, that not only, as we have just seen, are life and death dependent upon the most trifling accidents, but that the existence of the organised being in general is an ephemeral one, that animal and plant arise to-day and pass away to-morrow, and birth and death follow in quick succession, while to the unorganised things which stand so much lower an incomparably longer duration is assured, and an infinite duration to the absolutely formless matter alone, to which, indeed, we attribute this *a priori*,—then, I think, the thought must follow of its own accord, even from the purely empirical, but objective and unprejudiced comprehension of such an order of things, that this is only a superficial phenomenon, that such a constant arising and passing away can by no means touch the root of things, but can only be relative, nay, only apparent, in which the true inner nature of that thing is not included, the nature which everywhere evades our glance and is thoroughly mysterious, but rather that this continues to exist undisturbed by it; although we can neither apprehend nor conceive the manner in which this happens, and must therefore think of it only generally as a kind of *tour de passe-passe* which took place there. For that, while what is most imperfect, the lowest, the unorganised, continues to exist unassailed, it is just the most perfect beings, the living creatures, with their infinitely complicated and inconceivably ingenious organisations, which constantly arise, new from the very foundation, and after a brief span of time absolutely pass into nothingness, to make room for other new ones like them coming into existence out of nothing—this is something so obviously absurd that it can never be the true order of things, but rather a mere veil which conceals this, or, more accurately, a phenomenon conditioned by the nature of our intellect. Nay, the whole being and not being itself of these individuals, in relation to which death and life are opposites, can only be relative. Thus the language of nature, in which it is given us as absolute, cannot be the true and ultimate expression of the nature of things and of the order of the world, but indeed only a *patois du pays*, *i.e.*, something merely relatively true,—something to be understood *cum grano salis*, or, to speak properly, something conditioned by our intellect; I say, an immediate, intuitive conviction of the kind which I have tried to describe in words will press itself upon every one; *i.e.*, certainly only upon every one whose mind is not of an utterly ordinary species, which is absolutely only capable of knowing the particular simply and solely as such, which is strictly limited to the knowledge of individuals, after the manner of the intellect of the brutes. Whoever, on the other hand, by means of a capacity of an only somewhat higher power, even just begins to see in the individual beings their universal, their Ideas, will also, to a certain extent, participate in that conviction, and that indeed as an immediate, and therefore certain, conviction. In fact, it is also only small, limited minds that fear death quite seriously as their annihilation, and persons of decidedly superior capacity are completely free from such terrors. Plato rightly bases the whole of philosophy upon the knowledge of the doctrine of Ideas, *i.e.*, upon the perception of the universal in the particular. But the conviction here described, which proceeds directly from the comprehension of nature, must have been exceedingly vivid in those sublime authors of the Upanishads of the Vedas, who can scarcely be thought of as mere men, for it speaks to us so forcibly out of an innumerable number of their utterances that we must ascribe this immediate illumination of their mind to the fact that these wise men, standing nearer the origin of our race in time, comprehended the nature of things more clearly and profoundly than the already deteriorated race, *ὁιοι νυν βροτοι εισιν*, is able to do. But certainly their comprehension is assisted by the natural world of India, which is endowed with life in a very different degree from our northern world. However, thorough reflection, as pursued by Kant's great mind, leads by another path to the same result, for it teaches us that our intellect, in which that phenomenal world which changes so fast exhibits itself, does not comprehend the true ultimate nature of things, but merely its phenomenal manifestation, and indeed, as I add, because it is originally only destined to present the motives to our will, *i.e.*, to be serviceable to it in the pursuit of its paltry ends.

Let us, however, carry our objective and unprejudiced consideration of nature still further. If I kill a living creature, whether a dog, a bird, a frog, or even only an insect, it is really inconceivable that this being, or rather the original force by virtue of which such a marvellous phenomenon exhibited itself just the moment before, in its full energy and love of life, should have been annihilated by my wicked or thoughtless act. And again, on the other hand, the millions of animals of every kind which come into existence every moment, in infinite variety, full of force and activity, can never, before the act of their generation, have been nothing at all, and have attained from nothing to an absolute beginning. If now in this way I see one of these withdraw itself from my sight, without me knowing where it goes, and another appear without me knowing whence it comes; if, moreover, both have the same form, the same nature, the same character, and only not the same matter, which yet during their existence they continually throw off and renew; then certainly the assumption, that that which vanishes and that which appears in its place are one and the same, which has only experienced a slight alteration, a renewal of the form of its existence, and that consequently death is for the species what sleep is for the individual; this assumption, I say, lies so close at hand that it is impossible not to light upon it, unless the mind, perverted in early youth by the imprinting of false views, hurries it out of the way, even from a distance, with superstitious fear. But the opposite assumption that the birth of an animal is an arising out of nothing, and accordingly that its death is its absolute annihilation, and this with the further addition that man, who has also originated out of nothing, has yet an individual, endless existence, and indeed a conscious existence, while the dog, the ape, the elephant, are annihilated by death, is really something against which the healthy mind revolts and which it must regard as absurd. If, as is sufficiently often repeated, the comparison of the results of a system with the utterances of the healthy mind is supposed to be a touchstone of its truth, I wish the adherents of the system which was handed down from Descartes to the pre-Kantian eclectics, nay, which even now is still the prevailing view of the great majority of cultured people in Europe, would apply this touchstone here.

Throughout and everywhere the true symbol of nature is the circle, because it is the schema or type of recurrence. This is, in fact, the most universal form in nature, which it carries out in everything, from the course of the stars down to the death and the genesis of organised beings, and by which alone, in the ceaseless stream of time, and its content, a permanent existence, *i.e.*, a nature, becomes possible.

If in autumn we consider the little world of insects, and see how one prepares its bed to sleep the long, rigid winter-sleep; another spins its coccoon to pass the winter as a chrysalis, and awake in spring rejuvenated and perfected; and, finally, how most of them, intending themselves to rest in the arms of death, merely arrange with care the suitable place for their egg, in order to issue forth again from it some day renewed;—this is nature's great doctrine of immortality, which seeks to teach us that there is no radical difference between sleep and death, but the one endangers existence just as little as the other. The care with which the insect prepares a cell, or hole, or nest, deposits its egg in it, together with food for the larva that will come out of it in the following spring, and then quietly dies, is just like the care with which in the evening a man lays ready his clothes and his breakfast for the next morning, and then quietly goes to sleep; and at bottom it could not take place at all if it were not that the insect which dies in autumn is in itself, and according to its true nature, just as much identical with the one which is hatched out in the spring as the man who lies down to sleep is identical with the man who rises from it.

If now, after these considerations, we return to ourselves and our own species, then cast our glance forward far into the future, and seek to present to our minds the future generations, with the millions of their individuals in the strange form of their customs and pursuits, and then interpose with the question: Whence will all these come? Where are they now? Where is the fertile womb of that nothing, pregnant with worlds, which still conceals the coming races? Would not the smiling and true answer to this be, Where else should they be than there where alone the real always was and will be, in the present and its content?—thus with thee, the foolish questioner, who in this mistaking of his own nature is like the leaf upon the tree, which, fading in autumn and about to fall, complains at its destruction, and will not be consoled by looking forward to the fresh green which will clothe the tree in spring, but says lamenting, "I am not these! These are quite different leaves!" Oh, foolish leaf! Whither wilt thou? And whence should others come? Where is the nothing whose abyss thou fearest? Know thine own nature, that which is so filled with thirst for existence; recognise it in the inner, mysterious, germinating force of the tree, which, constantly *one* and the same in all generations of leaves, remains untouched by all arising and passing away. And now, *οιη περ φυλλων γενεη, τοιηδε και ανδρων* (*Qualis foliorum generatio, talis et hominum*). Whether the fly which now buzzes round me goes to sleep in the evening, and buzzes again to-morrow, or dies in the evening, and in spring another fly buzzes which has sprung from its egg: that is in itself the same thing; but therefore the knowledge which exhibits this as two fundamentally different things is not unconditioned, but relative; a knowledge of the phenomenon, not of the thing in itself. In the morning the fly exists again; it also exists again in the spring. What distinguishes for it the winter from the night? In Burdach's "Physiology," vol. i. § 275, we read, "Till ten o'clock in the morning no *Cercaria ephemera* (one of the infusoria) is to be seen (in the infusion), and at twelve the whole water swarms with them. In the evening they die, and the next morning they again appear anew." So it was observed by Nitzsch six days running.

So everything lingers but a moment, and hastens on to death. The plant and the insect die at the end of the summer, the brute and the man after a few years: death reaps unweariedly. Yet notwithstanding this, nay, as if this were not so at all, everything is always there and in its place, just as if everything were imperishable. The plant always thrives and blooms, the insect hums, the brute and the man exist in unwasted youth, and the cherries that have already been enjoyed a thousand times we have again before us every summer. The nations also exist as immortal individuals, although sometimes their names change; even their action, what they do and suffer, is always the same; although history always pretends to relate something different: for it is like the kaleidoscope, which at every turn shows a new figure, while we really always have the same thing before our eyes. What then presses itself more irresistibly upon us than the thought that that arising and passing away does not concern the real nature of things, but this remains untouched by it, thus is imperishable, and therefore all and each that *wills* to exist actually exists continuously and without end. Accordingly at every given point of time all species of animals, from the gnat to the elephant, exist together complete. They have already renewed themselves many thousand times, and withal have remained the same. They know nothing of others like them, who have lived before them, or will live after them; it is the species which always lives, and in the consciousness of the imperishable nature of the species and their identity with it the individuals cheerfully exist. The will to live manifests itself in an endless present, because this is the form of the life of the species, which, therefore, never grows old, but remains always young. Death is for it what sleep is for the individual, or what winking is for the eye, by the absence of which the Indian gods are known, if they appear in human form. As through the entrance of night the world vanishes, but yet does not for a moment cease to exist, so man and brute apparently pass away through death, and yet their true nature continues, just as undisturbed by it. Let us now think of that alternation of death and birth as infinitely rapid vibrations, and we have before us the enduring objectification of the will, the permanent Ideas of being, fixed like the rainbow on the waterfall. This is temporal immortality. In consequence of this, notwithstanding thousands of years of death and decay, nothing has been lost, not an atom of the matter, still less anything of the inner being, that exhibits itself as nature. Therefore every moment we can cheerfully cry, "In spite of time, death, and decay, we are still all together!"

Perhaps we would have to except whoever had once said from the bottom of his heart, with regard to this game, "I want no more." But this is not yet the place to speak of this.

But we have certainly to draw attention to the fact that the pain of birth and the bitterness of death are the two constant conditions under which the will to live maintains itself in its objectification, *i.e.*, our inner nature, untouched by the course of time and the death of races, exists in an everlasting present, and enjoys the fruit of the assertion of the will to live. This is analogous to the fact that we can only be awake during the day on condition that we sleep during the night; indeed the latter is the commentary which nature offers us for the understanding of that difficult passage.[1]

For the substratum, or the content, πληρωμα, or the material of the *present*, is through all time really the same. The impossibility of knowing this identity directly is just *time*, a form and limitation of our intellect. That on account of it, for example, the future event is not yet, depends upon an illusion of which we become conscious when that event has come. That the essential form of our intellect introduces such an illusion explains and justifies itself from the fact that the intellect has come forth from the hands of nature by no means for the apprehension of the nature of things, but merely for the apprehension of motives, thus for the service of an individual and temporal phenomenon of will.[2]

Whoever comprehends the reflections which here occupy us will also understand the true meaning of the paradoxical doctrine of the Eleatics, that there is no arising and passing away, but the whole remains immovable: "*Παρμενιδης και Μελισσος ανηρουν γενεσιν και φθοραν, δια το νομιξειν το παν ακινητον*" (*Parmenides et Melissus ortum et interitum tollebant, quoniam nihil moveri putabant*), *Stob. Ecl.*, i. 21. Light is also thrown here upon the beautiful passage of Empedocles which Plutarch has preserved for us in the book, "*Adversus Coloten*," c. 12:—

[1] The suspension of the *animal* functions is sleep, that of the *organic* functions is death.

[2] There is only *one present*, and this is always: for it is the sole form of actual existence. One must attain to the insight that the *past* is not *in itself* different from the present, but only in our apprehension, which has time as its form, on account of which alone the present exhibits itself as different from the past. To assist this insight, imagine all the events and scenes of human life, bad and good, fortunate and unfortunate, pleasing and terrible as they successively present themselves in the course of time and difference of places, in the most checkered multifariousness and variety, as *at once and together*, and always present in the *Nunc stans*, while it is only apparently that now this and now that is; then what the objectification of the will to live really means will be understood. Our pleasure also in *genre* painting depends principally upon the fact that it fixes the fleeting scenes of life. The dogma of metempsychosis has proceeded from the feeling of the truth which has just been expressed.

"Νηπιοι· όυ γαρ σφιν δολιχοφρονες εισι μεριμναι,
Οἱ δη γινεσθαι παρος ουκ εον ελπιζουσι,
Η τι καταθνησκειν και εξολλυσθαι ἁπαντη.
Ουκ αν ανηρ τοιαυτα σοφος φρεσι μαντευσαιτο,
Ὡς οφρα μεν τε βιωσι (το δη βιοτον καλεουσι),
Τοφρα μεν ουν εισιν, και σφιν παρα δεινα και ἐσθλα
Πριν τε παγεν τε βροτοι, και επει λυθεν, ουδεν αρ' ἐισιν."

(Stulta, et prolixas non admittentia curas
Pectora: qui sperant, existere posse, quod ante
Non fuit, aut ullam rem pessum protinus ire;—
Non animo prudens homo quod præsentiat ullus,
Dum vivunt (namque hoc vitaï nomine signant),
Sunt, et fortuna tum conflictantur utraque:
Ante ortum nihil est homo, nec post funera quidquam.)

The very remarkable and, in its place, astonishing passage in Diderot's "*Jacques le fataliste*," deserves not less to be mentioned here: "*Un château immense, au frontispice duquel on lisait: 'Je n'appartiens à personne, et j'appartiens à tout le monde: vous y étiez avant que d'y entrer, vous y serez encore, quand vous en sortirez.'*"

Certainly in the sense in which, when he is begotten, the man arises out of nothing, he becomes nothing through death. But really to learn to know this "nothing" would be very interesting; for it only requires moderate acuteness to see that this empirical nothing is by no means absolute, *i.e.*, such as would in every sense be nothing. We are already led to this insight by the observation that all qualities of the parents recur in the children, thus have overcome death. Of this, however, I will speak in a special chapter.

There is no greater contrast than that between the ceaseless flight of time, which carries its whole content with it, and the rigid immobility of what is actually present, which at all times is one and the same. And if from this point of view we watch in a purely objective manner the immediate events of life, the *Nunc stans* becomes clear and visible to us in the centre of the wheel of time. To the eye of a being of incomparably longer life, which at *one* glance comprehended the human race in its whole duration, the constant alternation of birth and death would present itself as a continuous vibration, and accordingly it would not occur to it at all to see in this an ever new arising out of nothing and passing into nothing; but just as to our sight the quickly revolving spark appears as a continuous circle, the rapidly vibrating spring as a permanent triangle, the vibrating cord as a spindle, so to this eye the species would appear as that which has being and permanence, death and life as vibrations.

We will have false conceptions of the indestructibility of our true nature by death, so long as we do not make up our minds to study it primarily in the brutes, but claim for ourselves alone a class apart from them, under the boastful name of immortality. But it is this pretension alone, and the narrowness of view from which it proceeds, on account of which most men struggle so obstinately against the recognition of the obvious truth that we are essentially, and in the chief respect, the same as the brutes; nay, that they recoil at every hint of our relationship with these. But it is this denial of the truth which more than anything else closes against them the path to real knowledge of the indestructibility of our nature. For if we seek anything upon a wrong path, we have just on that account forsaken the right path, and upon the path we follow we will never attain to anything in the end but late disillusion. Up, then, follow the truth, not according to preconceived notions, but as nature leads! First of all, learn to recognise in the aspect of every young animal the existence of the species that never grows old, which, as a reflection of its eternal youth, imparts to every individual a temporary youth, and lets it come forth as new and fresh as if the world were of to-day. Let one ask himself honestly whether the swallow of this year's spring is absolutely a different one from the swallow of the first spring, and whether really between the two the miracle of the creation out of nothing has repeated itself millions of times, in order to work just as often into the hands of absolute annihilation. I know well that if I seriously assured any one that the cat which now plays in the yard is still the same one which made the same springs and played the same tricks there three hundred years ago, he would think I was mad; but I also know that it is much madder to believe that the cat of to-day is through and through and in its whole nature quite a different one from the cat of three hundred years ago. One only requires truly and seriously to sink oneself in the contemplation of one of these higher vertebrates in order to become distinctly conscious that this unfathomable nature, taken as a whole, as it exists there, cannot possibly become nothing; and yet, on the other hand, one knows its transitoriness. This depends upon the fact that in this animal the infinite nature of its Idea (species) is imprinted in the finiteness of the individual. For in a certain sense it is of course true that in the individual we always have before us another being—in the sense which depends upon the principle of sufficient reason, in which are also included time and space, which constitute the *principium individuationis.* But in another sense it is not true—in the sense in which reality belongs to the permanent forms of things, the Ideas alone, and which was so clearly evident to Plato that it became his fundamental thought, the centre of his philosophy; and he made the comprehension of it the criterion of capacity for philosophising in general.

As the scattered drops of the roaring waterfall change with lightning rapidity, while the rainbow, whose supporter they are, remains immovably at rest, quite untouched by that ceaseless change, so every Idea, *i.e.*, every species of living creature remains quite untouched by the continual change of its individuals. But it is the Idea, or the species in which the will to live is really rooted, and manifests itself; and therefore also the will is only truly concerned in the continuance of the species. For example, the lions which are born and die are like the drops of the waterfall; but the *leonitas*, the Idea or form of the lion, is like the unshaken rainbow upon it. Therefore Plato attributed true being to the Ideas alone, *i.e.*, to the species; to the individuals only a ceaseless arising and passing away. From the profound consciousness of his imperishable nature really springs also the confidence and peace of mind with which every brute, and even human individual, moves unconcernedly along amid a host of chances, which may annihilate it any moment, and, moreover, moves straight on to death: out of its eyes, however, there shines the peace of the species, which that death does not affect, and does not concern. Even to man this peace could not be imparted by uncertain and changing dogmas. But, as was said, the contemplation of every animal teaches that death is no obstacle to the kernel of life, to the will in its manifestation. What an unfathomable mystery lies, then, in every animal! Look at the nearest one; look at your dog, how cheerfully and peacefully he lives! Many thousands of dogs have had to die before it came to this one's turn to live. But the death of these thousands has not affected the Idea of the dog; it has not been in the least disturbed by all that dying. Therefore the dog exists as fresh and endowed with primitive force as if this were its first day and none could ever be its last; and out of its eyes there shines the indestructible principle in it, the archæus. What, then, has died during those thousands of years? Not the dog—it stands unscathed before us; merely its shadow, its image in our form of knowledge, which is bound to time. Yet how can one even believe that that passes away which for ever and ever exists and fills all time? Certainly the matter can be explained empirically; in proportion as death destroyed the individuals, generation produced new ones. But this empirical explanation is only an apparent explanation: it puts one riddle in the place of the other. The metaphysical understanding of the matter, although not to be got so cheaply, is yet the only true and satisfying one.

Kant, in his subjective procedure, brought to light the truth that time cannot belong to the thing in itself, because it lies pre-formed in our apprehension. Now death is the temporal end of the temporal phenomenon; but as soon as we abstract time, there is no longer any end, and this word has lost all significance. But I, here upon the objective path, am trying to show the positive side of the matter, that the thing in itself remains untouched by time, and by that which is only possible through time, arising and passing away, and that the phenomena in time could not have even that ceaselessly fleeting existence which stands next to nothingness, if there were not in them a kernel of the infinite. Eternity is certainly a conception which has no perception as its foundation; accordingly it has also a merely negative content; it signifies a timeless existence. Time is yet merely an image of eternity, *ὁ χρονος εἰκων του αἰωνος*, as Plotinus has it; and in the same way our temporal existence is a mere image of our true nature. This must lie in eternity, just because time is only the form of our knowledge; but on account of this alone do we know our own existence, and that of all things as transitory, finite, and subject to annihilation.

In the second book I have shown that the adequate objectivity of the will as the thing in itself, at each of its grades, is the (Platonic) Idea; similarly in the third book that the Ideas of things have the pure subject of knowledge as their correlative; consequently the knowledge of them only appears exceptionally and temporarily under specially favourable conditions. For individual knowledge, on the other hand, thus in time, the *Idea* presents itself under the form of the *species*, which is the Idea broken up through its entrance into time. Therefore the species is the most immediate objectification of the thing in itself, *i.e.*, of the will to live. The inmost nature of every brute, and also of man, accordingly lies in the species; thus the will to live, which is so powerfully active, is rooted in this, not really in the individual. On the other hand, in the individual alone lies the immediate consciousness: accordingly it imagines itself different from the species, and therefore fears death. The will to live manifests itself in relation to the individual as hunger and the fear of death: in relation to the species as sexual instinct and passionate care for the offspring. In agreement with this we find nature, which is free from that delusion of the individual, as careful for the maintenance of the species as it is indifferent to the destruction of the individuals: the latter are always only means, the former is the end. Therefore a glaring contrast appears between its niggardliness in the endowment of the individuals and its prodigality when the species is concerned. In the latter case from *one* individual are often annually obtained a hundred thousand germs, and more; for example, from trees, fishes, crabs, termites, and many others. In the former case, on the contrary, only barely enough in the way of powers and organs is given to each to enable it with ceaseless effort to maintain its life. And, therefore, if an animal is injured or weakened it must, as a rule, starve. And where an incidental saving was possible, through the circumstance that one part could upon necessity be dispensed with, it has been withheld, even out of order. Hence, for example, many caterpillars are without eyes; the poor creatures grope in the dark from leaf to leaf, which, since they lack feelers, they do by moving three-fourths of their body back and forward in the air, till they find some object. Hence they often miss their food which is to be found close by. But this happens in consequence of the *lex parsimoniæ naturæ*, to the expression of which *natura nihil facit supervacaneum* one may add *et nihil largitur*. The same tendency of nature shows itself also in the fact that the more fit the individual is, on account of his age, for the propagation of the species, the more powerfully does the *vis naturæ medicatrix* manifest itself in him, and therefore his wounds heal easily, and he easily recovers from diseases. This diminishes along with the power of generation, and sinks low after it is extinct; for now in the eyes of nature the individual has become worthless.

If now we cast another glance at the scale of existences, with the whole of their accompanying gradations of consciousness, from the polyp up to man, we see this wonderful pyramid, kept in ceaseless oscillation certainly by the constant death of the individuals, yet by means of the bond of generation, enduring in the species through the infinite course of time. While, then, as was explained above, the *objective*, the species, presents itself as indestructible, the *subjective*, which consists merely in the self-consciousness of these beings, seems to be of the shortest duration, and to be unceasingly destroyed, in order, just as often, to come forth again from nothing in an incomprehensible manner. But, indeed, one must be very short-sighted to let oneself be deceived by this appearance, and not to comprehend that, although the form of temporal permanence only belongs to the objective, the subjective, *i.e.*, the will, which lives and manifests itself in all, and with it the subject of the *knowledge* in which all exhibits itself, must be not less indestructible; because the permanence of the objective, or external, can yet only be the phenomenal appearance of the indestructibility of the subjective or internal; for the former can possess nothing which it has not received on loan from the latter; and cannot be essentially and originally an objective, a phenomenon, and then secondarily and accidentally a subjective, a thing in itself, a self-consciousness. For clearly the former as a manifestation presupposes something which manifests itself, as being for other presupposes a being for self, and as object presupposes a subject; and not conversely: because everywhere the root of things must lie in that which they are for themselves, thus in the subjective, not in the objective, *i.e.*, in that which they are only for others, in a foreign consciousness. Accordingly we found in the first book that the right starting-point for philosophy is essentially and necessarily the subjective, *i.e.*, the idealistic starting-point; and also that the opposite starting-point, that which proceeds from the objective, leads to materialism. At bottom, however, we are far more one with the world than we commonly suppose: its inner nature is our will, its phenomenal appearance is our idea. For any one who could bring this unity of being to distinct consciousness, the difference between the continuance of the external world after his death and his own continuance after death would vanish. The two would present themselves to him as one and the same; nay, he would laugh at the delusion that could separate them. For the understanding of the indestructibility of our nature coincides with that of the identity of the macrocosm and the microcosm. Meanwhile one may obtain light upon what is said here by a peculiar experiment, performed by means of the imagination, an experiment which might be called metaphysical. Let any one try to present vividly to his mind the time, in any case not far distant, when he will be dead. Then he thinks himself away and lets the world go on existing; but soon, to his own astonishment, he will discover that he was nevertheless still there. For he intended to present the world to his mind without himself; but the ego is the immediate element in consciousness, through which alone the world is brought about, and for which alone it exists. This centre of all existence, this kernel of all reality, is to be abolished, and yet the world is to go on existing; it is a thought which can be conceived in the abstract, but not realised. The endeavour to accomplish this, the attempt to think the secondary without the primary, the conditioned without the condition, that which is supported without the supporter, always fails, much in the same way as the attempt to think an equilateral, right-angled triangle, or a destruction or origination of matter, and similar impossibilities. Instead of what was intended, the feeling here presses upon us that the world is not less in us than we in it, and that the source of all reality lies within us. The result is really this: the time when I shall not be will objectively come; but subjectively it can never come. It might therefore, indeed, be asked, how far every one, in his heart, actually believes in a thing which he really cannot conceive at all; or whether, since the profound consciousness of the indestructibleness of our true nature associates itself with that merely intellectual experiment, which, however, has already been made more or less distinctly by every one, whether, I say, our own death is not perhaps for us at bottom the most incredible thing in the world.

The deep conviction of the indestructibleness of our nature through death, which, as is also shown by the inevitable qualms of conscience at its approach, every one carries at the bottom of his heart, depends altogether upon the consciousness of the original and eternal nature of our being: therefore Spinoza expresses it thus: "*Sentimus, experimurque, nos æternos esse.*" For a reasonable man can only think of himself as imperishable, because he thinks of himself as without beginning, as eternal, in fact as timeless. Whoever, on the other hand, regards himself as having become out of nothing must also think that he will again become nothing; for that an eternity had passed before he was, and then a second eternity had begun, through which he will never cease to be, is a monstrous thought. Really the most solid ground for our immortality is the old principle: "*Ex nihilo nihil fit, et in nihilum nihil potest reverti.*" Theophrastus Paracelsus very happily says (Works, Strasburg, 1603, vol. ii. p. 6): "The soul in me has arisen out of something; therefore it does not come to nothing; for it comes out of something." He gives the true reason. But whoever regards the birth of the man as his absolute beginning must regard death as his absolute end. For both are what they are in the same sense; consequently every one can only think of himself as *immortal* so far as he also thinks of himself as *unborn*, and in the same sense. What birth is, that also is death, according to its nature and significance: it is the same line drawn in two directions. If the former is an actual arising out of nothing, then the latter is also an actual annihilation. But in truth it is only by means of the *eternity* of our real being that we can conceive it as imperishable, and consequently this imperishableness is not temporal. The assumption that man is made out of nothing leads necessarily to the assumption that death is his absolute end. Thus in this the Old Testament is perfectly consistent; for no doctrine of immortality is suitable to a creation out of nothing. New Testament Christianity has such a doctrine because it is Indian in spirit, and therefore more than probably also of Indian origin, although only indirectly, through Egypt. But to the Jewish stem, upon which that Indian wisdom had to be grafted in the Holy Land, such a doctrine is as little suited as the freedom of the will to its determinism, or as

> "*Humano capiti cervicem pictor equinam*
> *Jungere si velit.*"

It is always bad if one cannot be thoroughly original, and dare not carve out of the whole wood. Brahmanism and Buddhism, on the other hand, have quite consistently, besides the continued existence after death, an existence before birth to expiate the guilt of which we have this life. Moreover, how distinctly conscious they were of the necessary consistency in this is shown by the following passage from Colebrooke's "History of the Indian Philosophy" in the "Transac. of the Asiatic London Society,' vol. i. p. 577: "Against the system of the Bhagavatas which is but partially heretical, the objection upon which the chief stress is laid by Vyaso is, that the soul would not be eternal if it were a production, and consequently had a beginning." Further, in Upham's "Doctrine of Buddhism," p. 110, it is said: "The lot in hell of impious persons called Deitty is the most severe: these are they who, discrediting the evidence of Buddha, adhere to the heretical doctrine that all living beings had their beginning in the mother's womb, and will have their end in death."

Whoever conceives his existence as merely accidental must certainly fear that he will lose it by death. On the other hand, whoever sees, even only in general, that his existence rests upon some kind of original necessity will not believe that this which has produced so wonderful a thing is limited to such a brief span of time, but that it is active in every one. But he will recognise his existence as necessary who reflects that up till now, when he exists, already an infinite time, thus also an infinity of changes, has run its course, but in spite of this he yet exists; thus the whole range of all possible states has already exhausted itself without being able to destroy his existence. *If he could ever not be, he would already not be now.* For the infinity of the time that has already elapsed, with the exhausted possibility of the events in it, guarantees that *what exists, exists necessarily.* Therefore every one must conceive himself as a necessary being, *i.e.*, as a being whose existence would follow from its true and exhaustive definition if one only had it. In this line of thought, then, really lies the only immanent proof of the imperishableness of our nature, *i.e.*, the only proof of this that holds good within the sphere of empirical data. In this nature existence must inhere, because it shows itself as independent of all states which can possibly be introduced through the chain of causes; for these states have already done what they could, and yet our existence has remained unshaken by it, as the ray of light by the storm wind which it cuts through. If time, of its own resources, could bring us to a happy state, then we would already have been there long ago; for an infinite time lies behind us. But also: if it could lead us to destruction, we would already have long been no more. From the fact that we now exist, it follows, if well considered, that we must at all times exist. For we are ourselves the nature which time has taken up into itself in order to fill its void; consequently it fills the whole of time, present, past, and future, in the same way, and it is just as impossible for us to fall out of existence as to fall out of space. Carefully considered, it is inconceivable that what once exists in all the strength of reality should ever become nothing, and then not be, through an infinite time. Hence has arisen the Christian doctrine of the restoration of all things, that of the Hindus of the constantly repeated creation of the world by Brahma, together with similar dogmas of the Greek philosophers. The great mystery of our being and not being, to explain which these and all kindred dogmas have been devised, ultimately rests upon the fact that the same thing which objectively constitutes an infinite course of time is subjectively an indivisible, ever present present: but who comprehends it? It has been most distinctly set forth by Kant in his immortal doctrine of the ideality of time and the sole reality of the thing in itself. For it results from this that the really essential part of things, of man, of the world, lies permanently and enduringly in the *Nunc stans*, firm and immovable; and that the change of the phenomena and events is a mere consequence of our apprehension of them by means of our form of perception, which is time. Accordingly, instead of saying to men, "Ye have arisen through birth, but are immortal," one ought to say to them, "Ye are not nothing," and teach them to understand this in the sense of the saying attributed to Hermes Trismegistus, "*Το γαρ ὀν ἀει ἐσται*" (*Quod enim est, erit semper*), *Stob. Ecl.*, i. 43, 6. If, however, this does not succeed, but the anxious heart raises its old lament, "I see all beings arise through birth out of nothing, and after a brief term again return to this; my existence also, now in the present, will soon lie in the distant past, and I will be nothing!"—the right answer is, "Dost thou not exist? Hast thou not within thee the valuable present, after which ye children of time so eagerly strive, now within, actually within? And dost thou understand how thou hast attained to it? Knowest thou the paths which have led thee to it, that thou canst know they will be shut against thee by death? An existence of thyself after the destruction of thy body is not conceivable by thee as possible; but can it be more inconceivable to thee than thy present existence, and how thou hast attained to it? Why shouldst thou doubt but that the secret paths to this present, which stood open to thee, will also stand open to every future present?"

If, then, considerations of this kind are at any rate adapted to awaken the conviction that there is something in us which death cannot destroy, this yet only takes place by raising us to a point of view from which birth is not the beginning of our existence. But from this it follows that what is proved to be indestructible by death is not properly the individual, which, moreover, as having arisen through generation, and having in itself the qualities of the father and mother, presents itself as a mere difference of the species, but as such can only be finite. As, in accordance with this, the individual has no recollection of its existence before its birth, so it can have no remembrance of its present existence after death. But every one places his ego in *consciousness;* this seems to him therefore to be bound to individuality, with which, besides, everything disappears which is peculiar to him, as to this, and distinguishes him from others. His continued existence without individuality becomes to him therefore indistinguishable from the continuance of other beings, and he sees his ego sink. But whoever thus links his existence to the identity of consciousness, and therefore desires an endless existence after death for this, ought to reflect that he can certainly only attain this at the price of just as endless a past before birth. For since he has no remembrance of an existence before birth, thus his consciousness begins with birth, he must accept his birth as an origination of his existence out of nothing. But then he purchases the endless time of his existence after death for just as long a time before birth; thus the account balances without any profit for him. If, on the other hand, the existence which death leaves untouched is different from that of the individual consciousness, then it must be independent of birth, just as of death; and therefore, with regard to it, it must be equally true to say, "I will always be," and "I have always been;" which then gives two infinities for one. But the great equivocation really lies in the word "I," as any one will see at once who remembers the contents of our second book, and the separation which is made there of the willing from the knowing part of our nature. According as I understand this word I can say, "Death is my complete end;" or, "This my personal phenomenal existence is just as infinitely small a part of my true nature as I am of the world." But the "I" is the dark point in consciousness, as on the retina the exact point at which the nerve of sight enters is blind, as the brain itself is entirely without sensation, the body of the sun is dark, and the eye sees all except itself. Our faculty of knowledge is directed entirely towards without, in accordance with the fact that it is the product of a brain function, which has arisen for the purpose of mere self-maintenance, thus of the search for nourishment and the capture of prey. Therefore every one knows himself only as this individual as it presents itself in external perception. If, on the other hand, he could bring to consciousness what he is besides and beyond this, then he would willingly give up his individuality, smile at the tenacity of his attachment to it, and say, "What is the loss of this individuality to me, who bear in myself the possibility of innumerable individualities?" He would see that even if a continued existence of his individuality does not lie before him, it is yet quite as good as if he had such an existence, because he carries in himself complete compensation for it. Besides, however, it may further be taken into consideration that the individuality of most men is so miserable and worthless that with it they truly lose nothing, and that that in them which may still have some worth is the universal human element; but to this imperishableness can be promised. Indeed, even the rigid unalterableness and essential limitation of every individual would, in the case of an endless duration of it, necessarily at last produce such great weariness by its monotony that only to be relieved of this one would prefer to become nothing. To desire that the individuality should be immortal really means to wish to perpetuate an error infinitely. For at bottom every individuality is really only a special error, a false step, something that had better not be; nay, something which it is the real end of life to bring us back from. This also finds confirmation in the fact that the great majority, indeed really all men, are so constituted that they could not be happy in whatever kind of world they might be placed. In proportion as such a world excluded want and hardship, they would become a prey to ennui, and in proportion as this was prevented, they would fall into want, misery, and suffering. Thus for a blessed condition of man it would be by no means sufficient that he should be transferred to a "better world," but it would also be necessary that a complete change should take place in himself; that thus he should no longer be what he is, and, on the contrary, should become what he is not. But for this he must first of all cease to be what he is: this desideratum is, as a preliminary, supplied by death, the moral necessity of which can already be seen from this point of view. To be transferred to another world and to have his whole nature changed are, at bottom, one and the same. Upon this also ultimately rests that dependence of the objective upon the subjective which the idealism of our first book shows. Accordingly here lies the point at which the transcendent philosophy links itself on to ethics. If one considers this one will find that the awaking from the dream of life is only possible through the disappearance along with it of its whole ground-warp also. But this is its organ itself, the intellect together with its forms, with which the dream would spin itself out without end, so firmly is it incorporated with it. That which really dreamt this dream is yet different from it, and alone remains over. On the other hand, the fear that with death all will be over may be compared to the case of one who imagines in a dream that there are only dreams without a dreamer. But now, after an individual consciousness has once been ended by death, would it even be desirable that it should be kindled again in order to continue for ever? The greater part of its content, nay, generally its whole content, is nothing but a stream of small, earthly, paltry thoughts and endless cares. Let them, then, at last be stilled! Therefore with a true instinct, the ancients inscribed upon their gravestones: *Securitati perpetuæ*;—or *Bonæ quieti*. But if here, as so often has happened, a continued existence of the individual consciousness should be desired, in order to connect with it a future reward or punishment, what would really be aimed at in this would simply be the compatibility of virtue and egoism. But these two will never embrace: they are fundamentally opposed. On the other hand, the conviction is well founded, which the sight of noble conduct calls forth, that the spirit of love, which enjoins one man to spare his enemy, and another to protect at the risk of his life some one whom he has never seen before, can never pass away and become nothing.

The most thorough answer to the question as to the continued existence of the individual after death lies in Kant's great doctrine of the *ideality of time*, which just here shows itself specially fruitful and rich in consequences, for it substitutes a purely theoretical but well-proved insight for dogmas which upon one path as upon the other lead to the absurd, and thus settles at once the most exciting of all metaphysical questions. Beginning, ending, and continuing are conceptions which derive their significance simply and solely from time, and are therefore valid only under the presupposition of this. But time has no absolute existence; it is not the manner of being of the thing in itself, but merely the form of our *knowledge* of our existence and nature, and that of all things, which is just on this account very imperfect, and is limited to mere phenomena. Thus with reference to this knowledge alone do the conceptions of ceasing and continuing find application, not with reference to that which exhibits itself in these, the inner being of things in relation to which these conceptions have therefore no longer any meaning. For this shows itself also in the fact that an answer to the question which arises from those time-conceptions is impossible, and every assertion of such an answer, whether upon one side or the other, is open to convincing objections. One might indeed assert that our true being continues after death because it is false that it is destroyed; but one might just as well assert that it is destroyed because it is false that it continues: at bottom the one is as true as the other. Accordingly something like an antinomy might certainly be set up here. But it would rest upon mere negations. In it one would deny two contradictorily opposite predicates of the subject of the judgment, but only because the whole category of these predicates would be inapplicable to that subject. But if now one denies these two predicates, not together, but separately, it appears as if the contradictory opposite of the predicate which in each case is denied were proved of the subject of the judgment. This, however, depends upon the fact that here incommensurable quantities are compared, for the problem removes us to a scene where time is abolished, and yet asks about temporal properties which it is consequently equally false to attribute to, or to deny of the subject. This just means: the problem is transcendent. In this sense death remains a mystery.

On the other hand, adhering to that distinction between phenomenon and thing in itself, we can make the assertion that, as phenomenon, man is certainly perishable, but yet his true being will not be involved in this. Thus this true being is indestructible, although, on account of the elimination of time-conceptions which is connected with it, we cannot attribute to it continuance. Accordingly we would be led here to the conception of an indestructibility which would yet be no continuance. Now this is a conception which, having been obtained on the path of abstraction, can certainly also be thought in the abstract, but yet cannot be supported by any perception, and consequently cannot really become distinct; yet, on the other hand, we must here keep in mind that we have not, like Kant, absolutely given up the knowledge of the thing in itself, but know that it is to be sought for in the will. It is true that we have never asserted an absolute and exhaustive knowledge of the thing in itself, but rather have seen very well that it is impossible to know anything as it is absolutely and in itself. For as soon as I *know*, I have an idea; but this idea, just because it is *my* idea, cannot be identical with what is known, but repeats it in an entirely different form, for it makes a being for other out of a being for self, and is thus always to be regarded as a phenomenal appearance of the thing in itself. Therefore for a *knowing* consciousness, however it may be constituted, there can be always only phenomena. This is not entirely obviated even by the fact that it is my own nature which is known; for, since it falls within my *knowing* consciousness, it is already a reflex of my nature, something different from this itself, thus already in a certain degree phenomenon. So far, then, as I am a knowing being, I have even in my own nature really only a phenomenon; so far, on the other hand, as I am directly this nature itself, I am not a *knowing* being. For it is sufficiently proved in the second book that knowledge is only a secondary property of our being, and introduced by its animal nature. Strictly speaking, then, we know even our own will always merely as phenomenon, and not as it may be absolutely in and for itself. But in that second book, and also in my work upon the will in nature, it is fully explained and proved that if, in order to penetrate into the inner nature of things, leaving what is given merely indirectly and from without, we stick to the only phenomenon into the nature of which an immediate insight from within is attainable, we find in this quite definitely, as the ultimate kernel of reality, the will, in which therefore we recognise the thing in itself in so far as it has here no longer space, although it still has time, for its form consequently really only in its most immediate manifestation, and with the reservation that this knowledge of it is still not exhaustive and entirely adequate. Thus in this sense we retain here also the conception of will as that of the thing in itself.

The conception of ceasing to be is certainly applicable to man as a phenomenon in time, and empirical knowledge plainly presents death as the end of this temporal existence. The end of the person is just as real as was its beginning, and in the same sense as before birth we were not, after death we shall be no more. Yet no more can be destroyed by death than was produced by birth; thus not that through which birth first became possible. In this sense *natus et denatus* is a beautiful expression. But now the whole of empirical knowledge affords us merely phenomena; therefore only phenomena are involved in the temporal processes of coming into being and passing away, and not that which manifests itself in the phenomena, the thing in itself. For this the opposition of coming into being and passing away conditioned by the brain, does not exist at all, but has here lost meaning and significance. It thus remains untouched by the temporal end of a temporal phenomenon, and constantly retains that existence to which the conceptions of beginning, end, and continuance are not applicable. But the thing in itself, so far as we can follow it, is in every phenomenal being the will of this being: so also in man Consciousness, on the other hand, consists in knowledge. But knowledge, as activity of the brain, and consequently as function of the organism, belongs, as has been sufficiently proved, to the mere phenomenon, and therefore ends with this. The will alone, whose work, or rather whose image was the body, is that which is indestructible. The sharp distinction of will from knowledge, together with the primacy of the former, which constitutes the fundamental characteristic of my philosophy, is therefore the only key to the contradiction which presents itself in so many ways, and arises ever anew in every consciousness, even the most crude, that death is our end, and that yet we must be eternal and indestructible, thus the *sentimus, experimurque nos æternos esse* of Spinoza. All philosophers have erred in this: they place the metaphysical, the indestructible, the eternal element in man in the *intellect.* It lies exclusively in the *will,* which is entirely different from the intellect, and alone is original. The intellect, as was most fully shown in the second book, is a secondary phenomenon, and conditioned by the brain, therefore beginning and ending with this. The will alone is that which conditions, the kernel of the whole phenomenon, consequently free from the forms of the phenomenon to which time belongs, thus also indestructible. Accordingly with death consciousness is certainly lost, but not that which produced and sustained consciousness; life is extinguished, but not the principle of life also, which manifested itself in it. Therefore a sure feeling informs every one that there is something in him which is absolutely imperishable and indestructible. Indeed the freshness and vividness of memories of the most distant time, of earliest childhood, bears witness to the fact that something in us does not pass away with time, does not grow old, but endures unchanged. But what this imperishable element is one could not make clear to oneself. It is not consciousness any more than it is the body upon which clearly consciousness depends. But it is just that which, when it appears in consciousness, presents itself as *will*. Beyond this immediate manifestation of it we certainly cannot go; because we cannot go beyond consciousness; therefore the question what that may be when it does not come within consciousness, *i.e.*, what it is absolutely in itself, remains unanswerable.

In the phenomenon, and by means of its forms, time and space, as *principium individuationis*, what presents itself is that the human individual perishes, while the human race, on the contrary, always remains and lives. But in the true being of things, which is free from these forms, this whole distinction between the individual and the race also disappears, and the two are immediately one. The whole will to live is in the individual, as it is in the race, and therefore the continuance of the species is merely the image of the indestructibility of the individual.

Since, then, the infinitely important understanding of the indestructibility of our true nature by death depends entirely upon the distinction between phenomenon and thing in itself, I wish now to bring this difference into the clearest light by explaining it in the opposite of death, thus in the origin of the animal existence, *i.e.*, generation. For this process, which is just as mysterious as death, presents to us most directly the fundamental opposition between the phenomenal appearance and the true being of things, *i.e.*, between the world as idea and the world as will, and also the entire heterogeneity of the laws of these two. The act of procreation presents itself to us in a twofold manner: first, for self-conciousness, whose only object, as I have often shown, is the will, with all its affections; and then for the consciousness of other things, *i.e.*, the world of idea, or the empirical reality of things. Now, from the side of the will, thus inwardly, subjectively, for self-consciousness, that act presents itself as the most immediate and complete satisfaction of the will, *i.e.*, as sensual pleasure. From the side of the idea, on the other hand, thus externally, objectively, for the consciousness of other things, this act is just the woof of the most cunning of webs, the foundation of the inexpressibly complicated animal organism, which then only requires to be developed to become visible to our astonished eyes. This organism, whose infinite complication and perfection is only known to him who has studied anatomy, cannot, from the side of the idea, be otherwise conceived and thought of than as a system devised with the most ingenious forethought and carried out with the most consummate skill and exactness, as the most arduous work of profound reflection. But from the side of the will we know, through self-consciousness, the production of this organism as the work of an act which is exactly the opposite of all reflection, an impetuous, blind impulse, an exceedingly pleasurable sensation. This opposition is closely related to the infinite contrast, which is shown above, between the absolute facility with which nature produces its works, together with the correspondingly boundless carelessness with which it abandons them to destruction, and the incalculably ingenious and studied construction of these very works, judging from which they must have been infinitely difficult to make, and their maintenance should have been provided for with all conceivable care; while we have the opposite before our eyes. If now by this certainly very unusual consideration, we have brought together in the boldest manner the two heterogeneous sides of the world, and, as it were, grasped them with one hand, we must now hold them fast in order to convince ourselves of the entire invalidity of the laws of the phenomenon, or the world as idea, for that of will, or the thing in itself. Then it will become more comprehensible to us that while on the side of the idea, that is, in the phenomenal world, there exhibits itself to us now an arising out of nothing, and now an entire annihilation of what has arisen, from that other side, or in itself, a nature lies before us with reference to which the conceptions of arising and passing away have no significance. For, by going back to the root, where, by means of self-consciousness, the phenomenon and the thing in itself meet, we have just, as it were, palpably apprehended that the two are absolutely incommensurable, and the whole manner of being of the one, together with all the fundamental laws of its being, signify nothing, and less than nothing, in the other. I believe that this last consideration will only be rightly understood by a few, and that it will be displeasing and even offensive to all who do not understand it, but I shall never on this account omit anything that can serve to illustrate my fundamental thought.

At the beginning of this chapter I have explained that the great clinging to life, or rather fear of death, by no means springs from knowledge, in which case it would be the result of the known value of life; but that that fear of death has its root directly in the *will*, out of the original nature of which it proceeds, in which it is entirely without knowledge, and therefore blind will to live. As we are allured into life by the wholly illusory inclination to sensual pleasure, so we are retained in it by the fear of death, which is certainly just as illusory. Both spring directly from the will, which in itself is unconscious. If, on the contrary, man were merely a *knowing* being, then death would necessarily be to him not only indifferent, but even welcome. The reflection to which we have here attained now teaches that what is affected by death is merely the *knowing* consciousness, and the will, on the other hand, because it is the thing in itself, which lies at the foundation of every phenomenon, is free from all that depends upon temporal determinations, thus is also imperishable. Its striving towards existence and manifestation, from which the world results, is constantly satisfied, for this accompanies it as the shadow accompanies the body, for it is merely the visibility of its nature. That yet in us it fears death results from the fact that here knowledge presents its existence to it as merely in the individual phenomenon, whence the illusion arises that it will perish with this, as my image in a mirror seems to be destroyed along with it if the mirror is broken; this then, as contrary to its original nature, which is a blind striving towards existence, fills it with horror. From this now it follows that that in us which alone is capable of fearing death, and also alone fears it, the *will*, is not affected by it; and that, on the other hand, what is affected by it and really perishes is that which from its nature is capable of no fear, and in general of no desire or emotion, and is therefore indifferent to being and not being, the mere subject of knowledge, the intellect, whose existence consists in its relation to the world of idea, *i.e.*, the objective world, whose correlative it is, and with whose existence its own is ultimately one. Thus, although the individual consciousness does not survive death, yet that survives it which alone struggles against it—the will. This also explains the contradiction that from the standpoint of knowledge philosophers have always proved with cogent reasons that death is no evil; yet the fear of death remains inevitable for all, because it is rooted, not in knowledge, but in the will. It is also a result of the fact that only the will, and not the intellect, is indestructible, that all religions and philosophies promise a reward in eternity only to the virtues of the will, or heart, not to those of the intellect, or head.

The following may also serve to illustrate this consideration. The will, which constitutes our true being, is of a simple nature; it merely wills, and does not know. The subject of knowledge, on the other hand, is a secondary phenomenon, arising from the objectification of the will;

it is the point of unity of the sensibility of the nervous system, as it were the focus in which the rays of the activity of all the parts of the brain unite. With this, then, it must perish. In self-consciousness, as that which alone knows, it stands over against the will as its spectator, and, although sprung from it, knows it as something different from itself, something foreign to it, and consequently also only empirically, in time, by degrees, in its successive excitements and acts, and also learns its decisions only *a posteriori,* and often very indirectly. This explains the fact that our own nature is a riddle to us, *i.e.,* to our intellect, and that the individual regards itself as having newly arisen and as perishable; although its true nature is independent of time, thus is eternal. As now the *will* does not *know,* so conversely the intellect, or the subject of knowledge, is simply and solely *knowing,* without ever *willing.* This can be proved even physically in the fact that, as was already mentioned in the second book, according to Bichat, the various emotions directly affect all parts of the organism and disturb their functions, with the exception of the brain, which can only be affected by them very indirectly, *i.e.,* just in consequence of those disturbances (*De la vie et de la mort,* art. 6, § 2). But from this it follows that the subject of knowledge, for itself and as such, cannot take part or interest in anything, but for it the being or not being of everything, nay, even of its own self, is a matter of indifference. Now why should this purely neutral being be immortal? It ends with the temporal manifestation of the will, *i.e.,* the individual, as it arose with it. It is the lantern which is extinguished when it has served its end. The intellect, like the perceptible world which exists only in it, is a mere phenomenon; but the finiteness of both does not affect that of which they are the phenomenal appearance. The intellect is the function of the cerebral nervous system; but the latter, like the rest of the body, is the objectivity of the *will.* Therefore the intellect depends upon the somatic life of the organism; but this itself depends upon the will. The organised body may thus, in a certain sense, be regarded as the link between the will and the intellect; although really it is only the will itself exhibiting itself spatially in the perception of the intellect. Death and birth are the constant renewal of the consciousness of the will, in itself without end and without beginning, which alone is, as it were, the substance of existence (but each such renewal brings a new possibility of the denial of the will to live). Consciousness is the life of the subject of knowledge, or the brain, and death is its end. And therefore, finally, consciousness is always new, in each case beginning at the beginning. The will alone is permanent; and, moreover, it is it alone that permanence concerns; for it is the will to live. The knowing subject for itself is not concerned about anything. In the ego, however, the two are bound up together. In every animal existence the will has achieved an intellect which is the light by which it here pursues its ends. It may be remarked by the way that the fear of death may also partly depend upon the fact that the individual will is so loath to separate from the intellect which has fallen to its lot through the course of nature, its guide and guard, without which it knows that it is helpless and blind.

Finally, this explanation also agrees with the commonplace moral experience which teaches us that the will alone is real, while its objects, on the other hand, as conditioned by knowledge, are only phenomena, are only froth and vapour, like the wine which Mephistopheles provided in Auerbach's cellar: after every sensuous pleasure we also say, "And yet it seemed as I were drinking wine."

The terrors of death depend for the most part upon the false illusion that now the ego vanishes and the world remains. But rather is the opposite the case; the world vanishes, but the inmost kernel of the ego, the supporter and producer of that subject, in whose idea alone the world has its existence, remains. With the brain the intellect perishes, and with the intellect the objective world, its mere idea. That in other brains, afterwards as before, a similar world lives and moves is, with reference to the intellect which perishes, a matter of indifference. If, therefore, reality proper did not lie in the *will*, and if the moral existence were not that which extends beyond death, then, since the intellect, and with it its world, is extinguished, the true nature of things in general would be no more than an endless succession of short and troubled dreams, without connection among themselves; for the permanence of unconscious nature consists merely in the idea of time of conscious nature. Thus a world-spirit dreaming without end or aim, dreams which for the most part are very troubled and heavy, would then be all in all.

When, now, an individual experiences the fear of death, we have really before us the extraordinary, nay, absurd, spectacle of the lord of the worlds, who fills all with his being, and through whom alone everything that is has its existence, desponding and afraid of perishing, of sinking into the abyss of eternal nothingness;—while, in truth, all is full of him, and there is no place where he is not, no being in which he does not live; for it is not existence that supports him, but he that supports existence. Yet it is he who desponds in the individual who suffers from the fear of death, for he is exposed to the illusion produced by the *principium individuationis* that his existence is limited to the nature which is now dying. This illusion belongs to the heavy dream into which, as the will to live, he has fallen. But one might say to the dying individual: "Thou ceasest to be something which thou hadst done better never to become."

So long as no denial of the will takes place, what death leaves untouched is the germ and kernel of quite another existence, in which a new individual finds itself again, so fresh and original that it broods over itself in astonishment. What sleep is for the individual, death is for the will as thing in itself. It would not endure to continue the same actions and sufferings throughout an eternity without true gain, if memory and individuality remained to it. It flings them off, and this is lethe; and through this sleep of death it reappears refreshed and fitted out with another intellect, as a new being—"a new day tempts to new shores."

As the self-asserting will to live man has the root of his existence in the species. Accordingly death is the loss of one individuality and the assumption of another, consequently a change of individuality under the exclusive guidance of one's own will. For in this alone lies the eternal power which could produce its existence with its ego, yet, on account of its nature, was not able to maintain it in existence. For death is the *démenti* which the essence (*essentia*) of every one receives in its claim to existence (*existentia*), the appearance of a contradiction which lies in every individual existence:

> "For all that arises
> Is worthy of being destroyed."

But an infinite number of such existences, each with its ego, stands within reach of this power, thus of the will, which, however, will again prove just as transitory and perishable. Since now every ego has its separate consciousness, that infinite number of them is, with reference to such an ego, not different from a single one. From this point of view it appears to me not accidental that *ævum*, *αἰων*, signifies both the individual term of life and infinite time. Indeed from this point of view it may be seen, although indistinctly, that ultimately and in themselves both are the same; and according to this there would really be no difference whether I existed only through my term of life or for an infinite time.

Certainly, however, we cannot obtain an idea of all that

is said above entirely without time-concepts; yet when we are dealing with the thing in itself these ought to be excluded. But it belongs to the unalterable limitations of our intellect that it can never entirely cast off this first and most immediate form of all its ideas, in order to operate without it. Therefore we certainly come here upon a kind of metempsychosis, although with the important difference that it does not concern the whole ψυχη, not the *knowing* being, but the *will* alone; and thus, with the consciousness that the form of time only enters here as an unavoidable concession to the limitation of our intellect, so many absurdities which accompany the doctrine of metempsychosis disappear. If, indeed, we now call in the assistance of the fact, to be explained in chapter 43, that the character, *i.e.*, the will, is inherited from the father, and the intellect, on the other hand, from the mother, it agrees very well with our view that the will of a man, in itself individual, separated itself in death from the intellect received from the mother in generation, and in accordance with its now modified nature, under the guidance of the absolutely necessary course of the world harmonising with this, received through a new generation a new intellect, with which it became a new being, which had no recollection of an earlier existence; for the intellect, which alone has the faculty of memory, is the mortal part or the form, while the will is the eternal part, the substance. In accordance with this, this doctrine is more correctly denoted by the word palingenesis than by metempsychosis. These constant new births, then, constitute the succession of the life-dreams of a will which in itself is indestructible, until, instructed and improved by so much and such various successive knowledge in a constantly new form, it abolishes or abrogates itself.

The true and, so to speak, esoteric doctrine of Buddhism, as we have come to know it through the latest investigations, also agrees with this view, for it teaches not metempsychosis, but a peculiar palingenesis, resting upon a moral basis which it works out and explains with great profundity. This may be seen from the exposition of the subject, well worth reading and pondering, which is given in Spence Hardy's "Manual of Buddhism," pp. 394–96 (with which compare pp. 429, 440, and 445 of the same book), the confirmation of which is to be found in Taylor's "*Prabodh Chandro Daya*," London, 1812, p. 35; also in Sangermano's "Burmese Empire," p. 6, and in the "Asiatic Researches," vol. vi. p. 179, and vol. ix. p. 256. The very useful German compendium of Buddhism by Köppen is also right upon this point. Yet for the great mass of Buddhists this doctrine is too subtle; therefore to them simple metempsychosis is preached as a comprehensible substitute.

Besides, it must not be neglected that even empirical grounds support a palingenesis of this kind. As a matter of fact there does exist a connection between the birth of the newly appearing beings and the death of those that are worn out. It shows itself in the great fruitfulness of the human race which appears as a consequence of devastating diseases. When in the fourteenth century the black death had for the most part depopulated the old world, a quite abnormal fruitfulness appeared among the human race, and twin-births were very frequent. The circumstance was also very remarkable that none of the children born at this time obtained their full number of teeth; thus nature, exerting itself to the utmost, was niggardly in details. This is related by F. Schnurrer, "*Chronik der Seuchen*," 1825. Casper also, "*Ueber die wahrscheinliche Lebensdauer des Menschen*," 1835, confirms the principle that the number of births in a given population has the most decided influence upon the length of life and mortality in it, as this always keeps pace with the mortality: so that always and everywhere the deaths and the births increase and decrease in like proportion; which he places beyond doubt by an accumulation of evidence collected from many lands and their various provinces. And yet it is impossible that there can be a *physical* causal connection between my early death and the fruitfulness of a marriage with which I have nothing to do, or conversely. Thus here the metaphysical appears undeniably and in a stupendous manner as the immediate ground of explanation of the physical. Every new-born being indeed comes fresh and blithe into the new existence, and enjoys it as a free gift: but there is, and can be, nothing freely given. Its fresh existence is paid for by the old age and death of a worn-out existence which has perished, but which contained the indestructible seed out of which this new existence has arisen: they are *one* being. To show the bridge between the two would certainly be the solution of a great riddle.

The great truth which is expressed here has never been entirely unacknowledged, although it could not be reduced to its exact and correct meaning, which is only possible through the doctrine of the primacy and metaphysical nature of the will and the secondary, merely organic nature of the intellect. We find the doctrine of metempsychosis, springing from the earliest and noblest ages of the human race, always spread abroad in the earth as the belief of the great majority of mankind, nay, really as the teaching of all religions, with the exception of that of the Jews and the two which have proceeded from it: in the most subtle form, however, and coming nearest to the truth, as has already been mentioned, in Buddhism. Accordingly, while Christians console themselves with the thought of meeting again in another world, in which one regains one's complete personality and knows oneself at once, in those other religions the meeting again is already going on now, only incognito. In the succession of births, and by virtue of metempsychosis or palingenesis, the persons who now stand in close connection or contact with us will also be born along with us at the next birth, and will have the same or analogous relations and sentiments towards us as now, whether these are of a friendly or a hostile description. (*Cf.*, for example, Spence Hardy's "Manual of Buddhism," p. 162.) Recognition is certainly here limited to an obscure intimation, a reminiscence which cannot be brought to distinct consciousness, and refers to an infinitely distant time;—with the exception, however, of Buddha himself, who has the prerogative of distinctly knowing his own earlier births and those of others;—as this is described in the "Jâtaka." But, in fact, if at favourable moment one contemplates, in a purely objective manner, the action of men in reality; the intuitive conviction is forced upon one that it not only is and remains constantly the same, according to the (Platonic) Idea, but also that the present generation, in its true inner nature, is precisely and substantially identical with every generation that has been before it. The question simply is in what this true being consists. The answer which my doctrine gives to this question is well known. The intuitive conviction referred to may be conceived as arising from the fact that the multiplying-glasses, time and space, lose for a moment their effect. With reference to the universality of the belief in metempsychosis, Obry says rightly, in his excellent book, "*Du Nirvana Indien*," p. 13: "*Cette vieille croyance a fait le tour du monde, et était tellement répandue dans la haute antiquité, qu'un docte Anglican l'avait jugée sans père, sans mère, et sans généalogie*" (*Ths. Burnet, dans Beausobre, Hist. du Manichéisme*, ii. p. 391). Taught already in the "Vedas," as in all the sacred books of India, metempsychosis is well known to be the kernel of Brahmanism and Buddhism. It accordingly prevails at the present day in the whole of non-Mohammedan Asia, thus among more than half of the whole human race, as the firmest conviction, and with an incredibly strong practical influence. It was also the belief of the Egyptians (Herod., ii. 123), from whom it was received with enthusiasm by Orpheus, Pythagoras, and Plato: the Pythagoreans, however, specially retained it. That it was also taught in the mysteries of the Greeks undeniably follows from the ninth book of Plato's "Laws" (pp. 38 and 42, ed. Bip.) Nemesius indeed (*De nat. hom.*, c. 2) says: "*Κοινη μεν οὐν παντες Ἑλληνες, οἱ την ψυχην αθανατον αποφηναμενοι, την μετενσωματωσιν δογματιζουσι.*" (*Communiter igitur omnes Græci, qui animam immortalem statuerunt, eam de uno corpore in aliud transferri censuerunt.*) The "Edda" also, especially in the "Völuspá," teaches metempsychosis. Not less was it the foundation of the religion of the Druids (*Cæs. de bello Gall.*, vi.; *A. Pictet, Le mystère des Bardes de l'ile de Bretagne*, 1856). Even a Mohammedan sect in Hindostan, the Bohrahs, of which Colebrooke gives a full account in the "Asiatic Researches," vol. vii. p. 336 *sqq.*, believes in metempsychosis, and accordingly refrains from all animal food. Also among American Indians and negro tribes, nay, even among the natives of Australia, traces of this belief are found, as appears from a minute description given in the *Times* of 29th January 1841 of the execution of two Australian savages for arson and murder. It is said there: "The younger of the two prisoners met his end with a dogged and a determined spirit, as it appeared, of revenge; the only intelligible expressions made use of conveyed an impression that he would rise up a 'white fellow,' which it was considered strengthened his resolution." Also in a book by Ungewitter, "*Der Welttheil Australien*," it is related that the Papuas in Australia regarded the whites as their own relations who had returned to the world. According to all this, the belief in metempsychosis presents itself as the natural conviction of man, whenever he reflects at all in an unprejudiced manner. It would really be that which Kant falsely asserts of his three pretended Ideas of the reason, a philosopheme natural to human reason, which proceeds from its forms; and when it is not found it must have been displaced by positive religious doctrines coming from a different source. I have also remarked that it is at once obvious to every one who hears of it for the first time. Let any one only observe how earnestly Lessing defends it in the last seven paragraphs of his "*Erziehung des Menschengeschlechts.*" Lichtenberg also says in his "*Selbstcharacteristik:*" "I cannot get rid of the thought that I died before I was born." Even the excessively empirical Hume says in his sceptical essay on immortality, p. 23: "The metempsychosis is therefore the only system of this kind that philosophy can hearken to."[1] What resists this belief, which is spread over the whole human race and commends itself alike to the wise and to the vulgar, is Judaism, together with the two religions which have sprung from it, because they teach the creation of man out of nothing, and he has then the hard task of linking on to this the belief in an ondless existence *a parte post.* They certainly have succeeded, with fire and sword, in driving out of Europe and part of Asia that consoling primitive belief of mankind; it is still doubtful for how long. Yet how difficult this was is shown by the oldest Church histories. Most of the heretics were attached to this primitive belief; for example, Simonists, Basilidians, Valentinians, Marcionists, Gnostics, and Manichæans. The Jews themselves have in part fallen into it, as Tertullian and Justinus (in his dialogues) inform us. In the Talmud it is related that Abel's soul passed into the body of Seth, and then into that of Moses. Even the passage of the Bible, Matt. xvi. 13–15, only obtains a rational meaning if we understand it as spoken under the assumption of the dogma of metempsychosis. Luke, it is true, who also has the passage (ix. 18–20), adds the words *οτι προφητης τις των αρχαιων ανεστη*, and thus attributes to

[1] This posthumous essay is to be found in the "Essays on Suicide and the Immortality of the Soul" by the late David Hume, Basil, 1799, sold by James Decker. By this reprint at Bâle these two works of one of the greatest thinkers and writers of England were rescued from destruction, when in their own land, in consequence of the stupid and utterly contemptible bigotry which prevailed, they had been suppressed through the influence of a powerful and insolent priesthood, to the lasting shame of England. They are entirely passionless, coldly rational investigations of the two subjects named.

the Jews the assumption that such an ancient prophet can rise again body and all, which, since they know that he has already lain between six and seven hundred years in his grave, and consequently has long since turned to dust, would be a palpable absurdity. In Christianity, however, the doctrine of original sin, *i.e.*, the doctrine of punishment for the sins of another individual, has taken the place of the transmigration of souls and the expiation in this way of all the sins committed in an earlier life. Both identify, and that with a moral tendency, the existing man with one who has existed before; the transmigration of souls does so directly, original sin indirectly.

Death is the great reprimand which the will to live, or more especially the egoism, which is essential to this, receives through the course of nature; and it may be conceived as a punishment for our existence.[1] It is the painful loosing of the knot which the act of generation had tied with sensual pleasure, the violent destruction coming from without of the fundamental error of our nature: the great disillusion. We are at bottom something that ought not to be: therefore we cease to be. Egoism consists really in the fact that man limits all reality to his own person, in that he imagines that he lives in this alone and not in others. Death teaches him better, for it destroys this person, so that the true nature of man, which is his will, will henceforth live only in other individuals; while his intellect, which itself belonged only to the phenomenon, *i.e.*, to the world as idea, and was merely the form of the external world, also continues to exist in the condition of being idea, *i.e.*, in the *objective* being of things as such, thus also only in the existence of what was hitherto the external world. His whole ego thus lives from this time forth only in that which he had hitherto regarded as non-ego: for the difference between external and internal ceases. We call to mind

[1] Death says: Thou art the product of an act which should not have been; therefore to expiate it thou must die.

here that the better man is he who makes the least difference between himself and others, does not regard them as absolute non-ego, while for the bad man this difference is great, nay, absolute. I have worked this out in my prize essay on the foundation of morals. According to what was said above, the degree in which death can be regarded as the annihilation of the man is in proportion to this difference. But if we start from the fact that the distinction of outside me and in me, as a spatial distinction, is only founded in the phenomenon, not in the thing in itself, thus is no absolutely real distinction, then we shall see in the losing of our own individuality only the loss of a phenomenon, thus only an apparent loss. However much reality that distinction has in the empirical consciousness, yet from the metaphysical standpoint the propositions, "I perish, but the world endures," and "The world perishes but I endure," are at bottom not really different.

But, besides all this, death is the great opportunity no longer to be I;—to him who uses it. During life the will of man is without freedom: his action takes place with necessity upon the basis of his unalterable character in the chain of motives. But every one remembers much that he has done, and on account of which he is by no means satisfied with himself. If now he were to go on living, he would go on acting in the same way, on account of the unalterable nature of his character. Accordingly he must cease to be what he is in order to be able to arise out of the germ of his nature as a new and different being. Therefore death looses these bonds; the will again becomes free; for freedom lies in the *Esse,* not in the *Operari.* "*Finditur nodus cordis, dissolvuntur omnes dubitationes, ejusque opera evanescunt,*" is a very celebrated saying of the Vedas, which all Vedantic writers frequently repeat.[1] Death is the moment of that deliverance from the one-

[1] *Sancara, s. de theologumenis Vedanticorum,* ed. F. H. H. Windischmann, p. 37; "*Oupnekhat,*" vol. i. p. 387 *et* p. 78; Colebrooke's "Miscellaneous Essays," vol. i. p. 363.

sidedness of an individuality which does not constitute the inmost kernel of our being, but is rather to be thought of as a kind of aberration of it. The true original freedom re-enters at this moment, which, in the sense indicated, may be regarded as a *restitutio in integrum.* The peace and quietness upon the countenance of most dead persons seems to have its origin in this. Quiet and easy is, as a rule, the death of every good man: but to die willingly, to die gladly, to die joyfully, is the prerogative of the resigned, of him who surrenders and denies the will to live. For only he wills to die *really,* and not merely *apparently,* and consequently he needs and desires no continuance of his person. The existence which we know he willingly gives up: what he gets instead of it is in our eyes *nothing,* because our existence is, with reference to that, *nothing.* The Buddhist faith calls it Nirvana,[1] *i.e.,* extinction.

[1] The etymology of the word Nirvana is variously given. According to Colebrooke ("Transact. of the Royal Asiat. Soc.," vol. i. p. 566) it comes from *va,* "to blow," like the wind, and the prefixed negative *nir,* and thus signifies a calm, but as an adjective "extinguished." Obry, also, *Du Nirvana Indien,* p. 3, says: "*Nirvanam en sanscrit signifie à la lettre extinction, telle que celle d'un feu.*" According to the "Asiatic Journal," vol. xxiv. p. 735, the word is really Neravana, from *nera,* "without," and *vana,* "life," and the meaning would be *annihilatio.* In "Eastern Monachism," by Spence Hardy, p. 295, Nirvana is derived from *vana,* "sinful desires," with the negative *nir.* J. J. Schmidt, in his translation of the history of the Eastern Mongolians, says that the Sanscrit word Nirvana is translated into Mongolian by a phrase which signifies "departed from misery," "escaped from misery." According to the learned lectures of the same in the St. Petersburg Academy, Nirvana is the opposite of Sanfara, which is the world of constant re-birth, of longings and desires, of illusion of the senses and changing forms, of being born, growing old, becoming sick, and dying. In the Burmese language the word Nirvana, according to the analogy of other Sanscrit words, becomes transformed into Nieban, and is translated by "complete vanishing." See Sangermano's "Description of the Burmese Empire," translated by Tandy, Rome, 1833, § 27. In the first edition of 1819 I also wrote Nieban, because we then knew Buddhism only from meagre accounts of the Burmese.

CHAPTER XLII.

THE LIFE OF THE SPECIES.

In the preceding chapter it was called to mind that the (Platonic) Ideas of the different grades of beings, which are the adequate objectification of the will to live, exhibit themselves in the knowledge of the individual, which is bound to the form of time, as the *species, i.e.*, as the successive individuals of one kind connected by the bond of generation, and that therefore the species is the Idea (εἶδος, *species*) broken up in time. Accordingly the true nature of every living thing lies primarily in its species: yet the species again has its existence only in the individuals. Now, although the will only attains to self-consciousness in the individual, thus knows itself immediately only as the individual, yet the deep-seated consciousness that it is really the species in which his true nature objectifies itself appears in the fact that for the individual the concerns of the species as such, thus the relations of the sexes, the production and nourishment of the offspring, are of incomparably greater importance and consequence than everything else. Hence, then, arises in the case of the brutes, heat or rut (an excellent description of the vehemence of which will be found in Burdach's "Physiology," vol. i. §§ 247, 257), and, in the case of man, the careful and capricious selection of the other individual for the satisfaction of the sexual impulse, which can rise to the height of passionate love, to the fuller investigation of which I shall devote a special chapter: hence also, finally the excessive love of parents for their offspring.

In the supplements to the second book the will was compared to the root and the intellect to the crown of the tree; and this is the case inwardly or psychologically. But outwardly or physiologically the genitals are the root and the head the crown. The nourishing part is certainly not the genitals, but the villi of the intestines: yet not the latter but the former are the root; because through them the individual is connected with the species in which it is rooted. For physically the individual is a production of the species, metaphysically a more or less perfect picture of the Idea, which, in the form of time, exhibits itself as species. In agreement with the relation expressed here, the greatest vitality, and also the decrepitude of the brain and the genital organs, is simultaneous and stands in connection. The sexual impulse is to be regarded as the inner life of the tree (the species) upon which the life of the individual grows, like a leaf that is nourished by the tree, and assists in nourishing the tree; this is why that impulse is so strong, and springs from the depths of our nature. To castrate an individual means to cut him off from the tree of the species upon which he grows, and thus severed, leave him to wither: hence the degradation of his mental and physical powers. That the service of the species, *i.e.*, fecundation, is followed in the case of every animal individual by momentary exhaustion and debility of all the powers, and in the case of most insects indeed by speedy death, on account of which Celsus said, "*Seminis emissio est partis animæ jactura;*" that in the case of man the extinction of the generative power shows that the individual approaches death; that excessive use of this power at every age shortens life, while, on the other hand, temperance in this respect increases all the powers, and especially the muscular powers, on which account it was part of the training of the Greek athletes; that the same restraint lengthens the life of the insect even to the following spring; all this points to the fact that the life of the individual is at bottom only borrowed from the species, and that all vital force is, as it were, force of the species restricted by being dammed up. But this is to be explained from the fact that the metaphysical substratum of life reveals itself directly in the species and only by means of this in the individual. Accordingly the Lingam with the Yoni, as the symbol of the species and its immortality, is worshipped in India, and, as the counterpoise of death, is ascribed as an attribute to the very divinity who presides over death, Siva.

But without myth or symbol, the vehemence of the sexual impulse, the keen intentness and profound seriousness with which every animal, including man, pursues its concerns, shows that it is through the function which serves it that the animal belongs to that in which really and principally its true being lies, the *species;* while all other functions and organs directly serve only the individual, whose existence is at bottom merely secondary. In the vehemence of that impulse, which is the concentration of the whole animal nature, the consciousness further expresses itself that the individual does not endure, and therefore all must be staked on the maintenance of the species, in which its true existence lies.

To illustrate what has been said, let us now imagine a brute in rut, and in the act of generation. We see a seriousness and intentness never known in it at any other time. Now what goes on in it? Does it know that it must die, and that through its present occupation a new individual, which yet entirely resembles itself, will arise in order to take its place? Of all this it knows nothing, for it does not think. But it is as intently careful for the continuance of the species in time as if it knew all that. For it is conscious that it desires to live and exist, and it expresses the highest degree of this volition in the act of generation; this is all that then takes place in its consciousness. This is also quite sufficient for the permanence of the kind; just because the will is the radical and knowledge the adventitious. On this account the will does not require to be guided by knowledge throughout; but whenever in its primitive originality it has resolved, this volition will objectify itself of its own accord in the world of the idea. If now in this way it is that definite animal form which we have thought of that wills life and existence, it does not will life and existence in general, but in this particular form. Therefore it is the sight of its form in the female of its species that stimulates the will of the brute to the act of generation. This volition of the brute, when regarded from without and under the form of time, presents itself as such an animal form maintained through an infinite time by the constantly repeated replacement of one individual by another, thus by the alternation of death and reproduction, which so regarded appear only as the pulse-beats of that form (ιδεα, εἶδος, *species*) which endures through all time. They may be compared to the forces of attraction and repulsion in which matter consists. That which is shown here in the brute holds good also of man; for although in him the act of generation is accompanied by complete knowledge of its final cause, yet it is not guided by this knowledge, but proceeds directly from the will to live as its concentration. It is accordingly to be reckoned among instinctive actions. For in reproduction the brute is just as little guided by knowledge of the end as in mechanical instincts; in these also the will manifests itself, in the main, without the mediation of knowledge, which here, as there, is only concerned with details. Reproduction is, to a certain extent, the most marvellous of all instincts, and its work the most astonishing.

These considerations explain why the sexual desire has a very different character from every other; it is not only the strongest, but even specifically of a more powerful kind than any other. It is everywhere tacitly assumed as necessary and inevitable, and is not, like other desires, a matter of taste and disposition. For it is the desire which even constitutes the nature of man. In conflict with it no motive is so strong that it would be certain of victory. It is so pre-eminently the chief concern that no other pleasures make up for the deprivation of its satisfaction; and, moreover, for its sake both brute and man undertake every danger and every conflict. A very naive expression of this disposition is the well-known inscription on the door of the *fornix* at Pompeii, decorated with the phallus: "*Heic habitat felicitas:*" this was for those going in naïve, for those coming out ironical, and in itself humorous. On the other hand, the excessive power of the sexual passion is seriously and worthily expressed in the inscription which (according to Theon of Smyrna, *De Musica*, c. 47), Osiris had placed upon the column he erected to the eternal gods: "To Eros, the spirit, the heaven, the sun, the moon, the earth, the night, the day, and the father of all that is and that shall be;" also in the beautiful apostrophe with which Lucretius begins his work:

> "*Æneadum genetrix, hominum divomque voluptas,*
> *Alma Venus cet.*"

To all this corresponds the important *rôle* which the relation of the sexes plays in the world of men, where it is really the invisible central point of all action and conduct, and peeps out everywhere in spite of all veils thrown over it. It is the cause of war and the end of peace, the basis of what is serious, and the aim of the jest, the inexhaustible source of wit, the key to all allusions, and the meaning of all mysterious hints, of all unspoken offers and all stolen glances, the daily meditation of the young, and often also of the old, the hourly thought of the unchaste, and even against their will the constantly recurring imagination of the chaste, the ever ready material of a joke, just because the profoundest seriousness lies at its foundation. It is, however, the piquant element and the joke of life that the chief concern of all men is secretly pursued and ostensibly ignored as much as possible. But, in fact, we see it every moment seat itself, as the true and hereditary lord of the world, out of the fulness of its own strength, upon the ancestral throne, and looking down from thence with scornful glances, laugh at the preparations which have been made to bind it, imprison it, or at least to limit it and wherever it is possible to keep it concealed, or even so to master it that it shall only appear as a subordinate, secondary concern of life. But all this agrees with the fact that the sexual passion is the kernel of the will to live, and consequently the concentration of all desire; therefore in the text I have called the genital organs the focus of the will. Indeed, one may say man is concrete sexual desire; for his origin is an act of copulation and his wish of wishes is an act of copulation, and this tendency alone perpetuates and holds together his whole phenomenal existence. The will to live manifests itself indeed primarily as an effort to sustain the individual; yet this is only a step to the effort to sustain the species, and the latter endeavour must be more powerful in proportion as the life of the species surpasses that of the individual in duration, extension, and value. Therefore sexual passion is the most perfect manifestation of the will to live, its most distinctly expressed type; and the origin of the individual in it, and its primacy over all other desires of the natural man, are both in complete agreement with this.

One other remark of a physiological nature is in place here, a remark which throws light upon my fundamental doctrine expounded in the second book. As the sexual impulse is the most vehement of desires, the wish of wishes, the concentration of all our volition, and accordingly the satisfaction of it which exactly corresponds to the individual wish of any one, that is, the desire fixed upon a definite individual, is the summit and crown of his happiness, the ultimate goal of his natural endeavours, with the attainment of which everything seems to him to have been attained, and with the frustrating of which everything seems to him to have been lost:—so we find, as its physiological correlative, in the objectified will, thus in the human organism, the sperm or semen as the secretion of secretions, the quintessence of all animal fluids, the last result of all organic functions, and have in it a new proof of the fact that the body is only the objectivity of the will, *i.e.*, is the will itself under the form of the idea.

With reproduction is connected the maintenance of the offspring, and with the sexual impulse, parental love; and thus through these the life of the species is carried on. Accordingly the love of the brute for its young has, like the sexual impulse, a strength which far surpasses that of the efforts which merely concerns itself as an individual. This shows itself in the fact that even the mildest animals are ready to undertake for the sake of their young even the most unequal battle for life and death, and with almost all species of animals the mother encounters any danger for the protection of her young, nay, in many cases even faces certain death. In the case of man this instinctive parental love is guided and directed by reason, *i.e.*, by reflection. Sometimes, however, it is also in this way restricted, and with bad characters this may extend to the complete repudiation of it. Therefore we can observe its effects most purely in the lower animals. In itself, however, it is not less strong in man; here also, in particular cases, we see it entirely overcome self-love, and even extend to the sacrifice of life. Thus, for example, the French newspapers have just announced that at Cahors, in the department of Lot, a father has taken his own life in order that his son, who had been drawn for military service, should be the eldest son of a widow, and therefore exempt (*Galignani's Messenger* of 22d June 1843). Yet in the case of the lower animals, since they are capable of no reflection, the instinctive maternal affection (the male is generally ignorant of his paternity) shows itself directly and unsophisticated, and therefore with perfect distinctness and in its whole strength. At bottom it is the expression of the consciousness in the brute that its true being lies more immediately in the species than in the individual, and therefore, when necessary, it sacrifices its life that the species may be maintained in the young. Thus here, as also in the sexual impulse, the will to live becomes to a certain extent transcendent, for its consciousness extends beyond the individual, in which it is inherent, to the species. In order to avoid expressing this second manifestation of the life of the species in a merely abstract manner, and to present it to the reader in its magnitude and reality, I will give a few examples of the extraordinary strength of instinctive maternal affection.

The sea-otter, when pursued, seizes its young one and dives with it; when it comes up again to take breath, it covers the young one with its body, and receives the harpoon of the hunter while the young one is escaping. A young whale is killed merely to attract the mother, who hurries to it and seldom forsakes it so long as it still lives, even although she is struck with several harpoons (Scoresby's "Journal of a Whaling Voyage;" from the English of Kreis, p. 196). At Three Kings Island, near New Zealand, there are colossal seals called sea-elephants (*phoca proboscidea*). They swim round the island in regular herds and feed upon fishes, but yet have certain terrible enemies below water unknown to us, by whom they are often severely wounded; hence their swimming together requires special tactics. The females bring forth their young upon the shore; while they are suckling them, which lasts from seven to eight weeks, all the males form a circle round them in order to prevent them, driven by hunger, from entering the sea, and if this is attempted they prevent it by biting. Thus they all fast together for between seven and eight weeks, and all become very thin, simply in order that the young may not enter the sea before they are able to swim well and observe the necessary tactics which are then taught them with blows and bites (Freycinet, *Voy. aux terres Australes*, 1826). We also see here how parental affection, like every strong exertion of the will (*cf.* chap. xix. 6), heightens the intelligence. Wild ducks, white-throats, and many other birds, when the sportsman comes near their nest, fly in front of him with loud cries and flap about as if their wings were injured, in order to attract his attention from their young to themselves. The lark tries to entice the dog away from its nest by exposing itself. In the same way hinds and does induce the hunter to pursue them in order that their young may not be attacked. Swallows have flown into burning houses to rescue their young or perish with them. At Delfft, in a great fire, a stork allowed itself to be burnt in its nest rather than forsake its tender young, which could not yet fly (Hadr. Junius, *Descriptio Hollandiæ*). Mountain-cocks and woodcocks allow themselves to be taken upon the nest when brooding. *Muscicapa tyrannus* protects its nest with remarkable courage, and defends itself against eagles. An ant has been cut in two, and the fore half been seen to bring the pupæ to a place of safety. A bitch whose litter had been cut out of her belly crept up to them dying, caressed them, and began to whine violently only when they were taken from her (Burdach, *Physiologie als Erfahrungswissenschaft*, vol. ii. and iii).

CHAPTER XLIII.

ON HEREDITY.

THE most ordinary experience teaches that in generation the combined seed of the parents not only propagates the peculiarities of the species, but also those of the individual, as far as bodily (objective, external) qualities are concerned, and this has also always been recognised—

> "*Naturæ sequitur semina quisque suæ.*"
>
> —CATULL.

Now whether this also holds good of mental (subjective, internal) qualities, so that these also are transmitted by the parents to the children, is a question which has already often been raised, and almost always answered in the affirmative. More difficult, however, is the problem whether it is possible to distinguish what belongs to the father and what to the mother, thus what is the mental inheritance which we receive from each of our parents. If now we cast upon this problem the light of our fundamental knowledge that the will is the true being, the kernel, the radical element in man, and the intellect, on the other hand, is what is secondary, adventitious, the accident of that substance; before questioning experience we will assume it as at least probable that the father, as *sexus potior* and the procreative principle, imparts the basis, the radical element, of the new life, thus the *will*, and the mother, as *sexus sequior* and merely conceiving principle, imparts the secondary element, the *intellect;* that thus the man inherits his moral nature, his character, his inclinations, his heart, from the father, and, on the other hand, the grade, quality, and tendency of his intelligence from the mother. Now this assumption actually finds its confirmation in experience; only this cannot be decided by a physical experiment upon the table, but results partly from the careful and acute observation of many years, and partly from history.

One's own experience has the advantage of complete certainty and the greatest speciality, and this outweighs the disadvantage that arises from it, that its sphere is limited and its examples not generally known. Therefore, primarily, I refer every one to his own experience. First of all let him consider himself, confess to himself his inclinations and passions, his characteristic errors and weaknesses, his vices, and also his excellences and virtues, if he has any. Then let him think of his father, and he cannot fail to recognise all these characteristic traits in him also. On the other hand, he will often find his mother of an entirely different character, and a moral agreement with her will very seldom occur, indeed only through the exceptional accident of a similarity of the character of the two parents. Let him make this examination, for example, with reference to quick temper or patience, avarice or prodigality, inclination to sensuality, or to intemperance, or to gambling, hard-heartedness or kindliness, honesty or hypocrisy, pride or condescension, courage or cowardice, peaceableness or quarrelsomeness, placability or resentfulness, &c. Then let him make the same investigation with regard to all those whose characters and whose parents he has accurately known. If he proceeds attentively, with correct judgment, and candidly, the confirmation of our principle will not be lacking. Thus, for example, he will find the special tendency to lie, which belongs to many men, equally present in two brothers, because they have inherited it from the father; on this account also the comedy, "The Liar and his Son," is psychologically correct. However, two inevitable limitations must here be borne in mind, which only open injustice could interpret as evasions. First, *pater semper incertus.* Only a decided physical resemblance to the father removes this limitation; a superficial resemblance, on the other hand, is not sufficient to do so; for there is an after-effect of earlier impregnation by virtue of which the children of the second marriage have sometimes still a slight resemblance to the first husband, and children begotten in adultery to the legitimate father. Such an after-effect has been still more distinctly observed in the case of brutes. The second limitation is, that in the son the moral character of the father certainly appears, yet under the modification which it has received through another and often very different *intellect* (the inheritance from the mother), and thus a correction of the observation becomes necessary. This modification may be important or trifling in proportion to that difference, but it can never be so great that the fundamental traits of the paternal character do not always appear under it recognisably enough, like a man who has disguised himself by an entirely different kind of dress, wig, and beard. For example, if by inheritance from the mother a man is preeminently endowed with reason, thus with the power of reflection and deliberation, the passions inherited from his father are partly bridled by this, partly concealed, and accordingly only attain to a methodical, systematic, or secret manifestation, and thus a very different phenomenon from that of the father, who perhaps had only a very limited mind, will then result; and in the same way the converse case may occur. The inclinations and passions of the mother, on the other hand, do not reappear at all in the children, often indeed their opposite.

Historical examples have the advantage over those of private life of being universally known; but, on the other hand, they are of course impaired by the uncertainty and frequent falsification of all tradition, and especially also by the fact that as a rule they only contain the public, not the private life, and consequently only the political actions, not the finer manifestations of character. However, I wish to support the truth we are speaking of by a few historical examples, to which those who have made a special study of history can no doubt add a far larger number of equally pertinent cases.

It is well known that P. Decius Mus sacrificed his life for his country with heroic nobleness; for, solemnly committing himself and the enemy to the infernal deities, with covered face he plunged into the army of the Latins. About forty years later his son, of the same name, did exactly the same thing in the war against the Gauls (Liv. viii. 6; x. 28). Thus a thorough proof of the Horatian *fortes creantur fortibus et bonis:* the converse of which is thus given by Shakspeare—

> "Cowards father cowards, and base things sire base."
> —CYMBELINE, iv. 2.

Early Roman history presents to us whole families whose members in long succession distinguished themselves by devoted patriotism and courage; such were the *gens Fabia* and the *gens Fabricia.* Again, Alexander the Great was fond of power and conquest, like his father Philip. The pedigree of Nero which, with a moral intention, Suetonius (c. 4 *et* 5) gives at the beginning of his sketch of this monster is very well worth considering. It is the *gens Claudia* he describes, which flourished in Rome through six centuries, and produced not only capable, but arrogant and cruel men. From it sprang Tiberius, Caligula, and finally Nero. In his grandfather, and still more strongly in his father, all those atrocious qualities show themselves, which could only attain their perfect development in Nero, partly because his higher position afforded them freer scope, partly because he had for his mother the irrational Bacchante, Agrippina, who could impart to him no intellect to bridle his passions. Quite in our sense, therefore, Suetonius relates that at his birth *præsagio fuit etiam Domitii, patris, vox, inter gratulationes amicorum, negantis, quidquam ex se et Agrippina, nisi detestabile et malo publico nasci potuisse.* On the other hand, Cimon was the son of Miltiades, and Hannibal of Hamilcar, and the Scipios make up a whole family of heroes and noble defenders of their country. But the son of Pope Alexander VI. was his hideous image, Cæsar Borgia. The son of the notorious Duke of Alba was just as cruel and wicked a man as his father. The malicious and unjust Philip IV. of France, who is specially known by his cruel torture and execution of the knights templars, had for his daughter Isabella, wife of Edward II. of England, who rebelled against her husband, took him prisoner, and after he had signed his abdication, since the attempt to kill him by ill-usage was unsuccessful, caused him to be put to death in prison in a manner which is too horrible for me to care to relate. The blood-thirsty tyrant and *defensor fidei,* Henry VIII. of England had a daughter by his first marriage, Queen Mary, equally distinguished for bigotry and cruelty, who from her numerous burnings of heretics has won the name of Bloody Mary. His daughter by his second marriage, Elizabeth, received an excellent understanding from her mother, Anne Boleyn, which prevented bigotry and curbed the parental character in her, yet did not do away with it; so that it still always shone through on occasions, and distinctly appeared in her cruel treatment of Mary of Scotland. Van Geuns[1] tells a story, after Marcus Donatus, of a Scotch girl whose father had been burnt as a highway robber and a cannibal when she was only one year old. Although she was brought up among quite different people, there developed in her the same craving for human flesh, and being caught in the act of satisfying it, she was buried alive. In the *Freimüthigen* of the 13th July 1821 we read that in the department of Aube the police pursued a girl because she had murdered two children, whom she ought to have taken to the

[1] "*Disputatio de corporum habitudine, animæ, hujusque virium indice.*" *Harderov.*, 1789, § 9.

foundling hospital, in order to keep the little money given to the children. At last the police found the girl on the road to Paris, near Romilly, drowned, and her own father gave himself up as her murderer. Finally, let me mention a couple of cases which have occurred recently, and have therefore only the newspapers as their vouchers. In October 1836 a Count Belecznai was condemned to death in Hungary because he had murdered an official and severely wounded his own relations. His elder brother was executed earlier as a patricide, and his father also had been a murderer (*Frankfurter Postzeitung* of the 26th October 1836). A year later the youngest brother of this Count, in the same street where the latter had murdered the official, fired a pistol at the steward of his estates, but missed him (*Frankfurter Journal*, 16th September 1837). In the *Frankfurter Postzeitung* of the 19th November 1857 a correspondent in Paris announces the condemnation to death of a very dangerous highway robber, Lemaire, and his companions, and adds: "The criminal tendency seems hereditary in his family and in those of his confederates, as several of their race have died on the scaffold." It follows from a passage in the Laws of Plato that similar cases were already known in Greece (*Stob. Flor.*, vol. ii. p. 213). The annals of crime will certainly have many similar pedigrees to show. The tendency to suicide is specially hereditary.

On the other hand, when we see the excellent Marcus Aurelius have the wicked Commodus for a son, this does not not lead us astray; for we know that the *Diva Faustina* was a *uxor infamis*. On the contrary, we mark this case in order in analogous cases to presume an analogous reason; for example, that Domitian was the full brother of Titus I can never believe, but that Vespasian also was a deceived husband.

Now, as regards the second part of the principle set up thus the inheritance of the intellect from the mother, this enjoys a far more general acceptance than the first part, which in itself appeals to the *liberum arbitrium indifferentiæ,* while its separate apprehension is opposed by the doctrine of the simplicity and indivisibility of the soul. Even the old and popular expression "mother-wit" shows the early recognition of this second truth, which depends upon the experience both with regard to small and great intellectual endowments, that they are the possession of those whose mothers proportionately distinguished themselves by their intelligence. That, on the other hand, the intellectual qualities of the father are not transmitted to the son is proved both by the fathers and the sons of men distinguished by the most eminent faculties, for, as a rule, they are quite ordinary men, without a trace of the paternal mental gifts. But if now an isolated exception to this experience, so often confirmed, should appear; such, for example, as is presented by Pitt and his father, Lord Chatham, we are warranted in ascribing it to accident, nay, obliged to do so, although, on account of the exceptional rarity of great talents, it is certainly an accident of a most extraordinary kind. Here, however, the rule holds good: it is improbable that the improbable *never* happens. Besides, great statesmen (as was already mentioned in chapter 22) are so just as much through the qualities of their character, thus through what is inherited from the father, as through the superiority of their mind. On the other hand, among artists, poets, and philosophers, to whose works alone *genius* is properly ascribed, I know of no case analogous to that. Raphael's father was certainly a painter, but not a great one; Mozart's father, and also his son, were musicians, but not great ones. However, it is indeed wonderful that the fate which had destined a very short life to both of these men, each the greatest in his own sphere, as it were by way of compensation, took care, by letting them be born already in their workshop, that, without suffering the loss of time in youth which for the most part occurs in the case of other men of genius, they received even from childhood, through paternal example and instruction, the necessary introduction into the art to which they were exclusively destined. This secret and mysterious power which seems to guide the individual life I have made the subject of special investigations, which I have communicated in the essay, "*Ueber die scheinbare Absichtlichkeit im Schicksale des Einzelnen*" (*Parerga*, vol. i.). It is further to be observed here that there are certain scientific occupations which certainly presuppose good native faculties, yet not those which are really rare and extraordinary; while the principal requirements are zealous efforts, diligence, patience, early instruction, sustained study, and much practice. From this, and not from the inheritance of the intellect of the father, the fact is to be explained that, since the son always willingly follows the path that has been opened up by the father, and almost all businesses are hereditary in certain families, in some sciences also, which before everything demand diligence and persistence, individual families can show a succession of men of merit; such are the Scaligers, the Bernouillis, the Cassinis, the Herschels.

The number of proofs of the actual inheritance of the intellect of the mother would be much greater than it appears if it were not that the character and disposition of the female sex is such that women rarely give public proof of their mental faculties; and therefore these do not become historical, and thus known to posterity. Besides, on account of the weaker nature in general of the female sex, these faculties themselves can never reach the grade in them to which they may afterwards rise in the son; thus, with reference to themselves, we have to estimate their achievements higher in this proportion. Accordingly, in the first instance, only the following examples present themselves as proofs of our truth. Joseph II. was the son of Maria Theresia. Cardanus says in the third chapter, "*De vita propria:*" "*Mater mea fuit memoria et ingenio pollens.*" J. J. Rousseau says in the first book of the "Confessions:" "*La beauté de ma mère, son esprit, ses talents,—elle en avait de trop brillans pour son état,"* &c., and then quotes some delightful lines of hers. D'Alembert was the illegitimate son of Claudine de Tencin, a woman of superior mind, and the author of several romances and similar works, which met with great approbation in her day, and should even still be enjoyable (see her biography in the "*Blätter für litterarische Unterhaltung,*" March 1845, Nos. 71–73). That Buffon's mother was a remarkable woman is shown by the following passage from the "*Voyage à Montbar, par Hérault de Sechelles,*" which Flourens quotes in his "*Histoire des travaux de Buffon,*" p. 288: "*Buffon avait ce principe qu'en général les enfants tenaient de leur mère leurs qualités intellectuelles et morales: et lorsqu'il l'avait développé dans la conversation, il en faisait sur-le-champ l'application à lui-même, en faisant un éloge pompeux de sa mère, qui avait en effet, beaucoup d'esprit, des connaissances étandues, et une tête très bien organisée.*" That he includes the moral qualities is an error which is either committed by the reporter, or depends upon the fact that his mother had accidentally the same character as himself and his father. The contrary of this is shown in innumerable cases in which the mother and the son have opposite characters. Hence the greatest dramatists could present, in Orestes and Hamlet, mother and son in hostile conflict, in which the son appears as the moral representative and avenger of his father. On the other hand, the converse case, that the son should appear as the moral representative and avenger of the mother against the father, would be revolting and, at the same time, almost absurd. This depends upon the fact that between father and son there is actual identity of nature, which is the will, but between mother and son there is merely identity of intellect, and even this only in a conditioned manner. Between mother and son the greatest moral opposition can exist, between father and son only an intellectual opposition. From this point of view, also, one should recognise the necessity of the Salic law: the woman cannot carry on the race. Hume says in his short autobiography: "Our mother was a woman of singular merit." It is said of Kant's mother in the most recent biography by F. W. Schubert: "According to the judgment of her son himself, she was a woman of great natural understanding. For that time, when there was so little opportunity for the education of girls, she was exceptionally well instructed, and she also continued later to care for her further education by herself. In the course of walks she drew the attention of her son to all kinds of natural phenomena, and tried to explain to him through them the power of God." What a remarkably able, clever, and superior woman Goethe's mother was is now universally known. How much she has been spoken of in literature! while his father has not been spoken of at all; Goethe himself describes him as a man of subordinate faculties. Schiller's mother was susceptible to poetry, and made verses herself, a fragment of which will be found in his biography by Schwab. Bürger, that genuine poetic genius, to whom perhaps the first place after Goethe among German poets belongs—for compared with his ballads those of Schiller seem cold and laboured—has given an account of his parents which for us is significant, and which his friend and physician, Althof repeats in his biography which appeared in 1798, in these words: "Bürger's father was certainly provided with a variety of knowledge after the manner of study prevalent at the time, and was also a good, honourable man; but he loved his quiet comfort and his pipe of tobacco so much, that, as my friend used to say, he had always first to pull himself together if he was going to apply himself for a quarter of an hour or so to the instruction of his son. His wife was a woman of extraordinary mental endowments, which, however, were so little cultivated that she had scarcely learnt to write legibly. Bürger thought that with proper culture his mother would have been the most famous of her sex, although he several times expressed a strong disapproval of different traits of her moral character. However, he believed that he inherited from his mother some mental gifts, and from his father an agreement with his moral character." Walter Scott's mother was a poetess, and was in communication with the wits of her time, as we learn from the obituary notice of Walter Scott in the *Globe* of 24th September 1832. That poems of hers appeared in print in 1789 I find from an article entitled "Mother-wit," in the *Blätter für litterarische Unterhaltung* of 4th October 1841, published by Brockhaus, which gives a long list of clever mothers of distinguished men, from which I shall only take two: "Bacon's mother was a distinguished linguist, wrote and translated several works, and in all of them showed learning, acuteness, and taste. Boerhave's mother distinguished herself through medical knowledge." On the other hand, Haller has preserved for us a strong proof of the inheritance of the mental weakness of the mother, for he says: "*E duabus patriciis sororibus, ob divitias maritos nactis, quum tamen fatuis essent proximæ, novimus in nobilissimas gentes nunc a seculo retro ejus morbi manasse semina, ut etiam in quarta generatione, quintave, omnium posterorum aliqui fatui supersint*" (*Elementa physiol.*, Lib. xxix. § 8). Also, according to Esquirol, madness is more frequently inherited from the mother than the father. If, however, it is inherited from the father, I attribute this to the disposition of the character whose influence occasions it.

It seems to follow from our principle that sons of the same mother have equal mental capacity, and if one should be highly gifted the other must be so also. Sometimes it is so. Examples of this are the Carracci, Joseph and Michael Haydn, Bernard and Andreas Romberg, George and Frederic Cuvier. I would also add the brothers Schlegel, if it were not that the younger, Friedrich, made himself unworthy of the honour of being named along with his excellent, blameless, and highly distinguished brother, August Wilhelm, by the disgraceful obscurantism which in the last quarter of his life he pursued along with Adam

Müller. For obscurantism is a sin, possibly not against the Holy Spirit, but yet against the human spirit, which one ought therefore never to forgive, but always and everywhere implacably to remember against whoever has been guilty of it, and take every opportunity of showing contempt for him so long as he lives, nay, after he is dead. But just as often the above result does not take place; for example, Kant's brother was quite an ordinary man. To explain this I must remind the reader of what is said in the thirty-first chapter on the physiological conditions of genius. Not only an extraordinarily developed and absolutely correctly formed brain (the share of the mother) is required, but also a very energetic action of the heart to animate it, *i.e.*, subjectively a passionate will, a lively temperament: this is the inheritance from the father. But this quality is at its height only during the father's strongest years; and the mother ages still more quickly. Accordingly the highly gifted sons will, as a rule, be the eldest, begotten in the full strength of both parents; thus Kant's brother was eleven years younger than him. Even in the case of two distinguished brothers, as a rule, the elder will be the superior. But not only the age, but every temporary ebb of the vital force or other disturbance of health in the parents at the time when the child is begotten may interfere with the part of one or other, and prevent the appearance of a man of eminent talent, which is therefore so exceedingly rare a phenomenon. It may be said, in passing, that in the case of twins the absence of all the differences just mentioned is the cause of the quasi-identity of their nature.

If single cases should be found in which a highly gifted son had a mother who was not mentally distinguished at all, this may be explained from the fact that this mother herself had a phlegmatic father, and on this account her more than ordinarily developed brain was not adequately excited by a corresponding energy of the circulation—a necessary condition, as I have explained above in chapter 31. Nevertheless, her highly perfected nervous and cerebral system was transmitted to the son, in whose case a father with a lively and passionate disposition and an energetic action of the heart was added, and thus the other physical condition of great mental power first appeared here. Perhaps this was Byron's case, since we nowhere find the mental advantages of his mother mentioned. The same explanation is also to be applied to the case in which the mother of a son of genius who was herself distinguished for mental gifts had a mother who was by no means clever, for the father of the latter has been a man of a phlegmatic disposition.

The inharmonious, disproportionate, ambiguous element in the character of most men might perhaps be referred to the fact that the individual has not a simple origin, but derives the will from the father and the intellect from the mother. The more heterogeneous and ill-adapted to each other the two parents were, the greater will that want of harmony, that inner variance, be. While some excel through their heart and others through their head, there are still others whose excellence lies in a certain harmony and unity of the whole nature, which arises from the fact that in them heart and head are so thoroughly adapted that they mutually support and advance each other; which leads us to assume that the parents were peculiarly suited to each other, and agreed in an exceptional measure.

With reference to the physiological side of the theory set forth, I wish now to mention that Burdach, who erroneously assumes that the same psychical qualities may be inherited now from the father, now from the mother, yet adds (*Physiologie als Erfahrungswissenschaft*, vol. i. § 306): "As a whole, the male element has more influence in determining the irritable life, and the female element, on the other hand, has more influence on the sensibility." What Linné says in the "*Systema naturæ*," Tom. i. p. 8, is also in point here: "*Mater prolifera promit, ante genera-*

tionem, vivum compendium medullare novi animalis suique simillimi, carinam Malpighianam dictum, tanquam plumulam vegetabilium: hoc ex genitura Cor adsociat ramificandum in corpus. Punctum emin saliens ovi incubantis avis ostendit primum·cor micans, cerebrumque cum medulla: corculum hoc, cessans a frigore, excitatur calido halitu, premitque bulla aërea, sensim dilatata, liquores, secundum canales fluxiles. Punctum vitalitatis itaque in viventibus est tanquam a prima creatione continuata medullaris vitæ ramificatio, cum ovum sit gemma medullaris matris a primordio viva, licet non sua ante proprium cor paternum.

If we now connect the conviction we have gained here of the inheritance of the character from the father and the intellect from the mother with our earlier investigation of the wide gulf which nature has placed between man and man in a moral as in an intellectual regard, and also with our knowledge of the absolute unalterableness both of the character and of the mental faculties, we shall be led to the view that a real and thorough improvement of the human race might be attained to not so much from without as from within, thus not so much by instruction and culture as rather upon the path of generation. Plato had already something of the kind in his mind when in the fifth book of his Republic he set forth his wonderful plan for increasing and improving his class of warriors. If we could castrate all scoundrels, and shut up all stupid geese in monasteries, and give persons of noble character a whole harem, and provide men, and indeed complete men, for all maidens of mind and understanding, a generation would soon arise which would produce a better age than that of Pericles. But, without entering into such utopian plans, it might be taken into consideration that if, as, if I am not mistaken, was actually the case among certain ancient nations, castration was the severest punishment after death, the world would be delivered from whole races of scoundrels, all the more certainly as it is well known that most crimes are committed between the age of twenty and thirty.[1] In the same way, it might be considered whether, as regards results, it would not be more advantageous to give the public dowries which upon certain occasions have to be distributed, not, as is now customary, to the girls who are supposed to be the most virtuous, but to those who have most understanding and are the cleverest; especially as it is very difficult to judge as to virtue, for, as it is said, only God sees the heart. The opportunities for displaying a noble character are rare, and a matter of chance; besides, many a girl has a powerful support to her virtue in her plainness; on the other hand, as regards understanding, those who themselves are gifted with it can judge with great certainty after some examination. The following is another practical application. In many countries, among others in South Germany, the bad custom prevails of women carrying burdens, often very considerable, upon the head. This must act disadvantageously upon the brain, which must thereby gradually deteriorate in the female sex of the nation; and since from that sex the male sex receives its brain, the whole nation becomes ever more stupid; which in many cases is by no means necessary. Accordingly by the abolition of this custom the quantum of intelligence in the whole nation would be increased, which would positively be the greatest increase of the national wealth.

But if now, leaving such practical applications to others, we return to our special point of view, the ethico-metaphysical standpoint — since we connect the content of chapter 41 with that of the present chapter—the following

[1] Lichtenberg says in his miscellaneous writings (Göttingen, 1801, vol. ii. p. 447): "In England it was proposed to castrate thieves. The proposal is not bad: the punishment is very severe; it makes persons contemptible, and yet leaves them still fit for trades; and if stealing is hereditary, in this way it is not propagated. Moreover, the courage ceases, and since the sexual passion so frequently leads to thefts, this cause would also disappear. The remark that women would so much the more eagerly restrain their husbands from stealing is roguish, for as things are at present they risk losing them altogether."

result will present itself to us, which, with all its transcendence, has yet a direct empirical support. It is the same character, thus the same individually determined will, that lives in all the descendants of one stock, from the remote ancestor to the present representative of the family. But in each of these a different intellect is given with it, thus a different degree and a different kind of knowledge. Thus in each of these life presents itself to it from another side and in a different light: it receives a new fundamental view of it, a new instruction. It is true that, since the intellect is extinguished with the individual, that will cannot supplement the insight of one course of life with that of another. But in consequence of each fundamentally new view of life, such as only a renewed personality can impart to it, its willing itself receives a different tendency, thus experiences a modification from it, and what is the chief concern, the will, has, in this new direction, either to assert life anew or deny it. In this way does the arrangement of nature of an ever-changing connection of a will with an intellect, which arises from the necessity of two sexes for reproduction, become the basis of a method of salvation. For by virtue of this arrangement life unceasingly presents new sides to the will (whose image and mirror it is), turns itself about, as it were, without intermission before its sight, allows different and ever different modes of perception to try their effect upon it, so that upon each of these it must decide for assertion or denial, both of which constantly stand open to it, only that, if once denial is chosen, the whole phenomenon ceases for it with death. Now because, according to this, it is just the constant renewal and complete alteration of the intellect for the same will which, as imparting a new view of the world, holds open the path of salvation, and because the intellect comes from the mother, the profound reason may lie here on account of which all nations (with very few and doubtful exceptions) abominate and forbid the marriage of brothers and sisters, nay, even on account of which sexual love does not arise at all between brothers and sisters, unless in very rare exceptions, which depend upon an unnatural perversity of the instinct, if not upon the fact that one of the two is illegitimate. For from a marriage of brothers and sisters nothing could proceed but constantly ever the same will with the same intellect, as both already exist united in both the parents, thus the hopeless repetition of the phenomenon which has already been.

But if now, in the particular case and close at hand, we contemplate the incredibly great and yet manifest difference of characters—find one so good and philanthropic, another so wicked, nay, ferocious; again, behold one just, honest, and upright, and another completely false, as a sneak, a swindler, a traitor, an incorrigible scoundrel—there discloses itself to us a chasm in our investigation, for in vain we ponder, reflecting on the origin of such a difference. Hindus and Buddhists solve the problem by saying, "It is the consequence of the deeds of the preceding courses of life." This solution is certainly the oldest, also the most comprehensible, and has come from the wisest of mankind; but it only pushes the question further back. Yet a more satisfactory answer will hardly be found. From the point of view of my whole teaching, it remains for me to say that here, where we are speaking of the will as thing in itself, the principle of sufficient reason, as merely the form of the phenomenon, is no longer applicable; with it, however, all why and whence disappear. Absolute freedom just consists in this, that something is not subject at all to the principle of sufficient reason, as the principle of all necessity. Such freedom, therefore, only belongs to the thing in itself. And this is just the will. Accordingly, in its phenomenal manifestation, consequently in the *Operari*, it is subject to necessity; but in the *Esse*, where it has determined itself as thing in itself, it is free. Whenever, therefore, we come to this, as happens here, all explanation by means of reasons and consequents ceases, and nothing remains for us but to say that here manifests itself the true freedom of the will, which belongs to it because it is the thing in itself, which, however, just as such, is groundless, *i.e.*, knows no why. But on this account all understanding ceases for us here, because all our understanding depends upon the principle of sufficient reason, for it consists in the mere application of that principle.

CHAPTER XLIV.

THE METAPHYSICS OF THE LOVE OF THE SEXES.

"Ye wise men, highly, deeply learned,
Who think it out and know,
How, when, and where do all things pair?
Why do they kiss and love?
Ye men of lofty wisdom, say
What happened to me then;
Search out and tell me where, how, when,
And why it happened thus."

—BÜRGER.

THIS chapter is the last of four whose various reciprocal relations, by virtue of which, to a certain extent, they consitute a subordinate whole, the attentive reader will recognise without it being needful for me to interrupt my exposition by recalling them or referring to them.

We are accustomed to see poets principally occupied with describing the love of the sexes. This is as a rule the chief theme of all dramatic works, tragical as well as comical, romantic as well as classical, Indian as well as European. Not less is it the material of by far the largest part of lyrical and also of epic poetry, especially if we class with the latter the enormous piles of romances which for centuries every year has produced in all the civilised countries of Europe as regularly as the fruits of the earth. As regards their main contents, all these works are nothing else than many-sided brief or lengthy descriptions of the passion we are speaking of. Moreover, the most successful pictures of it—such, for example, as Romeo and Juliet, *La Nouvelle Héloïse*, and *Werther*—have gained immortal fame. Yet, when Rochefoucauld imagines that it is the same with passionate love as with ghosts, of which every one speaks, but which no one has seen; and Lichtenberg also in his essay, "*Ueber die Macht der Liebe,*" disputes and denies the reality and naturalness of that passion, they are greatly in error. For it is impossible that something which is foreign and contrary to human nature, thus a mere imaginary caricature, could be unweariedly represented by poetic genius in all ages, and received by mankind with unaltered interest; for nothing that is artistically beautiful can be without truth:—

> "*Rien n'est beau que le vrai; le vrai seul est aimable.*"
>
> —BOIL.

Certainly, however, it is also confirmed by experience, although not by the experience of every day, that that which as a rule only appears as a strong yet still controllable inclination may rise under certain circumstances to a passion which exceeds all others in vehemence, and which then sets aside all considerations, overcomes all obstacles with incredible strength and perseverance, so that for its satisfaction life is risked without hesitation, nay, if that satisfaction is still withheld, is given as the price of it. Werthers and Jacopo Ortis exist not only in romance, but every year can show at least half a dozen of them in Europe: *Sed ignotis perierunt mortibus illi;* for their sorrows find no other chroniclers than the writers of official registers or the reporters of the newspapers. Yet the readers of the police news in English and French journals will attest the correctness of my assertion. Still greater, however, is the number of those whom the same passion brings to the madhouse. Finally, every year can show cases of the double suicide of a pair of lovers who are opposed by outward circumstances. In such cases, however, it is inexplicable to me how those who, certain of mutual love, expect to find the supremest bliss in the enjoyment of this, do not withdraw themselves from all connections by taking the extremest steps, and endure all hardships, rather than give up with life a pleasure which is greater than any other they can conceive. As regards the lower grades of that passion, and the mere approaches to it, every one has them daily before his eyes, and, as long as he is not old, for the most part also in his heart.

So then, after what has here been called to mind, no one can doubt either the reality or the importance of the matter; and therefore, instead of wondering that a philosophy should also for once make its own this constant theme of all poets, one ought rather to be surprised that a thing which plays throughout so important a part in human life has hitherto practically been disregarded by philosophers altogether, and lies before us as raw material. The one who has most concerned himself with it is Plato, especially in the "Symposium" and the "Phædrus." Yet what he says on the subject is confined to the sphere of myths, fables, and jokes, and also for the most part concerns only the Greek love of youths. The little that Rousseau says upon our theme in the "*Discours sur l'inégalité*" (p. 96, ed. Bip.) is false and insufficient. Kant's explanation of the subject in the third part of the essay, "*Ueber das Gefühl des Schönen und Erhabenen*" (p. 435 *seq.* of Rosenkranz's edition), is very superficial and without practical knowledge, therefore it is also partly incorrect. Lastly, Platner's treatment of the matter in his "Anthropology" (§ 1347 *seq.*) every one will find dull and shallow. On the other hand, Spinoza's definition, on account of its excessive naïveté, deserves to be quoted for the sake of amusement: "*Amor est titillatio, concomitante idea causæ externæ* (*Eth.* iv., prop. 44, *dem.*) Accordingly I have no predecessors either to make use of or to refute. The subject has pressed itself upon me objectively, and has entered of its own accord into the connection of my consideration of the world. Moreover, least of all can I hope for approbation from those who are themselves under the power of this passion, and who accordingly seek to express the excess of their feelings in the sublimest and most ethereal images. To them my view will appear too physical, too material, however metaphysical and even transcendent it may be at bottom. Meanwhile let them reflect that if the object which to-day inspires them to write madrigals and sonnets had been born eighteen years earlier it would scarcely have won a glance from them.

For all love, however ethereally it may bear itself, is rooted in the sexual impulse alone, nay, it absolutely is only a more definitely determined, specialised, and indeed in the strictest sense individualised sexual impulse. If now, keeping this in view, one considers the important part which the sexual impulse in all its degrees and nuances plays not only on the stage and in novels, but also in the real world, where, next to the love of life, it shows itself the strongest and most powerful of motives, constantly lays claim to half the powers and thoughts of the younger portion of mankind, is the ultimate goal of almost all human effort, exerts an adverse influence on the most important events, interrupts the most serious occupations every hour, sometimes embarrasses for a while even the greatest minds, does not hesitate to intrude with its trash interfering with the negotiations of statesmen and the investigations of men of learning, knows how to slip its love letters and locks of hair even into ministerial portfolios and philosophical manuscripts, and no less devises daily the most entangled and the worst actions, destroys the most valuable relationships, breaks the firmest bonds, demands the sacrifice sometimes of life or health, sometimes of wealth, rank, and happiness, nay, robs those who are otherwise honest of all conscience, makes those who have hitherto been faithful, traitors; accordingly, on the whole, appears as a malevolent demon that strives to pervert, confuse, and overthrow everything; —then one will be forced to cry, Wherefore all this noise? Wherefore the straining and storming, the anxiety and want? It is merely a question of every Hans finding his Grethe.[1] Why should such a trifle play so important a part, and constantly introduce disturbance and confusion into the well-regulated life of man? But to the earnest investigator the spirit of truth gradually reveals the answer. It is no trifle that is in question here; on the contrary, the importance of the matter is quite proportionate to the seriousness and ardour of the effort. The ultimate end of all love affairs, whether they are played in sock or cothurnus, is really more important than all other ends of human life, and is therefore quite worthy of the profound seriousness with which every one pursues it. That which is decided by it is nothing less than *the composition of the next generation.* The *dramatis personæ* who shall appear when we are withdrawn are here determined, both as regards their existence and their nature, by these frivolous love affairs. As the being, the *existentia*, of these future persons is absolutely conditioned by our sexual impulse generally, so their nature, *essentia*, is determined by the individual selection in its satisfaction, *i.e.*, by sexual love, and is in every respect irrevocably fixed by this. This is the key of the problem: we shall arrive at a more accurate knowledge of it in its application if we go through the degrees of love, from the passing inclination to the vehement passion, when we shall also recognise that the difference of these grades arises from the degree of the individualisation of the choice.

The collective love affairs of the present generation taken together are accordingly, of the whole human race, the serious *meditatio compositionis generationis futuræ, e qua iterum pendent innumeræ generationes.* This high importance of the matter, in which it is not a question of individual weal or woe, as in all other matters, but of the existence and special nature of the human race in future times, and therefore the will of the individual appears

[1] I have not ventured to express myself distinctly here: the courteous reader must therefore translate the phrase into Aristophanic language.

at a higher power as the will of the species;—this it is on which the pathetic and sublime elements in affairs of love depend, which for thousands of years poets have never wearied of representing in innumerable examples; because no theme can equal in interest this one, which stands to all others which only concern the welfare of individuals as the solid body to the surface, because it concerns the weal and woe of the species. Just on this account, then, is it so difficult to impart interest to a drama without the element of love, and, on the other hand, this theme is never worn out even by daily use.

That which presents itself in the individual consciousness as sexual impulse in general, without being directed towards a definite individual of the other sex, is in itself, and apart from the phenomenon, simply the will to live. But what appears in consciousness as a sexual impulse directed to a definite individual is in itself the will to live as a definitely determined individual. Now in this case the sexual impulse, although in itself a subjective need, knows how to assume very skilfully the mask of an objective admiration, and thus to deceive our consciousness; for nature requires this stratagem to attain its ends. But yet that in every case of falling in love, however objective and sublime this admiration may appear, what alone is looked to is the production of an individual of a definite nature is primarily confirmed by the fact that the essential matter is not the reciprocation of love, but possession, *i.e.*, the physical enjoyment. The certainty of the former can therefore by no means console us for the want of the latter; on the contrary, in such a situation many a man has shot himself. On the other hand, persons who are deeply in love, and can obtain no return of it, are contented with possession, *i.e.*, with the physical enjoyment. This is proved by all forced marriages, and also by the frequent purchase of the favour of a woman, in spite of her dislike, by large presents or other sacrifices, nay, even by cases of rape. That this particular child shall be begotten is, although unknown to the parties concerned, the true end of the whole love story; the manner in which it is attained is a secondary consideration. Now, however loudly persons of lofty and sentimental soul, and especially those who are in love, may cry out here about the gross realism of my view, they are yet in error. For is not the definite determination of the individualities of the next generation a much higher and more worthy end than those exuberant feelings and supersensible soap bubbles of theirs? Nay, among earthly aims, can there be one which is greater or more important? It alone corresponds to the profoundness with which passionate love is felt, to the seriousness with which it appears, and the importance which it attributes even to the trifling details of its sphere and occasion. Only so far as this end is assumed as the true one do the difficulties encountered, the infinite exertions and annoyances made and endured for the attainment of the loved object, appear proportionate to the matter. For it is the future generation, in its whole individual determinateness, that presses into existence by means of those efforts and toils. Nay, it is itself already active in that careful, definite, and arbitrary choice for the satisfaction of the sexual impulse which we call love. The growing inclination of two lovers is really already the will to live of the new individual which they can and desire to produce; nay, even in the meeting of their longing glances its new life breaks out, and announces itself as a future individuality harmoniously and well composed. They feel the longing for an actual union and fusing together into a single being, in order to live on only as this; and this longing receives its fulfilment in the child which is produced by them, as that in which the qualities transmitted by them both, fused and united in one being, live on. Conversely, the mutual, decided and persistent aversion between a man and a maid is a sign that what they could produce would only be a badly organised, in itself inharmonious and unhappy being. Hence there lies a deeper meaning in the fact that Calderon, though he calls the atrocious Semiramis the daughter of the air, yet introduces her as the daughter of rape followed by the murder of the husband.

But, finally, what draws two individuals of different sex exclusively to each other with such power is the will to live, which exhibits itself in the whole species, and which here anticipates in the individual which these two can produce an objectification of its nature answering to its aims. This individual will have the will, or character, from the father, the intellect from the mother, and the corporisation from both; yet, for the most part, the figure will take more after the father, the size after the mother, —according to the law which comes out in the breeding of hybrids among the brutes, and principally depends upon the fact that the size of the fœtus must conform to the size of the uterus. Just as inexplicable as the quite special individuality of any man, which is exclusively peculiar to him, is also the quite special and individual passion of two lovers; indeed at bottom the two are one and the same: the former is *explicite* what the latter was *implicite.* The moment at which the parents begin to love each other—to fancy each other, as the very happy English expression has it—is really to be regarded as the first appearance of a new individual and the true *punctum saliens* of its life, and, as has been said, in the meeting and fixing of their longing glances there appears the first germ of the new being, which certainly, like all germs, is generally crushed out. This new individual is to a certain extent a new (Platonic) Idea; and now, as all Ideas strive with the greatest vehemence to enter the phenomenal world, eagerly seizing for this end upon the matter which the law of causality divides among them all, so also does this particular Idea of a human individuality strive with the greatest eagerness and vehemence towards its realisation in the phenomenon. This eagerness and vehemence is just the passion of the two future parents for each other. It has innumerable degrees, the two extremes of which may at any rate be described as *Αφροδιτη πανδημος* and *ουρανια*; in its nature, however, it is everywhere the same. On the other hand, it will be in degree so much the more powerful the more *individualised* it is; that is, the more the loved individual is exclusively suited, by virtue of all his or her parts and qualities, to satisfy the desire of the lover and the need established by his or her own individuality. What is really in question here will become clear in the further course of our exposition. Primarily and essentially the inclination of love is directed to health, strength, and beauty, consequently also to youth; because the will first of all seeks to exhibit the specific character of the human species as the basis of all individuality: ordinary amorousness (*Αφροδιτη πανδημος*) does not go much further. To these, then, more special claims link themselves on, which we shall investigate in detail further on, and with which, when they see satisfaction before them, the passion increases. But the highest degrees of this passion spring from that suitableness of two individualities to each other on account of which the will, *i.e.*, the character, of the father and the intellect of the mother, in their connection, make up precisely that individual towards which the will to live in general which exhibits itself in the whole species feels a longing proportionate to this its magnitude, and which therefore exceeds the measure of a mortal heart, and the motives of which, in the same way, lie beyond the sphere of the individual intellect. This is thus the soul of a true and great passion. Now the more perfect is the mutual adaptation of two individuals to each other in each of the many respects which have further to be considered, the stronger will be their mutual passion. Since there do not exist two individuals exactly alike, there must be for each particular man a particular woman—always with reference to what is to be produced—who corresponds most perfectly. A really passionate love is as rare as the accident of these two meeting. Since, however, the possibility of such a love is present in every one, the representations of it in the works of the poets are comprehensible to us. Just because the passion of love really turns about that which is to be produced, and its qualities, and because its kernel lies here, a friendship without any admixture of sexual love can exist between two young and good-looking persons of different sex, on account of the agreement of their disposition, character, and mental tendencies; nay, as regards sexual love there may even be a certain aversion between them. The reason of this is to be sought in the fact that a child produced by them would have physical or mental qualities which were inharmonious; in short, its existence and nature would not answer the ends of the will to live as it exhibits itself in the species. On the other hand, in the case of difference of disposition, character, and mental tendency, and the dislike, nay, enmity, proceeding from this, sexual love may yet arise and exist; when it then blinds us to all that; and if it here leads to marriage it will be a very unhappy one.

Let us now set about the more thorough investigation of the matter. Egoism is so deeply rooted a quality of all individuals in general, that in order to rouse the activity of an individual being egoistical ends are the only ones upon which we can count with certainty. Certainly the species has an earlier, closer, and greater claim upon the individual than the perishable individuality itself. Yet when the individual has to act, and even make sacrifices for the continuance and quality of the species, the importance of the matter cannot be made so comprehensible to his intellect, which is calculated merely with regard to individual ends, as to have its proportionate effect. Therefore in such a case nature can only attain its ends by implanting a certain illusion in the individual, on account of which that which is only a good for the species appears to him as a good for himself, so that when he serves the species he imagines he is serving himself; in which process a mere chimera, which vanishes immediately afterwards, floats before him, and takes the place of a real thing as a motive. This illusion is instinct. In the great majority of cases this is to be regarded as the sense of the species, which presents what is of benefit to *it* to the will. Since, however, the will has here become individual, it must be so deluded that it apprehends through the sense of the individual what the sense of the species presents to it, thus imagines it is following individual ends while in truth it is pursuing ends which are merely general (taking this word in its strictest sense). The external phenomenon of instinct we can best observe in the brutes where its rôle is most important; but it is in ourselves alone that we arrive at a knowledge of its internal process, as of everything internal. Now it is certainly supposed that man has almost no instinct; at any rate only this, that the new-born babe seeks for and seizes the breast of its mother. But, in fact, we have a very definite, distinct, and complicated instinct, that of the selection of another individual for the satisfaction of the sexual impulse, a selection which is so fine, so serious, and so arbitrary. With this satisfaction in itself, *i.e.*, so far as it is a sensual pleasure resting upon a pressing want of the individual, the beauty or ugliness of the other individual has nothing to do. Thus the regard for this which is yet pursued with such ardour, together with the careful selection which springs from it, is evidently connected, not with the chooser himself—although he imagines it is so—but with the true end, that which is to be produced, which is to receive the type of the species as purely and correctly as possible. Through a thousand physical accidents and moral aberrations there arise a great variety of deteriorations of the human form; yet its true type, in all its parts, is always again established: and this takes place under the guidance of the sense of beauty, which always directs the sexual impulse, and without which this sinks to the level of a disgusting necessity. Accordingly, in the first place, every one will decidedly prefer and eagerly desire the most beautiful individuals, *i.e.*, those in whom the character of the species is most purely impressed; but, secondly, each one will specially regard as beautiful in another individual those perfections which he himself lacks, nay, even those imperfections which are the opposite of his own. Hence, for example, little men love big women, fair persons like dark, &c. &c. The delusive ecstasy which seizes a man at the sight of a woman whose beauty is suited to him, and pictures to him a union with her as the highest good, is just the *sense of the species*, which, recognising the distinctly expressed stamp of the same, desires to perpetuate it with this individual. Upon this decided inclination to beauty depends the maintenance of the type of the species: hence it acts with such great power. We shall examine specially further on the considerations which it follows. Thus what guides man here is really an instinct which is directed to doing the best for the species, while the man himself imagines that he only seeks the heightening of his own pleasure. In fact, we have in this an instructive lesson concerning the inner nature of all instinct, which, as here, almost always sets the individual in motion for the good of the species. For clearly the pains with which an insect seeks out a particular flower, or fruit, or dung, or flesh, or, as in the case of the ichneumonidæ, the larva of another insect, in order to deposit its eggs there only, and to attain this end shrinks neither from trouble nor danger, is thoroughly analogous to the pains with which for his sexual satisfaction a man carefully chooses a woman with definite qualities which appeal to him individually, and strives so eagerly after her that in order to attain this end he often sacrifices his own happiness in life, contrary to all reason, by a foolish marriage, by love affairs which cost him wealth, honour, and life, even by crimes such as adultery or rape, all merely in order to serve the species in the most efficient way, although at the cost of the individual, in accordance with the will of nature which is everywhere sovereign. Instinct, in fact, is always an act which seems to be in accordance with the conception of an end, and yet is entirely without such a conception. Nature implants it wherever the acting individual is incapable of understanding the end, or would be unwilling to pursue it. Therefore, as a rule, it is given only to the brutes, and indeed especially to the lowest of them which have least understanding; but almost only in the case we are here considering it is also given to man, who certainly could understand the end, but would not pursue it with the necessary ardour, that is, even at the expense of his individual welfare. Thus here, as in the case of all instinct, the truth assumes the form of an illusion, in order to act upon the will. It is a voluptuous illusion which leads the man to believe he will find a greater pleasure in the arms of a woman whose beauty appeals to him than in those of any other; or which indeed, exclusively directed to a single individual, firmly convinces him that the possession of her will ensure him excessive happiness. Therefore he imagines he is taking trouble and making sacrifices for his own pleasure, while he does so merely for the maintenance of the regular type of the species, or else a quite special individuality, which can only come from these parents, is to attain to existence. The character of instinct is here so perfectly present, thus an action which seems to be in accordance with the conception of an end, and yet is entirely without such a conception, that he who is drawn by that illusion often abhors the end which alone guides it, procreation, and would like to hinder it; thus it is in the case of almost all illicit love affairs. In accordance with the character of the matter which has been explained, every lover will experience a marvellous disillusion after the pleasure he has at last attained, and will wonder that what was so longingly desired accomplishes nothing more than every other sexual satisfaction; so that he does not see himself much benefited by it. That wish was related to all his other wishes as the species is related to the individual, thus as the infinite to the finite. The satisfaction, on the other hand, is really only for the benefit of the species, and thus does not come within the consciousness of the individual, who, inspired by the will of the species, here served an end with every kind of sacrifice, which was not his own end at all. Hence, then, every lover, after the ultimate consummation of the great work, finds himself cheated; for the illusion has vanished by means of which the individual was here the dupe of the species. Accordingly Plato very happily says: "*ἡδονη ἁπαντων αλαζονεστατον*" (*voluptas omnium maxime vaniloqua*), *Phileb.* 319.

But all this reflects light on the instincts and mechanical tendencies of the brutes. They also are, without doubt, involved in a kind of illusion, which deceives them with the prospect of their own pleasure, while they work so laboriously and with so much self-denial for the species, the bird builds its nest, the insect seeks the only suitable place for its eggs, or even hunts for prey which, unsuited for its own enjoyment, must be laid beside the eggs as food for the future larvæ, the bees, the wasps, the ants apply themselves to their skilful dwellings and highly complicated economy. They are all guided with certainty by an illusion, which conceals the service of the species under the mask of an egotistical end. This is probably the only way to comprehend the inner or subjective process that lies at the foundation of the manifestations of instinct. Outwardly, however, or objectively, we find in those creatures which are to a large extent governed by instinct, especially in insects, a preponderance of the ganglion system, *i.e.*, the *subjective* nervous system, over the objective or cerebral system; from which we must conclude that they are moved, not so much by objective, proper apprehension as by subjective ideas exciting desire, which arise from the influence of the ganglion system upon the brain, and accordingly by a kind of illusion; and this will be the *physiological* process in the case of all instinct. For the sake of illustration I will mention as another example of instinct in the human species, although a weak one, the capricious appetite of women who are pregnant. It seems to arise from the fact that the nourishment of the embryo sometimes requires a special or definite modification of the blood which flows to it, upon which the food which produces such a modification at once presents itself to the pregnant woman as an object of ardent longing, thus here also an illusion arises. Accordingly woman has one instinct more than man; and the ganglion system is also much more developed in the woman. That man has fewer instincts than the brutes and that even these few can be easily led astray, may be explained from the great preponderance of the brain in his case. The sense of beauty which instinctively guides the selection for the satisfaction of sexual passion is led astray when it degenerates into the tendency to pederasty; analogous to the fact that the blue-bottle (*Musca vomitoria*), instead of depositing its eggs, according to instinct, in putrefying flesh, lays them in the blossom of the *Arum dracunculus*, deceived by the cadaverous smell of this plant.

Now that an instinct entirely directed to that which is to be produced lies at the foundation of all sexual love will receive complete confirmation from the fuller analysis of it, which we cannot therefore avoid. First of all we have to remark here that by nature man is inclined to inconstancy in love, woman to constancy. The love of the man sinks perceptibly from the moment it has obtained satisfaction; almost every other woman charms him more than the one he already possesses; he longs for variety. The love of the woman, on the other hand, increases just from that moment. This is a consequence of the aim of nature which is directed to the maintenance, and therefore to the greatest possible increase, of the species. The man can easily beget over a hundred children a year; the woman, on the contrary, with however many men, can yet only bring one child a year into the world (leaving twin births out of account). Therefore the man always looks about after other women; the woman, again, sticks firmly to the one man; for nature moves her, instinctively and without reflection, to retain the nourisher and protector of the future offspring. Accordingly faithfulness in marriage is with the man artificial, with the woman it is natural, and thus adultery on the part of the woman is much less pardonable than on the part of the man, both objectively on account of the consequences and also subjectively on account of its unnaturalness.

But in order to be thorough and gain full conviction that the pleasure in the other sex, however objective it may seem to us, is yet merely disguised instinct, *i.e.*, sense of the species, which strives to maintain its type, we must investigate more fully the considerations which guide us in this pleasure, and enter into the details of this, rarely as these details which will have to be mentioned here may have figured in a philosophical work before. These considerations divide themselves into those which directly concern the type of the species, *i.e.*, beauty, those which are concerned with physical qualities, and lastly, those which are merely relative, which arise from the requisite correction or neutralisation of the one-sided qualities and abnormities of the two individuals by each other. We shall go through them one by one.

The first consideration which guides our choice and inclination is age. In general we accept the age from the years when menstruation begins to those when it ceases, yet we give the decided preference to the period from the eighteenth to the twenty-eighth year. Outside of those years, on the other hand, no woman can attract us: an old woman, *i.e.*, one who no longer menstruates, excites our aversion. Youth without beauty has still always attraction; beauty without youth has none. Clearly the unconscious end which guides us here is the possibility of reproduction in general: therefore every individual loses attraction for the opposite sex in proportion as he or she is removed from the fittest period for begetting or conceiving. The second consideration is that of health. Acute diseases only temporarily disturb us, chronic diseases or cachexia repel us, because they are transmitted to the child. The third consideration is the skeleton, because it is the basis of the type of the species. Next to age and disease nothing repels us so much as a deformed figure; even the most beautiful face cannot atone for it; on the contrary, even the ugliest face when accompanied by a straight figure is unquestionably preferred. Further, we feel every disproportion of the skeleton most strongly; for example, a stunted, dumpy, short-boned figure, and many such; also a halting gait, where it is not the result of an extraneous accident. On the other hand, a strikingly beautiful figure can make up for all defects: it enchants us. Here also comes in the great value which all attach to the smallness of the feet: it depends upon the fact that they are an essential characteristic of the species, for no animal has the tarsus and the metatarsus taken together so small as man, which accords with his upright walk; he is a plantigrade. Accordingly Jesus Sirach also says (xxvi. 23, according to the revised translation by Kraus): "A woman with a straight figure and beautiful feet is like columns of gold in sockets of silver." The teeth also are important; because they are essential for nourishment and quite specially hereditary. The fourth consideration is a certain fulness of flesh; thus a predominance of the vegetative function, of plasticity; because this promises abundant nourishment for the fœtus; hence great leanness repels us in a striking degree. A full female bosom exerts an exceptional charm upon the male sex; because, standing in direct connection with the female functions of propagation, it promises abundant nourishment to the new-born child. On the other hand, excessively fat women excite our disgust: the cause is that this indicates atrophy of the uterus, thus barrenness; which is not known by the head, but by instinct. The last consideration of all is the beauty of the face. Here also before everything else the bones are considered; therefore we look principally for a beautiful nose, and a short turned-up nose spoils everything. A slight inclination of the nose downwards or upwards has decided the happiness in life of innumerable maidens, and rightly so, for it concerns the type of the species. A small mouth, by means of small maxillæ, is very essential as specifically characteristic of the human countenance, as distinguished from the muzzle of the brutes. A receding or, as it were, cut-away chin is especially disagreeable, because *mentum prominulum* is an exclusive characteristic of our species. Finally comes the regard for beautiful eyes and forehead; it is connected with the psychical qualities, especially the intellectual which are inherited from the mother.

The unconscious considerations which, on the other hand, the inclination of women follows naturally cannot be so exactly assigned. In general the following may be asserted: They give the preference to the age from thirty to thirty-five years, especially over that of youths who yet really present the height of human beauty. The reason is that they are not guided by taste but by instinct, which recognises in the age named the acme of reproductive power. In general they look less to beauty, especially of the face. It is as if they took it upon themselves alone to impart this to the child. They are principally won by the strength of the man, and the courage which is connected with this; for these promise the production of stronger children, and also a brave protector for them. Every physical defect of the man, every divergence from the type, may with regard to the child be removed by the woman in reproduction, through the fact that she herself is blameless in these respects, or even exceeds in the opposite direction. Only those qualities of the man have to be excepted which are peculiar to his sex, and which therefore the mother cannot give to the child: such are the manly structure of the skeleton, broad shoulders, slender hips, straight bones, muscular power, courage, beard, &c. Hence it arises that women often love ugly men, but never an unmanly man, because they cannot neutralise his defects.

The second class of the considerations which lie at the foundation of sexual love are those which regard psychical qualities. Here we shall find that the woman is throughout attracted by the qualties of the heart or character in the man, as those which are inherited from the father. The woman is won especially by firmness of will, decision, and courage, and perhaps also by honesty and goodheartedness. On the other hand, intellectual gifts exercise no direct and instinctive power over her, just because they are not inherited from the father. Want of understanding does a man no harm with women; indeed extraordinary mental endowment, or even genius, might sooner influence them unfavourably as an abnormity. Hence one often sees an ugly, stupid, and coarse fellow get the better of a cultured, able, and amiable man with women. Also marriages from love are sometimes consummated between natures which are mentally very different: for example, the man is rough, powerful, and stupid; the woman tenderly sensitive, delicately thoughtful, cultured, æsthetic, &c.; or the man is a genius and learned, the woman a goose:

> "*Sic visum Veneri; cui placet impares*
> *Formas atque animos sub juga aënea*
> *Sævo mittere cum joco.*"

The reason is, that here quite other considerations than the intellectual predominate,—those of instinct. In marriage what is looked to is not intellectual entertainment, but the production of children: it is a bond of the heart, not of the head. It is a vain and absurd pretence when women assert that they have fallen in love with the mind of a man, or else it is the over-straining of a degenerate nature. Men, on the other hand, are not determined in their instinctive love by the qualities of character of the woman; hence so many Socrateses have found their Xantippes; for example, Shakspeare, Albrecht Dürer, Byron, &c. The intellectual qualities, however, certainly influence here, because they are inherited from the mother. Yet their influence is easily outweighed by that of physical beauty, which acts directly, as concerning a more essential point. However, it happens, either from the feeling or the experience of that influence, that mothers have their daughters taught the fine arts, languages, and so forth in order to make them attractive to men, whereby they wish to assist the intellect by artificial means, just as, in case of need, they assist the hips and the bosom. Observe that here we are speaking throughout only of that entirely immediate instinctive attraction from which alone love properly so called grows. That a woman of culture and understanding prizes understanding and intellect in a man, that a man from rational reflection should test and have regard to the character of his bride, has nothing to do with the matter with which we are dealing here. Such things lie at the bottom of a rational choice in marriage, but not of the passionate love, which is our theme.

Hitherto I have only taken account of the *absolute* considerations, *i.e.*, those which hold good for every one: I come now to the *relative* considerations, which are individual, because in their case what is looked to is the rectification of the type of the species, which is already defectively presented, the correction of the divergences from it which the chooser's own person already bears in itself, and thus the return to the pure presentation of the type. Here, then, each one loves what he lacks. Starting from the individual constitution, and directed to the individual constitution, the choice which rests upon such relative considerations is much more definite, decided, and exclusive than that which proceeds merely from the absolute considerations; therefore the source of really passionate love will lie, as a rule, in these relative considerations, and only that of the ordinary and slighter inclination in the absolute considerations. Accordingly it is not generally precisely correct and perfect beauties that kindle great passions. For such a truly passionate inclination to arise something is required which can only be expressed by a chemical metaphor: two persons must neutralise each other, like acid and alkali, to a neutral salt. The essential conditions demanded for this are the following. First: all sex is one-sided. This one-sidedness is more distinctly expressed in one individual than in another; therefore in every individual it can be better supplemented and neutralised by one than by another individual of the opposite sex, for each one requires a one-sidedness which is the opposite of his own to complete the type of humanity in the new individual that is to be produced, the constitution of which is always the goal towards which all tends. Physiologists know that manhood and womanhood admit of innumerable degrees, through which the former sinks to the repulsive gynander and hypospadæus, and the latter rises to the graceful androgyne; from both sides complete hermaphrodism can be reached, at which point stand those individuals who, holding the exact mean between the two sexes, can be attributed to neither, and consequently are unfit to propagate the species. Accordingly, the neutralisation of two individualities by each other, of which we are speaking, demands that the definite degree of *his* manhood shall exactly correspond to the definite degree of *her* womanhood; so that the one-sidedness of each exactly annuls that of the other. Accordingly, the most manly man will seek the most womanly woman, and *vice versâ*, and in the same way every individual will seek another corresponding to him or her in degree of sex.

Now how far the required relation exists between two individuals is instinctively felt by them, and, together with the other relative considerations, lies at the foundation of the higher degrees of love. While, therefore, the lovers speak pathetically of the harmony of their souls, the heart of the matter is for the most part the agreement or suitableness pointed out here with reference to the being which is to be produced and its perfection, and which is also clearly of much more importance than the harmony of their souls, which often, not long after the marriage, resolves itself into a howling discord. Now, here come in the further relative considerations, which depend upon the fact that every one endeavours to neutralise by means of the other his weaknesses, defects, and deviations from the type, so that they will not perpetuate themselves, or even develop into complete abnormities in the child which is to be produced. The weaker a man is as regards muscular power the more will he seek for strong women; and the woman on her side will do the same. But since now a less degree of muscular power is natural and regular in the woman, women as a rule will give the preference to strong men. Further, the size is an important consideration. Little men have a decided inclination for big women, and *vice versâ;* and indeed in a little man the preference for big women will be so much the more passionate if he himself was begotten by a big father, and only remains little through the influence of his mother; because he has inherited from his father the vascular system and its energy, which was able to supply a large body with blood. If, on the other hand, his father and grandfather were both little, that inclination will make itself less felt. At the foundation of the aversion of a big woman to big men lies the intention of nature to avoid too big a race, if with the strength which *this* woman could impart to them they would be too weak to live long. If, however, such a woman selects a big husband, perhaps for the sake of being more presentable in society, then, as a rule, her offspring will have to atone for her folly. Further, the consideration as to the complexion is very decided. Blondes prefer dark persons, or brunettes; but the latter seldom prefer the former. The reason is, that fair hair and blue eyes are in themselves a variation from the type, almost an abnormity, analogous to white mice, or at least to grey horses. In no part of the world, not even in the vicinity of the pole, are they indigenous, except in Europe, and are clearly of Scandinavian origin. I may here express my opinion in passing that the white colour of the skin is not natural to man, but that by nature he has a black or brown skin, like our forefathers the Hindus; that consequently a white man has never originally sprung from the womb of nature, and that thus there is no such thing as a white race, much as this is talked of, but every white man is a faded or bleached one. Forced into the strange world, where he only exists like an exotic plant, and like this requires in winter the hothouse, in the course of thousands of years man became white. The gipsies, an Indian race which immigrated only about four centuries ago, show the transition from the complexion of the Hindu to our own.[1] Therefore in sexual love nature strives to return to dark hair and brown eyes as the primitive type; but the white colour of the skin has become a second nature, though not so that the brown of the Hindu repels us. Finally, each one also seeks in the particular parts of the body the corrective of his own defects and aberrations, and does so the more decidedly the more important the part is. Therefore snub-nosed individuals have an inexpressible liking for hook-noses, parrot-faces; and it is the same with regard to all other parts. Men with excessively slim, long bodies and limbs can find beauty in a body which is even beyond measure stumpy and short. The considerations with regard to temperament act in an

[1] The fuller discussion of this subject will be found in the "Parerga," vol ii. § 92 of the first edition (second edition, pp. 167-170).

analogous manner. Each will prefer the temperament opposed to his own; yet only in proportion as his one is decided. Whoever is himself in some respect very perfect does not indeed seek and love imperfection in this respect, but is yet more easily reconciled to it than others; because he himself insures the children against great imperfection of this part. For example, whoever is himself very white will not object to a yellow complexion; but whoever has the latter will find dazzling whiteness divinely beautiful. The rare case in which a man falls in love with a decidedly ugly woman occurs when, besides the exact harmony of the degree of sex explained above, the whole of her abnormities are precisely the opposite, and thus the corrective, of his. The love is then wont to reach a high degree.

The profound seriousness with which we consider and ponder each bodily part of the woman, and she on her part does the same, the critical scrupulosity with which we inspect a woman who begins to please us, the capriciousness of our choice, the keen attention with which the bridegroom observes his betrothed, his carefulness not to be deceived in any part, and the great value which he attaches to every excess or defect in the essential parts, all this is quite in keeping with the importance of the end. For the new being to be produced will have to bear through its whole life a similar part. For example, if the woman is only a little crooked, this may easily impart to her son a hump, and so in all the rest. Consciousness of all this certainly does not exist. On the contrary, every one imagines that he makes that careful selection in the interest of his own pleasure (which at bottom cannot be interested in it at all); but he makes it precisely as, under the presupposition of his own corporisation, is most in keeping with the interest of the species, to maintain the type of which as pure as possible is the secret task. The individual acts here, without knowing it, by order of something higher than itself, the species; hence the importance which it attaches to things which may and indeed must be, indifferent to itself as such. There is something quite peculiar in the profound unconscious seriousness with which two young persons of opposite sex who see each other for the first time regard each other, in the searching and penetrating glance they cast at one another, in the careful review which all the features and parts of their respective persons have to endure. This investigating and examining is the *meditation of the genius of the species* on the individual which is possible through these two and the combination of its qualities. According to the result of this meditation is the degree of their pleasure in each other and their yearning for each other. This yearning, even after it has attained a considerable degree, may be suddenly extinguished again by the discovery of something that had previously remained unobserved. In this way, then, the genius of the species meditates concerning the coming race in all who are capable of reproduction. The nature of this race is the great work with which Cupid is occupied, unceasingly active, speculating, and pondering. In comparison with the importance of his great affair, which concerns the species and all coming races, the affairs of individuals in their whole ephemeral totality are very trifling; therefore he is always ready to sacrifice these regardlessly. For he is related to them as an immortal to mortals, and his interests to theirs as infinite to finite. Thus, in the consciousness of managing affairs of a higher kind than all those which only concern individual weal or woe, he carries them on sublimely, undisturbed in the midst of the tumult of war, or in the bustle of business life, or during the raging of a plague, and pursues them even into the seclusion of the cloister.

We have seen in the above that the intensity of love increases with its individualisation, because we have shown that the physical qualities of two individuals can be such that, for the purpose of restoring as far as possible the type of the species, the one is quite specially and perfectly the completion or supplement of the other, which therefore desires it exclusively. Already in this case a considerable passion arises, which at once gains a nobler and more sublime appearance from the fact that it is directed to an individual object, and to it alone; thus, as it were, arises at the special order of the species. For the opposite reason, the mere sexual impulse is ignoble, because without individualisation it is directed to all, and strives to maintain the species only as regards quantity, with little respect to quality. But the individualising, and with it the intensity of the love, can reach so high a degree that without its satisfaction all the good things in the world, and even life itself, lose their value. It is then a wish which attains a vehemence that no other wish ever reaches, and therefore makes one ready for any sacrifice, and in case its fulfilment remains unalterably denied, may lead to madness or suicide. At the foundation of such an excessive passion there must lie, besides the considerations we have shown above, still others which we have not thus before our eyes. We must therefore assume that here not only the corporisation, but the *will* of the man and the *intellect* of the woman are specially suitable to each other, in consequence of which a perfectly definite individual can be produced by them alone, whose existence the genius of the species has here in view, for reasons which are inaccessible to us, since they lie in the nature of the thing in itself. Or, to speak more exactly, the will to live desires here to objectify itself in a perfectly definite individual, which can only be produced by this father with this mother. This metaphysical desire of the will in itself has primarily no other sphere of action in the series of existences than the hearts of the future parents, which accordingly are seized with this ardent longing, and now imagine themselves to desire on their own account what really for the present has only a purely metaphysical end, *i.e.*, an end which lies outside the series of actually existing things. Thus it is the ardent longing to enter existence of the future individual which has first become possible here, a longing which proceeds from the primary source of all being, and exhibits itself in the phenomenal world as the lofty passion of the future parents for each other, paying little regard to all that is outside itself; in fact, as an unparalleled illusion, on account of which such a lover would give up all the good things of this world to enjoy the possession of this woman, who yet can really give him nothing more than any other. That yet it is just this possession that is kept in view here is seen from the fact that even this lofty passion, like all others, is extinguished in its enjoyment—to the great astonishment of those who are possessed by it. It also becomes extinct when, through the woman turning out barren (which, according to Hufeland, may arise from nineteen accidental constitutional defects), the real metaphysical end is frustrated; just as daily happens in millions of germs trampled under foot, in which yet the same metaphysical life principle strives for existence; for which there is no other consolation than that an infinity of space, time, and matter, and consequently inexhaustible opportunity for return, stands open to the will to live.

The view which is here expounded must once have been present to the mind of Theophrastus Paracelsus, even if only in a fleeting form, though he has not handled this subject, and my whole system of thought was foreign to him; for, in quite a different context and in his desultory manner, he wrote the following remarkable words: "*Hi sunt, quos Deus copulavit, ut eam, quæ fuit Uriæ et David; quamvis ex diametro (sic enim sibi humana mens persuadebat) cum justo et legitimo matrimonio pugnaret hoc. . . . sed propter Salomonem,* QUI ALIUNDE NASCI NON POTUIT, *nisi ex Bathseba, conjuncto David semine, quamvis meretrice, conjunxit eos Deus*" (*De vita longa*, i. 5).

The longing of love, the ἵμερος, which the poets of all ages are unceasingly occupied with expressing in innumerable forms, and do not exhaust the subject, nay, cannot do it justice, this longing, which attaches the idea of endless happiness to the possession of a particular woman, and unutterable pain to the thought that this possession cannot be attained,—this longing and this pain cannot obtain their material from the wants of an ephemeral individual; but they are the sighs of the spirit of the species, which sees here, to be won or lost, a means for the attainment of its ends which cannot be replaced, and therefore groans deeply. The species alone has infinite life, and therefore is capable of infinite desires, infinite satisfaction, and infinite pain. But these are here imprisoned in the narrow breast of a mortal. No wonder, then, if such a breast seems like to burst, and can find no expression for the intimations of infinite rapture or infinite misery with which it is filled. This, then, affords the materials for all erotic poetry of a sublime kind, which accordingly rises into transcendent metaphors, soaring above all that is earthly. This is the theme of Petrarch, the material for the St. Preuxs, Werthers, and Jacopo Ortis, who apart from it could not be understood nor explained. For that infinite esteem for the loved one cannot rest upon some spiritual excellences, or in general upon any objective, real qualities of hers; for one thing, because she is often not sufficiently well known to the lover, as was the case with Petrarch. The spirit of the species alone can see at one glance what *worth* she has for *it*, for its ends. And great passions also arise, as a rule, at the first glance:

> "Who ever loved that loved not at first sight?"
> —SHAKSPEARE, "As You Like it," iii. 5.

In this regard a passage in the romance of "*Guzman de Alfarache*," by Mateo Aleman, which has been famous for 250 years, is remarkable: "*No es necessario, para que uno ame, que pase distancia de tiempo, que siga discurso, ni haga eleccion, sino que con aquella primera y sola vista, concurran juntamente cierta correspondencia ó consonancia, ó lo que acá solemos vulgarmente decir, una confrontacion de sangre, á que por particular influxo suelen mover las estrellas.*" (For one to love it is not necessary that much time should pass, that he should set about reflecting and make a choice; but only that at that first and only glance a certain correspondence and consonance should be encountered on both sides, or that which in common life we are wont to call a *sympathy of the blood*, and to which a special influence of the stars generally impels), P. ii. lib. iii. c. 5. Accordingly the loss of the loved one, through a rival, or through death, is also for the passionate lover a pain that surpasses all others, just because it is of a transcendental kind, since it affects him not merely as an individual, but attacks him in his *essentia æterna*, in the life of the species into whose special will and service he was here called. Hence jealousy is such torment and so grim, and the surrender of the loved one is the greatest of all sacrifices. A hero is ashamed of all lamentations except the lamentation of love, because in this it is not he but the species that laments. In Calderon's "Zenobia the Great" there is in the first act a scene between Zenobia and Decius in which the latter says:

> "*Cielos, luego tu me quieres?*
> *Perdiera cien mil victorias,*
> *Volviérame,*" &c.

(Heaven! then thou lovest me? For this I would lose a thousand victories, would turn about, &c.)

Here, honour, which hitherto outweighed every interest, is beaten out of the field as soon as sexual love, *i.e.*, the interest of the species, comes into play, and sees before it a decided advantage; for this is infinitely superior to every interest of mere individuals, however important it may be. Therefore to this alone honour, duty, and fidelity yield after they have withstood every other temptation, including the threat of death. In the same way we find in private life that conscientiousness is in no point so rare as in this: it is here sometimes set aside even by persons who are otherwise honest and just, and adultery is recklessly committed when passionate love, *i.e.*, the interest of the species, has mastered them. It even seems as if in this they believed themselves to be conscious of a higher right than the interests of individuals can ever confer; just because they act in the interest of the species. In this reference Chamfort's remark is worth noticing: "*Quand un homme et une femme ont l'un pour l'autre une passion violente, il me semble toujours que quelque soient les obstacles qui les séparent, un mari, des parens, etc., les deux amans sont l'un a l'autre, de par la Nature, qu'ils s'appartiennent de droit divin, malgré les lois et les conventions humaines.*" Whoever is inclined to be incensed at this should be referred to the remarkable indulgence which the Saviour shows in the Gospel to the woman taken in adultery, in that He also assumes the same guilt in the case of all present. From this point of view the greater part of the "Decameron" appears as mere mocking and jeering of the genius of the species at the rights and interests of individuals which it tramples under foot. Differences of rank and all similar circumstances, when they oppose the union of passionate lovers, are set aside with the same ease and treated as nothing by the genius of the species, which, pursuing its ends that concern innumerable generations, blows off as spray such human laws and scruples. From the same deep-lying grounds, when the ends of passionate love are concerned, every danger is willingly encountered, and those who are otherwise timorous here become courageous. In plays and novels also we see, with ready sympathy, the young persons who are fighting the battle of their love, *i.e.*, the interest of the species, gain the victory over their elders, who are thinking only of the welfare of the individuals. For the efforts of the lovers appear to us as much more important, sublime, and therefore right, than anything that can be opposed to them, as the species is more important than the individual. Accordingly the fundamental theme of almost all comedies is the appearance of the genius of the species with its aims, which are opposed to the personal interest of the individuals presented, and therefore threaten to undermine their happiness. As a rule it attains its end, which, as in accordance with poetical justice, satisfies the spectator, because he feels that the aims of the species are much to be preferred to those of the individual. Therefore at the conclusion he leaves the victorious lovers quite confidently, because he shares with them the illusion that they have founded their own happiness, while they have rather sacrificed it to the choice of the species, against the will and foresight of their elders. It has been attempted in single, abnormal comedies to reverse the matter and bring about the happiness of the individuals at the cost of the aims of the species; but then the spectator feels the pain which the genius of the species suffers, and is not consoled by the advantages which are thereby assured to the individuals. As examples of this kind two very well-known little pieces occur to me: "*La reine de 16 ans*," and "*Le marriage de raison*." In tragedies containing love affairs, since the aims of the species are frustrated, the lovers who were its tools, generally perish also; for example, in "Romeo and Juliet," "Tancred," "Don Carlos," "Wallenstein," "The Bride of Messina," and many others.

The love of a man often affords comical, and sometimes also tragical phenomena; both because, taken possession of by the spirit of the species, he is now ruled by this, and no longer belongs to himself: his conduct thereby becomes unsuited to the individual. That which in the higher grades of love imparts such a tinge of poetry and sublimeness to his thoughts, which gives them even a transcendental and hyperphysical tendency, on account of which he seems to lose sight altogether of his real, very physical aim, is at bottom this, that he is now inspired by the spirit of the species whose affairs are infinitely more important than all those which concern mere individuals, in order to found under the special directions of this spirit the whole existence of an indefinitely long posterity with this individual and exactly determined nature, which it can receive only from him as father and the woman he loves as mother, and which otherwise could never, *as such*, attain to existence, while the objectification of the will to live expressly demands this existence. It is the feeling that he is acting in affairs of such transcendent importance which raises the lover so high above everything earthly, nay, even above himself, and gives such a hyperphysical clothing to his very physical desires, that love becomes a poetical episode even in the life of the most prosaic man; in which last case the matter sometimes assumes a comical aspect. That mandate of the will which objectifies itself in the species exhibits itself in the consciousness of the lover under the mask of the anticipation of an infinite blessedness which is to be found for him in the union with this female individual. Now, in the highest grades of love this chimera becomes so radiant that if it cannot be attained life itself loses all charm, and now appears so joyless, hollow, and insupportable that the disgust at it even overcomes the fear of death, so that it is then sometimes voluntarily cut short. The will of such a man has been caught in the vortex of the will of the species, or this has obtained such a great predominance over the individual will that if such a man cannot be effective in the first capacity, he disdains to be so in the last. The individual is here too weak a vessel to be capable of enduring the infinite longing of the will of the species concentrated upon a definite object. In this case, therefore, the issue is suicide, sometimes the double suicide of the two lovers; unless, to save life, nature allows madness to intervene, which then covers with its veil the consciousness of that hopeless state. No year passes without proving the reality of what has been expounded by several cases of all these kinds.

Not only, however, has the unsatisfied passion of love

sometimes a tragic issue, but the satisfied passion also leads oftener to unhappiness than to happiness. For its demands often conflict so much with the personal welfare of him who is concerned that they undermine it, because they are incompatible with his other circumstances, and disturb the plan of life built upon them. Nay, not only with external circumstances is love often in contradiction, but even with the lover's own individuality, for it flings itself upon persons who, apart from the sexual relation, would be hateful, contemptible, and even abhorrent to the lover. But so much more powerful is the will of the species than that of the individual that the lover shuts his eyes to all those qualities which are repellent to him, overlooks all, ignores all, and binds himself for ever to the object of his passion—so entirely is he blinded by that illusion, which vanishes as soon as the will of the species is satisfied, and leaves behind a detested companion for life. Only from this can it be explained that we often see very reasonable and excellent men bound to termagants and she-devils, and cannot conceive how they could have made such a choice. On this account the ancients represented love as blind. Indeed, a lover may even know distinctly and feel bitterly the faults of temperament and character of his bride, which promise him a miserable life, and yet not be frightened away:—

"I ask not, I care not,
If guilt's in thy heart,
I know that I love thee
Whatever thou art."

For ultimately he seeks not his own things, but those of a third person, who has yet to come into being, although he is involved in the illusion that what he seeks is his own affair. But it is just this not seeking of one's own things which is everywhere the stamp of greatness, that gives to passionate love also a touch of sublimity, and makes it a worthy subject of poetry. Finally, sexual love is compatible even with the extremest hatred towards its object:

therefore Plato has compared it to the love of the wolf for the sheep. This case appears when a passionate lover, in spite of all efforts and entreaties, cannot obtain a favourable hearing on any condition:—

> "I love and hate her."
>
> —SHAKSPEARE, *Cymb.*, iii. 5.

The hatred of the loved one which then is kindled sometimes goes so far that the lover murders her, and then himself. One or two examples of this generally happen every year; they will be found in the newspapers. Therefore Goethe's lines are quite correct:—

> "By all despised love! By hellish element!
> Would that I knew a worse, that I might swear by!"

It is really no hyperbole if a lover describes the coldness of his beloved and the delight of her vanity, which feeds on his sufferings, as cruelty; for he is under the influence of an impulse which, akin to the instinct of insects, compels him, in spite of all grounds of reason, to pursue his end unconditionally, and to undervalue everything else: he cannot give it up. Not one but many a Petrarch has there been who was compelled to drag through life the unsatisfied ardour of love, like a fetter, an iron weight at his foot, and breathe his sighs in lonely woods; but only in the one Petrarch dwelt also the gift of poetry; so that Goethe's beautiful lines hold good of him:—

> "And when in misery the man was dumb
> A god gave me the power to tell my sorrow."

In fact, the genius of the species wages war throughout with the guardian geniuses of individuals, is their pursuer and enemy, always ready relentlessly to destroy personal happiness in order to carry out its ends; nay, the welfare of whole nations has sometimes been sacrificed to its humours. An example of this is given us by Shakspeare in "Henry VI.," pt. iii., act 3, sc. 2 and 3. All this depends upon the fact that the species, as that in which the root of our being lies, has a closer and earlier right to us than the individual; hence its affairs take precedence. From the feeling of this the ancients personified the genius of the species in Cupid, a malevolent, cruel, and therefore ill-reputed god, in spite of his childish appearance; a capricious, despotic demon, but yet lord of gods and men:

" Συ δ'ω θεων τυραννε κ'ανθρωπων, Ερως!"
(*Tu, deorum hominumque tyranne, Amor!*)

A deadly shot, blindness, and wings are his attributes. The latter signify inconstancy; and this appears, as a rule, only with the disillusion which is the consequence of satisfaction.

Because the passion depended upon an illusion, which represented that which has only value for the species as valuable for the individual, the deception must vanish after the attainment of the end of the species. The spirit of the species which took possession of the individual sets it free again. Forsaken by this spirit, the individual falls back into its original limitation and narrowness, and sees with wonder that after such a high, heroic, and infinite effort nothing has resulted for its pleasure but what every sexual gratification affords. Contrary to expectation, it finds itself no happier than before. It observes that it has been the dupe of the will of the species. Therefore, as a rule, a Theseus who has been made happy will forsake his Ariadne. If Petrarch's passion had been satisfied, his song would have been silenced from that time forth, like that of the bird as soon as the eggs are laid.

Here let me remark in passing that however much my metaphysics of love will displease the very persons who are entangled in this passion, yet if rational considerations in general could avail anything against it, the fundamental truth disclosed by me would necessarily fit one more than anything else to subdue it. But the saying of the old comedian will, no doubt, remain true: "*Quæ res in se neque consilium, neque modum habet ullum, eam consilio regere non potes.*"

Marriages from love are made in the interest of the species, not of the individuals. Certainly the persons concerned imagine they are advancing their own happiness; but their real end is one which is foreign to themselves, for it lies in the production of an individual which is only possible through them. Brought together by this aim, they ought henceforth to try to get on together as well as possible. But very often the pair brought together by that instinctive illusion, which is the essence of passionate love, will, in other respects, be of very different natures. This comes to light when the illusion vanishes, as it necessarily must. Accordingly love marriages, as a rule, turn out unhappy; for through them the coming generation is cared for at the expense of the present. "*Quien se casa por amores, ha de vivir con dolores*" (Who marries from love must live in sorrow), says the Spanish proverb. The opposite is the case with marriages contracted for purposes of convenience, generally in accordance with the choice of the parents. The considerations prevailing here, of whatever kind they may be, are at least real, and cannot vanish of themselves. Through them, however, the happiness of the present generation is certainly cared for, to the disadvantage of the coming generation, and notwithstanding this it remains problematical. The man who in his marriage looks to money more than to the satisfaction of his inclination lives more in the individual than in the species; which is directly opposed to the truth; hence it appears unnatural, and excites a certain contempt. A girl who, against the advice of her parents, rejects the offer of a rich and not yet old man, in order, setting aside all considerations of convenience, to choose according to her instinctive inclination alone, sacrifices her individual welfare to the species. But just on this account one cannot withhold from her a certain approbation; for she has preferred what is of most importance, and has acted in the spirit of nature (more exactly, of the species), while the parents advised in the spirit of individual egoism. In accordance with all this, it appears as if in making a marriage either the individual or the interests of the species must come off a loser. And this is generally the case; for that convenience and passionate love should go hand in hand is the rarest of lucky accidents. The physical, moral, or intellectual deficiency of the nature of most men may to some extent have its ground in the fact that marriages are ordinarily entered into not from pure choice and inclination, but from all kinds of external considerations, and on account of accidental circumstances. If, however, besides convenience, inclination is also to a certain extent regarded, this is, as it were, an agreement with the genius of the species. Happy marriages are well known to be rare; just because it lies in the nature of marriage that its chief end is not the present but the coming generation. However, let me add, for the consolation of tender, loving natures, that sometimes passionate sexual love associates itself with a feeling of an entirely different origin—real friendship based upon agreement of disposition, which yet for the most part only appears when sexual love proper is extinguished in its satisfaction. This friendship will then generally spring from the fact that the supplementing and corresponding physical, moral, and intellectual qualities of the two individuals, from which sexual love arose, with reference to the child to be produced, are, with reference also to the individuals themselves, related to each other in a supplementary manner as opposite qualities of temperament and mental gifts, and thereby form the basis of a harmony of disposition.

The whole metaphysics of love here dealt with stands in close connection with my metaphysics in general, and the light which it throws upon this may be summed up as follows.

We have seen that the careful selection for the satisfaction of the sexual impulse, a selection which rises through innumerable degrees up to that of passionate love, depends upon the highly serious interest which man takes in the special personal constitution of the next generation. Now this exceedingly remarkable interest confirms two truths which have been set forth in the preceding chapters. (1.) The indestructibility of the true nature of man, which lives on in that coming generation. For that interest which is so lively and eager, and does not spring from reflection and intention, but from the inmost characteristics and tendencies of our nature, could not be so indelibly present and exercise such great power over man if he were absolutely perishable, and were merely followed in time by a race actually and entirely different from him. (2.) That his true nature lies more in the species than in the individual. For that interest in the special nature of the species, which is the root of all love, from the passing inclination to the serious passion, is for every one really the highest concern, the success or failure of which touches him most sensibly; therefore it is called *par excellence* the affair of the heart. Moreover, when this interest has expressed itself strongly and decidedly, everything which merely concerns one's own person is postponed and necessarily sacrificed to it. Through this, then, man shows that the species lies closer to him than the individual, and he lives more immediately in the former than in the latter. Why does the lover hang with complete abandonment on the eyes of his chosen one, and is ready to make every sacrifice for her? Because it is his immortal part that longs after her; while it is only his mortal part that desires everything else. That vehement or intense longing directed to a particular woman is accordingly an immediate pledge of the indestructibility of the kernel of our being, and of its continued existence in the species. But to regard this continued existence as something trifling and insufficient is an error which arises from the fact that under the conception of the continued life of the species one thinks nothing more than the future existence of beings similar to us, but in no regard identical with us; and this again because, starting from knowledge directed towards without, one takes into consideration only the external form of the species as we apprehend it in perception, and not its inner nature. But it is just this inner nature which lies at the foundation of our own consciousness as its kernel, and hence indeed is more immediate than this itself, and, as thing in itself, free from the *principium individuationis*, is really the same and identical in all individuals, whether they exist together or after each other. Now this is the will to live, thus just that which desires life and continuance so vehemently. This accordingly is spared and unaffected by death. It can attain to no better state than its present one; and consequently for it, with life, the constant suffering and striving of the individuals is certain. To free it from this is reserved for the denial of the will to live, as the means by which the individual will breaks away from the stem of the species, and surrenders that existence in it. We lack conceptions for that which it now is; indeed all data for such conceptions are wanting. We can only describe it as that which is free to be will to live or not. Buddhism denotes the latter case by the word Nirvana, the etymology of which was given in the note at the end of chapter 41. It is the point which remains for ever unattainable to all human knowledge, just as such.

If now, from the standpoint of this last consideration, we contemplate the turmoil of life, we behold all occupied with its want and misery, straining all their powers to satisfy its infinite needs and to ward off its multifarious sorrows, yet without daring to hope anything else than simply the preservation of this tormented existence for a short span of time. In between, however, in the midst of the tumult, we see the glances of two lovers meet longingly: yet why so secretly, fearfully, and stealthily? Because these lovers are the traitors who seek to perpetuate the whole want and drudgery, which would otherwise speedily reach an end; this they wish to frustrate, as others like them have frustrated it before. This consideration already passes over into the subject of the following chapter.[1]

[[1] The appendix to this chapter was added only in the third edition of the German, and is meant to explain, in consistency with Schopenhauer's general principles, the wide prevalence of the practice of pederasty, among different nations and in different ages. It is omitted.—*Trs.*]

CHAPTER XLV.[1]

ON THE ASSERTION OF THE WILL TO LIVE.

If the will to live exhibited itself merely as an impulse to self-preservation, this would only be an assertion of the individual phenomenon for the span of time of its natural duration. The cares and troubles of such a life would not be great, and consequently existence would be easy and serene. Since, on the contrary, the will wills life absolutely and for all time, it exhibits itself also as sexual impulse, which has in view an endless series of generations. This impulse does away with that carelessness, serenity, and innocence which would accompany a merely individual existence, for it brings unrest and melancholy into the consciousness; misfortunes, cares, and misery into the course of life. If, on the other hand, it is voluntarily suppressed, as we see in rare exceptions, then this is the turning of the will, which changes its course. The will does not then transcend the individual, but is abolished in it. Yet this can only take place by means of the individual doing painful violence to itself. If, however, it does take place, then the freedom from care and the serenity of the purely individual existence is restored to the consciousness, and indeed in a higher degree. On the other hand, to the satisfaction of that most vehement of all impulses and desires is linked the origin of a new existence, thus the carrying out of life anew, with all its burdens, cares, wants, and pains; certainly in another individual; yet if the two who are different in the phe-

[1] This chapter is connected with § 60 of the first volume.

nomenon were so absolutely and in themselves, where would then be eternal justice? Life presents itself as a problem, a task to be worked out, and therefore, as a rule, as a constant conflict with necessity. Accordingly every one tries to get through with it and come off as well as he can. He performs life as a compulsory service which he owes. But who has contracted the debt?—His begetter, in the enjoyment of sensual pleasure. Thus, because the one has enjoyed this, the other must live, suffer, and die. However, we know and look back here to the fact that the difference of the similar is conditioned by space and time, which in this sense I have called the *principium individuationis.* Otherwise eternal justice could not be vindicated. Paternal love, on account of which the father is ready to do, to suffer, and to risk more for his child than for himself, and at the same time knows that he owes this, depends simply upon the fact that the begetter recognises himself in the begotten.

The life of a man, with its endless care, want, and suffering, is to be regarded as the explanation and paraphrase of the act of procreation, *i.e.,* the decided assertion of the will to live; and further, it is also due to this that he owes to nature the debt of death, and thinks with anxiety of this debt. Is this not evidence of the fact that our existence involves guilt? At any rate, we always exist, subject to the periodical payment of the toll, birth and death, and successively partake of all the sorrows and joys of life, so that none can escape us: this is just the fruit of the assertion of the will to live. Thus the fear of death, which in spite of all the miseries of life holds us firmly to it, is really illusory; but just as illusory is the impulse which has enticed us into it. This enticement itself may be seen objectively in the reciprocal longing glances of two lovers; they are the purest expression of the will to live, in its assertion. How soft and tender it is here! It wills wellbeing, and quiet pleasure, and mild joys for itself, for others, for all. It is the theme of Anacreon. Thus by allurements and flattery it makes its way into life. But when once it is there, misery introduces crime, and crime misery; horror and desolation fill the scene. It is the theme of Æschylus.

But now the act through which the will asserts itself and man arises is one of which all are, in their inmost being, ashamed, which they therefore carefully conceal; nay, if they are caught in it, are terrified as if they had been taken in a crime. It is an action of which in cold reflection one generally thinks with dislike, and in a lofty mood with loathing. Reflections which in this regard approach the matter more closely are offered by Montaigne in the fifth chapter of the third book, under the marginal heading: "*Ce que c'est que l'amour.*" A peculiar sadness and repentance follows close upon it, is yet most perceptible after the first performance of the act, and in general is the more distinct the nobler is the character. Hence even Pliny, the pagan, says: "*Homini tantum primi coitus pœnitentia, augurium scilicet vitæ, a pœnitenda origine*" (*Hist. Nat.*, x. 83). And, on the other hand, in Goethe's "Faust," what do devil and witches practise and sing of on their Sabbath? Lewdness and obscenity. And in the same work (in the admirable "Paralipomena" to "Faust") what does incarnate Satan preach before the assembled multitude? Lewdness and obscenity. But simply and solely by means of the continual practice of such an act as this does the human race subsist. If now optimism were right, if our existence were to be thankfully recognised as the gift of the highest goodness guided by wisdom, and accordingly in itself praiseworthy, commendable, and agreeable, then certainly the act which perpetuates it would necessarily have borne quite another physiognomy. If, on the other hand, this existence is a kind of false step or error; if it is the work of an originally blind will, whose most fortunate development is that it comes to itself in order to abolish itself; then the act which perpetuates that existence must appear precisely as it does appear.

With reference to the first fundamental truth of my doctrine, the remark deserves a place here that the shame mentioned above which attaches to the act of generation extends even to the parts which are concerned in this, although, like all other parts, they are given us by nature. This is again a striking proof that not only the actions but even the body of man is to be regarded as the manifestation, the objectification, of his will, and as its work. For he could not be ashamed of a thing which existed without his will.

The act of generation is further related to the world, as the answer is related to the riddle. The world is wide in space and old in time, and of an inexhaustible multiplicity of forms. Yet all this is only the manifestation of the will to live; and the concentration, the focus of this will is the act of generation. Thus in this act the inner nature of the world expresses itself most distinctly. In this regard it is indeed worth noticing that this act itself is also distinctly called "the will" in the very significant German phrase, "*Er verlangte von ihr, sie sollte ihm zu Willen sein*" (He desired her to comply with his wishes). As the most distinct expression of the will, then, this act is the kernel, the compendium, the quintessence of the world. Therefore from it we obtain light as to the nature and tendency of the world: it is the answer to the riddle. Accordingly it is understood under "the tree of knowledge," for after acquaintance with it the eyes of every one are opened as to life, as Byron also says:

> "The tree of knowledge has been plucked,—all's known."
> —*Don Juan*, i. 128.

It is not less in keeping with this quality that it is the great *αρρητον*, the open secret, which must never and nowhere be distinctly mentioned, but always and everywhere is understood as the principal matter, and is therefore constantly present to the thoughts of all, wherefore also the slightest allusion to it is instantly understood. The leading part which that act, and what is connected with it, plays in the world, because love intrigues are everywhere, on the one hand, pursued, and, on the other hand, assumed, is quite in keeping with the importance of this *punctum saliens* of the egg of the world. The source of the amusing is simply the constant concealment of the chief concern.

But see now how the young, innocent, human intellect, when that great secret of the world first becomes known to it, is startled at the enormity! The reason of this is that in the long course which the originally unconscious will had to traverse before it rose to intellect, especially to human, rational intellect, it became so strange to itself that it no longer knows its origin, that *pœnitenda origo*, and now, from the standpoint of pure, and therefore innocent, knowing, is horrified at it.

Since now the focus of the will, *i.e.*, its concentration and highest expression, is the sexual impulse and its satisfaction, this is very significantly and naïvely expressed in the symbolical language of nature through the fact that the individualised will, that is, the man and the brute, makes its entrance into the world through the door of the sexual organs.

The assertion of the will to live, which accordingly has its centre in the act of generation, is in the case of the brute infallible. For the will, which is the *natura naturans*, first arrives at reflection in man. To arrive at reflection means, not merely to know the momentary necessity of the individual will, how to serve it in the pressing present—as is the case with the brute, in proportion to its completeness and its necessities, which go hand in hand—but to have attained a greater breadth of knowledge, by virtue of a distinct remembrance of the past, an approximate anticipation of the future, and thereby a general survey of the individual life, both one's own life and that of others, nay, of existence in general. Really the life of every species of brute, through the thousands of years of its existence, is to a certain extent like a single moment; for it is mere consciousness of the present, without that of the past and the future, and consequently without that of death. In this sense it is to be regarded as a permanent moment, a *Nunc stans.* Here we see, in passing, most distinctly that in general the form of life, or the manifestation of the will with consciousness, is primarily and immediately merely the present. Past and future are added only in the case of man, and indeed merely in conception, are known *in abstracto,* and perhaps illustrated by pictures of the imagination. Thus after the will to live, *i.e.,* the inner being of nature, in the ceaseless striving towards complete objectification and complete enjoyment, has run through the whole series of the brutes,—which often occurs in the various periods of successive animal series each arising anew on the same planet,—it arrives at last at reflection in the being who is endowed with reason, man. Here now to him the thing begins to be doubtful, the question forces itself upon him whence and wherefore all this is, and chiefly whether the care and misery of his life and effort is really repaid by the gain? "*Le jeu vaut-il bien la chandelle?*" Accordingly here is the point at which, in the light of distinct knowledge, he decides for the assertion or denial of the will to live; although as a rule he can only bring the latter to consciousness in a mythical form. We have consequently no ground for assuming that a still more highly developed objectification of the will is ever reached, anywhere; for it has already reached its turning-point here.

CHAPTER XLVI.[1]

ON THE VANITY AND SUFFERING OF LIFE.

AWAKENED to life out of the night of unconsciousness, the will finds itself an individual, in an endless and boundless world, among innumerable individuals, all striving, suffering, erring; and as if through a troubled dream it hurries back to its old unconsciousness. Yet till then its desires are limitless, its claims inexhaustible, and every satisfied desire gives rise to a new one. No possible satisfaction in the world could suffice to still its longings, set a goal to its infinite cravings, and fill the bottomless abyss of its heart. Then let one consider what as a rule are the satisfactions of any kind that a man obtains. For the most part nothing more than the bare maintenance of this existence itself, extorted day by day with unceasing trouble and constant care in the conflict with want, and with death in prospect. Everything in life shows that earthly happiness is destined to be frustrated or recognised as an illusion. The grounds of this lie deep in the nature of things. Accordingly the life of most men is troubled and short. Those who are comparatively happy are so, for the most part, only apparently, or else, like men of long life, they are the rare exceptions, a possibility of which there had to be,—as decoy-birds. Life presents itself as a continual deception in small things as in great. If it has promised, it does not keep its word, unless to

[1] This chapter is connected with §§ 56–59 of the first volume. Also chapters 11 and 12 of the second volume of the "Parerga and Paralipomena" should be compared with it.

show how little worth desiring were the things desired: thus we are deluded now by hope, now by what was hoped for. If it has given, it did so in order to take. The enchantment of distance shows us paradises which vanish like optical illusions when we have allowed ourselves to be mocked by them. Happiness accordingly always lies in the future, or else in the past, and the present may be compared to a small dark cloud which the wind drives over the sunny plain: before and behind it all is bright, only it itself always casts a shadow. The present is therefore always insufficient; but the future is uncertain, and the past irrevocable. Life with its hourly, daily, weekly, yearly, little, greater, and great misfortunes, with its deluded hopes and its accidents destroying all our calculations, bears so distinctly the impression of something with which we must become disgusted, that it is hard to conceive how one has been able to mistake this and allow oneself to be persuaded that life is there in order to be thankfully enjoyed, and that man exists in order to be happy. Rather that continual illusion and disillusion, and also the nature of life throughout, presents itself to us as intended and calculated to awaken the conviction that nothing at all is worth our striving, our efforts and struggles, that all good things are vanity, the world in all its ends bankrupt, and life a business which does not cover its expenses;—so that our will may turn away from it.

The way in which this vanity of all objects of the will makes itself known and comprehensible to the intellect which is rooted in the individual, is primarily *time*. It is the form by means of which that vanity of things appears as their perishableness; for on account of this all our pleasures and joys disappear in our hands, and we afterwards ask astonished where they have remained. That nothingness itself is therefore the only *objective* element in time, *i.e.*, that which corresponds to it in the inner nature of things, thus that of which it is the expression. Just on this account time is the *a priori* necessary form of all our perceptions; in it everything must present itself, even we ourselves. Accordingly, first of all, our life is like a payment which one receives in nothing but copper pence, and yet must then give a discharge for: the copper pence are the days; the discharge is death. For at last time makes known the judgment of nature concerning the work of all the beings which appear in it, in that it destroys them:—

> "And rightly so, for all that arises
> Is worthy only of being destroyed.
> Hence were it better that nothing arose."

Thus old age and death, to which every life necessarily hurries on, are the sentence of condemnation on the will to live, coming from the hands of nature itself, and which declares that this will is an effort which frustrates itself. "What thou hast wished," it says, "ends thus: desire something better." Hence the instruction which his life affords to every one consists, as a whole, in this, that the objects of his desires continually delude, waver, and fall, and accordingly bring more misery than joy, till at last the whole foundation upon which they all stand gives way, in that his life itself is destroyed and so he receives the last proof that all his striving and wishing was a perversity, a false path:—

> "Then old age and experience, hand in hand,
> Lead him to death, and make him understand,
> After a search so painful and so long,
> That all his life he has been in the wrong."

We shall, however, enter into the details of the matter, for it is in these views that I have met with most contradiction. First of all, I have to confirm by the following remarks the proof given in the text of the negative nature of all satisfaction, thus of all pleasure and all happiness, in opposition to the positive nature of pain.

We feel pain, but not painlessness; we feel care, but

not the absence of care; fear, but not security. We feel the wish as we feel hunger and thirst; but as soon as it has been fulfilled, it is like the mouthful that has been taken, which ceases to exist for our feeling the moment it is swallowed. Pleasures and joys we miss painfully whenever they are wanting; but pains, even when they cease after having long been present, are not directly missed, but at the most are intentionally thought of by means of reflection. For only pain and want can be felt positively, and therefore announce themselves; well-being, on the other hand, is merely negative. Therefore we do not become conscious of the three greatest blessings of life, health, youth, and freedom, so long as we possess them, but only after we have lost them; for they also are negations. We only observe that days of our life were happy after they have given place to unhappy ones. In proportion as pleasures increase, the susceptibility for them decreases: what is customary is no longer felt as a pleasure. Just in this way, however, is the susceptibility for suffering increased, for the loss of what we are accustomed to is painfully felt. Thus the measure of what is necessary increases through possession, and thereby the capacity for feeling pain. The hours pass the quicker the more agreeably they are spent, and the slower the more painfully they are spent; because pain, not pleasure, is the positive, the presence of which makes itself felt. In the same way we become conscious of time when we are bored, not when we are diverted. Both these cases prove that our existence is most happy when we perceive it least, from which it follows that it would be better not to have it. Great and lively joy can only be conceived as the consequence of great misery, which has preceded it; for nothing can be added to a state of permanent satisfaction but some amusement, or the satisfaction of vanity. Hence all poets are obliged to bring their heroes into anxious and painful situations, so that they may be able to free them from them. Dramas and Epics accordingly always describe only fighting, suffering, tormented men; and every romance is a rareeshow in which we observe the spasms and convulsions of the agonised human heart. Walter Scott has naïvely expressed this æsthetic necessity in the conclusion to his novel, "Old Mortality." Voltaire, who was so highly favoured both by nature and fortune, says, in entire agreement with the truth proved by me: "*Le bonheur n'est qu'un rève, et la douleur est réelle.*" And he adds: "*Il y a quatre-vingts ans que je l'éprouve. Je n'y sais autre chose que me résigner, et me dire que les mouches sont nées pour être mangées par les araignées, et les hommes pour être dévorés par les chagrins.*"

Before so confidently affirming that life is a blessing worth desiring or giving thanks for, let one compare calmly the sum of the possible pleasures which a man can enjoy in his life with the sum of the possible sorrows which may come to him in his life. I believe the balance will not be hard to strike. At bottom, however, it is quite superfluous to dispute whether there is more good or evil in the world: for the mere existence of evil decides the matter. For the evil can never be annulled, and consequently can never be balanced by the good which may exist along with it or after it.

"*Mille piacer' non vagliono un tormento.*"—Petr.
(A thousand pleasures are not worth one torment.)

For that a thousand had lived in happiness and pleasure would never do away with the anguish and death-agony of a single one; and just as little does my present well-being undo my past suffering. If, therefore, the evils in the world were a hundred times less than is the case, yet their mere existence would be sufficient to establish a truth which may be expressed in different ways, though always somewhat indirectly, the truth that we have not to rejoice but rather to mourn at the existence of the world;—that its non-existence would be preferable to its existence;—

that it is something which at bottom ought not to be, &c., &c. Very beautiful is Byron's expression of this truth:—

> " *Our life is a false nature,*—'tis not in
> The harmony of things, this hard decree,
> This uneradicable taint of sin,
> This boundless Upas, this all-blasting tree
> Whose root is earth, whose leaves and branches be
> The skies, which rain their plagues on men like dew—
> Disease, death, bondage—all the woes we see—
> And worse, the woes we see not—which throb through
> The immedicable soul, with heart-aches ever new."

If the world and life were an end in themselves, and accordingly required theoretically no justification and practically no indemnification or compensation, but existed, for instance, as Spinoza and the Spinozists of the present day represent it, as the single manifestation of a God, who, *animi causa,* or else in order to mirror himself, undertook such an evolution of himself; and hence its existence neither required to be justified by reasons nor redeemed by results;—then the sufferings and miseries of life would not indeed have to be fully equalled by the pleasures and well-being in it; for this, as has been said, is impossible, because my present pain is never abolished by future joys, for the latter fill their time as the former fills its time: but there would have to be absolutely no suffering, and death also would either have not to be, or else to have no terrors for us. Only thus would life pay for itself.

But since now our state is rather something which had better not be, everything about us bears the trace of this, —just as in hell everything smells of sulphur—for everything is always imperfect and illusory, everything agreeable is displaced by something disagreeable, every enjoyment is only a half one, every pleasure introduces its own disturbance, every relief new difficulties, every aid of our daily and hourly need leaves us each moment in the lurch and denies its service, the step upon which we place our foot so often gives way under us, nay, misfortunes great and small are the element of our life; and, in a word, we are like Phineus, whose food was all tainted and made uneatable by the harpies.[1] Two remedies for this are tried: first, *ευλαβεια, i.e.*, prudence, foresight, cunning; it does not fully instruct us, is insufficient, and leads to defeat. Secondly, the stoical equanimity which seeks to arm us against all misfortunes by preparedness for everything and contempt of all: practically it becomes cynical renunciation, which prefers once for all to reject all means of relief and all alleviations—it reduces us to the position of dogs, like Diogenes in his tub. The truth is, we ought to be wretched, and we are so. The chief source of the serious evils which affect men is man himself: *homo homini lupus.* Whoever keeps this last fact clearly in view beholds the world as a hell, which surpasses that of Dante in this respect, that one man must be the devil of another. For this, one is certainly more fitted than another; an arch-fiend, indeed, more fitted than all others, appearing in the form of a conqueror, who places several hundred thousand men opposite each other, and says to them: "To suffer and die is your destiny; now shoot each other with guns and cannons," and they do so.

In general, however, the conduct of men towards each other is characterised as a rule by injustice, extreme unfairness, hardness, nay, cruelty: an opposite course of conduct appears only as an exception. Upon this depends the necessity of the State and legislation, and upon none of your false pretences. But in all cases which do not lie within the reach of the law, that regardlessness of his like, peculiar to man, shows itself at once; a regardlessness which springs from his boundless egoism, and sometimes also from wickedness. How man deals with man is shown, for example, by negro slavery, the final end of which is sugar and coffee. But we do not need to go so far:

[1] All that we lay hold of resists us because it has its own will, which must be overcome.

at the age of five years to enter a cotton-spinning or other factory, and from that time forth to sit there daily, first ten, then twelve, and ultimately fourteen hours, performing the same mechanical labour, is to purchase dearly the satisfaction of drawing breath. But this is the fate of millions, and that of millions more is analogous to it.

We others, however, can be made perfectly miserable by trifling misfortunes; perfectly happy, not by the world. Whatever one may say, the happiest moment of the happy man is the moment of his falling asleep, and the unhappiest moment of the unhappy that of his awaking. An indirect but certain proof of the fact that men feel themselves unhappy, and consequently are so, is also abundantly afforded by the fearful envy which dwells in us all, and which in all relations of life, on the occasion of any superiority, of whatever kind it may be, is excited, and cannot contain its poison. Because they feel themselves unhappy, men cannot endure the sight of one whom they imagine happy; he who for the moment feels himself happy would like to make all around him happy also, and says:

"*Que tout le monde ici soit heureux de ma joie.*"

If life were in itself a blessing to be prized, and decidedly to be preferred to non-existence, the exit from it would not need to be guarded by such fearful sentinels as death and its terrors. But who would continue in life as it is if death were less terrible? And again, who could even endure the thought of death if life were a pleasure! But thus the former has still always this good, that it is the end of life, and we console ourselves with regard to the suffering of life with death, and with regard to death with the suffering of life. The truth is, that the two inseparably belong to each other, for together they constitute a deviation from the right path, to return to which is as difficult as it is desirable.

If the world were not something which, expressed *practically*, ought not to be, it would also not be *theoretically* a problem; but its existence would either require no explanation, inasmuch as it would be so entirely self-evident that wonder concerning it or a question about it could arise in no mind, or its end would present itself unmistakably. Instead of this, however, it is indeed an insoluble problem; for even the most perfect philosophy will yet always contain an unexplained element, like an insoluble deposit or the remainder which the irrational relation of two quantities always leaves over. Therefore if one ventures to raise the question why there is not rather nothing than this world, the world cannot be justified from itself, no ground, no final cause of its existence can be found in itself, it cannot be shown that it exists for its own sake, *i.e.*, for its own advantage. In accordance with my teaching, this can certainly be explained from the fact that the principle of its existence is expressly one which is without ground, a blind will to live, which as thing in itself cannot be made subject to the principle of sufficient reason, which is merely the form of the phenomenon, and through which alone every why is justified. But this also agrees with the nature of the world, for only a blind will, no seeing will, could place itself in the position in which we behold ourselves. A seeing will would rather have soon made the calculation that the business did not cover the cost, for such a mighty effort and struggle with the straining of all the powers, under constant care, anxiety, and want, and with the inevitable destruction of every individual life, finds no compensation in the ephemeral existence itself, which is so obtained, and which passes into nothing in our hands. Hence, then, the explanation of the world from the Anaxagorean *νοῦς*, *i.e.*, from a will accompanied by *knowledge*, necessarily demands optimism to excuse it, which accordingly is set up and maintained in spite of the loudly crying evidence of a whole world full of misery. Life is there given out to be a gift, while it is evident that every one would have declined such a gift if he could have seen it and tested it beforehand; just as Lessing admired the understanding of his son, who, because he had absolutely declined to enter life, had to be forcibly brought into it with the forceps, but was scarcely there when he hurried away from it again. On the other hand, it is then well said that life should be, from one end to the other, only a lesson; to which, however, any one might reply: "For this very reason I wish I had been left in the peace of the all-sufficient nothing, where I would have had no need of lessons or of anything else." If indeed it should now be added that he must one day give an account of every hour of his life, he would be more justified in himself demanding an account of why he had been transferred from that rest into such a questionable, dark, anxious, and painful situation. To this, then, we are led by false views. For human existence, far from bearing the character of a *gift*, has entirely the character of a *debt* that has been contracted. The calling in of this debt appears in the form of the pressing wants, tormenting desires, and endless misery established through this existence. As a rule, the whole lifetime is devoted to the paying off of this debt; but this only meets the interest. The payment of the capital takes place through death. And when was this debt contracted? At the begetting.

Accordingly, if we regard man as a being whose existence is a punishment and an expiation, we then view him in a right light. The myth of the fall (although probably, like the whole of Judaism, borrowed from the Zend-Avesta: Bundahish, 15), is the only point in the Old Testament to which I can ascribe metaphysical, although only allegorical, truth; indeed it is this alone that reconciles me to the Old Testament. Our existence resembles nothing so much as the consequence of a false step and a guilty desire. New Testament Christianity, the ethical spirit of which is that of Brahmanism and Buddhism, and is therefore very foreign to the otherwise optimistic spirit of the Old Testament, has also, very wisely, linked itself on precisely to that myth: indeed, without this it would have found no point of connection with Judaism at all. If any one desires to measure the degree of guilt with which our existence is tainted, then let him look at the suffering that is connected with it. Every great pain, whether bodily or mental, declares what we deserve: for it could not come to us if we did not deserve it. That Christianity also regards our existence in this light is shown by a passage in Luther's Commentary on Galatians, chap. 3, which I only have beside me in Latin: "*Sumus autem nos omnes corporibus et rebus subjecti Diabolo, et hospites sumus in mundo, cujus ipse princeps et Deus est. Ideo panis, quem edimus, potus, quem bibimus, vestes, quibus utimur, imo aër et totum quo vivimus in carne, sub ipsius imperio est.*" An outcry has been made about the melancholy and disconsolate nature of my philosophy; yet it lies merely in the fact that instead of inventing a future hell as the equivalent of sin, I show that where guilt lies in the world there is also already something akin to hell; but whoever is inclined to deny this can easily experience it.

And to this world, to this scene of tormented and agonised beings, who only continue to exist by devouring each other, in which, therefore, every ravenous beast is the living grave of thousands of others, and its self-maintenance is a chain of painful deaths; and in which the capacity for feeling pain increases with knowledge, and therefore reaches its highest degree in man, a degree which is the higher the more intelligent the man is; to this world it has been sought to apply the system of optimism, and demonstrate to us that it is the best of all possible worlds. The absurdity is glaring. But an optimist bids me open my eyes and look at the world, how beautiful it is in the sunshine, with its mountains and valleys, streams, plants, animals, &c. &c. Is the world, then, a rareeshow? These things are certainly beautiful to *look at*, but to *be* them is something quite different. Then comes a teleologist, and praises to me the wise arrangement by virtue of which it is taken care that the planets do not run their heads together, that land and sea do not get mixed into a pulp, but are held so beautifully apart, also that everything is neither rigid with continual frost nor roasted with heat; in the same way, that in consequence of the obliquity of the ecliptic there is no eternal spring, in which nothing could attain to ripeness, &c. &c. But this and all like it are mere *conditiones sine quibus non.* If in general there is to be a world at all, if its planets are to exist at least as long as the light of a distant fixed star requires to reach them, and are not, like Lessing's son, to depart again immediately after birth, then certainly it must not be so clumsily constructed that its very framework threatens to fall to pieces. But if one goes on to the results of this applauded work, considers the players who act upon the stage which is so durably constructed, and now sees how with sensibility pain appears, and increases in proportion as the sensibility develops to intelligence, and then how, keeping pace with this, desire and suffering come out ever more strongly, and increase till at last human life affords no other material than this for tragedies and comedies, then whoever is honest will scarcely be disposed to set up hallelujahs. David Hume, in his "Natural History of Religion," §§ 6, 7, 8, and 13, has also exposed, mercilessly but with convincing truth, the real though concealed source of these last. He also explains clearly in the tenth and eleventh books of his "Dialogues on Natural Religion," with very pertinent arguments, which are yet of quite a different kind from mine, the miserable nature of this world and the untenableness of all optimism; in doing which he attacks this in its origin. Both works of Hume's are as well worth reading as they are unknown at the present day in Germany, where, on the other hand, incredible pleasure is found, patriotically, in the most disgusting nonsense of home-bred boastful mediocrities, who are proclaimed great men. Hamann, however, translated these dialogues; Kant went through the translation, and late in life wished to induce Hamann's son to publish them because the translation of Platner did not satisfy him (see Kant's biography by F. W. Schubert, pp. 81 and 165). From every page of David Hume there is more to be learned than from the collected philosophical works of Hegel, Herbart, and Schleiermacher together.

The founder of systematic optimism, again, is Leibnitz whose philosophical merit I have no intention of denying although I have never succeeded in thinking myself into the monadology, pre-established harmony, and *identitas indiscernibilium*. His "*Nouveaux essays sur l'entendement*" are, however, merely an excerpt, with a full yet weak criticism, with a view to correction, of Locke's work which is justly of world-wide reputation. He here opposes Locke with just as little success as he opposes Newton in the "*Tentamen de motuum cœlestium causis*," directed against the system of gravitation. The "Critique of Pure Reason" is specially directed against this Leibnitz-Wolfian philosophy, and has a polemical, nay, a destructive relation to it, just as it is related to Locke and Hume as a continuation and further construction. That at the present day the professors of philosophy are on all sides engaged in setting Leibnitz, with his juggling, upon his legs again, nay, in glorifying him, and, on the other hand, in depreciating and setting aside Kant as much as possible, has its sufficient reason in the *primum vivere;* the "Critique of Pure Reason" does not admit of one giving out Judaistic mythology as philosophy, nor of one speaking, without ceremony, of the "soul" as a given reality, a well-known and well-accredited person, without giving account of how one arrived at this conception, and what justification one has for using it scientifically. But *primum vivere, deinde philosophari!* Down with Kant, *vivat* our Leibnitz! To return, then, to Leibnitz, I cannot ascribe to the Théodicée, as a methodical and broad unfolding of optimism, any other merit than this, that it gave occasion later for the immortal "*Candide*" of the great Voltaire; whereby certainly Leibnitz's often-repeated and lame excuse for the evil of the world, that the bad sometimes brings about the good, received a confirmation which was unexpected by him. Even by the name of his hero Voltaire indicates that it only requires sincerity to recognise the opposite of optimism. Really upon this scene of sin, suffering, and death optimism makes such an extraordinary figure that one would be forced to regard it as irony if one had not a sufficient explanation of its origin in the secret source of it (insincere flattery, with insulting confidence in its success), which, as was mentioned above, is so delightfully disclosed by Hume.

But indeed to the palpably sophistical proofs of Leibnitz that this is the best of all possible worlds, we may seriously and honestly oppose the proof that it is the worst of all possible worlds. For possible means, not what one may construct in imagination, but what can actually exist and continue. Now this world is so arranged as to be able to maintain itself with great difficulty; but if it were a little worse, it could no longer maintain itself. Consequently a worse world, since it could not continue to exist, is absolutely impossible: thus this world itself is the worst of all possible worlds. For not only if the planets were to run their heads together, but even if any one of the actually appearing perturbations of their course, instead of being gradually balanced by others, continued to increase, the world would soon reach its end. Astronomers know upon what accidental circumstances—principally the irrational relation to each other of the periods of revolution—this depends, and have carefully calculated that it will always go on well; consequently the world also can continue and go on. We will hope that, although Newton was of an opposite opinion, they have not miscalculated, and consequently that the mechanical perpetual motion realised in such a planetary system will not also, like the rest, ultimately come to a standstill. Again, under the firm crust of the planet dwell the powerful forces of nature which, as soon as some accident affords them free play, must necessarily destroy that crust, with everything living upon it, as has already taken place at least three times upon our planet, and will probably take place oftener still. The earthquake of Lisbon, the earthquake of Haiti, the destruction of Pompeii, are only small, playful hints of what is possible. A small alteration of the atmosphere, which cannot even be chemically proved, causes cholera, yellow fever, black death, &c., which carry off millions of men; a somewhat greater alteration would extinguish all life. A very moderate increase of heat would dry up all the rivers and springs. The brutes have received just barely so much in the way of organs and powers as enables them to procure with the greatest exertion sustenance for their own lives and food for their offspring; therefore if a brute loses a limb, or even the full use of one, it must generally perish. Even of the human race, powerful as are the weapons it possesses in understanding and reason, nine-tenths live in constant conflict with want, always balancing themselves with difficulty and effort upon the brink of destruction. Thus throughout, as for the continuance of the whole, so also for that of each individual being the conditions are barely and scantily given, but nothing over. The individual life is a ceaseless battle for existence itself; while at every step destruction threatens it. Just because this threat is so often fulfilled provision had to be made, by means of the enormous excess of the germs, that the destruction of the individuals should not involve that of the species, for which alone nature really cares. The world is therefore as bad as it possibly can be if it is to continue to be at all. *Q. E. D.* The fossils of the entirely different kinds of animal species which formerly inhabited the planet afford us, as a proof of our calculation, the records of worlds the continuance of which was no longer possible, and which consequently were somewhat worse than the worst of possible worlds.

Optimism is at bottom the unmerited self-praise of the real originator of the world, the will to live, which views itself complacently in its works; and accordingly it is not only a false, but also a pernicious doctrine. For it presents life to us as a desirable condition, and the happiness of man as the end of it. Starting from this, every one then believes that he has the most just claim to happiness and pleasure; and if, as is wont to happen, these do not fall to his lot, then he believes that he is wronged, nay, that he loses the end of his existence; while it is far more correct to regard work, privation, misery, and suffering, crowned by death, as the end of our life (as Brahmanism and Buddhism, and also genuine Christianity do); for it is these which lead to the denial of the will to live. In the New Testament the world is represented as a valley of tears, life as a process of purifying or refining, and the symbol of Christianity is an instrument of torture. Therefore, when Leibnitz, Shaftesbury, Bolingbroke, and Pope brought forward optimism, the general offence which it gave depended principally upon the fact that optimism is irreconcilable with Christianity; as Voltaire states and explains in the preface to his excellent poem, "*Le désastre de Lisbonne,*" which is also expressly directed against optimism. This great man, whom I so gladly praise, in opposition to the abuse of venal German ink-slingers, is placed decidedly higher than Rousseau by the insight to which he attained in three respects, and which prove the greater depth of his thinking: (1) the recognition of the preponderating magnitude of the evil and misery of existence with which he is deeply penetrated; (2) that of the strict necessity of the acts of will; (3) that of the truth of Locke's principle, that what thinks may also be material: while Rousseau opposes all this with declamations in his "*Profession de foi du vicaire Savoyard,*" a superficial Protestant pastor's philosophy; as he also in the same spirit attacks the beautiful poem of Voltaire which has just been referred to with ill-founded, shallow, and logically false reasoning, in the interests of optimism, in his long letter to Voltaire of 18th August 1756, which is devoted simply to this purpose. Indeed, the fundamental characteristic and the πρωτον ψευδος of Rousseau's whole philosophy is this, that in the place of the Christian doctrine of original sin, and the original depravity of the human race, he puts an original goodness and unlimited perfectibility of it, which has only been led astray by civilisation and its consequences, and then founds upon this his optimism and humanism.

As in "*Candide*" Voltaire wages war in his facetious manner against optimism, Byron has also done so in his serious and tragic style, in his immortal masterpiece, "Cain," on account of which he also has been honoured with the invectives of the obscurantist, Friedrich Schlegel. If now, in conclusion, to confirm my view, I were to give what has been said by great men of all ages in this anti-optimistic spirit, there would be no end to the quotations, for almost every one of them has expressed in strong language his knowledge of the misery of this world. Thus, not to confirm, but merely to embellish this chapter, a few quotations of this kind may be given at the end of it.

First of all, let me mention here that the Greeks, far as they were from the Christian and lofty Asiatic conception of the world, and although they decidedly stood at the point of view of the assertion of the will, were yet deeply affected by the wretchedness of existence. This is shown even by the invention of tragedy, which belongs to them. Another proof of it is afforded us by the custom of the Thracians, which is first mentioned by Herodotus, though often referred to afterwards—the custom of welcoming the new-born child with lamentations, and recounting all the evils which now lie before it; and, on the other hand, burying the dead with mirth and jesting, because they are no longer exposed to so many and great sufferings. In a beautiful poem preserved for us by Plutarch (*De audiend. poët. in fine*) this runs thus :—

> " Τον φυντα θρηνειν, εις ὁσ' ερχεται κακα·
> Τον δ'αυ θανοντα και πονων πεπαυμενον
> Χαιροντας ευφημουντας εκπεμπειν δομων."

> (*Lugere genitum, tanta qui intrarit mala :*
> *At morte si quis finiisset miserias,*
> *Hunc laude amicos atque lætitia exsequi.*)

It is not to be attributed to historical relationship, but to the moral identity of the matter, that the Mexicans welcomed the new-born child with the words, " My child, thou art born to endure; therefore endure, suffer, and keep silence." And, following the same feeling, Swift (as Walter Scott relates in his Life of Swift) early adopted the custom of keeping his birthday not as a time of joy but of sadness, and of reading on that day the passage of the Bible in which Job laments and curses the day on which it was said in the house of his father a man-child is born.

Well known and too long for quotation is the passage in the " Apology of Socrates," in which Plato makes this wisest of mortals say that death, even if it deprives us of consciousness for ever, would be a wonderful gain, for a deep, dreamless sleep every day is to be preferred even to the happiest life.

A saying of Heraclitus runs : " *Τῳ ουν βιῳ ονομα μεν βιος, εργον δε θανατος.*" (*Vitæ nomen quidem est vita, opus autem mors. Etymologicum magnum, voce* **Βιος**; also *Eustath. ad Iliad.*, i. p. 31.)

The beautiful lines of the " Theogony " are famous :—

> " Αρχην μεν μη φυναι επιχθονιοισιν αριστον,
> Μηδ' εισιδειν αυγας οξεος ἠελιου·
> Φυντα δ' ὁπως ωκιστα πυλας Αϊδαο περησαι,
> Και κεισθαι πολλην γην επαμησαμενον."

> (*Optima sors homini natum non esse, nec unquam*
> *Adspexisse diem, flammiferumque jubar.*
> *Altera jam genitum demitti protinus Orco,*
> *Et pressum multa mergere corpus humo.*)

Sophocles, in "Œdipus Colonus" (1225), has the following abbreviation of the same :—

"Μη φυναι τον ἀπαντα νι-
κᾳ λογον· το δ' επει φανη,
βηναι κειθεν, ὁθεν περ ἡκει,
πολυ δευτερον, ὡς ταχιστα."

(*Natum non esse sortes vincit alias omnes : proxima autem est, ubi quis in lucem editus fuerit, eodem redire, unde venit, quam ocissime.*)

Euripides says :—

"Πας δ' οδυνηρος βιος ανθρωπων,
Κ'ουκ εστι πονων αναπαυσις."

(*Omnis hominum vita est plena dolore,*
Nec datur laborum remissio.)

—Hippol, 189.

And Homer already said :—

"Ου μεν γαρ τι που εστιν οἰζυρωτερον ανδρος
Παντων, ὁσσα δε γαιαν επι πνεει τε και ἑρπει."

(*Non enim quidquam alicubi est calamitosius homine*
Omnium, quotquot super terram spirantque et moventur.)

—Il. xvii. 446.

Even Pliny says : "*Quapropter hoc primum quisque in remediis animi sui habeat, ex omnibus bonis, quæ homini natura tribuit, nullum melius esse tempestiva morte*" (*Hist. Nat.* 28, 2).

Shakspeare puts the words in the mouth of the old king Henry IV. :—

"O heaven ! that one might read the book of fate,
And see the revolution of the times,
. . . . . . how chances mock,
And changes fill the cup of alteration
With divers liquors ! O, if this were seen,
The happiest youth,—viewing his progress through,
What perils past, what crosses to ensue,—
Would shut the book, and sit him down and die."

Finally, Byron :—

"Count o'er the joys thine hours have seen,
Count o'er thy days from anguish free,
And know, whatever thou hast been,
'Tis something better not to be."

Baltazar Gracian also brings the misery of our existence before our eyes in the darkest colours in the "Criticon," Parte i., Crisi 5, just at the beginning, and Crisi 7 at the end, where he explicitly represents life as a tragic farce.

Yet no one has so thoroughly and exhaustively handled this subject as, in our own day, Leopardi. He is entirely filled and penetrated by it: his theme is everywhere the mockery and wretchedness of this existence; he presents it upon every page of his works, yet in such a multiplicity of forms and applications, with such wealth of imagery, that he never wearies us, but, on the contrary, is throughout entertaining and exciting.

CHAPTER XLVII.[1]

ON ETHICS.

HERE is the great gap which occurs in these supplements, on account of the circumstance that I have already dealt with moral philosophy in the narrower sense in the two prize essays published under the title, "*Die Grundprobleme der Ethik*," an acquaintance with which is assumed, as I have said, in order to avoid useless repetition. Therefore there only remains for me here a small gleaning of isolated reflections which could not be discussed in that work, the contents of which were, in the main, prescribed by the Academies; least of all those reflections which demand a higher point of view than that which is common to all, and which I was there obliged to adhere to. Accordingly it will not surprise the reader to find these reflections here in a very fragmentary collection. This collection again has been continued in the eighth and ninth chapters of the second volume of the Parerga.

That moral investigations are incomparably more difficult than physical, and in general than any others, results from the fact that they are almost immediately concerned with the thing in itself, namely, with that manifestation of it in which, directly discovered by the light of knowledge, it reveals its nature as *will*. Physical truths, on the other hand, remain entirely in the province of the idea, *i.e.*, of the phenomenon, and merely show how the lowest manifestations of the will present themselves in the idea in conformity to law. Further, the considera-

[1] This chapter is connected with §§ 55, 62, 67 of the first volume.

tion of the world from the *physical* side, however far and successfully it may be pursued, is in its results without any consolation for us: on the *moral* side alone is consolation to be found; for here the depths of our own inner nature disclose themselves to the consideration.

But my philosophy is the only one which confers upon ethics its complete and whole rights; for only if the true nature of man is his own *will*, and consequently he is, in the strictest sense, his own work, are his deeds really entirely his and to be ascribed to him. On the other hand, whenever he has another origin, or is the work of a being different from himself, all his guilt falls back upon this origin, or originator. For *operari sequitur esse.*

To connect the force which produces the phenomenon of the world, and consequently determines its nature, with the morality of the disposition or character, and thus to establish a *moral* order of the world as the foundation of the *physical*,—this has been since Socrates the problem of philosophy. Theism solved it in a childish manner, which could not satisfy mature humanity. Therefore pantheism opposed itself to it whenever it ventured to do so, and showed that nature bears in itself the power by virtue of which it appears. With this, however, ethics had necessarily to be given up. Spinoza, indeed, attempts here and there to preserve it by means of sophistry, but for the most part gives it up altogether, and, with a boldness which excites astonishment and repugnance, explains the distinction between right and wrong, and in general between good and evil, as merely conventional, thus in itself empty (for example, *Eth.* iv., prop. 37, schol. 2). After having met with unmerited neglect for more than a hundred years, Spinoza has, in general, become too much esteemed in this century through the reaction caused by the swing of the pendulum of opinion. All pantheism must ultimately be overthrown by the inevitable demands of ethics, and then by the evil and suffering of the world. If the world is a theophany, then all that man, or even the brute, does is equally divine and excellent; nothing can be censurable, and nothing more praiseworthy than the rest: thus there is no ethics. Hence, in consequence of the revived Spinozism of our own day, thus of pantheism, the treatment of ethics has sunk so low and become so shallow that it has been made a mere instruction as to the proper life of a citizen and a member of a family, in which the ultimate end of human existence is supposed to consist: thus in methodical, complete, smug, and comfortable philistinism. Pantheism, indeed, has only led to such shallow vulgarisms through the fact that (by a shameful misuse of the *e quovis ligno fit Mercurius*) a common mind, Hegel, has, by the well-known means, been falsely stamped as a great philosopher, and a herd of his disciples, at first suborned, afterwards only stupid, received his weighty words. Such outrages on the human mind do not remain unpunished: the seed has sprouted. In the same spirit it was then asserted that ethics should have for its material not the conduct of individuals, but that of nations, that this alone was a theme worthy of it. Nothing can be more perverse than this view, which rests on the most vulgar realism. For in every individual appears the whole undivided will to live, the thing in itself, and the microcosm is like the macrocosm. The masses have no more content than each individual. Ethics is concerned not with actions and their results, but with willing, and willing itself takes place only in the individual. Not the fate of nations, which exists only in the phenomenon, but that of the individual is decided *morally*. Nations are really mere abstractions; individuals alone actually exist. Thus, then, is pantheism related to ethics. But the evil and misery of the world are not in accord even with theism; hence it sought assistance from all kinds of evasions, theodicies, which yet were irretrievably overthrown by the arguments of Hume and Voltaire. Pantheism, however, is completely untenable in the presence of that bad side of the world. Only when the world is regarded entirely from without and from the *physical* side alone, and nothing else is kept in view but the constant restorative order, and the comparative imperishableness of the whole which is thereby introduced, is it perhaps possible to explain it as a god, yet always only symbolically. But if one enters within, thus considers also the *subjective* and *moral* side, with its preponderance of want, suffering, and misery, of dissension, wickedness, madness, and perversity, then one soon becomes conscious with horror that the last thing imaginable one has before one is a theophany. I, however, have shown, and especially in my work "*Ueber den Willen in der Natur*" have proved, that the force which works and acts in nature is identical with the will in us. Thereby the moral order of the world is brought into direct connection with the force which produces the phenomenon of the world. For the phenomenon of the will must exactly correspond to its nature. Upon this depends the exposition of eternal justice given in §§ 63 and 64 of the first volume, and the world, although subsisting by its own power, receives throughout a *moral* tendency. Accordingly the problem which has been discussed from the time of Socrates is now for the first time really solved, and the demand of thinking reason directed to morality is satisfied. Yet I have never professed to propound a philosophy which leaves no questions unanswered. In this sense philosophy is really impossible: it would be the science of omniscience. But *est quadam prodire tenus, si non datur ultra:* there is a limit to which reflection can penetrate and can so far lighten the night of our existence, although the horizon always remains dark. My doctrine reaches this limit in the will to live, which in its own manifestation asserts or denies itself. To wish, however, to go beyond this is, in my eyes, like wishing to fly beyond the atmosphere. We must stop there; even although new problems arise out of those which have been solved. Besides this, however, we must refer to the fact that the validity of the principle of sufficient reason is limited to the phenomenon; this was the theme of my first essay on that principle, which was published as early as 1813.

I now go on to supplement particular points, and shall begin by supporting, with two passages from classical poetry, my explanation of weeping given in § 67 of the first volume, that it springs from sympathy the object of which is one's own self. At the end of the eighth book of the "Odyssey," Ulysses, who in all his many sorrows is never represented as weeping, bursts into tears, when, still unknown, he hears his early heroic life and deeds sung by the bard Demodocus in the palace of the Phæacian king, for this remembrance of the brilliant period of his life contrasts with his present wretchedness. Thus not this itself directly, but the objective consideration of it, the picture of his present summoned up by his past, calls forth his tears; he feels sympathy with himself. Euripides makes the innocently condemned Hypolytus, bemoaning his own fate, express the same feeling:

"Φευ· ειθ' ην εμαυτον προσβλεπειν εναντιον
σταυθ', ὡς εδακρυς', ὁια πασχομεν κακα" (1084).

(*Heu, si liceret mihi, me ipsum extrinsecus spectare, quantopere deflerem mala, quæ patior.*)

Finally, as a proof of my explanation, an anecdote may be given here which I take from the English journal *The Herald* of the 16th July 1836. A client, when he had heard his case set forth by his counsel in court, burst into a flood of tears, and cried, "I never knew I had suffered half so much till I heard it here to-day."

I have shown in § 55 of the first volume how, notwithstanding the unalterable nature of the character, *i.e.*, of the special fundamental will of a man, a real moral repentance is yet possible. I wish, however, to add the following explanation, which I must preface by a few definitions. *Inclination* is every strong susceptibility of the will for motives of a certain kind. *Passion* is an inclination so strong that the motives which excite it exercise a power over the will, which is stronger than that of every possible motive that can oppose them; thus its mastery over the will becomes absolute, and consequently with reference to it the will is *passive* or *suffering*. It must, however, be remarked here that passions seldom reach the degree at which they fully answer to the definition, but rather bear their name as mere approximations to it: therefore there are then still counter-motives which are able at least to restrict their effect, if only they appear distinctly in consciousness. The *emotion* is just as irresistible, but yet only a passing excitement of the will, by a motive which receives its power, not from a deeply rooted inclination, but merely from the fact that, appearing suddenly, it excludes for the moment the counter-effect of all other motives, for it consists of an idea, which completely obscures all others by its excessive vividness, or, as it were, conceals them entirely by its too close proximity, so that they cannot enter consciousness and act on the will, whereby, therefore, the capacity for reflection, and with it *intellectual freedom*, is to a certain extent abolished. Accordingly the emotion is related to the passion as delirium to madness.

Moral repentance is now conditioned by the fact that before the act the inclination to it did not leave the intellect free scope, because it did not allow it to contemplate clearly and fully the counter-motives, but rather turned it ever anew to the motives in its own favour. But now, after the act has been performed, these motives are, by this itself, neutralised, and consequently have become ineffective. Now reality brings before the intellect the counter-motives as the consequences of the act which have already appeared; and the intellect now knows that they would have been the stronger if it had only adequately contemplated and weighed them. Thus the man becomes conscious that he has done what was really not in accordance with his will. This knowledge is repentance, for he has not acted with full intellectual freedom; for all the motives did not attain to efficiency. What excluded the motives opposed to the action was in the case of the hasty action the emotion, and in the case of the deliberate action the passion. It has also often depended upon the circumstance that his reason certainly presented to him the counter-motives in the abstract, but was not supported by a sufficiently strong imagination to present to him their whole content and true significance in images. Examples of what has been said are the cases in which revenge, jealousy, or avarice have led to murder. After it is committed they are extinguished, and now justice, sympathy, the remembrance of former friendship, raise their voices and say all that they would have said before if they had been allowed to speak. Then enters the bitter repentance, which says, "If it were not done it would never happen." An incomparable representation of this is afforded by the old Scottish ballad, which has also been translated by Herder, "Edward, Edward." In an analogous manner, the neglect of one's own good may occasion an egotistical repentance. For example, when an otherwise unadvisable marriage is concluded in consequence of passionate love, which now is extinguished just by the marriage, and for the first time the counter-motives of personal interest, lost independence, &c., &c., come into consciousness, and speak as they would have spoken before if they had been allowed utterance. All such actions accordingly spring from a relative weakness of intellect, because it lets itself be mastered by the will, just where its function as the presenter of motives ought to have been inexorably fulfilled, without allowing itself to be disturbed by the will. The vehemence of the will is here only *indirectly* the cause, in that it interferes with the intellect, and thereby prepares for itself repentance. The *reasonableness* of the character σωφροσυνη, which is opposed to passionateness, really consists in this, that the will never overpowers the intellect to such an extent as to prevent it from correctly exercising its function of the distinct, full, and clear exposition of the motives in the abstract for the reason, in the concrete for the imagination. Now this may just as well depend upon the moderation and mildness of the will as upon the strength of the intellect. All that is required is that the latter should be *relatively* strong enough for the will that is present, thus that the two should stand in a suitable relation to each other.

The following explanations have still to be added to the fundamental characteristics of the philosophy of law expounded in § 62 of the first volume, and also in my prize essay on the foundation of morals, § 17.

Those who, with Spinoza, deny that there is a right apart from the State, confound the means for enforcing the right with the right itself. Certainly the right is insured protection only in the State. But it itself exists independently of the State. For by force it can only be suppressed, never abolished. Accordingly the State is nothing more than an institution for protection, which has become necessary through the manifold attacks to which man is exposed, and which he would not be able to ward off alone, but only in union with others. So, then, the aims of the State are—

(1.) First of all, outward protection, which may just as well become needful against lifeless forces of nature or wild beasts as against men, consequently against other nations; although this case is the most frequent and important, for the worst enemy of man is man: *homo homini lupus.* Since, in consequence of this aim, nations always set up the principle, in words if not with deeds, that they wish to stand to each other in a purely defensive, never in an aggressive relation, they recognise *the law of nations.* This is at bottom nothing but natural law, in the only sphere of its practical activity that remains to it, between nation and nation, where it alone must reign, because its stronger son, positive law, cannot assert itself, since it requires a judge and an executive. Accordingly the law of nations consists of a certain degree of morality in the dealings of nations with each other, the maintenance of which is a question of honour for mankind. The bar at which cases based on this law are tried is that of public opinion.

(2.) Protection within, thus protection of the members of a State against each other, consequently security of private right, by means of the maintenance of an honest state of things, which consists in this, that the concentrated forces of all protect each individual, from which arises an appearance as if all were honest, *i.e.*, just, thus as if no one wished to injure the others.

But, as is always the way in human affairs, the removal of one evil generally opens the way for a new one; thus the granting of that double protection introduces the need of a third, namely: (3.) Protection against the protector, *i.e.*, against him or those to whom the society has transferred the management of the protection, thus the guarantee of public right. This appears most completely attainable by dividing and separating from each other the threefold unity of the protective power, thus the legislature, the judicature, and the executive, so that each is managed by others, and independently of the rest. The great value, indeed the fundamental idea of the monarchy appears to me to lie in the fact that because men remain men one must be placed so high, and so much power, wealth, security, and absolute inviolability given him that there remains nothing for him to desire, to hope, and to fear for himself; whereby the egoism which dwells in him, as in every one, is annihilated, as it were, by neutralisation, and he is now able, as if he were no longer a man, to practise justice, and to keep in view no longer his own but only the public good. This is the source of the seemingly superhuman nature that everywhere accompanies royalty, and distinguishes it so infinitely from the mere presidency. Therefore it must also be hereditary, not elective; partly in order that no one may see his equal in the king; partly that the king himself may only be able to provide for his successors by caring for the welfare of the State, which is absolutely one with that of his family.

If other ends besides that of protection, here explained, are ascribed to the State, this may easily endanger the true end.

According to my explanation, the right of property arises only through the expenditure of labour upon things. This truth, which has already often been expressed, finds a noteworthy confirmation in the fact that it is asserted, even in a practical regard, in a declaration of the American ex-president, Quincey Adams, which is to be found in the *Quarterly Review* of 1840, No. 130; and also in French, in the "*Bibliothèque universelle de Genève*," July 1840, No. 55. I will give it here in German (English of *Quarterly Review*): "There are moralists who have questioned the right of the Europeans to intrude upon the possessions of the aboriginals in any case, and under any limitations whatsoever; but have they maturely considered the whole subject? The Indian right of possession itself stands, with regard to the greatest part of the country, upon a *questionable* foundation. Their cultivated fields, their constructed habitations, a space of ample sufficiency for their subsistence, and whatever they had annexed of themselves by personal labour, was undoubtedly by the laws of nature theirs. But what is the right of a huntsman to the forest of a thousand miles over which he has accidentally ranged in quest of prey?" &c. In the same way, those who in our own day have seen occasion to combat communism with reasons (for example, the Archbishop of Paris, in his pastoral of June 1851) have always brought forward the argument that property is the result of work, as it were only embodied work. This is further evidence that the right of property can only be established by the application of work to things, for only in this respect does it find free recognition and make itself morally valid.

An entirely different kind of proof of the same truth is afforded by the moral fact that while the law punishes poaching just as severely as theft, and in many countries more severely, yet civil honour, which is irrevocably lost by the latter, is really not affected by the former; but the poacher, if he has been guilty of nothing else, is certainly tainted with a fault, but yet is not regarded, like the thief, as dishonourable and shunned by all. For the principles of civil honour rest upon moral and not upon mere positive law; but game is not an object upon which labour is bestowed, and thus also is not an object of a morally valid possession: the right to it is therefore entirely a positive one, and is not morally recognised.

According to my view, the principle ought to lie at the basis of criminal law that it is not really the man but only the deed which is punished, in order that it may not recur. The criminal is merely the subject in whom the deed is punished, in order that the law in consequence of which the punishment is inflicted may retain its deterrent power. This is the meaning of the expression, "He is forfeited to the law." According to Kant's explanation, which amounts to a *jus talionis*, it is not the deed but the man that is punished. The penitentiary system also seeks not so much to punish the deed as the man, in order to reform him. It thereby sets aside the real aim of punishment, determent from the deed, in order to attain the very problematic end of reformation. But it is always a doubtful thing to attempt to attain two different ends by *one* means: how much more so if the two are in any sense opposite ends. Education is a benefit, punishment ought to be an evil; the penitentiary prison is supposed to accomplish both at once. Moreover, however large a share untutored ignorance, combined with outward distress, may have in many crimes, yet we dare not regard these as their principal cause, for innumerable persons living in the same ignorance and under absolutely similar circumstances commit no crimes. Thus the substance of the matter falls back upon the personal, moral character; but this, as I have shown in my prize essay on the freedom of the will, is absolutely unalterable. Therefore moral reformation is really not possible, but only determent from the deed through fear. At the same time, the correction of knowledge and the awakening of the desire to work can certainly be attained; it will appear what effect this can produce. Besides this, it appears to me, from the aim of punishment set forth in the text, that, when possible, the apparent severity of the punishment should exceed the actual: but solitary confinement achieves the reverse. Its great severity has no witnesses, and is by no means anticipated by any one who has not experienced it; thus it does not deter. It threatens him who is tempted to crime by want and misery with the opposite pole of human suffering, ennui: but, as Goethe rightly observes—

> "When real affliction is our lot,
> Then do we long for ennui."

The contemplation of it will deter him just as little as the sight of the palatial prisons which are built by honest men for rogues. If, however, it is desired that these penitentiary prisons should be regarded as educational institutions, then it is to be regretted that the entrance to them is only obtained by crimes, instead of which it ought to have preceded them.

That punishment, as Beccaria has taught, ought to bear a proper proportion to the crime does not depend upon the fact that it would be an expiation of it, but rather on the fact that the pledge ought to be proportionate to the value of that for which it answers. Therefore every one is justified in demanding the pledge of the life of another as a guarantee for the security of his own life, but not for the security of his property, for which the freedom, and so forth, of another is sufficient pledge. For the security of the life of the citizens capital punishment is therefore absolutely necessary. Those who wish to abolish it should be answered, "First remove murder from the world, and then capital punishment ought to follow." It ought also to be inflicted for the clear attempt to murder just as for murder itself; for the law desires to punish the deed, not to revenge its consequences. In general the injury to be guarded against affords the right measure for the punishment which is to be threatened, but it does not give the moral baseness of the forbidden action. Therefore the law may rightly impose the punishment of imprisonment for allowing a flower-pot to fall from a window, or impose hard labour for smoking in the woods during the summer, and yet permit it in the winter. But to impose the punishment of death, as in Poland, for shooting an ure-ox is too much, for the maintenance of the species of ure-oxen may not be purchased with human life. In determining the measure of the punishment, along with the magnitude of the injury to be guarded against, we have to consider the strength of the motives which impel to the forbidden action. Quite a different standard of punishment would be established if expiation, retribution, *jus talionis,* were its true ground. But the criminal code ought to be nothing but a register of counter-motives for possible criminal actions: therefore each of these motives must decidedly outweigh the motives which lead to these actions, and indeed so much the more the greater the evil is which would arise from the action to be guarded against, the stronger the temptation to it, and the more difficult the conviction of the criminal;—always under the correct assumption that the will is not free, but determinable by motives;—apart from this it could not be got at at all. So much for the philosophy of law.

In my prize essay on the freedom of the will (p. 50 *seq.*) I have proved the originality and unalterableness of the inborn character, from which the moral content of the course of life proceeds. It is established as a fact. But in order to understand problems in their full extent it is sometimes necessary to oppose opposites sharply to each other. In this case, then, let one recall how incredibly great is the inborn difference between man and man, in a moral and in an intellectual regard. Here nobleness and wisdom; there wickedness and stupidity. In one the goodness of the heart shines out of the eyes, or the stamp of genius is enthroned in his countenance. The base physiognomy of another is the impression of moral worthlessness and intellectual dulness, imprinted by the hands of nature itself, unmistakable and ineradicable; he looks as if he must be ashamed of existence. But to this outward appearance the inner being really corresponds. We cannot possibly assume that such differences, which transform the whole being of the man, and which nothing can abolish, which, further, in conflict with his circumstances, determine his course of life, could exist without guilt or merit on the part of those affected by them, and be merely the work of chance. Even from this it is evident that the man must be in a certain sense his own work. But now, on the other hand, we can show the source of these differences empirically in the nature of the parents; and besides this, the meeting and connection of these parents has clearly been the work of the most accidental circumstances. By such considerations, then, we are forcibly directed to the distinction between the phenomenon and the true being of things, which alone can contain the solution of that problem. The thing in itself only reveals itself by means of the forms of the phenomenon; therefore what proceeds from the thing in itself must yet appear in those forms, thus also in the bonds of causality. Accordingly it will present itself to us here as a mysterious and incomprehensible guidance of things, of which the external empirical connection would be the mere tool. Yet all that happens appears in this empirical connection introduced by causes, thus necessarily and determined from without, while its true ground lies in the inner nature of what thus manifests itself. Certainly we can here see the solution of the problem only from afar, and when we reflect upon it we fall into an abyss of thought—as Hamlet very truly says, "thoughts beyond the reaches of our souls." In my essay in the first volume of the

Parerga "On the Appearance of Intention in the Fate of Individuals" I have set forth my thoughts upon this mysterious guidance of things, a guidance which indeed can only be conceived symbolically.

In § 14 of my prize essay on the foundation of morals there will be found an exposition of egoism, as regards its nature; and the following attempt to discover its root may be looked upon as supplementary to that paragraph. Nature itself contradicts itself directly, according as it speaks from the individual or the universal, from within or from without, from the centre or the periphery. It has its centre in every individual; for each individual is the whole will to live. Therefore, even if this individual is only an insect or a worm, nature itself speaks out of it thus: "I alone am all in all: in my maintenance everything is involved; the rest may perish, it is really nothing." So speaks nature from the *particular* standpoint, thus from the point of view of self-consciousness, and upon this depends the egoism of every living thing. On the other hand, from the *universal* point of view,—which is that of the *consciousness of other things*, that of objective knowledge, which for the moment looks away from the individual with whom the knowledge is connected,—from without then, from the periphery nature speaks thus: "The individual is nothing, and less than nothing. I destroy millions of individuals every day, for sport and pastime: I abandon their fate to the most capricious and wilful of my children, chance, who harasses them at pleasure. I produce millions of new individuals every day, without any diminution of my productive power; just as little as the power of a mirror is exhausted by the number of reflections of the sun, which it casts on the wall one after another. The individual is nothing." Only he who knows how to really reconcile and eliminate this patent contradiction of nature has a true answer to the question as to the perishableness and imperishableness of his own self. I believe I have given, in the first four chapters of this fourth book of the supplements, an adequate introduction to such knowledge. What is said above may further be illustrated in the following manner. Every individual, when he looks within, recognises in his nature, which is his will, the thing in itself, therefore that which everywhere alone is real. Accordingly he conceives himself as the kernel and centre of the world, and regards himself as of infinite importance. If, on the other hand, he looks without, then he is in the province of the idea the mere phenomenon, where he sees himself as an individual among an infinite number of other individuals, accordingly as something very insignificant, nay, vanishing altogether. Consequently every individual, even the most insignificant, every I, when regarded from within, is all in all; regarded from without, on the other hand, he is nothing, or at least as good as nothing. Hence upon this depends the great difference between what each one necessarily is in his own eyes and what he is in the eyes of others, consequently the egoism with which every one reproaches every one else.

In consequence of this egoism our fundamental error of all is this, that with reference to each other we are reciprocally not I. On the other hand, to be just, noble, and benevolent is nothing else than to translate my metaphysics into actions. To say that time and space are mere forms of our knowledge, not conditions of things in themselves, is the same as to say that the doctrine of metempsychosis, "Thou shalt one day be born as him whom thou now injurest, and in thy turn shalt suffer like injury," is identical with the formula of the Brahmans, which has frequently been mentioned, *Tat twam asi,* "This thou art." All true virtue proceeds from the immediate and intuitive knowledge of the metaphysical identity of all beings, which I have frequently shown, especially in § 22 of my prize essay on the foundation of morals. But just on this account it is not the result of a special pre-eminence of intellect; on the contrary, even the weakest intellect is sufficient to see through the *principium indivi-*

duationis, which is what is required in this matter. Accordingly we may find the most excellent character even in the case of a very weak understanding. And further, the excitement of our sympathy is accompanied by no exertion of our intellect. It rather appears that the requisite penetration of the *principium individuationis* would be present in every one if it were not that the *will* opposes this, and by virtue of its immediate mysterious and despotic influence upon the intellect generally prevents it from arising; so that ultimately all guilt falls back upon the *will*, as indeed is in conformity with the fact.

The doctrine of metempsychosis, touched on above, deviates from the truth merely through the circumstance that it transfers to the future what already is now. It makes my true inner nature exist in others only after my death, while, according to the truth, it already lives in them now, and death merely removes the illusion on account of which I am not aware of this; just as an innumerable host of stars constantly shine above our heads, but only become visible to us when the one sun near the earth has set. From this point of view my individual existence, however much, like that sun, it may outshine everything, appears ultimately only as a hindrance which stands between me and the knowledge of the true extent of my being. And because every individual, in his knowledge, is subject to this hindrance, it is just individuation that keeps the will to live in error as to its own nature; it is the Mâyâ of Brahmanism. Death is a refutation of this error, and abolishes it. I believe that at the moment of death we become conscious that it is a mere illusion that has limited our existence to our person. Indeed empirical traces of this may be found in several states which are related to death by the abolition of the concentration of consciousness in the brain, among which the magnetic sleep is the most prominent; for in it, if it reaches a high degree, our existence shows itself through various symptoms, beyond our persons and in other beings, most strikingly by direct participation in the thoughts of another individual, and ultimately even by the power of knowing the absent, the distant, and even the future, thus by a kind of omnipresence.

Upon this metaphysical identity of the will, as the thing in itself, in the infinite multiplicity of its phenomena, three principal phenomena depend, which may be included under the common name of sympathies: (1) *sympathy proper*, which, as I have shown, is the basis of justice and benevolence, *caritas;* (2) *sexual love*, with capricious selection, *amor*, which is the life of the species, that asserts its precedence over that of the individual; (3) *magic*, to which animal magnetism and sympathetic cures also belong. Accordingly *sympathy* may be defined as the empirical appearance of the metaphysical identity of the will, through the physical multiplicity of its phenomena, whereby a connection shows itself which is entirely different from that brought about by means of the forms of the phenomenon which we comprehend under the principle of sufficient reason.

CHAPTER XLVIII.[1]

ON THE DOCTRINE OF THE DENIAL OF THE WILL TO LIVE.

MAN has his existence and being either *with* his will, *i.e.*, his consent, or *without* this; in the latter case an existence so embittered by manifold and insupportable sufferings would be a flagrant injustice. The ancients, especially the Stoics, also the Peripatetics and Academics, strove in vain to prove that virtue sufficed to make life happy. Experience cried out loudly against it. What really lay at the foundation of the efforts of these philosophers, although they were not distinctly conscious of it, was the assumed *justice* of the thing; whoever was without guilt ought to be free from suffering, thus happy. But the serious and profound solution of the problem lies in the Christian doctrine that works do not justify. Accordingly a man, even if he has practised all justice and benevolence, consequently the *αγαθον*, *honestum*, is yet not, as Cicero imagines, *culpa omni carens* (*Tusc.*, v. i.); but *el delito mayor del hombre es haber nacido* (the greatest guilt of man is that he was born), as Calderon, illuminated by Christianity, has expressed it with far profounder knowledge than these wise men. Therefore that man comes into the world already tainted with guilt can appear absurd only to him who regards him as just then having arisen out of nothing and as the work of another. In consequence of *this* guilt, then, which must therefore have pro-

[1] This chapter is connected with § 68 of the first volume. Chapter 14 of the second volume of the Parerga should also be compared with it.

ceeded from his will, man remains rightly exposed to physical and mental suffering, even if he has practised all those virtues, thus is not happy. This follows from the *eternal justice* of which I have spoken in § 63 of the first volume. That, however, as St. Paul (Rom. iii. 21), Augustine, and Luther teach, works cannot justify, inasmuch as we all are and remain essentially sinners, ultimately rests upon the fact that, because *operari sequitur esse*, if we acted as we ought, we would necessarily be as we ought. But then we would require no *salvation* from our present condition, which not only Christianity but also Brahmanism and Buddhism (under the name which is expressed in English by *final emancipation*) present as the highest goal, *i.e.*, we would not need to become something quite different from, nay, the very opposite of what we are. Since, however, we are what we ought not to be, we also necessarily do what we ought not to do. Therefore we need a complete transformation of our mind and nature; *i.e.*, the new birth, as the result of which salvation appears. Although the guilt lies in action, *operari*, yet the root of the guilt lies in our *essentia et existentia*, for out of these the *operari* necessarily proceeds, as I have shown in the prize essay on the freedom of the will. Accordingly our one true sin is really original sin. Now the Christian myth makes original sin first arise after man came into existence, and for this purpose ascribes to him, *per impossibile*, a free will. It does this, however, simply as myth. The inmost kernel and spirit of Christianity is identical with that of Brahmanism and Buddhism; they all teach a great guilt of the human race through its existence itself, only that Christianity does not proceed directly and frankly like these more ancient religions: thus does not make the guilt simply the result of existence itself, but makes it arise through the act of the first human pair. This was only possible under the fiction of a *liberum arbitrium indifferentiæ*, and only necessary on account of the Jewish fundamental dogma, in which that doctrine had here to be implanted. Because, according to the truth, the coming into existence of man himself is the act of his free will, and accordingly one with the fall, and therefore the original sin, of which all other sins are the result, appeared already with the *essentia* and *existentia* of man; but the fundamental dogma of Judaism did not admit of such an explanation. Thus Augustine taught, in his books *De libero arbitrio,* that only as Adam before the fall was man guiltless and possessed of a free will, but for ever after is involved in the necessity of sin. The law, ὁ νομος, in the Biblical sense, always demands that we shall change our doing, while our being remains unchanged. But because this is impossible, Paul says that no man is justified by the law; only the new birth in Jesus Christ, in consequence of the work of grace, on account of which a new man arises and the old man is abolished (*i.e.*, a fundamental change of mind or conversion), can transfer us from the state of sinfulness into that of freedom and salvation. This is the Christian myth with reference to ethics. But certainly the Jewish theism, upon which it was grafted, must have received wonderful additions to adapt itself to that myth. In it the fable of the fall presented the only place for the graft of the old Indian stem. It is to be attributed just to that forcibly surmounted difficulty that the Christian mysteries have received such an extraordinary appearance, conflicting with the ordinary understanding, which makes proselytising more difficult, and on account of which, from incapacity to comprehend their profound meaning, Pelagianism, or at the present day Rationalism, rises against them, and seeks to explain them away, but thereby reduces Christianity to Judaism.

But to speak without myth: so long as our will is the same, our world can be no other than it is. It is true all wish to be delivered from the state of suffering and death; they would like, as it is expressed, to attain to eternal blessedness, to enter the kingdom of heaven, only not upon their own feet; they would like to be carried there by the course of nature. That, however, is impossible. Therefore nature will never let us fall and become nothing; but yet it can lead us nowhere but always again into nature. Yet how questionable a thing it is to exist as a part of nature every one experiences in his own life and death. Accordingly existence is certainly to be regarded as an erring, to return from which is salvation: it also bears this character throughout. It is therefore conceived in this manner by the ancient Samana religions, and also, although indirectly, by real and original Christianity. Even Judaism itself contains at least in the fall (this its redeeming feature) the germ of such a view. Only Greek paganism and Islamism are entirely optimistic: therefore in the former the opposite tendency had to find expression at least in tragedy; but in Islamism, which is the worst, as it is the most modern, of all religions, it appeared as Sufism, that very beautiful phenomenon, which is completely of Indian spirit and origin, and has now continued for upwards of a thousand years. Nothing can, in fact, be given as the end of our existence but the knowledge that we had better not be. This, however, is the most important of all truths, which must therefore be expressed, however great the contrast in which it stands with the European manner of thought of the present day. On the other hand, in the whole of non-Mohammedan Asia it is the most universally recognised fundamental truth, to-day as much as three thousand years ago.

If now we consider the will to live as a whole and objectively, we have, in accordance with what has been said, to think of it as involved in an illusion, to escape from which, thus to deny its whole existing endeavour, is what all religions denote by self-renunciation, *abnegatio sui ipsius;* for the true self is the will to live. The moral virtues, thus justice and benevolence, since if they are pure they spring, as I have shown, from the fact that the will to live, seeing through the *principium individuationis*, recognises itself in all its manifestations, are accordingly primarily a sign, a symptom, that the self-manifesting will is no longer firmly held in that illusion, but the disillusion already begins to take place; so that one might metaphorically say it already flaps its wings to fly away from it. Conversely, injustice, wickedness, cruelty are signs of the opposite, thus of the deep entanglement in that illusion. Secondly, however, these virtues are a means of advancing self-renunciation, and accordingly the denial of the will to live. For true integrity, inviolable justice, this first and most important of cardinal virtues, is so hard a task that whoever professes it unconditionally and from the bottom of his heart has to make sacrifices that soon deprive life of the sweetness which is demanded to make it enjoyable, and thereby turn away the will from it, thus lead to resignation. Yet just what makes integrity honourable is the sacrifices which it costs; in trifles it is not admired. Its nature really consists in this, that the just man does not throw upon others, by craft or force, the burdens and sorrows which life brings with it, as the unjust man does, but bears himself what falls to his lot; and thus he has to bear the full burden of the evil imposed upon human life, undiminished. Justice thereby becomes a means of advancing the denial of the will to live, for want and suffering, those true conditions of human life, are its consequence, and these lead to resignation. Still more quickly does the virtue of benevolence, *caritas*, which goes further, lead to the same result; for on account of it one takes over even the sufferings which originally fell to the lot of others, therefore appropriates to oneself a larger share of these than in the course of things would come to the particular individual. He who is inspired with this virtue has recognised his own being in all others. And thereby he identifies his own lot with that of humanity in general; but this is a hard lot, that of care, suffering, and death. Whoever, then, by renouncing every accidental advantage, desires for himself no other lot than that of humanity in general cannot desire even this long. The clinging to life and its pleasures must now soon yield, and give place to a universal renunciation; consequently the denial of the will will take place. Since now, in accordance with this, poverty, privation, and special sufferings of many kinds are introduced simply by the perfect exercise of the moral virtues, asceticism in the narrowest sense, thus the surrender of all possessions, the intentional seeking out of what is disagreeable and repulsive, self-mortification, fasts, the hair shirt, and the scourge—all this is rejected by many, and perhaps rightly, as superfluous. Justice itself is the hair shirt that constantly harasses its owner and the charity that gives away what is needed, provides constant fasts.[1] Just on this account Buddhism is free from all strict and excessive asceticism, which plays a large part in Brahmanism, thus from intentional self-mortification. It rests satisfied with the celibacy, voluntary poverty, humility, and obedience of the monks, with abstention from animal food, as also from all worldliness. Since, further, the goal to which the moral virtues lead is that which is here pointed out, the Vedanta philosophy[2] rightly says that after the entrance of true knowledge, with entire resignation in its train, thus the new birth, then the morality or immorality of the past life is a matter of indifference, and uses here also the saying so often quoted by the Brahmans: "*Finditur nodus cordis, dissolvuntur omnes dubitationes, ejusque opera evanescunt, viso supremo illo*" (*Sancara, sloca* 32).

[1] If, on the contrary, asceticism is admitted, the list of the ultimate motives of human action, given in my prize essay on the foundation of morals, namely: (1) our own good, (2) the ill of others, and (3) the good of others, must be supplemented by a fourth, our own ill; which I merely mention here in passing in the interests of systematic consistency. In the essay referred to this fourth motive had to be passed over in silence, for the question asked was stated in the spirit of the philosophical ethics prevailing in Protestant Europe.

[2] *Cf.* F. H. H. Windischmann's *Sancara, sive de theologumenis Vedanticorum.* pp. 116, 117, 121; and also *Oupnekhat*, vol. i. pp. 340, 356, 360.

Now, however objectionable this view may be to many, to whom a reward in heaven or a punishment in hell is a much more satisfactory explanation of the ethical significance of human action, just as the good Windischmann rejects that doctrine, while he expounds it, yet whoever is able to go to the bottom of the matter will find that in the end it agrees with that Christian doctrine especially urged by Luther, that it is not works but only the faith which enters through the work of grace, that saves us, and that therefore we can never be justified by our deeds, but can only obtain the forgiveness of our sins through the merits of the Mediator. It is indeed easy to see that without such assumptions Christianity would have to teach infinite punishment for all, and Brahmanism endless re-births for all, thus no salvation would be reached by either. The sinful works and their consequences must be annulled and annihilated, whether by extraneous pardon or by the entrance of a better knowledge; otherwise the world could hope for no salvation; afterwards, however, they become a matter of indifference. This is also the *μετανοια και αφεσις ἁμαρτιων*, the announcement of which the risen Christ exclusively imposes upon His Apostles as the sum of their mission (Luke xxiv. 47). The moral virtues are really not the ultimate end, but only a step towards it. This step is signified in the Christian myth by the eating of the tree of the knowledge of good and evil, with which moral responsibility enters, together with original sin. The latter itself is in truth the assertion of the will to live: the denial of the will to live, in consequence of the appearance of a better knowledge, is, on the other hand, salvation. Between these two, then, lies the sphere of morality; it accompanies man as a light upon his path from the assertion to the denial of the will, or, mythically, from original sin to salvation through faith in the mediation of the incarnate God (Avatar); or, according to the teaching of the Vedas, through all re-births, which are the consequence of the works in each case, until right knowledge appears, and with it salvation (final emancipation), Mokscha, *i.e.*, reunion with Brahma. The Buddhists, however, with perfect honesty, only indicate the matter negatively, by Nirvana, which is the negation of this world, or of Sansara. If Nirvana is defined as nothing, this only means that the Sansara contains no single element which could assist the definition or construction of Nirvana. Just on this account the Jainas, who differ from the Buddhists only in name, call the Brahmans who believe in the Vedas Sabdapramans, a nickname which is meant to signify that they believe upon hearsay what cannot be known or proved ("Asiat. Researches," vol. vi. p. 474).

When certain ancient philosophers, such as Orpheus, the Pythagoreans, and Plato (*e.g.*, in the "Phædo," pp. 151, 183 *seq.*, Bip.; and see *Clem. Alex. strom.*, iii. p. 400 *seq.*), just like the Apostle Paul, lament the union of soul and body, and desire to be freed from it, we understand the real and true meaning of this complaint, since we have recognised, in the second book, that the body is the will itself, objectively perceived as a phenomenon in space.

In the hour of death it is decided whether the man returns into the womb of nature or belongs no more to nature at all, but —— —— ——: for this opposite we lack image, conception, and word, just because these are all taken from the objectification of the will, therefore belong to this, and consequently can in no way express the absolute opposite of it, which accordingly remains for us a mere negation. However, the death of the individual is in each case the unweariedly repeated question of nature to the will to live, "Hast thou enough? Wilt thou escape from me?" In order that it may occur often enough, the individual life is so short. In this spirit are conceived the ceremonies, prayers, and exhortations of the Brahmans at the time of death, as we find them preserved in the Upanischad in several places; and so also are the Christian provisions for the suitable employment of the hour of death by means of exhortation, confession, communion, and extreme unction: hence also the Christian prayers for deliverance from sudden death. That at the present day it is just this that many desire only proves that they no longer stand at the Christian point of view, which is that of the denial of the will to live, but at that of its assertion, which is the heathen point of view.

But he will fear least to become nothing in death who has recognised that he is already nothing now, and who consequently no longer takes any share in his individual phenomenon, because in him knowledge has, as it were, burnt up and consumed the will, so that no will, thus no desire for individual existence, remains in him any more.

Individuality inheres indeed primarily in the intellect; and the intellect, reflecting the phenomenon, belongs to the phenomenon, which has the *principium individuationis* as its form. But it inheres also in the will, inasmuch as the character is individual: yet the character itself is abolished in the denial of the will. Thus individuality inheres in the will only in its assertion, not in its denial. Even the holiness which is connected with every purely moral action depends upon the fact that such an action ultimately springs from the immediate knowledge of the numerical identity of the inner nature of all living things.[1] But this identity only really exists in the condition of the denial of the will (Nirvana), for the assertion of the will (Sansara) has for its form the phenomenal appearance of it in multiplicity. Assertion of the will to live, the phenomenal world, the diversity of all beings, individuality, egoism, hatred, wickedness, all spring from *one* root; and so also, on the other hand, do the world as thing in itself, the identity of all beings, justice, benevolence, the denial of the will to live. If now, as I have sufficiently proved, even the moral virtues spring from the consciousness of that identity of all beings, but this lies, not in the phenomenon, but only in the thing in itself, in

[1] Cf. *Die beiden Grundprobleme der Ethik*, p. 274 (second edition, p. 271).

the root of all beings, the moral action is a momentary passing through the point, the permanent return to which is the denial of the will to live.

It follows, as a deduction from what has been said, that we have no ground to assume that there are more perfect intelligences than that of human beings. For we see that even this degree of intelligence is sufficient to impart to the will that knowledge in consequence of which it denies and abolishes itself, upon which the individuality, and consequently the intelligence, which is merely a tool of individual, and therefore animal nature, perish. This will appear to us less open to objection if we consider that we cannot conceive even the most perfect intelligences possible, which for this end we may experimentally assume, existing through an endless time, which would be much too poor to afford them constantly new objects worthy of them. Because the nature of all things is at bottom one, all knowledge of them is necessarily tautological. If now this nature once becomes comprehended, as by those most perfect intelligences it soon would be comprehended, what would then remain but the wearisomeness of mere repetition through an infinite time? Thus from this side also we are pointed to the fact that the end of all intelligence can only be reaction upon the will; since, however, all willing is an error, it remains the last work of intelligence to abolish the willing, whose ends it had hitherto served. Accordingly even the most perfect intelligence possible can only be a transition step to that to which no knowledge can ever extend: indeed such an intelligence can, in the nature of things, only assume the position of the moment of the attainment of perfect insight.

In agreement with all these considerations, and also with what is proved in the second book as to the origin of knowledge in the will, the *assertion* of which it reflects in fulfilling the sole function of knowledge, that of being serviceable to the ends of the will, while true salvation lies in its *denial*, we see all religions at their highest point pass over into mysticism and mysteries, *i.e.*, into darkness and veiled obscurity, which for knowledge signify merely an empty spot, the point where knowledge necessarily ceases; therefore for thought this can only be expressed by negations, but for sense perception it is indicated by symbolical signs; in temples by dim light and silence; in Brahmanism indeed by the required suspension of all thought and perception for the sake of sinking oneself profoundly in the grounds of one's own being, mentally pronouncing the mysterious Oum.[1] Mysticism in the widest sense is every guidance to the immediate consciousness of that to which neither perception nor conception, thus in general no knowledge extends. The mystic is thus opposed to the philosopher by the fact that he begins from within, while the philosopher begins from without. The mystic starts from his inner, positive, individual experience, in which he finds himself to be the eternal and only being, &c. But nothing of this is communicable except the assertions which one has to accept upon his word; consequently he cannot convince. The philosopher, on the other hand, starts from what is common to all, from the objective phenomenon which lies before all, and from the facts of consciousness as they are present in all. His method is therefore reflection upon all

[1] If we keep in view the essential immanence of our knowledge and of all knowledge, which arises from the fact that it is a secondary thing which has only appeared for the ends of the will, it then becomes explicable to us that all mystics of all religions ultimately attain to a kind of ecstasy, in which all and every knowledge, with its whole fundamental form, object and subject, entirely ceases, and only in this sphere, which lies beyond all knowledge, do they claim to have reached their highest goal, for they have then attained to the sphere in which there is no longer any subject and object, and consequently no more knowledge, just because there is no more will, the service of which is the sole destiny of knowledge.

Now, whoever has comprehended this will no longer regard it as beyond all measure extravagant that Fakirs should sit down, and, contemplating the tip of their nose, seek to banish all thought and perception, and that in many passages of the Upanischads instructions are given to sink oneself, silently and inwardly pronouncing the mysterious Oum, in the depths of one's own being, where subject and object and all knowledge disappear.

this, and combination of the data given in it: accordingly he can convince. He ought therefore to beware of falling into the way of the mystics, and, for example, by the assertion of intellectual intuitions or pretended immediate apprehensions of the reason, to seek to make a vain show of positive knowledge of that which is for ever inaccessible to all knowledge, or at the most can be indicated by means of a negation. The value and worth of philosophy lies in the fact that it rejects all assumptions which cannot be established, and takes as its data only what can be certainly proved in the world given in external perception, in the forms of apprehension of this world, which are constitutive of our intellect, and in the consciousness of one's own self which is common to all. Therefore it must remain cosmology, and cannot become theology. Its theme must limit itself to the world; to express in all aspects what this *is*, what it is in its inmost nature, is all that it can honestly achieve. Now it answers to this that my system when it reaches its highest point assumes a *negative* character, thus ends with a negation. It can here speak only of what is denied, given up: but what is thereby won, what is laid hold of, it is obliged (at the conclusion of the fourth book) to denote as nothing, and can only add the consolation that it is merely a relative, not an absolute nothing. For if something is none of all the things which we know, it is certainly for us, speaking generally, nothing. But it does not yet follow from this that it is absolutely nothing, that from every possible point of view and in every possible sense it must be nothing, but only that we are limited to a completely negative knowledge of it, which may very well lie in the limitation of our point of view. Now it is just here that the mystic proceeds positively, and therefore it is just from this point that nothing but mysticism remains. However, any one who wishes this kind of supplement to the negative knowledge to which alone philosophy can guide him will find it in its most beautiful and richest form in the Oupnekhat, then also in the Enneads of Plotinus, in Scotus Erigena, in passages of Jakob Böhm, but especially in the marvellous work of Madame de Guion, *Les Torrens,* and in Angelus Silesius; finally also in the poems of the Sufis, of which Tholuk has given us a collection translated into Latin, and another translated into German, and in many other works. The Sufis are the Gnostics of Islam. Hence Sadi denotes them by a word which may be translated "full of insight." Theism, calculated with reference to the capacity of the multitude, places the source of existence without us, as an object. All mysticism, and so also Sufism, according to the various degrees of its initiation, draws it gradually back within us, as the subject, and the adept recognises at last with wonder and delight that he is it himself. This procedure, common to all mysticism, we find not only expressed by Meister Eckhard, the father of German mysticism, in the form of a precept for the perfect ascetic, "that he seek not God outside himself" (Eckhard's works, edited by Pfeiffer, vol. i. p. 626), but also very naïvely exhibited by Eckhard's spiritual daughter, who sought him out, when she had experienced that conversion in herself, to cry out joyfully to him, "Sir, rejoice with me, I have become God" (*loc. cit.*, p. 465). The mysticism of the Sufis also expresses itself throughout precisely in accordance with this spirit, principally as a revelling in the consciousness that one is oneself the kernel of the world and the source of all existence, to which all returns. Certainly there also often appears the call to surrender all volition as the only way in which deliverance from individual existence and its suffering is possible, yet subordinated and required as something easy. In the mysticism of the Hindus, on the other hand, the latter side comes out much more strongly, and in Christian mysticism it is quite predominant, so that pantheistic consciousness, which is essential to all mysticism, here only appears in a secondary manner, in consequence of the surrender of all volition, as union with

God. Corresponding to this difference of the conception, Mohammedan mysticism has a very serene character, Christian mysticism a gloomy and melancholy character, while that of the Hindus, standing above both, in this respect also holds the mean.

Quietism, *i.e.*, surrender of all volition, asceticism, *i.e.*, intentional mortification of one's own will, and mysticism, *i.e.*, consciousness of the identity of one's own nature with that of all things or with the kernel of the world, stand in the closest connection; so that whoever professes one of them is gradually led to accept the others, even against his intention. Nothing can be more surprising than the agreement with each other of the writers who present these doctrines, notwithstanding the greatest difference of their age, country, and religion, accompanied by the firm certainty and inward confidence with which they set forth the permanence of their inner experience. They do not constitute a *sect*, which adheres to, defends, and propagates a favourite dogma once laid hold of; indeed the Indian, Christian, and Mohammedan mystics, quietists, and ascetics are different in every respect, except the inner significance and spirit of their teaching. A very striking example of this is afforded by the comparison of the *Torrens* of Madame de Guion with the teaching of the Vedas, especially with the passage in the Oupnekhat, vol. i. p. 63, which contains the content of that French work in the briefest form, but accurately and even with the same images, and yet could not possibly have been known to Madame de Guion in 1680. In the "*Deutschen Theologie*" (the only unmutilated edition, Stuttgart, 1851) it is said in chapters 2 and 3 that both the fall of the devil and that of Adam consisted in the fact that the one as the other ascribed to himself the I and me, the mine and to me, and on p. 89 it is said: "In true love there remains neither I nor me, mine, to me, thou, thine, and the like." Now, corresponding to this, it is said in the "Kural," from the Tamilian by Graul, p. 8: "The passion of the mine directed outwardly, and that of the I directed inwardly, cease" (*cf.* ver. 346). And in the "Manual of Buddhism ' by Spence Hardy, p. 258, Buddha says: "My disciples reject the thoughts I am this, or this is mine." In general, if we look away from the forms which are introduced by external circumstances and go to the bottom of the matter, we will find that Sakya Muni and Meister Eckhard teach the same; only that the former dared to express his thoughts directly, while the latter is obliged to clothe them in the garments of the Christian myth and adapt his expressions to this. He carries this, however, so far that with him the Christian myth has become little more than a symbolical language, just as the Hellenic myth became for the Neo-Platonists: he takes it throughout allegorically. In the same respect it is worth noticing that the transition of St. Francis from prosperity to the mendicant life is similar to the still greater step of Buddha Sakya Muni from prince to beggar, and that, corresponding to this, the life of St. Francis, and also the order he founded, was just a kind of Sannyasiism. Indeed it deserves to be mentioned that his relationship with the Indian spirit appears also in his great love for the brutes and frequent intercourse with them, when he always calls them his sisters and brothers; and his beautiful Cantico also bears witness to his inborn Indian spirit by the praise of the sun, the moon, the stars, the wind, the water, the fire, and the earth.[1]

Even the Christian quietists must often have had little or no knowledge of each other; for example, Molinos and Madame de Guion of Tauler and the "*Deutsche Theologie*," or Gichtel of the former. In any case, the great difference of their culture, in that some of them, like Molinos, were learned, others, like Gichtel and many more, were the reverse, has no essential influence upon their teaching.

[1] *S. Bonaventuræ vita S. Francisci*, ch. 8. K. Hase, "*Franz von Assisi*," ch. 10. "*I cantici di S. Francesco*," *editi da Schlosser e Steinle.*, *Francoforto, s.M.*, 1842.

Their great internal agreement, along with the firmness and certainty of their utterances, proves all the more that they speak from real inward experience, from an experience which certainly is not accessible to all, but is possessed only by a few favoured individuals, and therefore has received the name of the work of grace, the reality of which, however, for the above reasons, is not to be doubted. But in order to understand all this one must read the mystics themselves, and not be contented with second-hand reports of them; for every one must himself be comprehended before one judges concerning him. Thus to become acquainted with quietism I specially recommend Meister Eckhard, the "*Deutsche Theologie,*" Tauler, Madame de Guion, Antoinette Bourignon, the English Bunyan, Molinos,[1] and Gichtel. In the same way, as practical proofs and examples of the profound seriousness of asceticism, the life of Pascal, edited by Reuchlin, together with his history of the Port-Royal, and also the *Histoire de Sainte Elisabeth, par le comte de Montalembert*, and *La vie de Rancé, par Chateaubriand*, are very well worth reading, but yet by no means exhaust all that is important in this class. Whoever has read such writings, and compared their spirit with that of ascetism and quietism as it runs through all works of Brahmanism and Buddhism, and speaks in every page, will admit that every philosophy, which must in consistency reject that whole mode of thought, which it can only do by explaining the representatives of it to be either impostors or madmen, must just on this account necessarily be false. But all European systems, with the exception of mine, find themselves in this position. Truly it must be an extraordinary madness which, under the most widely different circumstances and persons possible, spoke with such agree-

[1] *Michælis de Molinos manuductio spiritualis; hispanice* 1675, *italice* 1080, *latine* 1687, *gallice in libro non adeo raro, cui titulus: Recueil de diverses pièces concernant le quiétisme, ou Molinos et ses disciples. Amstd.*, 1688.

ment, and, moreover, was raised to the position of a chief doctrine of their religion, by the most ancient and numerous peoples of the earth, something like three-fourths of all the inhabitants of Asia. But no philosophy can leave the theme of quietism and asceticism undecided if the question is proposed to it; because this theme is, in its matter, identical with that of all metaphysics and ethics. Here then is a point upon which I expect and desire that every philosophy, with its optimism, should declare itself. And if, in the judgment of contemporaries, the paradoxical and unexampled agreement of my philosophy with quietism and asceticism appears as an open stumbling-block, I, on the contrary, see just in that agreement a proof of its sole correctness and truth, and also a ground of explanation of why it is ignored and kept secret by the *Protestant* universities.

For not only the religions of the East, but also true Christianity, has throughout that ascetic fundamental character which my philosophy explains as the denial of the will to live; although Protestantism, especially in its present form, seeks to conceal this. Yet even the open enemies of Christianity who have appeared in the most recent times have ascribed to it the doctrines of renunciation, self-denial, perfect chastity, and, in general, mortification of the will, which they quite correctly denote by the name of the "*anti-cosmic tendency*," and have fully proved that such doctrines are essentially proper to original and genuine Christianity. In this they are undeniably right. But that they set up this as an evident and patent reproach to Christianity, while just here lies its profoundest truth, its high value, and its sublime character,—this shows an obscuring of the mind, which can only be explained by the fact that these men's minds, unfortunately like thousands more at the present day in Germany, are completely spoiled and distorted by the miserable Hegelism, that school of dulness, that centre of misunderstanding and ignorance, that mind-destroying, spurious wisdom, which now at last begins to be recognised as such, and the veneration of which will soon be left to the Danish Academy, in whose eyes even that gross charlatan is a *summus philosophus,* for whom it takes the field:—

> "*Car ils suivront la créance et estude,*
> *De l'ignorante et sotte multitude,*
> *Dont le plus lourd sera reçu pour juge.*"
>
> —Rabelais.

In any case, the ascetic tendency is unmistakable in the genuine and original Christianity as it developed in the writings of the Church Fathers from its kernel in the New Testament; it is the summit towards which all strives upwards. As its chief doctrine we find the recommendation of genuine and pure celibacy (this first and most important step in the denial of the will to live), which is already expressed in the New Testament.[1] Strauss also, in his "Life of Jesus" (vol. i. p. 618 of the first edition), says, with reference to the recommendation of celibacy given in Matt. xix. 11 *seq.*, "That the doctrine of Jesus may not run counter to the ideas of the present day, men have hastened to introduce surreptitiously the thought that Jesus only praised celibacy with reference to the circumstances of the time, and in order to leave the activity of the Apostles unfettered; but there is even less indication of this in the context than in the kindred passage, 1 Cor. vii. 25 *seq.;* but we have here again one of the places where *ascetic principles,* such as prevailed among the Essenes, and probably still more widely among the Jews, appear in the teaching of Jesus also." This ascetic tendency appears more decidedly later than at the beginning, when Christianity, still seeking adherents, dared not pitch its demands too high; and by the beginning of the third century it is expressly urged. Marriage, in genuine Christianity, is merely a compromise with the sinful nature of man, as a concession, something allowed to those who lack

[1] Matt. xix. 11 *seq.;* Luke xx. 35–37; 1 Cor. vii. 1–11 and 25–40 (1 Thess. iv. 3; 1 John iii. 3); Rev. xiv. 4.

strength to aspire to the highest, an expedient to avoid greater evil: in this sense it receives the sanction of the Church in order that the bond may be indissoluble. But celibacy and virginity are set up as the higher consecration of Christianity through which one enters the ranks of the elect. Through these alone does one attain the victor's crown, which even at the present day is signified by the wreath upon the coffin of the unmarried, and also by that which the bride lays aside on the day of her marriage.

A piece of evidence upon this point, which certainly comes to us from the primitive times of Christianity, is the pregnant answer of the Lord, quoted by Clemens Alexandrinus (*Strom.* iii. 6 *et* 9) from the Gospel of the Egyptians: "*Τη Σαλωμη ὁ κυριος πυνθανομενη, μεχρι ποτε θανατος ισχυσει; μεχρις αν, ειπεν, ὑμεις, αἱ γυναικες, τικτετε*" (*Salomæ interroganti "quousque vigebit mors?" Dominus "quoadusque" inquit "vos, mulieres, paritis"*). "*Τουτ' εστι, μεχρις αν αἱ επιθυμιαι ενεργωσι*" (*Hoc est, quamdiu operabuntur cupiditates*), adds Clement, c. 9, with which he at once connects the famous passage, Rom. v. 12. Further on, c. 13, he quotes the words of Cassianus: "*Πυνθανομενης της Σαλωμης, ποτε γνωσθησεται τα περι ὡν ηρετο, εφη ὁ κυριος, Ὁταν της αισχυνης ενδυμα πατησητε, και ὁταν γενηται τα δυο ἑν, και το αρρεν μετα της θηλειας ουτε αρρεν, ουτε θηλυ*" (*Cum interrogaret Salome, quando cognoscentur ea, de quibus interrogabat, ait Dominus: "quando pudoris indumentum conculcaveritis, et quando duo facto fuerint unum, et masculum cum fœmina nec masculum nec fœmineum*"), *i.e.*, when she no longer needs the veil of modesty, since all distinction of sex will have disappeared.

With regard to this point the heretics have certainly gone furthest: even in the second century the Tatianites or Encratites, the Gnostics, the Marcionites, the Montanists, Valentinians, and Cassians; yet only because with reckless consistency they gave honour to the truth, and therefore, in accordance with the spirit of Christianity, they taught perfect continence; while the Church prudently declared to be heresy all that ran counter to its far-seeing policy. Augustine says of the Tatianites: "*Nuptias damnant, atque omnino pares eas fornicationibus aliisque corruptionibus faciunt: nec recipiunt in suum numerum conjugio utentem, sive marem, sive fœminam. Non vescuntur carnibus, easque abominantur.* (*De hæresi ad quod vult Deum. hær.*, 25.) But even the orthodox Fathers look upon marriage in the light indicated above, and zealously preach entire continence, the ἁγνεια. Athanasius gives as the cause of marriage: **Ὁτι υποπιπτοντες εσμεν τῃ του προπατορος καταδικῃ· . . . επειδη ὁ προηγουμενος σκοπος του θεου ην, το μη δια γαμου γενεσθαι ἡμας και φθορας· ἡ δε παραβασις της εντολης τον γαμον εισηγαγεν δια το ανομησαι τον Αδαμ.** (*Quia subjacemus condemnationi propatoris nostri; . . . nam finis, a Deo prælatus, erat, nos non per nuptias et corruptionem fieri: sed transgressio mandati nuptias introduxit, propter legis violationem Adæ.—Exposit. in psalm.* 50). Tertullian calls marriage *genus mali inferioris, ex indulgentia ortum* (*De pudicitia*, c. 16) and says: "*Matrimonium et stuprum est commixtio carnis; scilicet cujus concupiscentiam dominus stupro adæquavit. Ergo, inquis, jam et primas, id est unas nuptias destruis? Nec immerito: quoniam et ipsæ ex eo constant, quod est stuprum* (*De exhort. castit.*, c. 9). Indeed, Augustine himself commits himself entirely to this doctrine and all its results, for he says: "*Novi quosdam, qui murmurent: quid, si, inquiunt, omnes velint ab omni concubitu abstinere, unde subsistet genus humanum? Utinam omnes hoc vellent! dumtaxat in caritate, de corde puro et conscientia bona, et fide non ficta: multo citius Dei civitas compleretur, ut acceleraretur terminus mundi*" (*De bono conjugali*, c. 10). And again: "*Non vos ab hoc studio, quo multos ad imitandum vos excitatis, frangat querela vanorum, qui dicunt: quomodo subsistet genus humanum, si omnes fuerint continentes? Quasi propter aliud retardetur hoc seculum, nisi ut impleatur prædestinatus numerus ille sanctorum, quo citius impleto, profecto nec terminus seculi differetur* (*De bono individuitatis*, c. 23).

One sees at once that he identifies salvation with the end of the world. The other passages in the works of Augustine which bear on this point will be found collected in the "*Confessio Augustiniana e D. Augustini operibus compilata a Hieronymo Torrense,*" 1610, under the headings *De matrimonio, De cœlibatu,* &c., and any one may convince himself from these that in ancient, genuine Christianity marriage was only a concession, which besides this was supposed to have only the begetting of children as its end, that, on the other hand, perfect continence was the true virtue far to be preferred to this. To those, however, who do not wish to go back to the authorities themselves I recommend two works for the purpose of removing any kind of doubt as to the tendency of Christianity we are speaking about: Carové, "*Ueber das Cölibatgesetz,*" 1832, and Lind, "*De cœlibatu Christianorum per tria priora secula,*" *Havniæ,* 1839. It is, however, by no means the views of these writers themselves to which I refer, for these are opposed to mine, but solely to their carefully collected accounts and quotations, which deserve full acceptance as quite trustworthy, just because both these writers are opponents of celibacy, the former a rationalistic Catholic, and the other a Protestant candidate in theology, who speaks exactly like one. In the first-named work we find, vol. i. p. 166, in that reference, the following result expressed: "In accordance with the Church view, as it may be read in canonical Church Fathers, in the Synodal and Papal instructions, and in innumerable writings of orthodox Catholics, perpetual chastity is called a divine, heavenly, angelic virtue, and the obtaining of the assistance of divine grace for this end is made dependent upon earnest prayer. We have already shown that this Augustinian doctrine is by Canisius and in the decrees of the Council of Trent expressed as an unchanging belief of the Church. That, however, it has been retained as a dogma till the present day is sufficiently established by the June number, 1831, of the magazine "*Der Katholik.*"

It is said there, p. 263: "In Catholicism the observance of a perpetual chastity, for the sake of God, appears as in itself the highest merit of man. The view that the observance of continual chastity as an end in itself sanctifies and exalts the man is, as every instructed Catholic is convinced, deeply rooted in Christianity, both as regards its spirit and its express precepts. The decrees of the Council of Trent have abolished all possible doubt on this point. . . . It must at any rate be confessed by every unprejudiced person, not only that the doctrine expressed by "*Der Katholik*" is really Catholic, but also that the proofs adduced may be quite irrefutable for a Catholic reason, because they are drawn so directly from the ecclesiastical view, taken by the Church, of life and its destiny." It is further said in the same work, p. 270: "Although both Paul calls the forbidding to marry a false doctrine, and the still Judaistic author of the Epistle to the Hebrews enjoins that marriage shall be held in honour by all, and the bed kept undefiled (Heb. xiii 4), yet the main tendency of these two sacred writers is not on that account to be mistaken. Virginity is for both the perfect state, marriage only a make-shift for the weak, and only as such to be held inviolable. The highest effort, on the other hand, was directed to complete, material putting off of self. The self must turn and refrain from all that tends only to its own pleasure, and that only temporarily." Lastly, p. 288: "We agree with the Abbé Zaccaria, who asserts that celibacy (not the law of celibacy) is before everything to be deduced from the teaching of Christ and the Apostle Paul."

What is opposed to this specially Christian view is everywhere and always merely the Old Testament, with its *παντα καλα λιαν*. This appears with peculiar distinctness from that important third book of the Stromata of Clement, where, arguing against the encratistic heretics mentioned above, he constantly opposes to them only Judaism, with its optimistic history of creation, with which the world-denying tendency of the New Testament is certainly in contradiction. But the connection of the New Testament with the Old is at bottom only external, accidental, and forced; and the one point at which Christian doctrine can link itself on to the latter is only to be found, as has been said, in the story of the fall, which, moreover, stands quite isolated in the Old Testament, and is made no further use of. But, in accordance with the account in the Gospels, it is just the orthodox adherents of the Old Testament who bring about the crucifixion of the founder of Christianity, because they find his teaching in conflict with their own. In the said third book of the Stromata of Clement the antagonism between optimism with theism on the one hand, and pessimism with ascetic morality on the other, comes out with surprising distinctness. This book is directed against the Gnostics, who just taught pessimism and asceticism, that is, εγκρατεια (abstinence of every kind, but especially from all sexual satisfaction); on account of which Clement censures them vigorously. But, at the same time, it becomes apparent that even the spirit of the Old Testament stands in this antagonism with that of the New Testament. For, apart from the fall, which appears in the Old Testament like a *hors d'œuvre*, the spirit of the Old Testament is diametrically opposed to that of the New Testament—the former optimistic, the latter pessimistic. Clement himself brings this contradiction out prominently at the end of the eleventh chapter (προσαποτεινομενον τον Παυλον τῳ Κριστῃ κ. τ. λ.), although he will not allow that it is a real contradiction, but explains it as only apparent,—like a good Jew, as he is. In general it is interesting to see how with Clement the New and the Old Testament get mixed up together; and he strives to reconcile them, yet for the most part drives out the New Testament with the Old. Just at the beginning of the third chapter he objects to the Marcionites that they find fault with the creation, after the example of Plato and Pythagoras; for Marcion teaches that nature is bad, made out of bad materials (*φυσις κακη, εκ τε ὑλης κακης*); therefore one ought not to people this world, but to abstain from marriage (*μη βουλομενοι τον κοσμον συμπληρουν, απεχεσθαι γαμου*). Now Clement, to whom in general the Old Testament is much more congenial and convincing than the New, takes this very much amiss. He sees in it their flagrant ingratitude to and enmity and rebellion against him who has made the world, the just demiurgus, whose work they themselves are, and yet despise the use of his creatures, in impious rebellion "forsaking the natural opinion" (*αντιτασσομενοι τῳ ποιητῃ τῳ σφων, . . . εγκρατεις τῃ προς τον πεποιηκοτα εχθρᾳ, μη βουλομενοι χρησθαι τοις ὑπ' αυτου κτισθεισιν, . . ασεβει θεομαχιᾳ των κατα φυσιν εκσταντες λογισμων*). At the same time, in his holy zeal, he will not allow the Marcionites even the honour of originality, but, armed with his well-known erudition, he brings it against them, and supports his case with the most beautiful quotations, that even the ancient philosophers, that Heraclitus and Empedocles, Pythagoras and Plato, Orpheus and Pindar, Herodotus and Euripides, and also the Sibyls, lamented deeply the wretched nature of the world, thus taught pessimism. Now in this learned enthusiasm he does not observe that in this way he is just giving the Marcionites water for their mill, for he shows that

"All the wisest of all the ages"

have taught and sung what they do, but confidently and boldly he quotes the most decided and energetic utterances of the ancients in this sense. Certainly they cannot lead him astray. Wise men may mourn the sadness of existence, poets may pour out the most affecting lamentations about it, nature and experience may cry out as loudly as they will against optimism,—all this does not touch our Church Father: he holds his Jewish revelation in his hand, and remains confident. The demiurgus made the world. From this it is *a priori* certain that it is excellent, and it may look as it likes. The same thing then takes place with regard to the second point, the *εγκρατεια*, through which, according to his view, the Marcionites show their ingratitude towards the demiurgus (*αχαριστειν τῳ δημιουργῳ*) and the perversity with which they put from them all his gifts (*δἰ αντιταξιν προς τον δημιουργον, την χρησιν των κοσμικων παραιτουμενοι*). Here now the tragic poets have preceded the Encratites (to the prejudice of their originality) and have said the same things. For since they also lament the infinite misery of existence, they have added that it is better to bring no children into such a world; which he now again supports with the most beautiful passages, and, at the same time, accuses the Pythagoreans of having renounced sexual pleasure on this ground. But all this touches him not; he sticks to his principle that all these sin against the demiurgus, in that they teach that one ought not to marry, ought not to beget children, ought not to bring new miserable beings into the world, ought not to provide new food for death (*δἰ εγκρατειας ασεβουσι εις τε την κτισιν και τον ἁγιον δημιουργον, τον παντοκρατορα μονον θεον, και διδασκουσι, μη δειν παραδεχεσθαι γαμον και παιδοποιϊαν, μηδε αντεισαγειν τῳ κοσμῳ δυστυχησοντας ἑτερους, μηδε επιχορηγειν θανατῳ τροφην*—c. 6). Since the learned Church Father thus denounces *εγκρατεια*, he seems to have had no presentiment that just after his time the celibacy of the Christian priesthood would be more and more introduced, and finally, in the eleventh century, raised to the position of a law, because it is in keeping with the spirit of the New Testament. It is just this spirit which the Gnostics have grasped more profoundly and understood better than our Church Father, who is more Jew than Christian. The conception of the Gnostics comes out very clearly at the beginning of the ninth chapter, where the following passage is quoted from the Gospel of the Egyptians: *Αυτος ειπεν ὁ Σωτηρ, „ηλθον καταλυσαι τα εργα της θηλειας·„ θηλειας μεν, της επιθυμιας· εργα δε,* γενεσιν και φθοραν (*Ajunt enim dixisse Servatorem: "veni ad dissolvendum opera feminæ;" feminæ quidem, cupiditatis; opera autem, generationem et interitum*); but quite specially at the end of the thirteenth and the beginning of the fourteenth chapter. The Church certainly was obliged to consider how to set a religion upon its legs that could also walk and stand in the world as it is, and among men; therefore it declared these persons to be heretics. At the conclusion of the seventh chapter our Church Father opposes Indian asceticism, as bad, to Christian Judaism; whereby the fundamental difference of the spirit of the two religions is clearly brought out. In Judaism and Christianity everything runs back to obedience or disobedience to the command of God: ὑπακοη και παρακοη; as befits us creatures, ἡμιν, τοις πεπλασμενοις ὑπο της του Παντοκρατορος βουλησεως (*nobis, qui Omnipotentis voluntate effecti sumus*), chap. 14. Then comes, as a second duty, λατρευειν θεῳ ζωντι, to serve God, extol His works, and overflow with thankfulness. Certainly the matter has a very different aspect in Brahmanism and Buddhism, for in the latter all improvement and conversion, and the only deliverance we can hope for from this world of suffering, this Sansara, proceeds from the knowledge of the four fundamental truths: (1) *dolor;* (2) *doloris ortus;* (3) *doloris interitus;* (4) *octopartita via ad doloris sedationem* (*Dammapadam, ed. Fausböll, p.* 35 *et* 347). The explanation of these four truths will be found in Bournouf, "*Introduct. à l'hist. du Buddhisme,*" p. 629, and in all expositions of Buddhism.

In truth, Judaism, with its παντα καλα λιαν, is not related to Christianity as regards its spirit and ethical tendency, but Brahmanism and Buddhism are. But the spirit and ethical tendency are what is essential in a religion, not the myths in which these are clothed. I therefore cannot give up the belief that the doctrines of Christianity can in some way be derived from these primitive religions. I have pointed out some traces of this in the second volume of the Parerga, § 179 (second edition, § 180). I have to add to these that Epiphanias (*Hæretic.* xviii.) relates that the first Jewish Christians of Jerusalem, who called themselves Nazarenes, refrained from all animal food. On account of this origin (or, at least, this agreement) Christianity belongs to the ancient, true and sublime faith of mankind, which is opposed to the false, shallow, and injurious optimism which exhibits itself in Greek paganism, Judaism, and Islamism. The Zend religion holds to a certain extent the mean, because it has opposed to Ormuzd a pessimistic counterpoise in Ahriman. From this Zend religion the Jewish religion proceeded, as J. G. Rhode has thoroughly proved in his book, "*Die heilige Sage des Zendvolks;*" from Ormuzd has come Jehovah, and from Ahriman, Satan, who, however, plays only a very subordinate rôle in Judaism, indeed almost entirely disappears, whereby then optimism gains the upper hand, and there only remains the myth of the fall as a pessimistic element, which certainly (as the fable of Meschia and Meschiane) is derived from the Zend-Avesta. Yet even this falls into oblivion, till it is again taken up by Christianity along with Satan. Ormuzd himself, however, is derived from Brahmanism, although from a lower region of it; he is no other than Indra, that subordinate god of the firmament and the atmosphere, who is represented as frequently in rivalry with men. This has been very clearly shown by J. J. Schmidt in his work on the relation of the Gnostic-theosophic doctrines to the religions of the East. This Indra-Ormuzd-Jehovah had afterwards to pass over into Christianity, because this religion arose in Judæa. But on account of the cosmopolitan character of Christianity he laid aside his own name to be denoted in the language of each converted nation by the appellation of the superhuman beings he supplanted, as θεος, *Deus*, which comes from the Sanscrit *Deva* (from which also devil comes), or among the Gothico-Germanic peoples by the word God, *Gott*, which comes from *Odin, Wodan, Guodan, Godan.*

In the same way he assumed in Islamism, which also sprang from Judaism, the name of Allah, which also existed earlier in Arabia. Analogous to this, the gods of the Greek Olympus, when in prehistoric times they were transplanted to Italy, also assumed the names of the previously reigning gods: hence among the Romans Zeus is called Jupiter, Hera Juno, Hermes Mercury, &c. In China the first difficulty of the missionaries arose from the fact that the Chinese language has no appellation of the kind and also no word for creating; for the three religions of China know no gods either in the plural or in the singular.[1]

However the rest may be, that *παντα καλα λιαν* of the Old Testament is really foreign to true Christianity; for in the New Testament the world is always spoken of as something to which one does not belong, which one does not love, nay, whose lord is the devil.[2] This agrees with the ascetic spirit of the denial of one's self and the overcoming of the world which, just like the boundless love of one's neighbour, even of one's enemy, is the fundamental characteristic which Christianity has in common with Brahmanism and Buddhism, and which proves their relationship. There is nothing in which one has to distinguish the kernel so carefully from the shell as in Christianity. Just because I prize this kernel highly I sometimes treat the shell with little ceremony; it is, however, thicker than is generally supposed.

Protestantism, since it has eliminated asceticism and its

[1] Cf. "*Ueber den Willen in der Natur*," second edition, p. 124; third edition, p. 135.

[2] For example, John xii. 25, 31, xiv. 30, xv. 18, 19, xvi. 33; Col. ii. 20; Eph. ii. 1–3; 1 John ii. 15–17, iv. 4, 5. On this opportunity one may see how certain Protestant theologians, in their efforts to misinterpret the text of the New Testament in conformity with their rationalistic, optimistic, and unutterably shallow view of life, go so far that they actually falsify this text in their translations. Thus H. A. Schott, in his new version given with the Griesbach text of 1805, has translated the word *κοσμος*, John xv. 18, 19, by *Judæi*, 1 John iv. 4, by *profani homines*; and Col. ii. 20, *στοιχεια του κοσμου* by *elementa Judaica;* while Luther everywhere renders the word honestly and correctly by "*Welt*" (world).

central point, the meritoriousness of celibacy, has already given up the inmost kernel of Christianity, and so far is to be regarded as a falling away from it. This has become apparent in our own day by the gradual transition of Protestantism into shallow rationalism, this modern Pelagianism, which ultimately degenerates into the doctrine of a loving father, who has made the world, in order that things may go on very pleasantly in it (in which case, then, he must certainly have failed), and who, if one only conforms to his will in certain respects, will also afterwards provide a still more beautiful world (with regard to which it is only a pity that it has such a fatal entrance). That may be a good religion for comfortable, married, and enlightened Protestant pastors; but it is no Christianity. Christianity is the doctrine of the deep guilt of the human race through its existence alone, and the longing of the heart for deliverance from it, which, however, can only be attained by the greatest sacrifices and by the denial of one's own self, thus by an entire reversal of human nature. Luther may have been perfectly right from the practical point of view, *i.e.*, with reference to the Church scandal of his time, which he wished to remove, but not so from the theoretical point of view. The more sublime a doctrine is, the more it is exposed to abuse at the hands of human nature, which, on the whole, is of a low and evil disposition: hence the abuses of Catholicism are so much more numerous and so much greater than those of Protestantism. Thus, for example, monasticism, that methodical denial of the will practised in common for the sake of mutual encouragement, is an institution of a sublime description, which, however, for this very reason is for the most part untrue to its spirit. The shocking abuses of the Church excited in the honest mind of Luther a lofty indignation. But in consequence of this he was led to desire to limit as much as possible the claims of Christianity itself, and for this end he first confined it to the words of the Bible; but then, in his well-meant zeal, he went too far, for he attacked the very heart of Christianity in the ascetic principle. For after the withdrawal of the ascetic principle, the optimistic principle soon necessarily took its place. But in religions, as in philosophy, optimism is a fundamental error which obstructs the path of all truth. From all this it seems to me that Catholicism is a shamefully abused, but Protestantism a degenerate Christianity; thus, that Christianity in general has met the fate which befalls all that is noble, sublime, and great whenever it has to dwell among men.

However, even in the very lap of Protestantism, the essentially ascetic and encratistic spirit of Christianity has made way for itself; and in this case it has appeared in a phenomenon which perhaps has never before been equalled in magnitude and definiteness, the highly remarkable sect of the Shakers, in North America, founded by an Englishwoman, Anne Lee, in 1774. The adherents of this sect have already increased to 6000, who are divided into fifteen communities, and inhabit a number of villages in the states of New York and Kentucky, especially in the district of New Lebanon, near Nassau village. The fundamental characteristic of their religious rule of life is celibacy and entire abstention from all sexual satisfaction. It is unanimously admitted, even by the English and Americans who visit them, and who laugh and jeer at them in every other respect, that this rule is strictly and with perfect honesty observed; although brothers and sisters sometimes even occupy the same house, eat at the same table, nay, *dance* together in the religious services in church. For whoever has made that hardest of all sacrifices may *dance* before the Lord; he is a victor, he has overcome. Their singing in church consists in general of cheerful, and partly even of merry, songs. The church-dance, also, which follows the sermon is accompanied by the singing of the rest. It is a lively dance, performed in measured time, and concludes with a galop, which is carried on till the dancers are exhausted. Between each dance one of their teachers cries aloud, "Think, that ye rejoice before the Lord for having slain your flesh; for this is here the only use we make of our refractory limbs." To celibacy most of the other conditions link themselves on of themselves. There are no families, and therefore there is no private property, but community of goods. All are clothed alike, in Quaker fashion, and with great neatness. They are industrious and diligent: idleness is not endured. They have also the enviable rule that they are to avoid all unnecessary noise, such as shouting, door-slamming, whip-cracking, loud knocking, &c. Their rule of life has been thus expressed by one of them: "Lead a life of innocence and purity, love your neighbours as yourself, live at peace with all men, and refrain from war, bloodshed, and all violence against others, as well as from all striving after worldly honour and distinction. Give to each his own, and follow after holiness, without which no man can see the Lord. Do good to all so far as your opportunity and your power extends." They persuade no one to join them, but test those who present themselves by a novitiate of several years. Moreover, every one is free to leave them; very rarely is any one expelled for misconduct. Adopted children are carefully educated, and only when they are grown up do they voluntarily join the sect. It is said that in the controversies of their ministers with Anglican clergy the latter generally come off the worse, for the arguments consist of passages from the New Testament. Fuller accounts of them will be found particularly in Maxwell's "Run through the United States," 1841; also in Benedict's "History of all Religions," 1830; also in the *Times*, November 4, 1837, and in the German magazine *Columbus*, May number, 1831. A German sect in America, very similar to them, who also live in strict celibacy and continence, are the Rappists. An account of them is given in F. Loher's "*Geschichte und Zustande der Deutschen in Amerika*," 1853.

In Russia also the Raskolniks are a similar sect. The Gichtelians live also in strict chastity. But among the ancient Jews we already find a prototype of all these sects, the Essenes, of whom even Pliny gives an account (*Hist. Nat.*, v. 15), and who resembled the Shakers very much, not only in celibacy, but also in other respects; for example, in dancing during divine service, which leads to the opinion that the founder of the Shakers took the Essenes as a pattern. In the presence of such facts as these how does Luther's assertion look: "*Ubi natura, quemadmodum a Deo nobis insita est, fertur ac rapitur,* FIERI NULLO MODO POTEST, *ut extra matrimonium caste vivatur*"? (*Catech. maj.*)

Although Christianity, in essential respects, taught only what all Asia knew long before, and even better, yet for Europe it was a new and great revelation, in consequence of which the spiritual tendency of the European nations was therefore entirely transformed. For it disclosed to them the metaphysical significance of existence, and therefore taught them to look away from the narrow, paltry, ephemeral life of earth, and to regard it no longer as an end in itself, but as a condition of suffering, guilt, trial, conflict, and purification, out of which, by means of moral achievements, difficult renunciation, and denial of oneself, one may rise to a better existence, which is inconceivable by us. It taught the great truth of the assertion and denial of the will to live in the clothing of allegory by saying that through Adam's fall the curse has come upon all, sin has come into the world, and guilt is inherited by all; but that, on the other hand, through the sacrificial death of Jesus all are reconciled, the world saved, guilt abolished, and justice satisfied. In order, however, to understand the truth itself that is contained in this myth one must not regard men simply in time, as beings independent of each other, but must comprehend the (Platonic) Idea of man, which is related to the series of men, as eternity in itself is related to eternity drawn out as time;

hence the eternal Idea *man* extended in time to the series of men through the connecting bond of generation appears again in time as a whole. If now we keep the Idea of man in view, we see that Adam's fall represents the finite, animal, sinful nature of man, in respect of which he is a finite being, exposed to sin, suffering, and death. On the other hand, the life, teaching, and death of Jesus Christ represent the eternal, supernatural side, the freedom, the salvation of man. Now every man, as such and *potentiâ*, is both Adam and Jesus, according as he comprehends himself, and his will thereupon determines him; in consequence of which he is then condemned and given over to death, or saved and attains to eternal life. Now these truths, both in their allegorical and in their real acceptation, were completely new as far as Greeks and Romans were concerned, who were still entirely absorbed in life, and did not seriously look beyond it. Let whoever doubts this see how Cicero (*Pro Cluentio*, c. 61) and Sallust (*Catil.*, c. 47) speak of the state after death. The ancients, although far advanced in almost everything else, remained children with regard to the chief concern, and were surpassed in this even by the Druids, who at least taught metempsychosis. That one or two philosophers, like Pythagoras and Plato, thought otherwise alters nothing as regards the whole.

That great fundamental truth, then, which is contained in Christianity, as in Brahmanism and Buddhism, the need of deliverance from an existence which is given up to suffering and death, and the attainableness of this by the denial of the will, thus by a decided opposition to nature, is beyond all comparison the most important truth there can be; but, at the same time, it is entirely opposed to the natural tendency of the human race, and in its true grounds it is difficult to comprehend; as indeed all that can only be thought generally and in the abstract is inaccessible to the great majority of men. Therefore for these men there was everywhere required, in order to bring that great truth within the sphere of its practical application, *a mythical vehicle* for it, as it were a receptacle, without which it would be lost and dissipated. The truth had therefore everywhere to borrow the garb of the fable, and also constantly to endeavour to connect itself with what in each case was historically given, already familiar, and already revered. What *sensu proprio* remained inaccessible to the great mass of mankind of all ages and lands, with their low tone of mind, their intellectual stupidity and general brutality, had, for practical purposes, to be brought home to them *sensu allegorico*, in order to become their guiding star. So, then, the religions mentioned above are to be regarded as the sacred vessels in which the great truth, known and expressed for several thousand years, indeed perhaps since the beginning of the human race, which yet in itself, for the great mass of mankind always remains a mystery, is, according to the measure of their powers, made accessible to them, preserved and transmitted through the centuries. Yet, because all that does not through and through consist of the imperishable material of pure truth is subject to destruction, whenever this fate befalls such a vessel, through contact with a heterogeneous age, its sacred content must in some way be saved and preserved for mankind by another. But it is the task of philosophy, since it is one with pure truth, to present that content pure and unmixed, thus merely in abstract conceptions, and consequently without that vehicle, for those who are capable of thinking, who are always an exceedingly small number. It is therefore related to religions as a straight line to several curves running near it: for it expresses *sensu proprio*, thus reaches directly, what they show in veiled forms and reach by circuitous routes.

If now, in order to illustrate what has just been said by an example, and also to follow a philosophical fashion of my time, I should wish perhaps to attempt to solve the profoundest mystery of Christianity, that of the

Trinity, in the fundamental conception of my philosophy, this could be done, with the licence permitted in such interpretations, in the following manner. The Holy Ghost is the distinct denial of the will to live: the man in whom this exhibits itself *in concreto* is the Son; He is identical with the will which asserts life, and thereby produces the phenomenon of this perceptible world, *i.e.*, with the Father, because the assertion and denial are opposite acts of the same will whose capability for both is the only true freedom. However, this is to be regarded as a mere *lusus ingenii.*

Before I close this chapter I wish to adduce a few proofs in support of what in § 68 of the first volume I denoted by the expression Δευτερος πλους, the bringing about of the denial of the will by one's own deeply felt suffering, thus not merely by the appropriation of the suffering of others, and the knowledge of the vanity and wretchedness of our existence introduced by this. We can arrive at a comprehension of what goes on in the heart of a man, in the case of an elevation of this kind and the accompanying purifying process, by considering what every emotional man experiences on beholding a tragedy, which is of kindred nature to this. In the third and fourth acts perhaps such a man is distressed and disturbed by the ever more clouded and threatened happiness of the hero; but when, in the fifth act, this happiness is entirely wrecked and shattered, he experiences a certain elevation of the soul, which affords him an infinitely higher kind of pleasure than the sight of the happiness of the hero, however great it might be, could ever have given. Now this is the same thing, in the weak water-colours of sympathy which is able to raise a well-known illusion, as that which takes place with the energy of reality in the feeling of our own fate when it is heavy misfortune that drives the man at last into the haven of entire resignation. Upon this occurrence depend all those conversions which completely transform men such as are described in the text. I may give here in a few words the story of the conversion of the Abbé Rancé, as it is strikingly similar to that of Raymond Lully, which is told in the text, and besides this is memorable on account of its result. His youth was devoted to enjoyment and pleasure; finally, he lived in a relation of passion with a Madame de Montbazon. One evening, when he visited her, he found her room empty, in disorder and darkness. He struck something with his foot; it was her head, which had been severed from the trunk, because after her sudden death her corpse could not otherwise be got into the lead coffin that stood beside it. After overcoming an immense sorrow, Rancé now became, in 1663, the reformer of the order of the Trappists, which at that time had entirely relaxed the strictness of its rules. He joined this order, and through him it was led back to that terrible degree of renunciation which is still maintained at ths present day at La Trappe, and, as the methodically carried out denial of the will, aided by the severest renunciation and an incredibly hard and painful manner of life, fills the visitor with sacred awe, after he has been touched at his reception by the humility of these genuine monks, who, emaciated by fasting, by cold, by night watches, prayers and penances, kneel before him, the worldling and the sinner, to implore his blessing. Of all orders of monks, this one alone has maintained itself in perfection in France, through all changes; which is to be attributed to the profound earnestness which in it is unmistakable, and excludes all secondary ends. It has remained untouched even by the decline of religion, because its root lies deeper in human nature than any positive system of belief.

I have mentioned in the text that this great and rapid change of the inmost being of man which we are here considering, and which has hitherto been entirely neglected by philosophers, appears most frequently when, with full consciousness, he stands in the presence of a violent and certain death, thus in the case of executions. But, in order to bring this process much more distinctly before our eyes, I regard it as by no means unbecoming to the dignity of philosophy to quote what has been said by some criminals before their execution, even at the risk of incurring the sneer that I encourage gallows' sermons. I certainly rather believe that the gallows is a place of quite peculiar revelations, and a watch-tower from which the man who even then retains his presence of mind obtains a wider, clearer outlook into eternity than most philosophers over the paragraphs of their rational psychology and theology. The following speech on the gallows was made on the 15th April, 1837, at Gloucester, by a man called Bartlett, who had murdered his mother-in-law: "Englishmen and fellow countrymen,—I have a few words to say to you, and they shall be but very few. Yet let me entreat you, one and all, that these few words that I shall utter may strike deep into your hearts. Bear them in your mind, not only now while you are witnessing this sad scene, but take them to your homes, take them, and repeat them to your children and friends. I implore you as a dying man—one for whom the instrument of death is even now prepared—and these words are that you may loose yourselves from the love of this dying world and its vain pleasures. Think less of it and more of your God. Do this: repent, repent, for be assured that without deep and true repentance, without turning to your heavenly Father, you will never attain, nor can hold the slightest hope of ever reaching those bowers of bliss to which I trust I am now fast advancing" (*Times*, 18th April 1837).

Still more remarkable are the last words of the well-known murderer, Greenacre, who was executed in London on the 1st of May 1837. The English newspaper the *Post* gives the following account, which is also reprinted in *Galignani's Messenger* of the 6th of May 1837: "On the morning of his execution a gentleman advised him to put his trust in God, and pray for forgiveness through the mediation of Jesus Christ. Greenacre replied that forgiveness through the mediation of Christ was a matter of opinion; for his part, he believed that in the sight of the highest Being, a Mohammedan was as good as a Christian and had just as much claim to salvation. Since his imprisonment he had had his attention directed to theological subjects, and he had become convinced that the gallows is a passport to heaven." The indifference displayed here towards positive religions is just what gives this utterance greater weight, for it shows that it is no fanatical delusion, but individual immediate knowledge that lies at its foundation. The following incident may also be mentioned which is given by *Galignani's Messenger* of the 15th August 1837, from the *Limerick Chronicle:* "Last Monday Maria Cooney was executed for the revolting murder of Mrs. Anderson. So deeply was this wretched woman impressed with the greatness of her crime that she kissed the rope which was put round her neck, while she humbly implored the mercy of God." Lastly this: the *Times,* of the 29th April 1845 gives several letters which Hocker, who was condemned for the murder of Delarue, wrote the day before his execution. In one of these he says: "I am persuaded that unless the natural heart be broken, and renewed by divine mercy, however noble and amiable it may be deemed by the world, it can never think of eternity without inwardly shuddering." These are the outlooks into eternity referred to above which are obtained from that watch-tower; and I have had the less hesitation in giving them here since Shakspeare also says—

> "Out of these convertites
> There is much matter to be heard and learned."
> —*As You Like it,* last scene.

Strauss, in his "Life of Jesus," has proved that Christianity also ascribes to suffering as such the purifying and sanctifying power here set forth (*Leben Jesu,* vol. i. ch. 6, §§ 72 and 74). He says that the beatitudes in the Sermon on the Mount have a different sense in Luke (vi.

21) from that which they have in Matt. (v. 3), for only the latter adds *τῳ πνευματι* to *μακαριοι ὁι πτωχοι*, and *την δικαιοσυνην* to *πεινωντες*. Thus by him alone are the simple-minded, the humble, &c., meant, while by Luke are meant the literally poor; so that here the contrast is that between present suffering and future happiness. With the Ebionites it is a capital principle that whoever takes his portion in this age gets nothing in the future, and conversely. Accordingly in Luke the blessings are followed by as many *ουαι*, woes, which are addressed to the rich, *ὁι πλουσιοι*, the full, *ὁι εμπεπλησμενοι*, and to them that laugh, *ὁι γελωντες*, in the Ebionite spirit. In the same spirit, he says, p. 604, is the parable (Luke xvi. 19) of the rich man and Lazarus given, which nowhere mentions any fault of the former or any merit of the latter, and takes as the standard of the future recompense, not the good done or the wickedness practised, but the evil suffered here and the good things enjoyed, in the Ebionite spirit. "A like estimation of outward poverty," Strauss goes on, "is also attributed to Jesus by the other synoptists (Matt. xix. 16; Mark x. 17; Luke xviii. 18), in the story of the rich young man and the saying about the camel and the eye of a needle."

If we go to the bottom of the matter we will recognise that even in the most famous passages of the Sermon on the Mount there is contained an indirect injunction to voluntary poverty, and thereby to the denial of the will to live. For the precept (Matt. v. 40 *seq.*) to consent unconditionally to all demands made upon us, to give our cloak also to him who will take away our coat, &c., similarly (Matt. vi. 25–34) the precept to cast aside all care for the future, even for the morrow, and so to live simply in the present, are rules of life the observance of which inevitably leads to absolute poverty, and which therefore just say in an indirect manner what Buddha directly commands his disciples and has confirmed by his own example: throw everything away and become bhikkhu, *i.e.*, beggars. This appears still more decidedly in the passage Matt. x. 9–15, where all possessions, even shoes and a staff, are forbidden to the Apostles, and they are directed to beg. These commands afterwards became the foundation of the mendicant order of St. Francis (*Bonaventuræ vita S. Francisci*, c. 3). Hence, then, I say that the spirit of Christian ethics is identical with that of Brahmanism aud Buddhism. In conformity with the whole view expounded here Meister Eckhard also says (Works, vol. i. p. 492): "The swiftest animal that bears thee to perfection is suffering."

CHAPTER XLIX.

THE WAY OF SALVATION.

THERE is only one inborn error, and that is, that we exist in order to be happy. It is inborn in us because it is one with our existence itself, and our whole being is only a paraphrase of it, nay, our body is its monogram. We are nothing more than will to live and the successive satisfaction of all our volitions is what we think in the conception of happiness.

As long as we persist in this inborn error, indeed even become rigidly fixed in it through optimistic dogmas, the world appears to us full of contradictions. For at every step, in great things as in small, we must experience that the world and life are by no means arranged with a view to containing a happy existence. While now by this the thoughtless man only finds himself tormented in reality, in the case of him who thinks there is added to his real pain the theoretical perplexity why a world and a life which exist in order that one may be happy in them answer their end so badly. First of all it finds expression in pious ejaculations, such as, "Ah! why are the tears on earth so many?" &c. &c. But in their train come disquieting doubts about the assumptions of those preconceived optimistic dogmas. One may try if one will to throw the blame of one's individual unhappiness now upon the circumstances, now upon other men, now upon one's own bad luck, or even upon one's own awkwardness, and may know well how all these have worked together to produce it; but this in no way alters the result that one has missed the real end of life, which consists indeed in being happy. The consideration of this is, then, often very depressing, especially if life is already on the wane; hence the countenances of almost all elderly persons wear the expression of that which in English is called disappointment. Besides this, however, hitherto every day of our life has taught us that joys and pleasures, even if attained, are in themselves delusive, do not perform what they promise, do not satisfy the heart, and finally their possession is at least embittered by the disagreeables that accompany them or spring from them; while, on the contrary, the pains and sorrows prove themselves very real, and often exceed all expectation. Thus certainly everything in life is calculated to recall us from that original error, and to convince us that the end of our existence is not to be happy. Indeed, if we regard it more closely and without prejudice, life rather presents itself as specially intended to be such that we shall *not* feel ourselves happy in it, for through its whole nature it bears the character of something for which we have no taste, which must be endured by us, and from which we have to return as from an error that our heart may be cured of the passionate desire of enjoyment, nay, of life, and turned away from the world. In this sense, it would be more correct to place the end of life in our woe than in our welfare. For the considerations at the conclusion of the preceding chapter have shown that the more one suffers the sooner one attains to the true end of life, and that the more happily one lives the longer this is delayed. The conclusion of the last letter of Seneca corresponds with this: *bonum tunc habebis tuum, quum intelliges infelicissimos esse felices;* which certainly seems to show the influence of Christianity. The peculiar effect of the tragic drama also ultimately depends upon the fact that it shakes that inborn error by vividly presenting in a great and striking example the vanity of human effort and the nothingness of this whole existence, and thus discloses the profound significance of life; hence it is recognised as the sublimest form of poetry. Whoever now has returned by one or other path from that error which dwells in us *a priori*, that πρωτον ψευδος of our existence, will soon see all in another light, and will now find the world in harmony with his insight, although not with his wishes. Misfortunes of every kind and magnitude, although they pain him, will no longer surprise him, for he has come to see that it is just pain and trouble that tend towards the true end of life, the turning away of the will from it. This will give him indeed a wonderful composedness in all that may happen, similar to that with which a sick person who undergoes a long and painful cure bears the pain of it as a sign of its efficacy. In the whole of human existence suffering expresses itself clearly enough as its true destiny. Life is deeply sunk in suffering, and cannot escape from it; our entrance into it takes place amid tears, its course is at bottom always tragic, and its end still more so. There is an unmistakable appearance of intention in this. As a rule man's destiny passes through his mind in a striking manner, at the very summit of his desires and efforts, and thus his life receives a tragic tendency by virtue of which it is fitted to free him from the passionate desire of which every individual existence is an example, and bring him into such a condition that he parts with life without retaining a single desire for it and its pleasures. Suffering is, in fact, the purifying process through which alone, in most cases, the man is sanctified, *i.e.*, is led back from the path of error of the will to live. In accordance with this, the salutary nature of the cross and of suffering is so often explained in Christian books of edification, and in general the cross, an instrument of suffering, not of doing, is very suitably the symbol of the Christian religion. Nay, even the Preacher, who is still Jewish, but so very philosophical, rightly says: "Sorrow is better than laughter: for by the sadness of the countenance the heart is made better" (Eccles. vii. 3). Under the name of the δευτερος πλους I have presented suffering as to a certain extent a substitute for virtue and holiness; but here I must make the bold assertion that, taking everything into consideration, we have more to hope for our salvation and deliverance from what we suffer than from what we do. Precisely in this spirit Lamartine very beautifully says in his "*Hymne à la douleur*," apostrophising pain:—

> "*Tu me traites sans doute en favori des cieux,*
> *Car tu n'épargnes pas les larmes à mes yeux.*
> *Eh bien! je les reçois comme tu les envoies,*
> *Tes maux seront mes biens, et tes soupirs mes joies.*
> *Je sens qu'il est en toi, sans avoir combattu,*
> *Une vertu divine au lieu de ma vertu,*
> *Que tu n'es pas la mort l'âme, mais sa vie,*
> *Que ton bras, en frappant, guérit et vivifie.*"

If, then, suffering itself has such a sanctifying power, this will belong in an even higher degree to death, which is more feared than any suffering. Answering to this, a certain awe, kindred to that which great suffering occasions us, is felt in the presence of every dead person, indeed every case of death presents itself to a certain extent as a kind of apotheosis or canonisation; therefore we cannot look upon the dead body of even the most insignificant man without awe, and indeed, extraordinary as the remark may sound in this place, in the presence of every corpse the watch goes under arms. Dying is certainly to be regarded as the real aim of life: in the moment of death all that is decided for which the whole course of life was only the preparation and introduction. Death is the result, the *Résumé* of life, or the added up sum which expresses at once the instruction which life gave in detail, and bit by bit; this, that the whole striving whose manifestation is life was a vain, idle, and self-contradictory effort, to have returned from which is a deliverance. As the whole, slow vegetation of the plant is related to the fruit, which now at a stroke achieves a hundredfold what the plant achieved gradually and bit by bit, so life, with its obstacles, deluded hopes, frustrated plans, and constant suffering, is related to death, which at one stroke destroys all, all that the man has willed, and so crowns the instruction which life gave him. The completed course of life upon which the dying man looks back has an effect upon the whole will that objectifies itself in this perishing individuality, analogous to that which a motive exercises upon the conduct of the man. It gives it a new direction, which accordingly is the moral and essential result of the life. Just because a sudden death makes this retrospect impossible, the Church regards such a death as a misfortune, and prays that it should be averted. Since this retrospect, like the distinct foreknowledge of death, as conditioned by the reason, is possible only in man, not in the brute, and accordingly man alone really drinks the cup of death, humanity is the only material in which the will can deny itself and entirely turn away from life. To the will that does not deny itself every birth imparts a new and different intellect,—till it has learned the true nature of life, and in consequence of this wills it no more.

In the natural course, in age the decay of the body coincides with that of the will. The desire for pleasures soon vanishes with the capacity to enjoy them. The occasion of the most vehement willing, the focus of the will, the sexual impulse, is first extinguished, whereby the man is placed in a position which resembles the state of innocence which existed before the development of the genital system. The illusions, which set up chimeras as exceedingly desirable benefits, vanish, and the knowledge of the vanity of all earthly blessings takes their place. Selfishness is repressed by the love of one's children, by means of which the man already begins to live more in the ego of others than in his own, which now will soon be no more. This course of life is at least the desirable one; it is the euthanasia of the will. In hope of this the Brahman is ordered, after he has passed the best years of his life, to forsake possessions and family, and lead the life of a hermit (*Menu*, B. 6). But if, conversely, the desire outlives the capacity for enjoyment, and we now regret particular pleasures in life which we miss, instead of seeing the emptiness and vanity of all; and if then gold, the abstract representative of the objects of desire for which the sense is dead, takes the place of all these objects themselves, and now excites the same vehement passions which were formerly more pardonably awakened by the objects of actual pleasure, and thus now with deadened senses a lifeless but indestructible object is desired with equally indestructible eagerness; or, also, if, in the same way, existence in the opinion of others takes the place of existence and action in the real world, and now kindles the same passions;—then the will has become sublimated and etherealised into avarice or ambition; but has thereby thrown itself into the last fortress, in which it can only now be besieged by death. The end of existence has been missed.

All these considerations afford us a fuller explanation of that purification, conversion of the will and deliverance, denoted in the preceding chapter by the expression δευτερος πλους which is brought about by the suffering of life, and without doubt is the most frequent. For it is the way of sinners such as we all are. The other way, which leads to the same goal, by means of mere knowledge and the consequent appropriation of the suffering of a whole world, is the narrow path of the elect, the saints, and therefore to be regarded as a rare exception. Therefore without that first way for most of us there would be no salvation to hope for. However, we struggle against entering upon it, and strive rather to procure for ourselves a safe and agreeable existence, whereby we chain our will ever more firmly to life. The conduct of the ascetics is the opposite of this. They make their life intentionally as poor, hard, and empty of pleasure as possible, because they have their true and ultimate welfare in view. But fate and the course of things care for us better than we ourselves, for they frustrate on all sides our arrangements for an utopian life, the folly of which is evident enough from its brevity, uncertainty, and emptiness, and its conclusion by bitter death; they strew thorns upon thorns in our path, and meet us everywhere with healing sorrow, the panacea of our misery. What really gives its wonderful and ambiguous character to our life is this, that two diametrically opposite aims constantly cross each other in it; that of the individual will directed to chimerical happiness in an ephemeral, dream-like, and delusive existence, in which, with reference to the past, happiness and unhappiness are a matter of indifference, and the present is every moment becoming the past; and that of fate visibly enough directed to the destruction of our happiness, and thereby to the mortification of our will and the abolition of the illusion that holds us chained in the bonds of this world.

The prevalent and peculiarly Protestant view that the end of life lies solely and immediately in the moral virtues, thus in the practice of justice and benevolence, betrays its insufficiency even in the fact that so miserably little real and pure morality is found among men. I am not speaking at all of lofty virtue, nobleness, magnanimity, and self-sacrifice, which one hardly finds anywhere but in plays and novels, but only of those virtues which are the duty of every one. Let whoever is old think of all those with whom he has had to do; how many persons will he have met who were merely really and truly *honest?* Were not by far the greater number, in spite of their shameless indignation at the slightest suspicion of dishonesty or even untruthfulness, in plain words, the precise opposite? Were not abject selfishness, boundless avarice, well-concealed knavery, and also poisonous envy and fiendish delight in the misfortunes of others so universally prevalent that the slightest exception was met with surprise? And benevolence, how very rarely it extends beyond a gift of what is so superfluous that one never misses it. And is the whole end of existence to lie in such exceedingly rare and weak traces of morality? If we place it, on the contrary, in the entire reversal of this nature of ours (which bears the evil fruits just mentioned) brought about by suffering, the matter gains an appearance of probability and is brought into agreement with what actually lies before us. Life presents itself then as a purifying process, of which the purifying lye is pain. If the process is carried out, it leaves behind it the previous immorality and wickedness as refuse, and there appears what the Veda says: "*Finditur nodus cordis, dissolvuntur omnes dubitationes, ejusque opera evanescunt.*" As agreeing with this view the fifteenth sermon of Meister Eckhard will be found very well worth reading.

CHAPTER L.

EPIPHILOSOPHY.

AT the conclusion of my exposition a few reflections concerning my philosophy itself may find their place. My philosophy does not pretend to explain the existence of the world in its ultimate grounds: it rather sticks to the facts of external and internal experience as they are accessible to every one, and shows the true and deepest connection of them without really going beyond them to any extra-mundane things and their relations to the world. It therefore arrives at no conclusions as to what lies beyond all possible experience, but affords merely an exposition of what is given in the external world and in self-consciousness, thus contents itself with comprehending the nature of the world in its inner connection with itself. It is consequently *immanent,* in the Kantian sense of the word. But just on this account it leaves many questions untouched; for example, why what is proved as a fact is as it is and not otherwise, &c. All such questions, however, or rather the answers to them, are really transcendent, *i.e.*, they cannot be thought by the forms and functions of our intellect, do not enter into these; it is therefore related to them as our sensibility is related to the possible properties of bodies for which we have no senses. After all my explanations one may still ask, for example, whence has sprung this will that is free to assert itself, the manifestation of which is the world, or to deny itself, the manifestation of which we do not know. What is the fatality lying beyond all experience which has placed it in the very doubtful dilemma of either appearing as a world in which suffering and death reign, or else denying its very being?—or again, what can have prevailed upon it to forsake the infinitely preferable peace of blessed nothingness? An individual will, one may add, can only turn to its own destruction through error in the choice, thus through the fault of knowledge; but the will in itself, before all manifestation, consequently still without knowledge, how could it go astray and fall into the ruin of its present condition? Whence in general is the great discord that permeates this world? It may, further, be asked how deep into the true being of the world the roots of individuality go; to which it may certainly be answered: they go as deep as the assertion of the will to live; where the denial of the will appears they cease, for they have arisen with the assertion. But one might indeed even put the question, "What would I be if I were not will to live?" and more of the same kind To all such questions we would first have to reply that the expression of the most universal and general form of our intellect is the *principle of sufficient reason;* but that just on this account that principle finds application only to the phenomenon, not to the being in itself of things. Yet all whence and why depend upon that principle alone. As a result of the Kantian philosophy it is no longer an *æterna veritas*, but merely the form, *i.e.*, the function, of our intellect, which is essentially cerebral, and originally a mere tool in the service of the will, which it therefore presupposes together with all its objectifications. But our whole knowing and conceiving is bound to its forms; accordingly we must conceive everything in time, consequently as a before and after, then as cause and effect, and also as above and below, whole and part, &c., and cannot by any means escape from this sphere in which all possibility of our knowledge lies. Now these forms are utterly unsuited to the problems raised here, nor are they fit or able to comprehend their solution even if it were given. Therefore with our intellect, this mere tool of the will, we are everywhere striking upon insoluble problems, as against the walls of our prison. But, besides this, it may at least be assumed as probable that not only *for us* is knowledge of all that has been asked about impossible, but no such knowledge is possible in general, thus never and in no way; that these relations are not only relatively but absolutely insusceptible of investigation; that not only does no one know them, but that they are in themselves unknowable, because they do not enter into the form of knowledge in general. (This corresponds to what Scotus Erigena says, *de mirabili divina ignorantia, qua Deus non intelligit quid ipse sit.* Lib. ii.) For knowableness in general, with its most essential, and therefore constantly necessary form of subject and object, belongs merely to the phenomenal appearance, not to the being in itself of things. Where knowledge, and consequently idea, is, there is also only phenomenon, and we stand there already in the province of the phenomenal; nay, knowledge in general is known to us only as a phenomenon of brain, and we are not only unjustified in conceiving it otherwise, but also incapable of doing so. What the world is as world may be understood: it is phenomenal manifestation; and we can know that which manifests itself in it, directly from ourselves, by means of a thorough analysis of self-consciousness. Then, however, by means of this key to the nature of the world, the whole phenomenal manifestation can be deciphered, as I believe I have succeeded in doing. But if we leave the world in order to answer the questions indicated above, we have also left the whole sphere in which, not only connection according to reason and consequent, but even knowledge itself is possible; then all is *instabilis tellus, innabilis unda.* The nature of things before or beyond the world, and consequently beyond the will, is open to no investigation; because knowledge in general is itself only a phenomenon, and therefore exists only in the world as the world exists only in it. The inner being in itself of things is nothing that knows, no intellect, but an unconscious; knowledge is only added as an accident, a means of assistance to the phenomenon of that inner being, and can therefore apprehend that being itself only in proportion to its own nature, which is designed with reference to quite different ends (those of the individual will), consequently very imperfectly. Here lies the reason why a perfect understanding of the existence, nature, and origin of the world, extending to its ultimate ground and satisfying all demands, is impossible. So much as to the limits of my philosophy, and indeed of all philosophy.

The *ἑν και παν*, *i.e.*, that the inner nature in all things is absolutely one and the same, my age had already grasped and understood, after the Eleatics, Scotus Erigena, Giordano Bruno, and Spinoza had thoroughly taught, and Schelling had revived this doctrine. But *what* this one is, and how it is able to exhibit itself as the many, is a problem the solution of which is first found in my philosophy. Certainly from the most ancient times man had been called the microcosm. I have reversed the proposition, and shown the world as the macranthropos: because will and idea exhaust its nature as they do that of man. But it is clearly more correct to learn to understand the world from man than man from the world; for one has to explain what is indirectly given, thus external perception from what is directly given, thus self-consciousness—not conversely.

With the Pantheists, then, I have certainly that *ἑν και παν* in common, but not the *παν θεος*; because I do not go beyond experience (taken in its widest sense), and still less do I put myself in contradiction with the data which lie before me. Scotus Erigena, quite consistently with the spirit of Pantheism, explains every phenomenon as a theophany; but then this conception must also be applied to the most terrible and abominable phenomena. Fine theophanies! What further distinguishes me from Pantheism is principally the following. (1). That their *θεος* is an x, an unknown quantity; the will, on the other hand, is of all possible things the one that is known to us most exactly, the only thing given immediately, and therefore exclusively fitted for the explanation of the rest. For what is unknown must always be explained by what is better known; not conversely. (2). That their θεος manifests himself *animi causa,* to unfold his glory, or, indeed, to let himself be admired. Apart from the vanity here attributed to him, they are placed in the position of being obliged to sophisticate away the colossal evil of the world; but the world remains in glaring and terrible contradiction with that imagined excellence. With me, on the contrary, the *will* arrives through its objectification however this may occur, at self-knowledge, whereby its abolition, conversion, salvation becomes possible. And accordingly, with me alone ethics has a sure foundation and is completely worked out in agreement with the sublime and profound religions, Brahmanism, Buddhism, and Christianity, not merely with Judaism and Mohammedanism. The metaphysic of the beautiful also is first fully cleared up as a result of my fundamental truth, and no longer requires to take refuge behind empty words. With me alone is the evil of the world honestly confessed in its whole magnitude: this is rendered possible by the fact that the answer to the question as to its origin coincides with the answer to the question as to the origin of the world. On the other hand, in all other systems, since they are all optimistic, the question as to the origin of evil is the incurable disease, ever breaking out anew, with which they are affected, and in consequence of which they struggle along with palliatives and quack remedies. (3.) That I start from experience and the natural self-consciousness given to every one, and lead to the will as that which alone is metaphysical; thus I adopt the ascending, analytical method. The Pantheists, again, adopt the opposite method, the descending or synthetical. They start from their θεος, which they beg or take by force, although sometimes under the name *substantia,* or absolute, and this unknown is then supposed to explain everything that is better known. (4.) That with me the world does not fill the whole possibility of all being, but in this there still remains much room for that which we denote only negatively as the denial of the will to live. Pantheism, on the other hand, is essentially optimism: but if the world is what is best, then the matter may rest there. (5.) That to the Pantheists the perceptible world, thus the world of idea, is just the intentional manifestation of the God indwelling in it, which contains no real explanation of its appearance, but rather requires to be explained itself. With me, on the other hand, the world as idea appears merely *per accidens*, because the intellect, with its external perception, is primarily only the medium of motives for the more perfect phenomena of will, which gradually rises to that objectivity of perceptibility, in which the world exists. In this sense its origin, as an object of perception, is really accounted for, and not, as with the Pantheists, by means of untenable fictions.

Since, in consequence of the Kantian criticism of all speculative theology, the philosophisers of Germany almost all threw themselves back upon Spinoza, so that the whole series of futile attempts known by the name of the post-Kantian philosophy are simply Spinozism tastelessly dressed up, veiled in all kinds of unintelligible language, and otherwise distorted, I wish, now that I have explained the relation of my philosophy to Pantheism in general, to point out its relation to Spinozism in particular. It stands, then, to Spinozism as the New Testament stands to the Old. What the Old Testament has in common with the New is the same God-Creator. Analogous to this, the world exists, with me as with Spinoza, by its inner power and through itself. But with Spinoza his *substantia æterna*, the inner nature of the world, which he himself calls God, is also, as regards its moral character and worth, Jehovah, the God-Creator, who applauds His own creation, and finds that all is very good, *παντα καλα*

λιαν. Spinoza has deprived Him of nothing but personality. Thus, according to him also, the world and all in it is wholly excellent and as it ought to be: therefore man has nothing more to do than *vivere, agere, suum Esse conservare ex fundamento proprium utile quœrendi* (*Eth.*, iv. pr. 67); he is even to rejoice in his life as long as it lasts; entirely in accordance with Ecclesiastes ix. 7–10. In short, it is optimism: therefore its ethical side is weak, as in the Old Testament; nay, it is even false, and in part revolting.[1] With me, on the other hand, the will, or the inner nature of the world, is by no means Jehovah, it is rather, as it were, the crucified Saviour, or the crucified thief, according as it resolves. Therefore my ethical teaching agrees with that of Christianity, completely and in its highest tendencies, and not less with that of Brahmanism and Buddhism. Spinoza could not get rid of the Jews; *quo semel est imbuta recens servabit odorem.* His contempt for the brutes, which, as mere things for our use, he also declares to be without rights, is thoroughly Jewish, and, in union with Pantheism, is at the same time absurd and detestable (*Eth.*, iv., appendix, c. 27). With all this Spinoza remains a very great man. But in order to estimate his work correctly we must keep in view his relation to Descartes. The latter had sharply divided nature into mind and matter, *i.e.*, thinking and extended substance, and had also placed God and the world in complete opposition to each other; Spinoza also, so long as he was a Cartesian, taught all that in his "*Cogitatis Metaphysicis*," c. 12, i. I., 1665. Only in his later years did he see the fundamental falseness of that double dualism; and accordingly his own philosophy principally consists of the indirect abolition of these two antitheses. Yet partly to avoid injuring his teacher, partly in order to be less offensive, he

[1] *Unusquisque tantum juris habet, quantum potentiâ valet* (*Tract. pol.*, c. 2 § 8). *Fides alicui data tamdiu rata manet, quamdiu ejus, qui fidem dedit, non mutatur voluntas* (*Ibid.*, § 12). *Uniuscujusque jus potentiâ ejus definetur* (*Eth.* iv., *pr.* 37, *schol.* I.) Especially chap. 16 of the *Tractatus theologico-politicus* is the true compendium of the immorality of Spinoza's philosophy.

gave it a positive appearance by means of a strictly dogmatic form, although its content is chiefly negative. His identification of the world with God has also this negative significance alone. For to call the world God is not to explain it: it remains a riddle under the one name as under the other. But these two negative truths had value for their age, as for every age in which there still are conscious or unconscious Cartesians. He makes the mistake, common to all philosophers before Locke, of starting from conceptions, without having previously investigated their origin, such, for example, as substance, cause, &c., and in such a method of procedure these conceptions then receive a much too extensive validity. Those who in the most recent times refused to acknowledge the Neo-Spinozism which had appeared, for example, Jacobi, were principally deterred from doing so by the bugbear of fatalism. By this is to be understood every doctrine which refers the existence of the world, together with the critical position of mankind in it, to any absolute necessity, *i.e.*, to a necessity that cannot be further explained. Those who feared fatalism, again, believed that all that was of importance was to deduce the world from the free act of will of a being existing outside it; as if it were antecedently certain which of the two was more correct, or even better merely in relation to us. What is, however, especially assumed here is the *non datur tertium,* and accordingly hitherto every philosophy has represented one or the other. I am the first to depart from this; for I have actually established the *Tertium:* the act of will from which the world arises is our own. It is free; for the principle of sufficient reason, from which alone all necessity derives its significance, is merely the form of its phenomenon. Just on this account this phenomenon, if it once exists, is absolutely necessary in its course; in consequence of this alone we can recognise in it the nature of the act of will, and accordingly *eventualiter* will otherwise.

APPENDIX.

ABSTRACT

OF

SCHOPENHAUER'S ESSAY ON THE FOURFOLD ROOT OF THE PRINCIPLE OF SUFFICIENT REASON (Fourth Edition, Edited by FRAUENSTÄDT. The First Edition appeared in 1813).

THIS essay is divided into eight chapters. The first is introductory. The second contains an historical review of previous philosophical doctrines on the subject. The third deals with the insufficiency of the previous treatment of the principle, and prescribes the lines of the new departure. The fourth, fifth, sixth, and seventh treat of the four classes of objects for the subject, and the forms of the principle of sufficient reason which respectively characterise these classes. The eighth contains general remarks and results. It will be convenient to summarise these chapters severally.

CHAPTER I.

Schopenhauer points out that Plato and Kant agree in recommending, as the method of all knowledge, obedience to two laws:—that of Homogeneity, and that of Specification. The former bids us, by attention to the points of resemblance and agreement in things, get at their kinds, and combine them into species, and these species again into genera, until we have arrived at the highest concept of all, that which embraces everything. This law being transcendental, or an essential in our faculty of reason, assumes that nature is in harmony with it, an assumption which is expressed in the old rule: *Entia præter necessitatem non esse multiplicanda.* The law of Specification, on the other hand, is stated by Kant in these words: *Entium varietates non temere esse minuendas.* That is to say, we must carefully distinguish the species which are united under a genus, and the lower kinds which in their turn are united under these species; taking care not to make a leap, and subsume the lower kinds and individuals under the concept of the genus, since this is always capable of division, but never descends to the object of pure perception. Plato and Kant agree that these laws are transcendental, and that they presuppose that things are in harmony with them.

The previous treatment of the principle of sufficient reason, even by Kant, has been a failure, owing to the neglect of the second of these laws. It may well be that we shall find that this principle is the common expression of more than one fundamental principle of knowledge, and that the necessity, to which it refers, is therefore of different kinds. It may be stated in these words: *Nihil est sine ratione cur potius sit, quam non sit.* This is the general expression for the different forms of the assumption which everywhere justifies that question "Why?" which is the mother of all science.

CHAPTER II.

Schopenhauer in this chapter traces historically the forms in which the principle had been stated by his predecessors, and their influence. He points out that in Greek philosophy it appeared in two aspects—that of the necessity of a ground for a logical judgment, and that of a cause for every physical change—and that these two aspects were systematically confounded. The Aristotelian division, not of the forms of the principle itself, but of one of its aspects, the causal, exemplified a confusion which continued throughout the Scholastic period. Descartes succeeds no better. His proof of the existence of God that the immensity of His nature is a *cause or reason* beyond which no cause is needed for His existence, simply illustrates the gross confusion between cause and ground of knowledge which underlies every form of this ontological proof. "That a miserable fellow like Hegel, whose entire philosophy is nothing but a monstrous amplification of the ontological proof, should dare to defend this proof against Kant's criticism of it is an alliance of which the ontological proof itself, little as it knows of shame, might well feel ashamed. It is not to be expected I should speak respectfully of people who have brought philosophy into disrespect." Spinoza made the same confusion when he laid it down that the cause of existence was either contained in the nature and definition of the thing as it existed, or was to be found outside that thing. It was through this confusion of the ground of knowledge with the efficient cause that he succeeded in identifying God with the world. The true picture of Spinoza's "*Causa sui*" is Baron Munchhausen encircling his horse with his legs, and raising himself and the horse upwards by means of his pigtail, with the inscription "*Causa sui*" written below. Leibnitz was the first to place the principle of sufficient reason in the position of a first principle, and to indicate the difference between its two meanings. But it was Wolff who first completely distinguished them, and divided the doctrine into three kinds: *principium fiendi* (cause), *principium essendi* (possibility), and *principium cognoscendi.* Baumgarten, Reimarus, Lambert, and Platner added nothing to the work of Wolff, and the next great step was Hume's question as to the validity of the principle. Kant's distinction of the logical or formal principle of knowledge—Every *proposition* must have its ground; from the transcendental or material principle, Every *thing* must have its ground—was followed out by his immediate successors. But when we come to Schelling we find the proposition that gravitation is the *reason* and light the *cause* of things, a proposition which is quoted simply as a curiosity, for such a piece of nonense deserves no place among the opinions of earnest and honest inquirers. The chapter concludes by pointing out the futility of the attempts to prove the principle. Every proof is the exhibition of the ground of a judgment which has been expressed, and of which, just because that ground is exhibited, we predicate truth The principle of sufficient reason is just this expression of the demand for such a ground, and he who seeks a proof, *i.e.*, the exhibition of a ground for this principle itself, presupposes it as true, and so falls into the circle of seeking a proof of the justification of the demand for proof.

CHAPTER III.

In the third chapter Schopenhauer points out that the two applications of the principle of sufficient reason distinguished by his predecessors, to judgments, which must have a ground, and to the changes of real objects, which must have a cause, are not exhaustive. The reason why the three sides of a certain triangle are equal is that the angles are equal, and this is neither a logical deduction nor a case of causation. With a view to stating exhaustively the various kinds into which the application of the principle falls it is necessary to determine the nature of the principle itself. All our ideas are objects of the subject, and all objects of the subject are our ideas. But our ideas stand to one another as a matter of fact in an orderly connection, which is always determinable *a priori* in point of form, and on account of which nothing that is in itself separate and wholly independent of other things can be the object of our consciousness. It is this connection which the principle of sufficient reason in its generality expresses. The relations which constitute it are what Schopenhauer calls its root, and they fall into four classes, which are discussed in the four following chapters.

CHAPTER IV.

In the fourth chapter Schopenhauer deals with the first class of objects for the subject and the form of the principle of sufficient reason which obtains in it. This first class is that of those complete ideas of perception which form part of our experience, and which are referable to some sensation of our bodies. These ideas are capable of being perceived only under the forms of Space and Time. If time were the only form there would be no coexistence, and therefore no persistence. If space were their only form there would be no succession, and therefore no change. Time may therefore be defined as the possibility of mutually exclusive conditions of the same thing. But the union of these two forms of existence is the essential condition of reality, and this union is the work of the understanding (see "World as Will and Idea," vol. i. § 4, and the table of predicables annexed to vol. ii., chap. 4). In this class of objects for the subject the principle of sufficient reason appears as the law of causality or the principle of sufficient reason of becoming, and it is through it that all objects which present themselves in perception are bound together through the changes of their states. When a new state of one or more objects makes its appearance it must have been preceded by another on which it regularly follows. This is causal sequence, and the first state is the cause, the second the effect. The law has thus to do exclusively with the *changes* of objects of external experience, and not with things themselves, a circumstance which is fatal to the validity of the cosmological proof of the existence of God. It follows also from the essential connection of causality with succession that the notion of reciprocity, with its contemporaneous existence of cause and effect, is a delusion. The chain of causes and effects does not affect either matter, which is that in which all changes take place, or the original forces of nature, through which causation becomes possible, and which exist apart from all change, and in this sense out of time, but which yet are everywhere present (*e.g.*, chemical forces; see *supra*, vol. i., § 26). In nature causation assumes three different forms; that of cause in the narrow sense, of stimulus, and of motive, on which differences depend the true distinctions between inorganic bodies, plants, and animals. It is only of cause properly so called that Newton's third law of the equality of action and reaction is true, and only here do we find the degree of the effect proportionate to that of the cause. The absence of this feature characterises stimulation. Motive demands knowledge as its condition, and intelligence is therefore the true characteristic of the animal. The three forms are in principle identical, the difference being due to the degrees of receptivity in existence. What is called freedom of the will is therefore an absurdity, as is also Kant's "Practical Reason." These results are followed by an examination of the nature of vision, which Schopenhauer sums up in these words : "I have examined all these visual processes in detail in order to show that the understanding is active in all of them, the understanding which, by apprehending every change as an effect and referring it to its cause, creates on the basis of the *a priori* and fundamental intuitions or perceptions of space and time, the objective world, that phenomenon of the brain, for which the sensations of the senses afford only certain data. And this task the understanding accomplishes only through its proper form, the law of causality, and accomplishes it directly without the aid of reflection, that is, of abstract knowledge through concepts and words, which are the material of secondary knowledge, of thought, thus of the Reason." "What understanding knows aright is reality; what reason knows aright is truth, *i.e.*, a judgment which has a ground; the opposite of the former being illusion (what is falsely perceived), of the latter error (what is falsely thought)." All understanding is an immediate apprehension of the causal relation, and this is the sole function of understanding, and not the complicated working of the twelve Kantian Categories, the theory of which is a mistaken one. A consequence of this conclusion is, that arithmetical processes do not belong to the understanding, concerned as they are with abstract conceptions. But it must not be forgotten that between volition and the apparently consequential action of the body there is no causal relation, for they are the same thing perceived in two different ways. Section 23 contains a detailed refutation of Kant's proof of the *a priori* nature of the causal relation in the "Second Analogy of Experience" of the Critique of Pure Reason, the gist of the objection being that the so-called subjective succession is as much objective in reality as what is called objective by Kant: "Phenomena may well follow one another, without following *from* one another."

CHAPTER V.

The fifth chapter commences with an examination of the distinction between man and the brutes. Man possesses *reason,* that is to say, he has a class of ideas of which the brutes are not capable, *abstract* ideas as distinguished from those ideas of perception from which the former kind are yet derived. The consequence is, that the brute neither speaks nor laughs, and lacks all those qualities which make human life great. The nature of *motives,* too, is different where abstract ideas are possible. No doubt the actions of men follow of necessity from their causes, not less than is the case with the brutes, but the kind of sequence through thought which renders choice, *i.e.,* the conscious conflict of motives, possible is different. Our abstract ideas, being incapable of being objects of perception, would be outside consciousness, and the operations of thought would be impossible, were it not that they are fixed for sense by arbitrary signs called words, which therefore always indicate *general* conceptions. It is just because the brutes are incapable of general conceptions that they have no faculty of speech. But thought does not consist in the mere presence of abstract ideas in consciousness, but in the union and separation of two or more of them, subject to the manifold restrictions and modifications which logic deals with. Such a clearly expressed conceptual relation is a judgment. In relation to judgments the principle of sufficient reason is valid in a new form: that of the ground of knowing. In this form it asserts that if a judgment is to express knowledge it must have a ground; and it is just because it has a ground that it has ascribed to it the predicate true. The grounds on which a judgment may depend are divisible into four kinds. A judgment may have another judgment as its ground, in which case its truth is formal or *logical.* There is no truth except in the relation of a judgment to something outside it, and intrinsic truth, which is sometimes distinguished from extrinsic logical truth, is therefore an absurdity. A judgment may also have its ground in sense-perception, and its truth is then material truth. Again, those forms of knowledge which lie in the understanding and in pure sensibility, as the conditions of the possibility of experience, may be the ground of a judgment which is then synthetical *a priori*. Finally, those formal conditions of all thinking which lie in the reason may be the ground of a judgment, which may in that case be called metalogically true. Of these metalogical judgments there are four, and they were long ago discovered and called laws of thought. (1.) A subject is equal to the sum of its predicates. (2.) A subject cannot at once have a given predicate affirmed and denied of it. (3.) Of two contradictorily opposed predicates one must belong to every subject. (4.) Truth is the relation of a judgment to something outside it as its sufficient reason. Reason, it may be remarked, has no material but only formal truth.

CHAPTER VI.

The third class of objects for the subject is constituted by the formal element in perception, the forms of outer and inner sense, space and time. This class of ideas, in which time and space appear as pure intuitions, is distinguished from that other class in which they are objects of perception by the presence of matter which has been shown to be the perceptibility of time and space in one aspect, and causality which has become objective, in another. Space and time have this property, that all their parts stand to one another in a relation in which each is determined and conditioned by another. This relation is peculiar, and is intelligible to us neither through understanding nor through reason, but solely through pure intuition or perception *a priori*. And the law according to which the parts of space and time thus determine one another is called the law of sufficient reason of *being*. In space every position is determined with reference to every other position, so that the first stands to the second in the relation of a consequence to its ground. In time every moment is conditioned by that which precedes it. The ground of being, in the form of the law of sequence, is here very simple owing to the circumstance that time has only one dimension. On the nexus of the position of the parts of space depends the entire science of geometry. Ground of *knowledge* produces *conviction* only, as distinguished from *insight* into the ground of *being.* Thus it is that the attempt, which even Euclid at times makes, to produce *conviction,* as distinguished from insight into the ground of being, in geometry, is a mistake, and induces aversions to mathematics in many an admirable mind.

CHAPTER VII.

The remaining class of objects for the subject is a very peculiar and important one. It comprehends only one object, the immediate object of inner sense, the subject in volition which becomes an object of knowledge, but only in inner sense, and therefore always in time and never in space; and in time only under limitations. There can be no knowledge of knowledge, for that would imply that the subject had separated itself from knowledge, and yet knew knowledge, which is impossible. The subject is the condition of the existence of ideas, and can never itself become idea or object. It knows itself therefore never as *knowing,* but only as *willing.* Thus what we know in ourselves is never what knows, but what wills, the will. The identity of the subject of volition with the subject of knowledge, through which the word "I" includes both, is the insoluble problem. The identity of the knowing with the known is inexplicable, and yet is immediately present. The operation of a motive is not, like that of all other causes, known only from without, and therefore indirectly, but also from within. Motivation is, in fact, causality viewed from within.

CHAPTER VIII.

In this, the concluding chapter, Schopenhauer sums up his results. Necessity has no meaning other than that of the irresistible sequence of the effect where the cause is given. All necessity is thus conditioned, and absolute or unconditioned necessity is a contradiction in terms. And there is a fourfold necessity corresponding to the four forms of the principle of sufficient reason:—(1.) The logical form, according to the principle of the ground of knowledge; on account of which, if the premisses are given, the conclusion follows. (2.) The physical form, according to the law of causality; on account of which, if the cause is given, the effect must follow. (3.) The mathematical form, according to the law of being; on account of which every relation expressed by a true geometrical proposition is what it is affirmed to be, and every correct calculation is irrefutable. (4.) The moral form, on account of which every human being and every brute must, when the motive appears, perform the only act which accords with the inborn and unalterable character. A consequence of this is, that every department of science has one or other of the forms of the principle of sufficient reason as its basis. In conclusion, Schopenhauer points out that just because the principle of sufficient reason belongs to the *a priori* element in intelligence, it cannot be applied to the entirety of things, to the universe as inclusive of intelligence. Such a universe is mere phenomenon, and what is only true because it belongs to the form of intelligence can have no application to intelligence itself. Thus it is that it cannot be said that the universe and all things in it exist because of something else. In other words, the cosmological proof of the existence of God is inadmissible.

INDEX.[1]

ABORIGINALS, interference with, iii. 411.

Absolute, conception of, has reality only in matter, ii. 94; how not to be conceived, ii. 94; misuse of, ii. 94, 215, 216, 393.

Abstract, idea, knowledge, dependent on idea of perception, i. 45, 52, 53, ii. 258; insufficiency of, i. 72, ii. 248-251; opposite of idea of perception, i. 7; philosophy must not start from, ii. 261 *seq.*; relation to intuitive knowledge, ii. 54, 55, 91; use of, ii. 235, 238.

Absurd, sphere of, ii. 242; supremacy of, i. 418.

Academies, relation of, to great men, ii. 496.

Accident. See *Substance.*

Actors, why madness common among, iii. 168.

Adultery, iii. 351, 364, 365.

Æschylus, iii. 213, 378.

Æsthetic mode of contemplation, i. 253 *seq.*, iii. 127 *seq.*

Agamemnon, i. 199, iii. 213.

Alemann, Matteo, iii. 363.

Alfieri, i. 247.

Allegory, nature of, use and abuse in art, i. 305-313.

America, compared with Old World in physical regard, iii. 57, 58.

Ampere, iii. 44.

Anacreon, iii. 377.

Analytical method, ii. 309.

Anatomy, what it teaches, iii. 38; value of comparative anatomy, i. 187, iii. 84.

Anaxagoras, iii. 2, 34, 73, 390.

Ancients, the, their architecture iii. 185, 188, 190; defects in religion, iii. 452; freedom of thought, ii. 394; inferiority of tragedy, iii. 213, 214; historians, i. 317, 318; philosophy, ii. 400; sculpture, i. 269, 291.

Angelus Silesius, i. 167, 492, iii. 432.

Anger, evidence of primacy of will, ii. 442; psychological effect of, ii. 429.

Animals, lower, distinctive characteristics of animal life, i. 25, ii. 228, 232; essential identity with man, i. 192; difference from man, i. 45, 47, 112, see *Man;* do not laugh, ii. 280; nor weep, i. 486; naïveté of, i. 204; no passions proper, iii. 16; no knowledge of death, iii. 249; yet fear death, iii. 251; right of man over, i. 481 n.

Animal magnetism, iii. 76, 418, 419.

Anselm of Canterbury, ii. 125, 126.

Anticipation in art, i. 287, 288; in nature, iii. 103, 104.

Antinomies, criticism of Kantian, i, 39, ii. 107 *seq.;* the two of natural science, i. 37 *seq.*

Antisthenes, i. 115, ii. 357.

Anwari Soheili, ii. 283.

Απαγωγη and επαγωγη, ii. 290.

Apollo Belvedere, i. 230.

Apperception, transcendental unity of, ii. 333.

A priori knowledge, meaning and explanation of. ii. 33; directness, necessity, and universality of,

[1] [In preparing this Index Frauenstädt's *Schopenhauer-Lexikon* has been freely used.—*Trs.*]

i. 88; table of *prœdicabilia a priori*, ii. 221; the basis of ontology, ii. 220.

Apuleius, ii. 352.

Architecture, its problem as a fine art, i. 276; solution of problem, i. 277 *seq.*, iii. 182 *seq.;* beauty and grace in, i. 277, iii. 188, 189; combines beauty with usefulness, i. 280; its relation to light, i. 279, 280; to music, iii. 239 *seq.;* to plastic arts and poetry, i. 280; its effects dynamical as well as mathematical, i. 279; comparison of antique and Gothic, iii. 189–192.

Aristippus, ii. 319, 363.

Aristo of Chios, ii. 319.

Aristocracy of intellect, ii. 342.

Aristotle, his logic, i. 62; on scientific knowledge, i. 95; his *forma substantialis,* i. 186; on essential conflict in nature, i. 192; his method, i. 239; on Platonic Ideas, i. 273, iii. 124; on derivation of ηθη, i. 378; his style, ii. 21; denies reciprocity, ii. 66; on the necessary and contingent, ii. 70; contented with abstract conceptions, ii. 71; on quality and quantity, ii. 76; his categories, ii. 85; on existence as subject, ii. 101; on infinity of world in space, ii. 110; atomism not necessary, ii. 111; infinity *potentia* not *actu*, ii. 115; refutation of ontological proof, ii. 129; νους πρακτικος of, ii. 133; the seat of the virtues, ii. 137; treatment of art, ii. 153; an infinitely large body immovable, ii. 203; relation of number and time, ii. 205; Topi of, ii. 212; division of causes, ii. 217; on pure matter, ii. 219; on origin of things, ii. 220; real things and conceptions, ii. 244; meaning of his *nihil est in intellectu nisi quod ante fuerit in sensu,* ii. 258; eight spheres of, ii. 265; rhetorics of, ii. 285; his επαγωγη and απαγωγη, ii. 290; his syllogistic figures, ii. 297; analysis of syllogisms, ii. 303; on the prudent man, ii. 347; his ethics eudæmonistic, ii. 349; wonder the origin of philosophy, ii. 360; view of the Sophists, ii. 362; necessity of metaphysics, ii. 379; on invertebrate animals, ii. 481; on plants, iii. 34; difference between efficient and final cause, iii. 82; his freedom from physico-theology, iii. 94; merits of his teaching as to organised and unorganised nature, iii. 95; nature a demon, iii. 106; music a cathartic of the feelings, iii. 174; poetry better than history, iii. 220.

Arithmetic, depends on *a priori* intuition of time, i. 99, ii. 204.

Arrian, ii. 355 *seq.*

Art, source and aim of, i. 238, 239, 286 *seq.*, iii. 126, 179; object of, see *Idea;* subject of, see *Genius;* relation to and difference from philosophy, iii. 176, 177, 178; contrasted with history, i. 298, 315, iii. 224; inborn and acquired, i. 252; the two extremes in series of, i. 274 *seq.*, 280; value and importance of, i. 345, 346, iii. 132; opposition between useful and fine, iii. 181.

Art, works of, tendency of, iii. 177; relation of conception to execution of, iii. 180; the abstract concept barren in, i. 303, 304, iii. 179, 180; why Idea more easily comprehended in than in nature, i. 252, iii. 132; co-operation of the beholder required for enjoyment of, iii. 177; why they do not give all to the senses, iii. 178 *seq.;* superiority of those dashed off in moment of conception, iii. 178, 180.

Asceticism, its source, i, 490 *seq.;* its way of manifesting itself, i. 492, 493, 506, iii. 425; identity of its spirit in different countries and religions, i. 502, 503, iii. 433; difference of spirit of cynicism, ii. 352, 353.

Assertion, definition of, ii. 308.

Association of ideas, its root, ii. 324; kinds of, ii. 324; apparent exceptions to law of, ii. 327; the will secretly controls the law of, ii. 328.

Astronomy, what it teaches, iii. 37; source of its certainty and com-

prehensibility, i. 86; its method, i. 87; Ptolemaic, i. 64.
Athanasius, iii. 439.
Atheism, what strengthens the reproach of, ii. 379; not necessarily materialism, ii. 131, 132.
Atom, assumption of, not necessary, iii. 44 *seq.;* has no reality, ii. 223; defence of, from porosity refuted, iii. 47.
Attraction and repulsion, forces of, constitute space-occupation, ii. 224.
Augustine, recognises identity of all things with will, i. 165; cause of beauty of vegetable world, i. 260 n.; on original sin, i. 524; the will not free, i. 525; dogmatics of, i. 525 n.; beginner of Scholasticism, ii. 12; on moral systems of ancients, ii. 349; spirit of his anti-Pelagianism, ii. 368, iii. 421; on affections of will, ii. 412 n.; his *de civit. Dei,* iii. 117 n.
Autobiography. See *Biography.*
Avarice, the vice of old age, iii. 465.
Avatar, iii. 426.
Axiom, definition, ii. 308.

BACON, his conception of philosophy, i. 109; all movement preceded by perception, i. 137 n.; on atheism, ii. 131; his philosophical method, ii. 212; on the intellect, ii. 433; his moral character, ii. 447; influence of climate upon intellect, iii. 18; rejected teleology, iii. 91; on final causes, iii. 93; on Democritus, iii. 95; on rarity of genius, iii. 158.
Basilidians, iii. 305.
Bass. See *Music.*
Baumgarten, his æsthetics, ii. 153.
Beard, its efficient and final cause in man, iii. 88.
Beauty, the beautiful, two elements of, i. 270; source of pleasure in, i. 253 *seq.;* everything beautiful, i. 271; why one thing more beautiful than another, i. 272; distinguished from grace, i. 289; distinguished from the sublime, i. 270; effect of natural beauty, i. 255, iii. 173, 174; beauty in art. See *Painting, Sculpture,* &c.
Beccaria, iii. 413.
Being, as the most general conception, ii. 236; in the professorial philosophy, ii. 288; relation of thought to. See *Thing in itself;* limitation of individual being the cause of philosophy, i. 135; contrast of seeing and being, iii. 392.
Bell, Sir Ch., i. 133, iii. 6.
Benedict, iii. 450.
Berkeley, on rareness of thought, i. 50; his idealism, ii. 15, 29, 41, 163, 165, 175, iii. 59, 261.
Bhagavad-gita, i. 366, iii. 75, 262.
Bible, one metaphysical truth in Old Testament, iii. 423; ascetic spirit of New Testament, iii. 437, 458 *seq.;* opposition of Old and New Testaments, i. 420, iii. 281, 441, 445; its historical material unsuited for paintings, i. 300.
Bichat, "*Sur la vie et la mort,*" ii. 470, 488; on circulation of blood, ii. 478; on organic and animal life, ii. 489; only animal life can be educated, ii. 491; Flourens' attack on, ii. 494 *seq.;* nervous and muscular systems in children, iii. 161; effect of emotions on organism, iii. 296.
Bio, on relation of science and philosophy, ii. 319.
Biography, superiority to history, i. 319 *seq.;* difficulty of dissimulating in autobiographies, i. 320.
Biot, on colour rings, ii. 338.
Blood, the primitive fluid of organism, ii. 478–481.
Body, the, an object among objects, i. 5, 14, 23, 25, 129, ii. 167; its identity with will, i. 129 *seq.;* 137–142, ii. 428, 468, 471–493; relation of physiological and metaphysical explanations of, i. 139 *seq.*, ii. 492, 493; its design, i. 140 *seq.;* knowledge of, key to nature of things, i. 136, 141 *seq.;* criticism of antithesis of body and soul as two substances, ii. 101–104, 378, iii. 11.
Böhm, Jakob, everything half dead, i. 191; "*De signatura rerum,*" i. 284 n., iii. 432.

Bolingbroke, iii. 397.
Books, not so instructive as reality, ii. 244, 245; why they cannot take the place of experience, ii. 248, 249.
Boswell, his Life of Johnson, ii. 446.
Boureguon, Antoinette, iii. 435.
Brahmanism, recognises no beginning of world, ii. 94, 95, 108, 109; teaches metempsychosis, iii. 303.
Brain, metaphysically considered, ii. 468, 485, 486; physiologically considered, its origin and function, ii. 411, 462, 463, 470, iii. 9; its share in perception, ii. 185; its relation to the ganglia, ii. 483; the seat of motives, ii. 473; develops with organism, ii. 416, iii. 13, 14; as necessary for thought as stomach for digestion, ii. 237; the regulator of the will, ii. 470; the condition of self-consciousness, iii. 12 *seq.*; influence of its development upon intellect at different periods of life, ii. 425, 454 *seq.*; necessity of sleep for, ii. 464; effect of over-work on, ii. 255, 256; its variation in man the cause of individual character, i. 171; its activity in dreams, ii. 464; the brain of genius, iii. 159, 160; influence on agility of limbs, iii. 21; influence of noise on, ii. 196, 197.
Brandis, Ch. A., ii. 264.
Brandis, J. D., ii. 488.
Bridgewater Treatise Men, iii. 91.
Brougham, Lord, iii. 91.
Brown, Thomas, "On Cause and Effect," ii. 207, iii. 92.
Bruno, Giordano, started from real in his philosophy, i. 33; his view of life, i. 366; lonely position in his age, ii. 13 n.; on finiteness of world, ii. 110; infinitely large body immovable, ii. 203; matter incorporeal, ii. 208, iii. 51, 54; no space beyond the world, ii. 265; his death, iii. 106; his motto, iii. 144.
Buddhism, its pre-eminence over all religions, ii. 371; superiority to Brahmanism, i. 460, iii. 430; compared with Christianity, iii. 445 *seq.*; its pessimism, i. 372; iii. 397; its mysticism, iii. 435; teaches that nature expects salvation from man, i. 492; its doctrine of metempsychosis, iii. 302; doctrine of Nirvana, iii. 308, 427.
Buffon, on intelligence of animals, i. 29; on style, ii. 247.
Bunyan, John, iii. 435.
Bundahish, iii. 391.
Burdach, sleep the original state, ii. 463; formation of muscles from blood, ii. 478; heart independent of nervous system and sensibility, ii. 479; reciprocal support of vegetable and insect world, iii. 90; on bees, iii. 100; on the burrying beetle, iii. 102; on *cercaria ephemera*, iii. 269; on maternal affection of animals, iii. 317.
Bürger, his place in German poetry, iii. 327; his parents, iii. 327; on love, iii. 336.
Burke, on the beautiful, ii. 153; on the apprehension of words, ii. 239.
Byron, an instance of connection of genius and madness, i. 247; brain weighed 6 lbs., iii. 160; quoted, i. 234, 324, 258, 342, 432, 458, iii. 379, 398, 400.

Cabanis, on arterial and venous systems, ii. 257; his materialism, ii. 378; on passions of children, ii. 424; "*Des rapports du physique au moral*," iii. 6.
Cæsar, Jul., on Druids, iii. 304.
Calderon, life a dream, i. 22; steadfast prince, i. 327; a crime to be born, i. 328, 458, iii. 420; his Semiramis, iii. 343; "Zenobia the Great," iii. 364.
Camerarius, J., collection of emblems, i. 309.
Cannibalism, most palpable example of wrong, i. 431; hereditary, iii. 322.
Canisius, iii. 440.
Canova, iii. 195.
Caravaggio, iii. 197.
Caricature, character of species annulled by that of individual, i. 291.
Carové, iii. 440.

Carracci, Hannibal, his allegorical paintings, i. 306, 308.
Casper, on length of human life, iii. 301.
Castration, its significance, iii. 310; its use as a punishment, iii. 331.
Categories, criticism of the Kantian, ii. 48–51.
Catholicism, compared with Protestantism in an ethical regard, iii. 448, 449.
Catullus, iii. 318.
Caucasian, an original race, iii. 58.
Cause, Causality, law of, ii. 214; *a priori* nature of law of, i. 154 *seq.*, ii. 206 *seq.*; corollary from it the permanence of substance, ii. 79; difference of cause and force, i. 144, 145; mysteriousness of connection between cause and effect, i. 174; temporal relation between cause and effect, ii. 209, 210; three kinds of causes, i. 149, 150; truth of doctrine of occasional causes, i. 178 *seq.*; falseness of proposition "the effect cannot contain more than the cause," ii. 213; a "first cause" inconceivable, ii. 214; to determine the cause of an effect, ii. 154.
Celibacy, from Christian and ethical point of view, iii. 425, 437, 438, 449, 450, 451.
Cellini, Benvenuto, his conversion, i. 510.
Celsus, on generation, iii. 310.
Certainty, distinguished from scientific completeness of knowledge, i. 83; superiority of immediate to indirect, i. 89, 90.
Cervantes, i. 311; ii. 246.
Chamfort, iii., 157, 158, 365.
Champollion, i. 313.
Change, nature of, i. 11; always conditioned by a cause, i. 170, ii. 211 *seq.*
Character, as a force of nature, i. 370; difference between that of man and brutes, i. 170, 386, 387; that of man individual, i. 290; empirical, ii. 407; constant, i. 378, ii. 441, 491; inherited from father, iii. 320 *seq.*; relation of intelligible to empirical, i. 203, 207, 373 *seq.*; a false inference from unalterableness of, i. 389; the acquired, i. 391–397; explanation of inharmonious nature of, iii. 330; abolition of, i. 520 *seq.*
Chatham, Lord, iii. 324.
Chateaubriand, iii. 435.
Chemistry, what it teaches, iii. 38; antinomy of, i. 37 *seq.*
Chevreul, experiments on light, iii. 62.
Childhood, character of, iii. 161 *seq.*
Chiliasts, ii. 243.
Chinese, philosophy, i. 187, 188, 343; garden, iii. 157.
Chladni, i. 344.
Choice, man larger sphere of, than brutes, i. 388; not freedom of individual volition, *loc. cit.*
Christianity, different constituent parts of, i. 500, 501, iii. 422; its connection with Brahmanism and Buddhism, iii. 391, 421, 459; pessimistic spirit of, ii. 372, iii. 397, 436; kernel of, i. 424, 523–524, ii. 149, iii. 421, 452; symbol of, iii. 462.
Chrysippus, i. 116, 118, 389, ii. 72, 349.
Cicero, i. 116 n., 117, 247, 389, ii. 72, 137, 138, 140, 141, 270, 272, 348, 356, 358, 444, iii. 147, 253 n., 452.
Circle, the symbol of nature, iii. 267.
Classics, advantage of studying, ii. 239.
Classical poetry, distinguished from romantic, iii. 209.
Cleanthes, i. 118, ii. 128.
Clemens Alexandrinus, "Stromata" referred to, i. 425, ii. 98, iii. 427, 438, 442, 443.
Clouds, illustration of opposition between Idea and phenomenon, i. 235.
Colebrooke, i. 491, 494 n., iii. 281, 304, 307, 308 n.
Comedy, distinguished from tragedy, iii. 218.
Composer, musical, i. 336.
Concept, conception, see *Abstract*; their construction the function of reason, i. 7, 50, ii. 235 *seq.*; content and extent of, ii. 236; spheres, i. 55, 64; representatives of, i. 51; relation to word, i. 51;

ii. 234, 238; relation to Idea, i. 301, 302; simple, ii. 236; distinct, ii. 237; abstract and concrete, i. 53; pure, ii. 385; advantages and disadvantages of, i. 45, 47 *seq.*, 68–75, ii. 234–243, 345 *seq.*
Concrete, union of form and matter, ii. 215.
Condillac, his materialism, ii. 175, 187, iii. 45.
Condorcet, ii. 187.
Connections among men, foundation of, ii. 450.
Conscience, presupposes intelligible character, i. 474; is only affected by deeds, i. 387; anguish of, i. 471 *seq.;* the good, i. 482.
Consciousness, only a property of animal beings, ii. 336, 337, 414; origin, aim, and seat of, ii. 475; what common to all, and what distinguishes one from another, ii. 414, iii. 17 *seq.;* self-consciousness and that of other things, ii. 259, 412, 468, iii. 126; limited to phenomena, i. 358 n., iii. 74, 285 *seq.;* as opposed to unconsciousness, ii. 328; fragmentary nature of, ii. 330 *seq.;* what gives it unity and connection, iii. 333; extinguished in death, iii. 255 *seq.*
Considering things, ways of, i. 239; iii. 121 *seq.*
Contingent, contingency, conception of, ii. 67; misuse of word by pre-Kantian dogmatists, ii. 70.
Conversation, ii. 343.
Copula, ii. 287, 288.
Coriolanus, ii. 136.
Corneille, iii. 203.
Correct, distinguished from true, real, &c., ii. 208.
Correggio, i. 300, 306, 307, 531.
Cosmogony, of Laplace, iii. 71, 72.
Cosmological proof, Kant's refutation of, ii. 130.
Cousin, M., iii. 45.
Cramp, ii. 484.
Crime, chief cause of, iii. 412. See *Punishment.*
Criticism, the Kantian, ii. 6–11.
Crystal, its one manifestation of life, i. 202; its individuality, i. 171; becomes rigid in the moment of movement, iii. 37.
Culture, cannot make up for want of understanding, ii. 253 *seq.*, 343.
Cuvier, ii. 204, 318, 479, iii. 98, 160, 165.
Cynicism, spirit and fundamental thought of, ii. 350 *seq.*, iii. 388.

Da Capo, i. 342.
Dæmon, i. 349, iii. 99.
Dante, i. 258, 419, ii. 315.
Davis, iii. 207.
Death, i. 356 *seq.*, 506–509, iii. 249–308, 312, 389, 463; sudden death, why prayed against, iii., 428.
Decameron, iii. 365.
Deductive method, ii. 310.
Delamark, ii. 318, 378.
Delirium, distinguished from madness, i. 248.
Democritus, i. 33, 159, 160, ii. 131, 140, 177, 378, iii. 61, 62, 64, 95.
Denial. See *Will.*
Descartes, vortex of, i. 159; identifies will with judgment, 377, 385; his thought not free, ii. 13; on repetition, ii. 21, 25; ontological proof, ii. 126; made philosophy start from self-consciousness, ii. 164, 165, 201, 400, iii. 59; the quantity of a motion, ii. 226; opinion of mathematics, ii. 323; slept a great deal, ii. 465; criticism of his doctrines, ii. 494–496; relation to Spinoza, iii. 475.
Desire, the universal nature of things, i. 165, iii. 34; in a psychological regard, ii. 429.
Determinism, iii. 67–69.
Δευτερος πλους, the second way of the denial of the will, i. 506, iii. 454, 465.
Dialectic, definition of, ii. 285.
Diderot, ii. 341, iii. 233, 272.
Diodorus the Megaric, ii. 72.
Diogenes the Cynic, i. 151, ii. 351, 352, iii. 388.
Diogenes, Laertius, i. 118, 151, 169, ii. 319, 351, 355, 363, iii. 255.
Dionysius the Areopagite, ii. 264.
Discovery, the work of understanding, i. 26, 27.
Disease, its nature, ii. 487.
Disgusting, the, i. 269.

Dissimulation, i. 47, iii. 231.
Divisibility, infinite, of time, i. 13, ii. 221 ; of matter, iii. 46.
Dog, intelligence of, ii. 230-232 ; wags its tail, ii. 280.
Dogmas, their relation to virtue and morality, i. 475 *seq.*
Dogmatism, philosophical, opposed to criticism, ii. 10, 11 ; its fundamental error, iii. 27.
Domenichino, iii. 193.
Donatello, iii. 193.
Don Quixote, i. 311.
Drama, the, i. 321–330, iii. 211–219.
Drapery in sculpture, i. 296.
Dreams, distinguished from real life, i. 20 *seq.*
Duns Scotus, i. 111, ii. 237.
Dutch paintings, i. 269.

EBIONITES, iii. 458.
Eckermann, "Conversations of Goethe," i. 362, iii. 240.
Eckhard, Meister, i. 492, 500, iii. 432, 435, 467.
Edda, the, iii. 304.
Ego, conception of, i. 132, 324, ii. 413, 487, iii. 3, 13, 284, 285 ; the logical ego, ii. 333.
Egoism, origin, nature, and scope of, i. 427, iii. 416, 417 ; theoretical egoism, i. 135.
Egyptians, gospel of, iii. 436, 444.
Eleatics, i. 33, 61, 93, ii. 85, 113, iii. 271.
Election, doctrine of, i. 378, ii. 149.
Elephant, intelligence of, i. 29, ii. 232, 233.
Eloquence, ii. 305, 306.
Emblems, i. 312, 313.
Emotion, its origin and effect, ii. 346, iii. 407, 408.
Empedocles, i. 192, 288, 530, iii. 8, 34, 95, 271.
Encratites, iii. 438.
English, the, their faults, ii. 131, iii. 92.
ἐν και παν, iii. 65, 471.
Ennui, i. 402, 404, iii. 413.
Ens realissimum, ii. 125–127.
Envy, iii, 389.
επαγωγη and *απαγωγη*, ii. 290.
Epic poetry, i. 324, 413, iii. 211.
Epicurus, Epicureans, i. 33, 37, ii. 131, 145, 177, 378, iii. 255, 261.
Epictetus, i. 115, 116 n., 386, ii. 354, 356.
Epiphanias, iii. 446.
Equivocation, i. 79.
Erigena, Scotus, ii. 319, iii. 432, 470, 471.
Error, definition of, i. 30, 103–105 ; difference between man and brutes with regard to, ii. 243, *seq.*; pernicious nature of, i. 45, ii. 241 *seq.*; tragic and comic side of, ii. 243 ; how perpetuated, ii. 243, 341.
Esquirol, iii. 117, 328.
Essenes, iii. 437, 451.
Essentia and *existentia*, their relation, ii. 129, 130 ; their union in pure matter, ii. 218.
Eternity, conception of, i. 228, 360 *seq.*, iii. 276.
Ethics, i. 441–443, 474 *seq.*, iii. 402–409 ; criticism of Kantian, ii. 133 *seq.*; of ancients, ii. 348, iii. 213, 214, 452.
Ethiopian, an original race, iii. 58.
Etiology, subject and scope of, i. 124 *seq.*; its relation to the philosophy of nature, i. 182 *seq.*
Euchel, Isaak, his "Prayers of the Jews," ii. 98.
Euclid, criticism of his method, i. 90–100, ii. 33, 164, 321–323.
Eudæmonism, ii. 348 *seq.*
ευκολος and *δυσκολος*, i. 407.
Euler, i. 55, 165, ii. 172 n., 187–189, 192, 341.
Euripides, i. 328, 453, iii. 214, 218, 400, 406, 443.
Evidence, distinction between empirical and *a priori*, i. 85 ; the predicate "evident" defined, ii. 308.
Evil, meaning of word, i. 426 ; the *punctum pruriens* of metaphysics, ii. 375. See *Pessimism.*
Existence, vanity of, iii. 382 *seq.*; the end of, ii. 695.
Experience, ii. 234 *seq.*, 388 *seq.*
Experiment, ii. 268.
Explanation, i. 105 *seq.*, 125.
Extension. See *Matter.*
Eye, i. 301, ii. 194, iii. 162.

FAME, i. 305, iii. 151.
Fanaticism, i. 466 n.
Fate, Fatalism, i. 389, 390, iii. 475.

Fear, effect of, ii. 429 *seq.;* origin of belief in God, ii. 130.
Feeling, as sense of touch, ii. 195 ; as opposite of knowing, i. 66–68.
Fénélon, i. 499.
Fernow, i. 293.
Fichte, i. 16, 33, 40–43, ii. 22, 31, 176, iii. 13.
Fit Arari, ii. 444.
Flagellants, ii. 243.
Flourens, ii. 133, 416, 417, 479, 494–496, iii. 165, 326.
Folly, a species of the ludicrous, i. 77 *seq.*, ii. 277 ; a characteristic of genius, iii. 153.
Force, distinguished from cause, i. 144, 145, 174–178, ii. 217 ; inseparable from matter, iii. 54 *seq.*
Form and matter, i. 162, 168, ii. 215, iii. 26, 53–57.
Forms of thought, ii. 86 *seq.;* their relation to parts of speech, ii. 85, 86.
Francis, St., i. 496, iii. 434, 459.
Frauenstädt, ii. 225.
Frederick the Great, ii. 133.
Freedom, as a metaphysical quality, i. 369 *seq.;* intellectual, iii. 407 ; of the will, i. 376 *seq.*, 388, 389, 520 *seq.;* criticism of Kant's doctrine, ii. 117 *seq.*
French, national charcter of, i. 510 ; philosophy of, ii. 18, iii. 44, 45 ; poetry, iii. 209 ; music, iii. 244.
Friendship, i. 485.
Fright, effect of, ii. 429.
Froriep, ii. 209.
Future. See *Present.*

GALL, ii. 469, 494, 495.
Galenus, ii. 297.
Gallows, iii. 456, 457.
Ganglia, their function in organism, ii. 484 *seq.*
Gardening, landscape, i. 282 ; difference between English and old French, iii. 175.
Garrick, ii. 279, iii. 21.
Gemüth, distinguished from mind, ii. 458, 459.
Generatio æquivoca, i. 184 *seq.;* iii. 54–56.
Generation, and death essential moments in life of species, i. 365, iii. 270–273 ; instinctive nature of act, iii. 309 ; act viewed subjectively and objectively, iii. 292, 293 ; inner significance of act, i. 423 *seq.*, iii. 379 ; reason of shame connected with, i. 423, iii. 378 ; existence a paraphrase of, iii. 377.
Genius, i. 238–247, 251–253, ii. 245-249, iii. 138–166.
Genital organs, the opposite pole of the brain, i. 425, iii. 87, 310 ; independence of knowledge, i. 150, 426 ; difference of plants, animals, and man in respect of, i. 204, iii. 35 ; shame connected with, iii. 379 ; symbolical language of, iii. 380.
Genus, distinguished from species, iii. 123 *seq.;* construction of logical genus, ii. 103, 104.
Geometry, content of, i. 9 ; method of, i. 90 *seq.;* ii. 321 *seq.*
Genre painting, i. 298.
Gichtel, iii. 434, 435.
Gilbert, ii. 196.
Giordano, Luca, iii. 198.
Given, the, ii. 23, 84.
Gleditsch, iii. 102, 110.
Gnostics, iii. 305, 432, 438, 442, 444.
γνωθι σαυτον, ii. 423.
God, origin of the word, iii. 446 ; egotistical origin of belief in, ii. 130 ; an asserted "consciousness of God," ii. 129, 141, 142 ; criticism of proofs for existence of, ii. 128–133.
Goethe, his theory of colours, i. 26, 160, 245, ii. 433 ; on genius, i. 247, iii. 19, 147, 151, 153, 156 ; on effect of human beauty, i. 285 ; on Laocoon, i. 293 ; on painting of music, i. 295 ; on fable of Proserpine and pomegranate, i. 311, 424 ; his songs, i. 323, iii. 210 ; on indestructibility of human spirit, i. 362 n. ; "Confessions of beautiful soul," i. 497 ; power of sight of suffering, i. 512 ; on persistency of error, ii. 4, 8 ; unknown to Kant, ii. 152 ; sensitive to noise, ii. 198 ; metamorphosis of plants, ii. 225, iii. 85 ; on skeletons of rodents, ii. 318 ; on Kant, ii.

340 ; never over-worked, ii, 427 ; example of folly of childhood, ii. 456 ; on sleep, ii. 466 ; "*Wahlverwandtschaften*," iii. 37, 151, 164 ; his love of natural sciences, iii. 39 ; his height, iii. 160 ; his childishness, iii. 163 ; his mother, iii. 327 ; quoted, i. 314, 366, ii. 14, 22, 294, iii. 132, 136, 369.
Good, the conception, i. 464 *seq.* ; nature of the good man, 465, 480, iii. 306, 307.
Gorgias, ii. 281, 286.
Gothic architecture compared with antique, iii. 189–192.
Gozzi, Carlo, i. 237, ii. 276, iii. 169.
Grace, distinguished from beauty, i. 289 ; Christian doctrine of, i. 522 *seq.*, 528, ii. 149.
Gracian, Balthasar, i. 311, ii. 250, iii. 401.
Grammar, relation to Logic, ii. 85–87, 89.
Gravitas, iii. 152.
Gravitation, i. 13, 26, 195, 212, 213, 398, ii. 225, 226, iii. 52, 394.
Greatness in spiritual sense, iii. 150.
Guicciardini, ii. 447.
Guido Reni, iii. 191.
Guilt, i. 204, 454, iii. 390, 415, 418, 420 *seq.*, 448.
Guion, Mme. de, i. 497, 505, iii. 432, 434, 435.

HALL, MARSHALL, i. 151, ii. 133, 483, 484, iii. 6.
Haller, ii. 479, 488, iii. 328.
Hamilton, Sir W., ii. 323.
Happiness, is negative, i. 411–413 ; from standpoint of higher knowledge, i. 456 ; impossible in an existence like ours, iii. 382, 383 ; and virtue, i. 466, iii. 420 *seq.*
Hardy, Spence, i. 497, iii. 301, 303, 308 n., 434.
Hauz, iii. 45.
Haydn, i. 304.
Head, relation of, to trunk in brutes and man, i. 230 ; opposite pole of genitals, i. 425, iii. 87, 310 ; and heart, ii. 450 *seq.*
Health, i. 190 *seq.*, iii. 385.
Hearing, sense of, ii. 195–199.
Heart, the centre and *primum mobile* of life, ii. 428, 479–481 ; opposition between head and heart, ii. 450 *seq.* ; why love affairs are called affairs of the heart, iii. 373.
Heathen, ii. 97.
Heavens, sublime effect of, i. 266, 267.
Hegel, ii. 8, 22, 31, 171, 243, 261, 266, iii. 45, 224, 225, 394, 404, 436.
Heine, Heinrich, ii. 283.
Hell, i. 419, iii. 387, 388, 392.
Helvetius, i. 288 n., ii. 256, 444, 446, iii. 8.
Heraclitus, i. 8, ii. 256, iii. 399.
Herder, i. 52, ii. 153, iii. 163.
Heredity, iii. 318–335.
Hermaphrodism, iii. 356.
Herodotus, ii. 347, iii. 303, 398.
Hesiod, i. 425.
History and science, i. 82, iii. 220, 221 ; and philosophy, iii. 223 ; and poetry, i. 315 *seq.*, iii. 224 ; and biography, i. 319 ; the philosophy of, i. 236, 237, iii. 224–226 ; true value of, iii. 227 *seq.* ; untrustworthiness of, i. 238, 316, 317, iii. 223 ; history of world and history of the saints, i. 497, 498.
Hobbes, i. 21, 361 n., 441, 446, 451, ii. 263, 453.
Holberg, ii. 379.
Holiness, inner nature of, i. 494, 495 ; its independence of dogmas, i. 495, 509.
Hollbach, ii. 176.
Home, ii. 153, 270.
Homer, i. 236, 295, 311, 314, 324, iii. 400.
Hooke, i. 26, ii. 225, 226.
Hope, ii. 431.
Horace, ii. 139, 140, 274, iii. 181.
Horizon, mental, ii. 338.
Huber, iii. 101.
Human race. See *Man.*
Humboldt, Alex. von, ii. 64, iii. 112.
Hume, David, i. 15, 52, 89, ii. 8, 129, 130, 156, 157, 173, 207, 209, iii. 92, 92 n., 305, 327, 393, 394, 395.
Humour, ii. 282–284.
Hutcheson, ii. 270.
Hydraulics, science, of iii. 38 ; as a fine art, i. 281, 282.

Hypothesis, correct, ii. 309 ; effect of, on mind, ii. 432.

I. See *Ego.*
Idea (*Vorstellung*), what it is, ii. 400 ; common form of all classes of, i. 3 ; form of combination of all classes of, i. 5 ; chief distinction among, i. 7 ; idea of perception, i. 7–45, ii. 163–227 ; abstract, i. 45–120, ii. 228–395 ; subjective correlative of, i. 13 (Cf. *Object* and *World*) ; the Platonic Idea (*Idee*) defined, i. 168, iii. 122 ; distinguished from thing in itself, i. 209, 226 *seq.*, 232, iii. 122 *seq.;* empirical correlative of, iii. 123 ; relation to individual things, i. 227, 233, iii. 275 ; knowledge of, i. 220–228, 271, ii. 335–336, iii. 122, 126 *seq.;* grades of, in nature, i. 195–199, 202 ; the object of art, see *Art ;* misuse of word, i. 168, ii. 99, 100 ; association of, see *Association* ; Kant's Ideas of reason, ii. 23 *seq.*
Ideal, in art, i. 287, 288 ; opposition between ideal and real, ii. 400 *seq.*
Idealism, as opposed to realism, i. 3 *seq.*. ii. 28 *seq.*, 163, 167 ; difference between empirical and transcendental, ii. 170, 184 ; absolute, i. 134, 135.
Identity, law of, ii. 86–88 ; philosophy of, i. 32, ii. 8, 400.
Idyll, the, why it must be short, i. 413.
Iffland, ii. 426.
Illusion distinguished from error, i. 28, 103, 104.
Imagination, an instrument of thought, ii. 240, 245 ; an essential element of genius, i. 241 *seq.*, iii. 141, 142.
Imitation, in art, i. 304 ; of idiosyncrasies of others, i. 395.
Immanent knowledge, opposed to transcendent and transcendental, i. 224, ii. 387, iii. 430 n., 468.
Immortality, iii. 75. See *Indestructibility.*
Impenetrability of matter, i, 13, ii. 103, 223 *seq.*, iii. 52.
Inclination, definition, iii. 406.
Indestructibility, of our true nature by death, Ch. 41 *passim*, iii. 249–308.
Indian, mysticism, iii. 432 ; sculpture, i. 309 ; philosophy, iii. 281, 282 ; caste i. 459, 460 (Cf. *Buddhism* and *Brahmanism*).
Individuality, as phenomenon rooted in the thing in itself, i. 147, 219, 354, 357, 358, iii. 74, 428, 469 ; at the different grades of nature, i. 170–172 ; language of nature with reference to, i. 355, 356, iii. 108 *seq.*, 416, 417 ; destruction of, by death, iii. 286, 298 *seq.*
Induction, ii. 310.
Infinite, true conception of, ii. 115.
Inquisition, i. 466 n.
Innocence, of plants, i. 204.
Insects, fertilisation of plants by, iii. 90 ; life of severed parts of, ii. 483 ; ephemeral nature of, iii. 267. See *Instinct.*
Instinct, an act directed to an unknown end, i. 148, 150, 197, iii. 96, 346 *seq.;* relation of, to guidance by motives, iii. 96 *seq.;* relation to somnambulism, iii. 98 ; throws light on organising work of nature, iii. 96–100, 103 ; in man, iii. 346 *seq.*
Intellect, pure, ii. 179, 180 ; empirical, secondary nature of, ii. 411–467, iii. 3 *seq.*, 291 ; end of, i. 199, 228, ii. 336, 485, iii. 21 *seq.*; degrees of, in series of animals and in man, iii. 29, 30 ; parsimony of nature in imparting, iii. 20 ; limitation of, to phenomena, iii. 21–29 ; imperfections of, ii. 330–344.
Interesting, distinguished from beautiful, i. 229.
Ionic school, i. 33.
Irritability as objectification of will, ii. 472 *seq.;* its connection with blood, ii. 478.
Isaiah ii. 437.
Islamism, iii. 423, 446.

JACOBI, i. 225 n., ii. 169.
Jealousy, iii. 364.
Johnson, Dr. Samuel, i. 328.
Jones, Sir W., i. 8, 501 n.
Joy, i. 410, ii. 429 *seq.*
Judaism, i. 300, iii. 305, 446.
Judgment, faculty of, i. 30, 84 *seq.*, ii. 152 *seq.*, 266 *seq.*

Julian, Emperor, ii. 350.
Jung Stilling, ii. 243.
Justinius, iii. 305.
Justice, as a virtue, i. 478, 479, iii. 424; retributive, i. 452; eternal, i. 427, 452–458, 461, iii. 405, 421; poetical, i. 328.

KANT, abstract and perceptible knowledge, ii. 25, 32, 80, 213; æsthetic, ii. 32, 33, 189; amphiboly, ii. 38; analytic, ii. 33–89; antinomy, i. 39, ii. 104–125, iii. 45; *a priori* nature of space and time, i. 6, 8, 154, 155, ii. 169, 201, 202, iii. 276 *seq.*; on the beautiful, iii. 189; categories, i. 57, ii. 43–47, 403; causality, i. 16, ii. 58 *seq.*, 173, 208, 209, 217, 385, 386, iii. 469; character, empirical and intelligible, i. 138, 203, 349, 373; chief result of Kantian philosophy, ii. 405; childish in old age, ii. 427; conceptions, philosophy a science of, ii. 259, 384; cosmological proof, ii. 130; cosmology, i. 194, ii. 225, iii. 72; critical philosophy, ii. 6–11; criticism of functions of the brain, ii. 174, 185; critique of judgment, ii. 152–159; critique of practical reason, ii. 133–150; critique of pure reason, ii. 3–133 (fundamental thought of, ii. 18–20), 237, 377; dialectic, ii. 89–133; "*Die Falsche Spitzfindigkeit,*" ii. 300; dreams distinguished from reality, i. 20, 21; editions of Critique, ii. 29; error, source of, i. 103; ethics, i. 79, 110, 140, ii. 12, 133–150; freedom and necessity, ii. 377; God, ii. 129, 130; laws of homogeneity and specification, i. 83; idealism of, ii. 29, 163, 164, 400 *seq.*; infinity, ii. 115; judgment, reflective and subsuming, i. 85; judgments, table of, ii. 56–78; philosophy of law, i. 433, ii. 150–152; logic, transcendental, ii. 33–133; on love, iii. 338; theory of ludicrous, ii. 270; influence of Kantian doctrine on mathematics, i. 94, 385; explanation of matter, i. 12 n., iii. 54; "Metaphysical First Principles of Natural Science," i. 88, ii. 111, 219, 224, 225; metaphysics, impossibility of, ii. 386 *seq.*; method of, ii. 53–55, iii. 5; Kant's mother, iii. 327; negative result of philosophy, ii. 17; *nihil privativum,* i. 528; sensitive to noise, ii. 198; ontological proof, ii. 129, 130; object of perception, ii. 33–43; permanence of substance, ii. 78–81; phenomenon and thing in itself, i. 9, 41, 155, 220, ii. 6–12, 28, 181, 379, 389, 399, 486; physico-theological proof, ii. 130; relation to Plato, i. 223 *seq.*; psychology, refutation of rational, ii. 100–104; reason, conception of, i. 49; ideas of, i. 169, ii. 96–100; ideal of, ii. 125–133, principle of, ii. 90–96; reciprocity, category of, ii. 61 *seq.*; schematism of categories, ii. 48–51; Scholastic dogmatism overthrown by, ii. 12–16, iii. 27; Schopenhauer gone further than, iii. 28, 59; his sleep, ii. 465; speculative theology, refutation of, ii. 128–133, iii. 473; spiritualism, refutation of, ii. 177; style of, ii. 20, 21, 340; subject, system starts from, i. 42; theory of, sublime, i. 265; love of symmetry, ii. 22, 47, 69, 76, 78, 106, 133; synthetic unity of apperception, ii. 51, 52, 333, 476, iii. 12; thing in itself, ii. 3, 31, 169, 381, 407; transcendent, transcendental and immanent, i. 124, ii. 3, 87, iii. 24; *das Vernünfteln* ii. 263; weight an *a priori* quality of matter, i. 13.
Kemble, i. 295.
Kepler, i. 87, 94, 137 n., iii. 41.
Kerner, Justinus, ii. 481.
Kielmayer, ii. 318.
Kieser, ii. 326, iii. 99.
Kirby, iii. 91, 101, 103.
Kleist, i. 311.
Klettenberg, Fr. von, i. 497.
Knowledge, whence the need of, iii. 7, 8; physiological and metaphysical view of, ii. 486, iii. 290, 291, 470; aim of, ii. 475; kinds of, i. 199, 230; degrees of, iii. 29, 30; why no knowledge of knowing, ii. 487; influence of

will upon, iii. 134; influence of, on degree of sensibility and suffering, i. 400, iii. 16.
Köppen, iii. 301.
Koran, ii. 361.
Körösi, Csoma, ii. 371.
Kosack, i. 96.
Krishna, iii. 262.

Lactantius, ii. 98.
Lalita-Vistara, iii. 168.
Lamarck, i. 185.
Lambert, i. 55, ii. 303.
Landscape painting, i. 282.
Language, the first production and tool of reason, i. 47, 48, 51; connection of conception with word, ii. 238; capacity for, depends on association of ideas, ii. 325; the acquisition of several an important mental culture, ii. 238, 239; against the modern habit of curtailing words, ii. 310 *seq*
Laocoon, i. 292, iii. 198.
Laplace, i. 194, ii. 225, iii. 72, 73.
Latin, as universal language of scientific literature, ii. 310 *seq.*
La Trappe, i. 510, iii. 455.
Laughter, as a psychical act, i. 76 *seq.*, ii. 270; peculiar to man, ii. 280; why pleasant, ii. 279; insulting and bitter, ii. 281; a test of moral worth, ii. 281.
Lavater, i. 312.
Law, philosophy of, i. 442, 452, ii. 150–152, iii. 409–414.
Learning, on the subordinate value of, ii. 253 *seq.*
Lee, Anne, iii. 449.
Legislation, i. 446, 447.
Leibnitz, i. 49, 111, 342, ii. 11, 81 *seq.*, 141, 237, 391, iii. 91, 394 *seq.*
Leibnitz-Wolfian philosophy, i. 64, ii. 8, 127, 129, 141, iii. 394.
Leopardi, iii. 401.
Lessing, i. 292, ii. 16, 153, 169, iii. 305.
Leszczynski, iii. 203 n.
Leucippus, ii. 177, 378, iii. 61, 64.
Lichtenberg, ii. 113, 172 n., 198, 445. iii. 21, 203 n., 305, 332 n.
Lie, the, origin and end of, i. 434 *seq.*
Liebig, iii. 42.
Life, nature of, iii. 36; conflict with mechanical and chemical forces, i. 190; opposition between organic and animal, ii. 489–492; blind striving, iii. 105–118; relation to dreams, i. 20, 415; tragic and comic side of, i. 415, 416; misery of, i. 401–407, 417, iii. 114, 382–401; aim of, iii. 376, 384–391.
Light, mechanical explanations of, iii. 44 *seq.*; relation to heat, i. 262, 263; explanation of pleasure given by, i. 258, iii. 137; connection with architecture, i. 279, 280.
Locke, i. 49, ii. 6, 7, 45, 81 *seq.*, 141, 173 *seq.*, 185 *seq.*, 212, 213, 258, 259, 402, iii. 5, 23, 59, 394.
Logic, definition of, i. 58, ii. 285; value of, i. 57–59, ii. 286; on what its certainty depends, ii. 268.
Love, nature of all true and pure, i. 484 *seq.*; root and significance of sexual love, iii, 419, 339–343, 360; degrees of it, iii. 344–361; the *rôle* of instinct in it, iii. 345–349, 350–360; independence of friendship, iii. 345; sublime and comic sides of, iii. 366 *seq.*
Lucretius, i. 403, 411, 412, iii. 91, 93, 313.
Lully, Raymond, i. 510, iii. 455.
Lupus, Rutilius, ii. 286.
Luther, i. 500, 525, ii. 145, 368, iii. 392, 421, 448–451.
Lyric, subjectivity of, i. 321; nature of the song, i. 322–324.

Machiavelli, ii. 135, iii. 158.
Macrocosm, i. 212, iii. 404.
Madness, nature of, i. 30, 248 *seq.*, iii. 167; criterion of, iii. 167 *seq.*; relation of knowledge of madman to that of the brutes, i. 249, ii. 243; relation of, to genius, i. 246, 247; prevalence among actors, iii. 168; origin of, i. 249 *seq.*, iii. 169, 170; *mania sine delirio*, iii. 171, 172.
Magnetism, animal, ii. 466, 467, iii. 76, 419.
Maine de Biran, ii. 206, 507, 217.
Malebranche, i. 178, 179, 522, ii. 15.
Man, the human race, connection with rest of nature, i. 200 *seq.*, 403, ii. 377; identity of essence

of man and the brutes, i. 192; difference between man and brutes, i. 46–48, 110–112, 170, 171, 230, 384, 385, ii. 228–233, 358, iii. 14–17, 380, 381; transcendent unity of human race, iii. 75, 76; turning-point of will to live, i. 491 *seq.*, iii. 381, 426; origin of, iii. 358; gradual degradation of. ii. 362.
Manichæans, iii. 305.
Mannerists, i. 304, 305.
Manzoni, ii. 352.
Marcionists, iii. 305, 438, 442, 443.
Marcus Aurelius, ii. 356. iii. 323.
Marriage, iii. 333, 334, 336–375.
Materialism, i. 34 *seq.*, ii. 175 *seq.*, iii. 60–64, 261, 262.
Mathematics, scientific nature of, i. 81, 82; ground of certainty of, i. 157, ii. 268; and genius, i. 246, 247; method of, i. 95 *seq.;* and logic, ii. 202; value of, ii. 323.
Matter, i. 10–13, 175, 275, 276, ii. 79, 103, 104, 218–224, iii. 48–54.
Maupertius, ii. 225.
Maximus of Tyre, ii. 264.
Maxwell, iii. 450.
Mâyâ, i. 9, 21, 425, 454, 455, 471, 478, 481, 482, 489, 490, 514, 515, ii. 8, 10, 108 n., iii. 69, 418.
Mechanics, iii. 37, 39, 43 *seq.*
Medwin, iii. 160 n.
Meister, J. C. F., ii. 152.
Melancholy, i. 512.
Melissus, ii. 264.
Memnon, ii. 198.
Memory, as a function of intellect, ii. 335, iii. 300; difference between that of men and brutes, ii. 229, 230; the influences acting upon, i. 30, 248–251, ii. 200, 334, 438 *seq.*
Menenius Agrippa, i. 311.
Mens as opposed to *animus*, ii. 458.
Menu, laws of, i. 433, 501 n., iii. 465.
Merck, ii. 446, iii. 200.
Metaphysics, i. 107, ii. 20, 359–395, iii. 40.
Metempsychosis, doctrine of, i. 458–460, iii. 300–306, 417, 418.
Method, i. 100, 108, ii. 53, 210, 259, 309, 310, 393.
Metre, i. 314, ii. 205–207.
Mind, presence of, ii. 430.
Minor key, i. 337, iii. 243, 244.
Missionaries, i. 460.
Mnemonics, ii. 325.
Modality, categories of, ii. 66–75.
Modesty, i. 303, iii. 202, 203.
Mohammedanism, ii. 361, 362, iii. 423, 433, 472.
Molinos, iii. 434, 435, 435 n.
Molock, ii. 243.
Monarchy, i. 443, iii. 410.
Monasticism, i. 499, iii. 448.
Mongolian race, iii. 58.
Montaigne, i. 463 n., ii. 315, 465, iii. 378.
Montalembert, iii. 435.
Montanists, iii. 438.
Monuments, value of historical, iii. 229.
Moon, æsthetic effect of, iii. 136.
Morality, i. 343, 477, iii. 405, 415, 423–428 (Cf. *Ethics*).
Morphology, i. 124, 125, 183.
Mortality, iii. 301–302.
Motives, Motivation, what they determine, i. 138, 212, 213, iii. 115; what imparts power to, iii. 97; intellectual condition of action of, i. 380, 381; influence of nearness upon strength of, ii. 346; influence upon intellect, ii. 436; distinguished from instinct, iii. 97; intellect as medium of, i. 199, ii. 336, 485, iii. 21 *seq.*
Movement, i. 194, ii. 226, 227, 483, 484, iii 39.
Mozart, iii. 163.
Müller, ii. 479.
Multiplicity, i. 145, 146, 166, 167, iii. 69 *seq.*, 274, 275.
Münchhausen, Baron, i. 34, ii. 278.
Murder, i. 432, iii. 413, 414.
Music, metaphysics of, i. 330–346, iii. 231–248.
Mysteries essential to religion, ii. 367, 368, iii. 430.
Mysticism, Mystics, i. 499, 500, iii. 430 n., 430–434.

NAKEDNESS, i. 296.
Nature, what it means, iii. 1; works of nature and works of art, iii. 1, 69, 70, 79; inner nature of, i. 140 *seq.*, 148, 152 *seq.*, iii. 32, 33, 39; perfection of works of, iii. 69, 70; the circle of, iii. 267;

grades of, i. 195 *seq.*, 202–206 ; continuity of, ii. 232, iii. 36, 85 ; the conflict in, i. 191, 210, 211 ; design of, i. 201–211, iii. 77 *seq.*, 95 ; relation to species and individual, i. 356, 425, 426, iii. 194, 277, 278, 396 ; æsthetic effect of, i. 255, iii. 173, 174 ; naïveté of, i. 203, 204, 356, 362, 423, 491, iii. 380 ; moral quality of, i. 518, iii. 106 ; laws of, i. 126, 172, 175 *seq.*, 183 ; forces of, i. 126, 162, 169–182, 202, ii. 217, 218, iii. 73, 259 ; investigator of, ii. 318, 319, 383.

Necessity, origin and meaning of conception, i. 97 ; relation to the actual and possible, ii. 72 *seq.* ; relation to contingent, ii. 67, 68 ; as opposed to freedom, iii. 67, 69 ; absolute necessity, ii. 70.

Nerves, i. 131, ii. 173, 185, 481–485.

Newton, Isaac, i. 26, 64, 160, 165, 245, ii. 226, 268, 338.

Nirvana, i. 460, iii. 308 n., 374, 427, 428.

Nitzsch, iii. 269.

Noise, ii. 198, 199, iii. 450.

Nominalism, ii. 85, iii. 125.

νοουμενον and *φαινομενον*, i. 93, ii. 85.

Nothing, relativity of conception, i. 528, iii. 272.

Nourishment, i. 357.

Numenius, ii. 98.

νους, ii. 459, iii. 390.

Nunc stans, the, i. 227, 361 n., iii. 381.

Object, conditioned by subject, i. 3, 6, 16, *seq.*, 123, 124, ii. 166–169, 170, 173, 179, 381.

Objectification, i. 130, 166–168, ii. 468.

Objectivity, of genius and in art, i. 240, 321, 324, ii. 417, iii. 144, 210.

Obscurantism, iii. 328, 329.

Obry, iii. 303, 308 n.

Ocelius Lucanus, ii. 113.

Opera, iii. 92, 233, 234.

Optimism, i. 420, ii. 391, iii. 390–397, 436, 443, 449, 471 *seq.*

Organism, ii. 468, iii. 77 *seq.*

Original sin, iii. 306, 421 *seq.*, 426.

Orpheus, iii. 303, 427, 433, 443.

Osiander, i. 151.

Ossian, i. 324.

Ought, the absolute, i. 350, ii. 144.

Oum, iii. 430, 430 n.

Oupnekhat, i. 459, 501, iii. 425 n. 432, 433.

Ovid, i. 396, 410.

Owen, R., ii. 131, 203 n., iii. 82, 86, 91.

Pæstum, iii. 185.

Pain, i. 386, 410, 412, 413, iii. 384, 385.

Paine, T., i. 231.

Painting, i. 282–292, 297–301, 306–310, iii. 193, 196–198.

Palingenesis, iii. 300, 301.

Pander, ii. 318.

Pantheism, iii. 106, 114, 403, 404, 471–475.

Paracelsus, Theophrastus, iii. 280, 362.

Parmenides, i. 141, 425.

Parody, ii. 275, 276.

Particles, logical, ii. 288, 315.

Pascal i. 476, iii. 435.

Passions, ii. 216, iii. 406, 407.

Past, the, i. 359, 360.

Pedantry, i. 78, ii. 250 *seq.*

Pelagianism, i. 525, ii. 368, 369, iii. 422, 448.

Penitentiary system, i. 404, iii. 412.

Perception, intellectuality of, i. 14–16, ii. 40, 174, 185, 192 ; share of senses and brain in, ii. 185 ; object of, i. 7, ii. 40 ; relation to thing in itself, ii. 174, 401 ; significance for knowledge, science, art, philosophy, and virtue, ii. 244–269, iii. 131, 141 *seq.*

Perfection, ii. 15.

Peripatetics, ii. 137, 145.

Permanence of substance, ii. 78.

Perpetual motion, ii. 65, iii. 395.

Pessimism, can be demonstrated, iii. 395 ; the ground of distinction among religions, ii. 372 *seq.* ; of the most significant religions, i. 420, iii. 423 ; of great men of all ages, iii. 398 *seq.*

Petitio principii, definition of, ii. 308.

Petit-Thouars, Admiral, iii. 55.

Petrarch, i. 487, 512, ii. 313, iii. 210, 363, 369, 370, 386.

Petronius, ii. 130.
Pettigrew, i. 178 n.
Phidias iii. 195.
Philosopher, the, nature of, i. 21, 109, ii. 319, 359, 360, iii. 146, 147 ; distinguished from poet, iii. 146, 147 ; distinguished from sophist, ii. 362, 363.
Philosophy, source of, i. 135, ii. 359–361, 374 ; task of, i. 107, 168, 350, 352, 495 ; distinguished from science, i. 107, ii. 317 ; as opposed to theology, ii. 367, 395, iii. 431, 453 ; relation to art, iii. 176, 177 ; relation to history, iii. 223 ; method of, ii. 53, 210, 259, 393 ; division of, i. 349 ; cause of small progress of, ii. 395 ; limits of, ii. 362, 363, iii. 27, 405 ; professors of, ii. 362, 363.
Phlegmatic temperament, iii. 18, 161.
Physics, subject of, ii. 375 ; relation to metaphysics, ii. 376–384, iii. 40.
Physiognomy, i. 74, 74 n.
Physiology, i. 125, ii. 317, iii. 38.
Pico de Mirandula, ii. 240.
Pictet, iii. 304.
Picturesque, iii. 130.
Pindar, i. 21.
Pitt, iii. 324.
Plagiarism, ii. 225, 226.
Plants, chief characteristics of, i. 357, ii. 29 ; inner nature of, i. 152, iii. 34–36 ; distinguished from animals, i. 25, 150, iii. 13 ; form and physiognomy of, i. 203, 204 ; metamorphosis of, iii. 85 ; æsthetic effect of, i. 260, 288, 289.
Platner, ii. 270.
Plato, on *a priori* knowledge, ii. 201 ; on being and becoming, i. 9 ; relation to Giordano Bruno, ii. 114 n. ; figure of the cave, i. 311, ii. 8 ; improper use of conceptions, ii. 211, 261, 264 ; his Dæmon, i. 349 ; his dialectic, ii. 309 ; source of error, i. 103 ; errors in syllogistic reasoning, i. 93 ; his ethics, i. 114, ii. 145, 149, 348 ; ευκολος and δυσκολος, i. 407 ; hope the dream of waking, ii. 431 ; his Ideas, i. 168, 220, 273, ii. 85, 99, 322, iii. 123, 274, 275 ; on love, iii. 338 ; on materialism, ii. 176 ; on mathematics, ii. 323 ; on metempsychosis, iii. 303 ; his method, i. 239 ; on music, i. 336 ; on nature of nothing, i. 529 ; on the nature of the philosopher, i. 21, 41, 109, 143 ; ii. 369, 374 ; on plants, iii. 34 ; on punishment, i. 451 ; on reason, ii. 141 ; on science, i. 83 ; on sensual pleasure, iii. 349, 369 ; his world of shadows, ii. 10 ; on existence of soul, ii. 102 ; his theism, ii. 98.
Pliny, iii. 378, 400, 451.
Plotinus, ii. 218, iii. 51, 54, 432.
Plouquet, i. 55.
Plutarch, ii. 98, 319, iii. 124, 271, 399.
Poaching, a positive, not a moral fault, iii. 411, 412.
Poet, the, grade of, iii, 202 ; marks of genuine, iii. 207 ; bad influence of mediocre, i. 317 n. ; distinguished from philosopher, iii. 146, 147.
Poetical justice, i. 328.
Poetry, i. 313–330, iii. 38, 200–219.
Point, extensionless, ii. 223 ; immovable, ii. 219.
Polarity, i. 187.
Polier, Mme. de, i. 492, 501 n., ii. 109.
Position, i. 9.
Possibility, ii. 69, 72.
Pouchet, iii. 56.
Poussin, i. 306.
Praxiteles, iii. 195.
Predestination, i, 378, ii. 149.
Pre-existence, iii. 253, 254.
Prejudice, ii. 268.
Preller, ii. 357,
Present, the, i. 358–360, iii. 271, 271 n.
Priestley, i. 373, ii. 111, 224, 225, iii. 46.
Priests, i. 466 n., ii. 362.
Principium individuationis, i. 145, 146, 166, 454 *seq.*, 481, iii. 274, 417, 418.
Principle of sufficient reason, is *a priori*, i. preface xi., 6, iii. 469 ; sphere of validity of, i. 7, 16, 17, 41, 106, iii. 405, 469 ; importance of, i. 96, 107, ii. 316 ; indemonstrable nature of, i. 96,

106; fourfold root of, i. 7 (Cf. *Appendix* to vol. iii.)
Property, right of, i. 432, 433 n., iii. 411.
Prose, as distinguished from poetry, i, 313, iii. 204–206.
Protestantism. See *Catholicism.*
Prudence, i. 27, 245, 456.
Psychology, ii. 412–467.
Punishment, distinguished from revenge, i. 449; end of, i. 448–450, iii. 412, 413; measure of, iii. 413, 414.
Pyramids, i. 267, iii. 229.
Pythagoras, iii. 303.
Pythagoreans, i. 33, 86, 92, 95, 188, 343, ii. 319, iii. 95, 124, 427, 442, 452.

QUALITY, of judgments, ii. 57, 87; as determination of matter, iii. 54; natural forces as *qualitates occultæ*, i. 126, 162, 170, 182, ii. 376.
Quid pro quo, i. 79.
Quieter of will, i. 301, 326, 327, 367, 396, 489, 490.
Quietism, iii. 433–4?5,

RABELAIS, iii. 437.
Radius, Justus, ii. 191.
Rameau, i. 58.
Rancé, Abbé, i. 510, iii. 455.
Raphael, i. 295, 300, 531, iii. 162.
Rationalism in theology, ii. 369.
Reading, disadvantage of much, ii. 253–255.
Realism, ii. 85, iii. 125.
Reality, definition, i. 30; the present is the form of, i. 359, 360, iii. 271 n.; of external world, i. 22, 23, ii. 169, 184.
Reason, the word, i. 48, ii. 141, 241; function of, i. 50, ii. 137; theoretical and practical, i. 30, 113, ii. 138, 139, 345, iii. 408, prerogative of man, i. 46–48, 110–112, 384, 385, ii. 228–233, iii. 380, 381; relation of language to, i. 47–51, ii. 238; advantages and disadvantages, i. 45, 47, 68–75, ii. 234–243, 345 *seq.*; compatible with want of understanding and with moral badness, ii. 136; opposed to revelation, ii. 142; Kant's Ideas of, i. 169, ii. 96–100; ideal of, ii. 125–133; principle of, ii. 90–96.
Reflection, definition, i. 46; relation to perceptive knowledge, ii. 54 *seq.*
Reflex movements, ii. 483–484.
Reid, Dr. Thomas, ii. 189, 191, 207, 240.
Reil, i. 140, 159.
Religion, significance of, ii. 367 *seq.*; value of, ii. 370; fundamental distinction between, ii. 372 *seq.*; mysteries essential to, ii. 367; demoralising influence of, i. 466 n.; conflict with culture and science, ii. 370; philosophy of, ii. 370 (Cf. *Buddhism*, *Brahmanism*, *Christianity*, *Judaism*, and *Mohammedanism*).
Repentance, i. 382, iii. 406, 407.
Reproduction. See *Generation.*
Republics tend to anarchy, i. 448.
Resignation. See *Will, denial of.*
Resolve, i. 387.
Revenge, distinguished from punishment, i. 449; relation to wickedness, i. 470; a characteristic of human nature which is not to be confounded with revenge, i. 462.
Rhetoric, i. 63, ii. 285, 286, 305, 306.
Rhyme. See *Poetry.*
Rhythm, in music, i. 339 *seq.* See *Poetry.*
Richter, Jean Paul, ii. 22, 198, 270, 283, iii. 141, 143, 145.
Right, negative nature of conception, i. 437, 444; independent of State, i. 439, iii. 409; positive i. 444, 446; of property, i. 432 433 n., iii. 411.
Ritter, ii. 357.
Romantic, distinguished from classical, iii. 209.
Rösch, ii. 478, 480.
Rosenkranz, i. 203 n., ii. 29, 36, 117, 120, 121, 146–148, 204 n., 212, 217, 225, 377.
Rosini, ii. 447.
Rousseau, i. 247, 343, ii. 136, 353, iii. 106, 325, 338, 397.
Ruins, sublime effect of, i. 267; analogous to *cadenza* in music, iii. 241.
Ruisdael, i. 255.

St. Hilaire, August, iii. 55.
St. Hilaire, Geoffroi, ii. 318, iii. 82.
Sakya Muni, iii. 168, 434.
Salvation, the way of, iii. 460–467.
Sangermano, iii. 301, 308 n.
Sannyasis, i. 496, ii. 352.
Saphir, ii. 274.
Sceptics, i. 123, 124.
Schelling, i. 187, ii. 22, 31, 116, 169, 176, 236, 261, iii. 62, 471.
Schiller, i. 79, 318, ii. 148, 276, 321, iii. 215, 217.
Schleiermacher, i. 67, 262, iii. 394.
Schlegel, iii. 75.
Schmidt, J. J., ii. 371, iii. 308 n.
Schnürrer, iii. 301.
Scholastics, Scholasticism, i. 82, 146, 162, 198 n., ii. 12, 13, 85, 100, 125, 126, iii. 125.
Scholiast, ii. 319.
Schultz, ii. 480.
Schulze, ii. 312.
Science, nature of, i. 36, 58, 80–90, 105, 106, 229, 238, ii. 53, 252, 267.
Scott, Sir Walter, ii. 427, 457, iii. 328, 386, 399.
Scopas, iii. 195.
Sculpture, as opposed to painting, i. 292, iii. 193; æsthetic effect of, iii. 200, 201; significance of drapery in, i. 296; antique, i. 309, iii. 194, 195; modern, iii. 195.
Secundus, Johannes, iii. 195.
Selfishness. See *Egoism*.
Self-knowledge, ii. 423.
Self-renunciation, meaning of, iii. 423; the appearance of freedom in the phenomenon, i. 388, 389
Seneca, i. 75, 246, 379, ii. 149, 234, 347, 350, 355–358, 458.
Sensation, ii. 186–191.
Senses, ii. 193–200.
Sensibility, i. 13.
Sentimentality, i. 512, 513.
Serenity, i. 422, iii. 376.
Seriousness, as the opposite of laughter, ii. 280; as determining the tendency of life, iii. 149.
Sex, degree of, iii. 356.
Sextus Empiricus, i. 62, 93, 343, ii. 127.
Sexual impulse, difference between man and brute with reference to, i. 171, iii. 309; significance and power of, i. 423, 425, iii. 310, 312–314, 376; physiological correlative of, iii. 314; its relation to happiness of life, iii. 376; voluntary renunciation of satisfaction of, i. 430, iii. 376.
Shaftesbury, iii. 397.
Shakers, iii. 449.
Shakspeare, i. 21, 268, 511, ii. 239, 254, 306, 315, iii. 210, 214, 216, 321, 363, 369, 400, 457.
Shame, i. 424, iii. 379.
Shenstone, ii. 275.
Siècle, iii. 112 n.
Sight, sense of, ii. 193 *seq.*
Simonists, iii. 305.
Simplicius, ii. 157.
Sirach, Jesus, iii. 352.
Sketches, value of, iii. 178.
Skull, explained from vertebræ, iii. 85.
Slavery, as a wrong, i. 432.
Sleep, necessity of, ii. 337, 428, 462, 463, 466; action of vital force in, ii. 463, 466; positive character of, ii. 464; relation to brain life, ii. 465; relation to death, i. 358, iii. 267 *seq.*
Socialists, iii. 250.
Socrates, i. 288, 343, ii. 107, 281, 363, iii. 299, 249, 252, 405.
Somnambulism, ii. 467, iii. 98 *seq.*
Sömmering, iii. 21.
Sophist, distinguished from philosopher, ii. 362, 363.
Sophistry, i. 63, ii. 263, 264.
Sophocles, i. 21, 295, 328, iii. 214.
Soul, historical, iii. 2, 3, 13; opposition between soul and body, ii. 102–104, 378; in what sense the word should be used, iii. 105; a motive which has led to the assumption of, ii. 409; theoretical and practical results of assumption, ii. 77, 409, 494.
Southey, ii. 427.
Space, ideality of, ii. 201–204, 221; opposition between space and time with reference to abstract knowledge, i. 69, 70; union of space and time the condition of duration and matter, i. 10–13, ii. 78; the framework of the phenomenal world, i. 187, 188; whether the world is limited in

space, ii. 109 (Cf. *Principium individuationis*).
Spallanzani, ii. 469.
Species, iii. 123.
Spectator, ii. 233.
Spinal cord, ii. 483–484.
Spinoza, on benevolence, i. 486; biography of, i. 497; explanation and use of concepts, i. 111, ii. 241, 266; ethical teaching of, i. 114, 367, iii. 403; God of, iii. 106; on knowledge of Ideas, i. 231, 232 n.; on immortality, iii. 280, 291; on love, iii. 338; method of, i. 100 n., 108, ii. 212; his place in western philosophy, ii. 13 n.; rejection of spiritualism, ii. 177; conception of substance, i. 33, ii. 373, 391; rejection of teleology, iii. 91, 93, 94; on will, i. 164, 377, 385, ii. 120.
Spiritualism, ii, 177.
Stahl, i. 64.
State, the, i. 442–448, 451, iii. 409–411.
Statics, ii. 226.
Stewart, Dugald, ii. 226, 240.
Stobæus, i. 114, 117, 118, 378, 506 n., ii. 137, 319, 350.
Stoics, Stoicism, i. 113–120, ii. 453–358.
Strauss, D. F., iii. 437, 457.
Stupidity, i. 30.
Style, ii. 44, 246, 247.
Suarez, i. 146, 162, 198 n., ii. 13, 89, 100.
Subject, the, has two parts, i. 132; of will, iii. 126; of knowing, i. 3, 6, 16, 123, 124, ii. 166–169, 170 *seq.*; pure, will-less subject of knowing, i. 253 *seq.*, iii. 128 *seq.*
Sublime, the, i. 259–268.
Substance, origin and content of concept, ii. 103, 104; principle of permanence of, ii. 78 *seq.*; and accident, i. 12 *seq.*, ii. 79, 80.
Succession, i. 9.
Suetonius, iii. 321.
Suffering, universality of, i. 399 *seq.*; sanctifying power of, i. 511; of life, i. 401–407, 417, iii. 114.
Sufism, iii. 423, 432.
Suicide, i, 408, 514-520, iii. 117.
Suidas, ii. 98.
Sulzer, ii. 141.
Supernaturalism, ii. 369
Swift, iii. 399.
Swoon, the twin-brother of death, iii. 256.
Sybarites, ii. 199.
Syllogism, ii. 292–304.
Symbolism, i. 308 *seq.*
Symmetry, analogy with rhythm iii. 240, 241.
Sympathy, definition and division, iii. 419.
Systems, philosophical, ground of interest in, ii. 360, 361; contrast between Schopenhauer's and others, i. 32, ii. 180, 393; division of those starting from object, i. 33; error of those which proceed historically, i. 352; criteria of truth of, ii. 391.

Tatianites, iii. 439.
Tauler, iii. 434, 435.
Teleology, i. 201–210, iii. 77–95.
Tennemann, i. 67, ii. 12.
Termini technici, iii. 312.
Tersteegen, i. 496.
Tertullian, ii. 368, iii. 305, 439.
Thales, i. 33.
Theodicy, iii. 394, 404.
Theon of Smyrna, iii. 313.
Thilo, iii. 158.
Thing in itself, as opposed to phenomenon, i. 40, 44, 128, 142, 145, 157, 166, ii. 31, 168, 169, 402, 403, iii. 292; how knowledge of it can be attained, i. 41, 128, ii. 31, 174, 175, 404, 405; in what sense it is the *will*, i. 142, ii. 407; why our knowledge of it is not exhaustive, i. 157, ii. 406, iii. 9, 24, 25, 27, 286 *seq.*; in history of philosophy, i. 220, ii. 30, 117, 174, 185, 380, 390, iii. 45.
Tholuk, iii. 432.
Thorwaldsen, iii. 195.
Thracians, iii. 398.
Tiedemann, ii. 470.
Tien, ii. 97.
Time, nature of, i. 9, 44, ii. 205, iii. 12; ideality of, ii. 201, 204; *prædicabilia a priori* of, ii. 121 *seq.* (Cf. *Space*).
Times, the, i. 178 n., ii. 459, iii. 304, 450.
Tourtual, ii. 187.

Tragedy, i., 326-330, iii. 212-216, 454.
Transcendent, ii. 387.
Transcendental knowledge, i. 224 ; philosophy, ii. 11.
Travelling, æsthetic effect of, iii. 131.
Trent, decrees of Council of, iii. 441.
Treviranus, ii. 470, iii. 35.
Truth, definition, i. 30, ii. 308 ; foundation of, i. 100-103 ; difference between conceivability and truth, ii. 278 ; relation to proof, i. 83, 84 ; power of, i. 45, 179.

UNDERSTANDING, function of, i. 13, 14 ; identity of nature at different grades, i. 26, 28, 29 ; why sensibility is everywhere accompanied by, i. 30, 31, 228 ; misuse of word, ii. 241 ; defects and advantages of knowledge of, ii. 253 ; keenness of, i. 27, 245.
Ungewitter, iii. 304.
Universal, two kinds of, i. 301-303, iii. 124, 125 ; knowledge of, ii. 335, 336 ; universal truths, ii. 308.
Upham, iii. 282.
Utopias, i. 451, iii. 331.

VALENTINIANS, iii. 305, 438.
Vaninus, Jul. Cæsar, iii. 32, 106.
Vauvenarque, ii. 251.
Vedas, 9, 21, 114, 234, 266, 364 n., 458, 501, ii. 108 n., 362, iii. 303, 307, 426, 427, 433, 467.
Velocity, ii. 226, 227.
Virgil, i. 293, 295.
Virtue, source of genuine, i. 475, 477, ii. 149, 252 ; cannot be taught, i. 475, ii. 149 ; relation to happiness, i. 466, iii. 420 ; distinguished from reasonableness, ii. 134 ; transition to asceticism, iii. 424, 425.
Voltaire, i. 327, 329, ii. 157, 277, 428, 469, iii. 178, 252, 368, 395. 398, 404.
Vyaso, iii. 282.

WEEPING, i. 486-488, iii. 406.
Weighing, two ways of, ii. 227.
Whewell, ii. 323.
Wieland, i. 246, ii. 427, iii. 200.
Will, subject of, iii. 126 ; identity of subject of will and knowledge, 132 ; as the thing in itself, i. 142, ii. 407 ; contrast between will and its phenomenal appearance, i. 145, 166, 213-215, iii. 69-71 ; objectification of, i. 130, 166-168, ii. 468 ; assertion of, i. 421-427, iii. 376-381 ; denial of, i. 488-514, iii. 420-459.
Windischmann, iii. 307, 425 n.
Winkelmann, i. 289, 290, 292, 295, 309, 318, ii. 153.
Winkelried, Arnold von, ii. 134.
Wirklichkeit, i. 10.
Wit, i. 77, ii. 268, 277.
Wolf, i. 111, ii. 70 n., 90, 97, 102, 127, 225, 479, iii. 85.
Wordsworth, ii. 427.
Wrong, conception of, i. 431-437.

XENOPHANES, ii. 220, iii. 8.
Xenophon, i. 288.

YAMA, iii. 258.
Yang, i. 187.
Yin, i. 187.
Y-King, i. 188, 343.
Youth, i. 324, iii. 304.
Yunghahn, iii. 112.

ZACCARIA, Abbé, iii. 441.
Zend Avesta, iii. 391, 446.
Zeno, i. 117 118.

CORRIGENDA AND ADDENDA

IN VOL. I.

Page xxxii. *insert*

PREFACE TO THE THIRD EDITION.

WHAT is true and genuine would more easily gain room in the world if it were not that those who are incapable of producing it are also sworn to prevent it from succeeding. This fact has already hindered and retarded, when indeed it has not choked, many a work that should have been of benefit to the world. For me the consequence of this has been, that although I was only thirty years old when the first edition of this work appeared, I live to see this third edition not earlier than my seventy-second year. Yet for this I find comfort in the words of Petrarch: *Si quis tota die currens, pervenit ad vesperam satis est* (*de vera Sapientia*, p. 140). If I also have at last arrived, and have the satisfaction at the end of my course of seeing the beginning of my influence, it is with the hope that, according to an old rule it will endure long in proportion to the lateness of its beginning.

In this third edition the reader will miss nothing that was contained in the second, but will receive considerably more, for, on account of the additions that have been made in it, it has, with the same type, 136 pages more than the second.

Seven years after the appearance of the second edition I published two volumes of "Parerga and Paralipomena." What is included under the latter name consists of additions to the systematic exposition of my philosophy, and would have found its right place in these volumes, but I was obliged to find a place for it then where I could, as it was very doubtful whether I would live to see this third edition. It will be found in the second volume of the said "Parerga," and will be easily recognised from the headings of the chapters.

FRANKFORT-ON-THE-MAINE,
September 1859.

Page xiv. line 9, *for* "pancorum" *read* "paucorum."

" xix. " 17, *for* "alchemists" *read* "adepts."

" xx. " 10, *after* "there" *insert* "unanimous."

" xxi. " 3, *for* "will appeal to any thinking mind no matter when it comprehends it" *read* "will also some time be comprehended by another thinking mind."

" xxii. last line, *after* "not" *insert* "in this case."

" xxiii. line 26, *for* "conceptions" *read* "conception."

" " " 32, *for* "origin" *read* "stem."

" xxiv. " 20, *for* "a chromatic" *read* "an achromatic."

" 6, line 15, *for* "universality" *read* "common or reciprocal nature."

" 21, " 31, *for* "Σιδωλ" *read* "Ειδωλ."

" 31, " 7, *for* "micrometre" *read* "micrometer."

" 41, " 11, *for* "θαυμαξειν" *read* "θαυμαζειν."

" 45, " 22, *after* "its" *insert* "iron."

" 45, " 23, *for* "extend to" *read* "quench."

" 48, " 31, *for* "λογιμον" *read* "λογικον."

" 49, " 22, *after* "to" *insert* "abstract.

" 50, " 14, *after* "function" *insert* "the construction of the concept."

" 62, " 26, *for* "Kallisthenes" read "Callisthenes."

" 75, " 1, *for* "fictum" *read* "fictam."

" 91, " 18, *for* "latter" *read* "former."

" 93, lines 8 and 33, *for* "νουμενον" *read* "νοουμενον."

" 99, line 17, *for* "42" *read* "32."

" 114, " 7, *for* "ευδαι μονειν" *read* "ενδαιμονειν."

" 116 note, *for* "εφαρμοεξειν" *read* "εφαρμοζειν."

" 117, line, 30, *for* "ψνχης" *read* "ψυχης."

" 118, lines 10, 12, *for* "Kleanthes" *read* "Cleanthes."

" 119, line 7, *for* "philospher" *read* "philosopher."

" 141, " 18, *for* "Σστιν" *read* "Εστιν."

" 146, " 23, *for* "became" *read* "become."

" 157, line 4, *for* "casuality" *read* "causality."

" 166, " 3, *insert* § 25.

" 169, " 5, *for* "Laertes" *read* "Laertius."

" 172, " 32, *for* "casuality" *read* "causality."

" 182, " 8, *for* "quidities" *read* "quiddities."

" 184, " 30, *for* "this" *read* "thus."

" 205, " 35, *for* "casuality" *read* "causality."

" 220, " 32, *for* "ειδῆ" *read* "ἔιδη."

" 222, " 24, *for* "casuality" *read* "causality."

" 223, lines 4 and 33, *for* "casuality" *read* "causality."

" 224, line 8, *for* "casuality" *read* "causality."

" 230, " 19, *for* "Apollo of Belvedere" *read* "Apollo Belvedere."

" 231, last line, *for* "Meus" *read* "Mens."

Page 247, line 17, *for* "Great wits to madness sure are near allied" *read* "Great wits are sure to madness near allied." The lines are not from Pope, as Schopenhauer says, but from Dryden's "Absalom and Achitophel," Pt. i., l. 163.

„ 251, „ 15, *for* "appear" *read* "appears."

„ 258, „ 18, *for* "Ahrimines" *read* "Ahriman."

„ 276, lines 9 and 11, *for* "casuality" and "casual" *read* "causality" and "causal;" line 23, *for* "Timaus" *read* "Timæus."

„ 382, line 32, *for* "as" *read* "but."

„ 396, „ 5, *for* "αναγκη" *read* "αναγκῃ."

„ 423, „ 35, *for* "principiu mindividuationis" *read* "principium individuationis."

„ 425, „ 7, *no comma after* "βασιλειαν."

„ 429, „ 25, *after* "chapter" *insert* "of his."

„ 445, last line, *for* "ζην" *read* "ζῃν."

„ 453, lines 4 and 5, *for* "παρ" *read* "πας."

„ 455, line 10, *for* "prineipium" *read* "principium."

„ 463, „ 27, *for* "ever" *read* "every."

„ 467, „ 5, *for* "πρως" *read* "προς."

„ 496, „ 25, *for* "Wiedergeborennen" *read* "Wiedergeborenen."

„ 520, „ 9, *for* "though this is hard to find out" *read* "which is certainly hard to explain."

„ 531, „ 16, *for* "wish to fruition" *read* "desire to aversion."